Web Gateway Tools

Connecting IBM and Lotus Applications to the Web

Edited by:

Josephine Cheng

Susan Malaika

WILEY COMPUTER PUBLISHING

John Wiley & Sons, Inc.

NEW YORK • CHICHESTER • WEINHEIM • BRISBANE • SINGAPORE • TORONTO

Executive Publisher: Katherine Schowalter
Editor: Robert M. Elliott
Managing Editor: Brian Snapp
Text Design & Composition: North Market Street Graphics, Lancaster, PA

Designations used by companies to distinguish their products are often claimed as trademarks. In all instances where John Wiley & Sons, Inc., is aware of a claim, the product names appear in initial capital or ALL CAPITAL LETTERS. Readers, however, should contact the appropriate companies for more complete information regarding trademarks and registration.

This text is printed on acid-free paper.

Copyright © 1997 International Business Machines Incorporated.

Published by John Wiley & Sons, Inc.

All rights reserved. Published simultaneously in Canada.

This publication is designed to provide accurate and authoritative information in regard to the subject matter covered. However, no representation is made, nor warranty given, that the information presented is without error or inaccuracy, or that computer program examples presented will compile or function error-free, or that URLs discussed will be resolvable by Internet servers. It is sold with the understanding that the publisher is not engaged in rendering legal, accounting, or other professional service. If legal advice or other expert assistance is required, the services of a competent professional person should be sought.

Reproduction or translation of any part of this work beyond that permitted by section 107 or 108 of the 1976 United States Copyright Act without the permission of the copyright owner is unlawful. Requests for permission or further information should be addressed to the Permissions Department, John Wiley & Sons, Inc.

Library of Congress Cataloging-in-Publication Data:

Web gateway tools : connecting IBM and Lotus applications to the Web /
   [edited by] Josephine Cheng, Susan Malaika.
      p.   cm.
   Includes index.
   ISBN 0-471-17555-2 (paper : acid-free paper)
    1. World Wide Web (Information retrieval system)   2. Application software.   I. Cheng, Josephine, 1953–   .   II. Malaika, Susan, 1953–   .
TK5105.888.W373   1997
005.2'76—dc21   96-29922
                                                                                CIP

Printed in the United States of America
10 9 8 7 6 5 4 3 2 1

Contents

About the Editors and Authors   viii
Acknowledgments   xi
Introduction   xiii

SECTION 1
Introduction and System Considerations   1

Chapter 1: Introduction to the Internet and Intranet   3

The Internet and the Community   4
A Brief History of the Internet   6
Introduction to the World Wide Web   7
Intranet: Client and Server Revisited   16
Present and Future Internet Trends   18

Chapter 2: Business Applications on the Web   25

Why Go Online?   25
So You Want To Make Money Online?   28
Which Applications Belong Online?   28
Examples of Intranet Applications   39
Planning Your Applications on the Web   42

Chapter 3: Internet and Web Security   49

    Security Risk Example   50
    Security Basics   52
    Secure Sockets Layer and Secure HyperText Transport Protocol   58
    Firewall   67

SECTION 2
Application Development   79

Chapter 4: Integrating Your Applications with the Web   81

    HTTP Overview   82
    Accessing Existing Applications and Data   87
    Guidelines for the User Interface   90
    Conclusion   101

Chapter 5: Server-side Programming Techniques   103

    Introduction   103
    Web Forms Programming   104
    Common Gateway Interface   110
    Managing Browser Session State   113
    When to Update Databases and Files   119
    Security   120
    Multimedia   121
    Conclusion   121

Chapter 6: Client-side Programming Techniques   123

    Java   123
    JavaScript   134
    NetRexx   141
    Specialized Non-Java Clients   142
    Conclusion   142

Chapter 7: Visual Programming for the Web   145

    The Pizza Scenario   148
    The Pizza Application   149

Contents   v

      Advanced Applications   166
      Conclusion   170
      Web Connection Parts   170

SECTION 3
Integrating Database Applications on the Web   173

Chapter 8: Using Net.Data to Access Databases and Files   175

      Dynamic Web Pages   176
      Building a Simple Database Application   181
      Customizing Reports   191
      Postprocessing of Data   203
      Accessing Files   212
      Accessing non-HTML Data   214
      Access Control by the Database   215
      Related Work   216
      Conclusion   219

Chapter 9: Lotus Internet Applications   221

      Lotus Extensions to the Classic Web Server   223
      Extending the Domino Server with Lotus Internet Applications   225
      Domino.Action   226
      Lotus Internet Publishing   228
      Domino.Merchant—Lotus Internet Commerce Solution   233
      Lotus Internet Customer Service   235
      Customizing the Domino Server for the World Wide Web   236
      The Strategic Direction for Lotus Internet Applications   251

SECTION 4
Integrating Transaction Systems with the Internet   253

Chapter 10: Transaction Processing Systems and the Internet   255

      Transaction Processing Background   255
      What Is a Transaction?   257

More on Transactions and Units of Recovery	258
What Is Conversational Programming?	261
Transaction Processing Facilities	263
Evolution of Transaction Processing Systems	264
Evolution of Web Server Environments	265
Web Server and Transaction Processing Differences	266
Transaction Processing and the Web	269
Conclusion	271

Chapter 11: Accessing CICS Applications from the Internet — 273

CICS Overview	273
CICS Internet Gateway	277
The MVS/ESA Web Server CGI Sample Program for CICS	291
Using the Lotus Domino Server to Access CICS	293
The CICS Gateway for Java	294
The CICS Web Interface	301
Choosing among the Access Methods	314
CICS Web Interface Application in 370 Assembler	315
CICS Web Interface Sample Converter in C	321

Chapter 12: Accessing Encina, IMS TM, and MQSeries Applications from the Internet — 331

Encina Overview	332
Accessing Encina Applications from the Web	336
IMS Overview	339
Accessing IMS Applications from the Web	341
MQSeries Overview	343
Accessing MQSeries Applications from the Web	347
Conclusion	354

Chapter 13: Electronic Commerce on the Internet — 355

Introduction	355
The Internet Is Worldwide: Implications	357
The Secure Electronic Transaction (SET) Protocol	359
Protecting Copyright Information on the Internet	360

Transaction Processing and Its Role in Electronic Commerce	361
Conclusion	366

SECTION 5
A Case Study — 367

Chapter 14: An Application Server — 369

Web Server Application Programming Interfaces	370
Web Application Platforms	371
Designing a Web Application Server	372
Extending the Application Server	378
Maintaining State in a Web Application Server	378
Embedding Content from Another Website	384
Connecting to Databases (Relational and Nonrelational)	391
Building Directed HTML	391
Designing a Director/Daemon Application Server	392
Conclusion	395

List of URLs — **397**

Glossary of Terms and Acronyms — **405**

For Further Reference — **433**

Index — **437**

About the Editors and Authors

Josephine Cheng is an IBM Distinguished Engineer at the Database Technology Institute at IBM's Santa Teresa Laboratory. She is responsible for the advanced technology for IBM database products including the development of DB2 World Wide Web Connection and Net.Data, mobile database strategies, object-relational technology, and new application areas. Josephine has filed many patents in query processing and optimization. She is a recipient of YWCA's 1996 Tribute to Women and Industry Award. She has B.S. and M.S. degrees in computer science from the University of California, Los Angeles. Josephine is the co-editor and author of the Introduction and Chapters 1 and 2 of this book.

Susan Malaika has worked for IBM in the United Kingdom for many years. Her area of specialization is transaction processing software and its interfaces to database management systems. Other areas in which Susan has been involved include data recovery and integrity, advanced transaction models, and distributed applications. In 1995, she became an Internet specialist and initiated a number of projects to provide Internet access to legacy systems. Susan has worked on software products and contributed to IBM manuals and documents. Before joining IBM, Susan was a database systems and application programmer. She has an M.S. degree in computer science from London University. Susan is the co-editor and author of Chapters 2, 4, 5, 6, 10, 11, 12, and 13 of this book.

David Fallside created the original idea and prototype for the Web parts that are now implemented in IBM's VisualAge products. He has a broad range of Internetwork experience, starting as a graduate student in the 1980s at Carnegie Mellon University, and more recently as the Webmaster of a nonprofit organization's 2000-plus page Website (www.awa.org). Today, David works for IBM on Internet strategy and technology in the database area. He received his B.S. degree in experimental psychology from Sussex University, England, and his Ph.D. degree in cognitive psychology from Carnegie Mellon University. David is the author of Chapter 7.

Keith McCall is the Director of Internet Applications at Lotus Development Corporation in Cambridge, Massachusetts. Before joining Lotus, he spent six years at IBM Canada Ltd. in software development, marketing, and sales. Keith's achievements include implementing the initial release of the Distributed Computing Environment for MVS and AS/400, initiating and prototyping DB2 World Wide Web Connection, implementing the most successful Internet Commerce site to date—the 1996 Atlanta Olympic Games Ticket Server—and architecting, designing, and developing IBM's Net.Commerce system. He holds a B.S. degree from the University of British Columbia. Keith is the author of Chapters 9 and 14.

Tam M. Nguyen is a Solutions Development Manager in the IBM Telecommunications and Media Industry. He was an architect of DB2 World Wide Web Connection. Tam was previously a research staff member at the IBM Thomas J. Watson Research Center, where he led a team to develop networked multimedia solutions for interactive television. His areas of interest include interactive multimedia applications and distributed network computing through the Internet. Tam received his Ph.D. in computer systems from the University of California, Berkeley. Tam is the co-author of Chapter 8.

HongHai Shen is a member of the Database Technology Institute at IBM's Santa Teresa Laboratory. His accomplishments include implementing mobile replication, designing the security configurations related to DB2 World Wide Web Connection, and architecting and prototyping mobile query and transaction agents. HongHai has filed several patents and published several papers in mobile computing and groupware systems. He received his B.S. and M.S. degrees in computer science from Fudan University, China, and M.S. and Ph.D. degrees in computer science from Purdue University. HongHai is the author of Chapter 3.

V. Srinivasan was an architect of Net.Data, and a designer and developer of DB2 World Wide Web Connection at IBM's Santa Teresa Laboratory. Previously, he played leading roles in building an object-relational gateway and a lightweight object-oriented database management system. V. Srinivasan has published research papers in the areas of accessing databases from the Internet, object-oriented databases, online processing in large-scale transaction systems, real-time systems, and distributed file systems. He received his Bachelor of Technology degree in computer science from the Indian Institute of Technology, Madras, and his M.S. and Ph.D. degrees in computer science from the University of Wisconsin, Madison. Srinivasan is the co-author of Chapter 8.

Emma Allfree is an information developer at IBM Hursley within the CICS information development group. She received her B.A. degree in technical communication from Coventry University, England. Emma is the co-author of Chapter 9.

Acknowledgments

For us, writing the acknowledgments is like seeing the light at the end of the tunnel—completion of our book! We started the writing project as a bunch of enthusiasts, authors who had no idea of what it would be like to take on two full-time jobs with equally aggressive schedules. We enjoyed writing this book for you, but we are happy to be regaining our lives!

Writing a book is not a simple task, and we would like to thank the many people who contributed along the way: James Sherwin for his clear illustrations; In Chung Niall, Clifford, Ken Cochran, Adrian Colyer, Patrick Dantressangle, Ken Davies, Andrew Dean, Emma Eldergill, Remy James, Peter Havercan, Chris Holloway, Wayne Jerves, Dave Kappos, Barbara Klein, Allen Lee, Steve Longhurst, Peter Niblett, Dennis Plum, Brian Pong, Michael Pong, Chris Sharp, Fong Shen, Michael Spradbury, Patrick Stephenson, Steve Wall, and Steve Wood for the samples they provided, as well as their advice and support; colleagues in the IBM Raleigh development lab, especially Pat Mueller and Martin Nally, who worked to make the Web parts a reality; Mark Davis and the IBM NetSP team for help in developing and testing the firewall configuration for Net.Data; the Net.Data team; colleagues at IBM Santa Teresa Laboratory and Hursley for providing the opportunity to discover the Internet; and Don Haderle for his sustenance.

We would like to thank Maggie Cutler, our copyeditor, for her thoughtful editing and her patience. We would also like to thank Bob Elliott, senior editor at Wiley, for his ongoing advice and suggestions for improvement, and Brian Calandra and his colleagues on the Wiley staff who supported the production of this book.

Last, but not least, we would like to thank our families and friends for their support, and for their understanding of our many disappearances late into the night to write the book.

Introduction

> *The Internet gets the human species back*
> *to what it's evolved to do—interact.*
>
> —*Trip Hawkins, Chief Executive Officer*
> *3DO Corporation*[1]

A common interest in the Internet brought together the authors of this book even though they are geographically dispersed across multiple cities, states, and even continents. However, the remote locations of the authors did not inhibit the collaborative writing process, and the writing of this book is a real-life demonstration of the power of the Internet for collaboration and information sharing. In addition, we have placed information for the readers of this book on the Internet at **http://www.ibm.com/technology/books/wcbgate/**

Although the Internet has been around for more than two decades, it has been used mainly by the research and academic communities. Its usage profile changed dramatically in the early 1990s, when it became more commercialized. Business on the Internet is still in its infancy, but it is expected that more and more business applications will connect to the Internet

---

1. *Information Week,* Quote of the Week, p. 10, July 29, 1996.

because of its global market, low entry cost, and accessibility to an ever-increasing number of users. The introduction of the World Wide Web (the Web), with its user-friendly, "one-click" browser available on all hardware and software platforms, further enhances the ease of use of the Internet.

Thanks to the Intranet, the benefits of the Internet technologies can be enjoyed within an enterprise too, without ever going outside the enterprise network. Because people outside the enterprise cannot access Intranet applications, many security issues usually associated with the Internet do not apply. Therefore, the implementation of Intranet applications is expected to be even more rapid than that of Internet applications.

Because many Internet and Intranet applications have to process data from files and/or databases, we devote one section of this book to the integration of database applications such as DATABASE 2 (DB2), Information Management System (IMS), and Lotus Notes databases on the Web. The deployment of databases leads to the installation of transaction systems to ensure data integrity across heterogeneous data sources as well as enhance support for the running of a large number of transactions. We therefore devote another section of the book to the issue of integrating transaction systems such as Transarc's Encina Monitor, IBM's Customer Information Control System (CICS), and Information Management System Transaction Manager (IMS TM), and messaging systems such as MQSeries, with the Internet. To reduce development costs, many enterprises want to reuse their existing applications as much as possible for Web exploitation. This book is therefore devoted to helping you to (1) connect your existing database applications and transaction systems to the Web and (2) develop new applications for both mainframe and desktop users. Various programming techniques using Java, and JavaScript for Web connection are discussed as well as the use of HyperText Markup Language (HTML).

Many tools and products are available to ease the implementation of Internet and Intranet applications. As lead developers of many of these tools and products, we share our insights into the technology behind them. We introduce each tool and describe in detail how to use it for designing and coding an Internet or Intranet application. Tools and products that we cover in this book are VisualAge, CICS Internet Gateway, MQSeries Internet Gateway, IMS Web, DB2 World Wide Web Connection, Net.Data, Olympic Games Ticket Server, and Net.Commerce—from IBM; and Lotus Domino Server, Domino.Action, Domino.Merchant, Domino.Broadcast for PointCast, and Internet Customer Service Solutions—from Lotus; and Transarc's DE-Light Web Client and Gateway.

In addition to the numerous examples of building Internet and Intranet applications with different techniques, this book includes a case study on building application servers such as the Olympic Games Ticket Server and Net.Commerce. The author of the case study is the architect of both products. He shares the experiences he gained during the development of the servers, as well as some of the challenges he encountered, such as state maintenance, security, reliability, performance, and scalability. You will find the discussion of the challenges and the suggested solutions relevant to any large-scale Web applications.

Who Is the Audience?

This book is intended for readers who would like to learn about techniques for launching applications on the Web and tools for integrating existing applications with the Internet and Web. Many detailed examples are included to illustrate Web application development.

To summarize, this book is written for:

- Information technology (IT) managers who want to establish a Website that makes their existing enterprise systems available through an Intranet
- Application developers who want to make their existing DB2, IMS, CICS, Encina, and Lotus Notes applications available through the Internet
- Application developers who want to develop new Web applications that access data stored in a mainframe or desktop database
- Anyone who wants to learn how to put an enterprise system online
- Anyone who wants to build an application server on the Web

How Is the Book Organized?

The book is organized into five sections:

- Section 1 focuses on the concepts and terminology of the Internet and Intranet.
- Section 2 focuses on application development techniques for Web programming and includes writing applications in Java, JavaScript, and NetRexx; the use of visual programming tools is also discussed.

- Section 3 focuses on Internet connections to database applications; gateway tools to connect new and existing applications are described.
- Section 4 focuses on Internet connections to transaction and messaging-based systems.
- Section 5 is a case study of developing an application server.

Sections 2, 3, and 4 are independent and can be read in any sequence. Section 5 assumes that you are familiar with the techniques described in Sections 2 through 4.

Section 1 Introduction and System Considerations

Chapter 1	Introduction to the Internet and Intranet
Chapter 2	Business Applications on the Web
Chapter 3	Security Considerations

Section 1 presents background information about the Internet and Intranet and gives a general description of Web applications. Chapter 1 introduces users to the concepts and terminology of the Internet and Intranet. The impacts of the Internet on our community and future Internet trends are discussed. Readers who are familiar with the Internet may choose to skip this chapter or browse through sections of interest.

Chapter 2 focuses on business applications on the Web. It begins by explaining the reasons why companies are eager to move their applications onto the Web and describes different types of applications running on the Web. The remainder of the chapter focuses on the many factors that you must take into account to successfully launch an application on the Web: server considerations, performance and capacity considerations, application and security considerations, and build-or-buy decisions.

Information system (IS) managers often cite security as the main reason why they are hesitant to implement an Internet solution. Consumers have also listed security as the main reason why they are not buying merchandise on the Internet. Therefore, Chapter 3 is dedicated to security considerations and explains techniques for protecting users and the enterprise. The techniques include authentication, secure communication channels, discretionary access control, firewalls, and proxy servers.

Section 2 Application Development

Chapter 4	Integrating Your Applications with the Web
Chapter 5	Server-side Programming Techniques
Chapter 6	Client-side Programming Techniques
Chapter 7	Visual Programming for the Web

Section 2 focuses on application development on the Web. Various techniques such as visual programming and programming in Java and JavaScript are discussed. These programming techniques can be used to connect database applications as well as transaction or messaging-based applications to the Web. We conclude this section with an explanation of a user-friendly approach, that is, a visual programming environment, to Web application development. We recommend the use of visual programming as much as possible because of its ease of use and rapid development capability. However, sophisticated users who want to develop their own programs to gain the best performance or make use of a system-level protocol may choose to use the Java programming techniques for both client-side and server-side development.

Chapter 4 describes three major approaches for accessing various data sources and applications from the Web: server-side programming, client-side programming, and HyperText Transfer Protocol (HTTP) integration. Examples and a comparison of the three approaches are discussed. User interface guidelines for Web applications and Website guidelines are provided.

The first generation of Web programmers use the common gateway interface (CGI) with programs written in Perl, C, and C++. Most gateway products are developed with this technique. The second generation of Web programmers use a Web server application program interface (API) for better performance. Because the program is executed on the server side and most likely resides on the Web server, this programming technique is called *server-side programming*. Chapter 5 describes server-side programming techniques, including invocation, parameter passing, and dynamic HTML. It also covers the issues and suggested solutions in managing browser sessions for a sequence of requests from a particular user.

You cannot talk about application development for the Internet without including Java. A compact, portable, object-oriented, interpretive language, Java is widely accepted as an Internet programming language. Chapter 6 describes the basic principles behind Java, the use of Java in clients and servers, the Internet inter-object request broker protocol (IIOP) and the remote method invocation (RMI), and Java database connectivity (JDBC) as well as advanced techniques for building Java client and server applications. Client-side programming techniques that use JavaScript, NetRexx, and specialized non-Java clients are also discussed.

Chapter 7 describes a visual programming environment that can be used to develop Web applications without the need to program a single line of code. The author of this chapter is the inventor of the Web Connection parts that enable IBM's VisualAge visual programming environment to be used for Web application development. He illustrates how to build a Web pizza-ordering application with VisualAge and describes how to use VisualAge's construction-by-parts paradigm to create Web applications that have DB2 data access and IMS, CICS, and MQSeries application connections.

Section 3 Integrating Database Applications on the Web

Chapter 8	Using Net.Data to Access Databases and Files
Chapter 9	Lotus Internet Applications

Section 3 focuses on gateway tools to "glue" new and existing programs onto the Web. Because the Web browser serves HTML documents, and existing programs do not deal with HTML tags, these gateway tools handle the HTML interface to the Web server so that applications can remain intact with no change in their application logic. Most Web gateway tools perform a conversion of a source document or a user front-end by adding HTML tags that the browser can understand. Examples are Lotus InterNotes for Notes documents and CICS Internet Gateway for CICS applications. Net.Data, a Web gateway tool for data access, provides a simple but powerful mechanism for users to customize report generation on the basis of the data retrieved.

In Chapter 8, the two architects of DB2 World Wide Web Connection and Net.Data share with you the design principles of both products. Although a relatively new product, DB2 World Wide Web Connection is already being used by many production Web applications, and it is also embedded in Internet applications such as Net.Commerce (Internet Mall), and the Olympic Games Server, which reported on the activities of the 1996 Olympic Games at a peak rate of 8.6 million visits to the Website per day. The development of Net.Data was motivated by feedback from customers on the success of DB2 World Wide Web Connection. Net.Data allows application logic written in programming languages such as Java, Perl, REXX, C, and C++. It also provides the capability to access files and databases by using simple file READ and WRITE functions and standard structured query language (SQL) without programming. Net.Data supports access to a variety of data sources such as files, Lotus Notes databases, IMS, DB2, and other relational databases. Chapter 8 includes hands-on examples of developing a Web application with Net.Data so that you can easily learn the features of the product.

Lotus Notes is a successful and popular groupware product. Users can enjoy Web technology using the Lotus Domino Server, which integrates Lotus Notes and a Web server. This integration enables a Web client to participate in Notes applications securely. Lotus Domino Server supports the uniform resource locator (URL) syntax for direct addressing of objects stored in a Notes database in addition to file-system-based URLs. With the Lotus Domino Server, you can deploy existing Lotus Notes applications on the Web and continue to use the tool set that Lotus Notes provides. Chapter 9 describes the Lotus Domino Server environment and a new set of Internet applications for rapid development of a broad range of Internet and Intranet business applications. The set of Internet applications includes Domino.Action, Domino.Merchant, Domino.Broadcast for PointCast, Lotus Notes:Newsstand, and Internet Customer Service.

Section 4 Integrating Transaction Systems with the Internet

Chapter 10	Transaction Processing Systems and the Internet
Chapter 11	Accessing CICS Applications from the Internet
Chapter 12	Accessing Encina, IMS TM, and MQSeries Applications from the Internet
Chapter 13	Electronic Commerce on the Internet

Section 4 is devoted to integrating transaction management systems on the Web. Chapter 10 describes the principles of transaction processing and their relationship with the Web. The general issues of integrating transaction processing systems with the Internet are discussed.

CICS is an application server that provides online transaction processing and transaction management for mission-critical applications on both IBM and non-IBM platforms. Many large corporations throughout the world are CICS customers. Chapter 11 focuses on accessing CICS applications on the Web. A number of approaches are discussed: HTTP support in CICS/ESA, CICS Gateway for Java, CICS Internet Gateway, and CICS Internet SupportPacs for the MVS Web server.

Transarc's Encina Monitor provides an environment to develop, run and administer distributed transaction processing applications. IMS TM is IBM's transaction monitor for environments that use both relational and hierarchical data stores and require the utmost in integrity, capacity, availability, and performance for distributed computing environments. MQSeries messaging software enables business applications to exchange information across different operating system platforms in a way that is straightforward and easy for programmers to implement. Chapter 12 describes the Web connection for Encina, IMS TM, and MQSeries.

More and more companies are setting up their storefronts on the Internet for marketing and direct sales. Many are creating virtual companies that do business solely on the Internet, not from a physical store. Chapter 13 examines electronic commerce and the issues associated with buying and selling on the Internet. Examples of electronic commerce, such as the Web Object Manager and Net.Commerce, are included.

Section 5 A Case Study

Chapter 14 An Application Server

Section 5 presents a case study in building a large-scale Web application server. Chapter 14 brings together all of the concepts discussed in the previous chapters and reiterates the importance of considering all of the technical components required to develop an Internet application server. An application server is intended to satisfy a particular need, such as merchandising, publications, or communications, by pulling together Web technology and interfacing it with data access and transaction technologies.

First, a Web application platform consisting of secure Web browsers and servers is presented with special emphasis on using Java applets (Java code executed in the client), accessing data, and tying the pieces together to solve a specific problem. Next, the user interface that an end user (for example, a customer) will use to communicate with the application server is described. Finally, the possible interfaces that can be used between a Web server and the application server are discussed, as well as the performance and portability tradeoffs that a developer or architect must make when designing the server. An example, including code, is given to demonstrate how to integrate a Web server and some data stored in a database for an application server product.

Conclusion

Numerous techniques and Web gateway tools are introduced in this book with hands-on examples. The techniques and tools are independent of, but also complement, each other. For example, the Java client-side programming technique can be used to develop Java applets used in VisualAge, Net.Data, and the Lotus Domino Server. Often, users choose a technique according to their platform, their environment, and the tools with which they are most comfortable. A Lotus Notes user may choose to use the Lotus Domino Server to access enterprise data, whereas a non-Lotus-Notes user may choose VisualAge to develop Web database applications. Users who simply want to access data from the Web may choose to use Net.Data, whereas others may choose to write their own programs in Perl or Java to connect their Web applications. Throughout the book, we discuss the benefits and limitations of each approach and provide guidelines for selecting the appropriate tools.

SECTION 1

Introduction and System Considerations

CHAPTER 1

Introduction to the Internet and Intranet

The Internet (also called the Net, information superhighway, cyberspace, or the Web) is the world's largest computer network, connecting more than four million computers and 45 million users to one another. Some analysts believe that the number of Internet users will grow to 200 million by the year 2000. Since the introduction of Web technology, anyone—individuals, small businesses, universities, and large corporations—can now do global publishing inexpensively. Internet Web pages have become the world's largest networked multimedia digital library. For example, Digital Equipment Corporation's Web search product, AltaVista, provides retrieval services for more than 30 million pages on 275,600 servers and more than four million articles from 14,000 Usenet news groups. Every month, six thousand servers are added to Lycos, another Web search product. Yahoo! reports 20 million "hits" per day.

Besides facilitating publishing and thus providing many educational opportunities, the Internet affects the daily lives of us all. In this chapter, you will discover the impact of the Internet on our community, and look at the history and main technologies of the Internet and the Web. Because the Internet also affects software development within an enterprise, it is important to examine the similarity between the Intranet (the Internet within a corporation) and client and server technology, as well as present and future trends of the Internet and Intranet.

THE INTERNET AND THE COMMUNITY

No one will dispute the importance of the telephone and television in our lives. They are ubiquitous, and they are one of the primary communication devices for information sharing. The Internet, designed with global information sharing in mind, is destined to have an impact on every person in the world that is orders of magnitude greater than that of telephones and TVs.

Are you aware that your name, address, and phone number can be easily found through the Internet? If you are listed in a local phone book in any city in the United States, chances are that your name can be found in the "Ultimate White Pages" (see Figure 1.1), http://www.infochase.com/ref/ultimates. In that online phone book, you can find phone numbers and addresses without paying the cost for directory assistance. If you have someone's phone number, you can perform a reverse search for his or her address, or, if you have an address, you can get a map showing the location

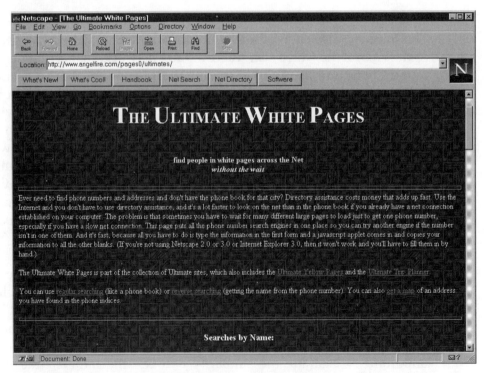

Figure 1.1 The Ultimate White Pages, http://www.infochase.com/ref/ultimates.

of that address. All this can be done easily and instantly, anywhere, any time, if you have access to the Internet.

By surfing or cruising the Net (that is, accessing information), you can read more than 850 magazines and 880 newspapers online, have a sneak preview of hundreds of movies, find out what happened at the Olympic Games, or cast a vote for your favorite presidential candidate for a news survey. You can look up plane and train schedules and get the weather forecasts for any part of the world (see Figure 1.2). You can do home banking and shop around for the lowest-priced merchandise before you make any purchase. All this is made possible by any one of the popular Web browsers.

The Internet is not only for adults. Kids can make friends on the Internet just as adults can and find all kinds of games. The http://www.4Kids.org Web page, designed for kids only, highlights fun, educational, and safe spots for kids to visit on the Web. See Figure 1.3 for another example of a

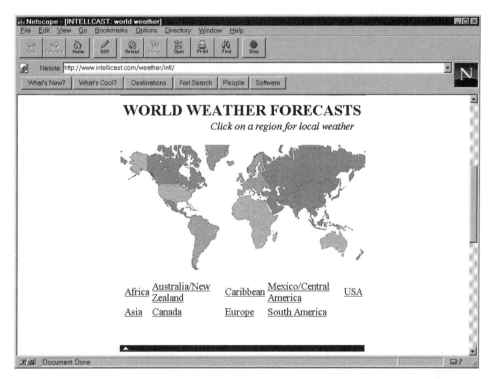

Figure 1.2 World weather report sections, http://www.intellicast.com/weather/intl. (Imagery courtesy of INTELLICAST, a registered trademark of WSI Corporation.)

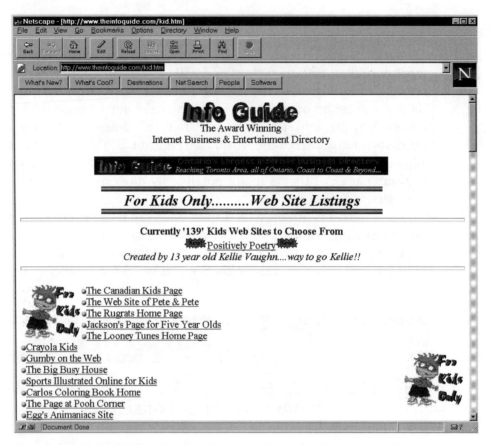

Figure 1.3 Info Guide—For Kids Only, http://www.theinfoguide.com/kid.htm.

website for children only. Some schools place homework assignments on the Internet for kids who are absent. Other schools let faculty reserve periodicals and books from their libraries through the Internet. Some universities are planning to allow students to submit applications for admission through the Internet. Indeed it would not be surprising to find a Parents Teachers Association (PTA) meeting conducted through the chat facility from a browser!

A BRIEF HISTORY OF THE INTERNET

Although the Internet has received a tremendous amount of attention recently, as the number of users has grown exponentially, it has been around since the late 1960s. In 1969, the U.S. Department of Defense funded a research and development project to create a network to connect computers among universities, government agencies, and companies that have government contracts for information sharing. Thus the Advanced Research Projects Administration Network (ARPANET) was born. In 1975, ARPANET was converted from an experimental network to an operational network, and the administration of the network was transferred to the Defense Communications Agency (DCA). The data communication protocol used in ARPANET underwent many revisions to become the basic Transmission Control Protocol/Internet Protocol (TCP/IP) that computers on the Internet use to communicate with each other.

TCP/IP was adopted as a military standard in 1983 when the government mandated that all computers connected to the ARPANET must convert to using TCP/IP. At the same time, ARPANET was divided into MILNET and ARPANET. MILNET is used exclusively by the military. ARPANET is used by universities and other organizations. The Internet encompasses both MILNET and ARPANET.

Besides being an open protocol standard, TCP/IP is independent of any physical network hardware. It can be run over Ethernet, token-ring, modem, X.25, logical unit 6.2 (LU 6.2), and other networks. Two protocol services, Serial Line Interface Protocol (SLIP) and Point-to-Point Protocol (PPP), are provided to allow fast access through modems to interface with TCP/IP systems.

INTRODUCTION TO THE WORLD WIDE WEB

Initially, the most popular application on the Internet was electronic mail (e-mail). In 1989, Tim Berners-Lee of the Conseil Europeen pour la Recherche Nucleaire, (CERN), the European Laboratory for Particle Physics in Geneva, introduced the hypertext language, HyperText Markup Language (HTML), in a paper entitled "Information Management: A Proposal." In 1990, the name *World Wide Web* was introduced. The first Web program was built on NeXT computers. In February 1993, the National Center for Supercomputing Applications (NCSA) at the University of Illinois introduced Mosaic, a graphical, user-friendly browser for X-Windows that enables users to click on an icon to get to the linked document. It was not until November 1993, however, that Mosaic became popular, when it was ported to Intel and Macintosh platforms. Around the same time, much of the software on the Web, including source code, became available free of charge for users to download. Free software, especially browsers, probably did as much to popularize the Net as anything else. In 1994, Marc Andreessen, one of the original developers of Mosaic, left the university to become a co-founder of Netscape Communications Corporation, one of the leading companies in Internet technology.

The Web became popular primarily because of its ease of use and the simplicity with which you can access and deliver objects anywhere on the Internet—thanks to the following technologies:

- Web browsers
- HTML
- HyperText Transport Protocol (HTTP)
- Uniform Resource Locator (URL)

The W3C, a nonprofit Web consortium consisting of companies such as IBM, Microsoft, Netscape Communications Corporation, and Sun Microsystems, has adopted HTML, URL, and HTTP for standardization. Next, we describe in detail each of the technologies listed above and other Internet service protocols. We also discuss a survey on Web usage and the database retrieval systems on the Web.

Web Browser

A browser is a program that runs in the client environment to retrieve information from the Internet. It is most commonly used to browse through an HTML document, sometimes referred to as a *page*. Users can get to an HTML document through a URL, the Internet addressing scheme for a document or a request. Users can also get documents by searching with one of the many Internet search products, such as Yahoo!, AltaVista, Lycos, or Infoseek.

Built by NCSA in 1993, Mosaic was the first graphical user interface browser enabling users to get to different documents easily. Today, browsers are being introduced with more and more functions, such as reading news and forums, receiving and sending mail, and participating interactively in video conferences. Many browsers come with their own HTML editors for users to create and edit HTML pages. They also support the downloading of a Java applet (a small application written in the Java programming language) from a server to the client and provide a Java interpreter to interpret the applet. This latest capability enables the server-centric Internet to provide more customization at the client by offloading some of the workload to the client side. Netscape, Spyglass, and Microsoft remain the leading providers of browser technology.

HTML

HTML is a document scripting language invented by Tim Berners-Lee while at CERN. HTML is derived from the Standard Generalized Markup Language (SGML). It consists of tags starting with a left angle bracket (<), a tag name, and a right angle bracket (>), for example, <H1> for Heading1.

HTML is used for document publishing on the Web. An HTML document can be viewed from a browser, which retrieves the document from a Web server through the HTTP. HTML provides two fundamental functions: *hyperlink,* a capability to reference or link to other documents, and *hypermedia,* a capability to include multimedia documents such as image, audio, video, and animation.

Because the creation of HTML pages requires only basic word processing skills, and not programming skills, the Web is extremely easy to use for publishing documents. You can learn more about HTML from various books on HTML, or from the following documents on the Web:

> **A Guide to HTML:**
> http://www.ncsa.uiuc.edu/General/Internet/WWW/HTMLPrimer.html
>
> **HTML 3.2 specification:**
> http://www.w3.org/pub/WWW/MarkUp/Wilbur
>
> **HTML 2.0 specification:**
> http://www.w3.org/pub/WWW/Markup/html-spec

You can use any text editor to write an HTML document. You can also use many page-building tools such as Adobe PageMill, Microsoft FrontPage, and NetObjects Fusion to design your Web page. Many publishing tools, such as WordPerfect 5.1 and Lotus Word Pro, also provide an option for converting their documents into HTML documents. As a matter of fact, HTML has become so popular that you are certain to find an HTML converter for any tools you use. For example, the Lotus Freelance Graphics 96 Edition provides an option to convert your Freelance presentation into

HTML pages, Lotus Approach 97 Edition can "Websize" your Approach applications for the Web, and IBM BookServer can convert BookManager documents into HTML pages. Other converters can be found at http://www.yahoo.com/Computers_and_Internet/Software/Internet/World_Wide_Web/HTML_Converters/Commercial_Products.

HyperText Transport Protocol (HTTP)

HTTP is an application-level protocol for retrieving documents with a fast response time over the Internet. It is a generic, stateless, object-oriented protocol. An HTTP server is commonly implemented as a *daemon* listening for the request of a particular port. As a result, it is also called HyperText Transport Protocol Daemon (HTTPD). The browser is commonly used as a user front end to specify the HTTP when a document is served through a URL.

The W3C has standardized HTTP, and its specification can be found on the W3C home page (http://www.w3.org). You can download from the Internet many implementations of HTTP servers. Many newer HTTP servers provide better performance with multithreaded connections, inline caching of images, and streaming of audio and video contents. There are also two security protocols for the Web server: Netscape Communications Corporation's Secure Socket Level (SSL) and Enterprise Integration Technologies (EIT's)/Terisa's Secure HTTP (SHTTP). SSL provides mutual authentication, data encryption, and data integrity to protect any higher level protocol built on sockets, such as File Transfer Protocol (FTP) and HTTP. SHTTP authenticates HTTP transactions only. Clients and/or servers can sign and/or encrypt with a public key or private key. Chapter 3 describes both SSL and SHTTP in detail. Among the providers of new-generation HTTP and secure HTTP servers are Netscape Communications Corporation, Microsoft, and IBM.

Most HTTP servers provide a CGI to execute user programs which can then maintain the necessary states that the programs require. Next, we discuss the CGI in detail.

Common Gateway Interface (CGI)

The CGI provides a simple mechanism to execute within an HTTP server a program requested by the returned HTML document. The HTTP server passes control to the program to be executed with the user's input parameters in the form of "Name=Value" pairs. The program can interface with other resources outside a normal HTTP server to read from or write to a

Introduction to the Internet and Intranet

file, make a database request, or perform other operations. Most existing applications use the CGI.

Although the CGI is easy to use, it is rather inefficient in executing programs because when a client requests a CGI program, a new copy of the CGI program is created and terminated for each request. As a result, many servers have introduced their own application programming interface (API) to interface with user programs. Some examples of these APIs are the Netscape server application program interface (NSAPI), IBM Internet connection server application program interface (ICAPI), and Microsoft Internet server application program interface (ISAPI). Many gateway products and user applications are switching from CGI to support these APIs for better performance.

Uniform Resource Locator (URL)

A URL is a scheme for addressing distributed requests over the Internet. It indicates which Internet service is used, where to send the request, and what the request is. The browser retrieves a document specified by a URL. A URL is used in an HTML document to reference or link to another document.

A URL has the following format:

URL Format

Protocol://hostname[:domain_port] path[/request]

where:
- Protocol can be one of the following:
    - *file* for local file
    - *ftp* for file transfer
    - *gopher* for gopher service
    - *http* for hypertext documents
    - *mailto* for outgoing mail
    - *news* or *nttp* for usenet news
    - *telnet* for connecting to other computers
    - *wais* for wais database search
- hostname is the name of the host computer

(continued)

> - domain_port is the network port number, and it is optional.
>   The default is 80 for http; 70 for gopher.
> - path is the path to get to the request
> - request can be a filename.file_extension or a query.
>   If no request is given, the default is the home page of the hostname.

Other Internet service protocols such as FTP, gopher, and WAIS, are discussed in the next section. Here are some examples of URLs.

> **Examples of URLs**
>
> HTTP request of IBM home page
>   http://www.ibm.com
>
> Query with parameters to find out more about HTML
>   http://www.altavista.digital.com/cgi-bin/
>   query?pg=q&what=web&fmt=.&q=HTML
>
> Partial request of mypage
>   mypage.html

Once you have retrieved a document by means of a URL, any subsequent reference to a URL from within that document with the same protocol, hostname, port number, and path can be a partial URL consisting of only the file name or request. The third example above is a partial URL, and it is equivalent to writing http://hostname[:domain_port]path/mypage.html. Partial URLs simplify the specification of a URL inside a document and make it easier to move the document to another server.

File Transfer Protocol (FTP)

FTP is used mainly for sending and retrieving files over the Internet. To perform an FTP operation between your computer and a remote computer, you must have a logon ID to the remote computer, unless an anonymous ID with null password has been set up. Once you have logged on to a remote server with the FTP service, you can see the directory of files that you can transfer. Most browsers support URLs with the FTP service. More information about FTP shareware and freeware can be found at http://www.yahoo.com/Computers_and_Internet/Software/Internet/FTP/

Telnet

Telnet is another method of connecting to a remote computer with a user logon ID and password. Once you are connected, you can perform operations as if you were on your local machine. Because Telnet requires a user logon ID and password and familiarity with the organization of information in the remote machine, it is not commonly used in a URL.

Gopher

Gopher is an Internet protocol and software that enables users to search and browse distributed documents held on servers. Hypertext documents are not supported with Gopher. The flexibility of the Web subsumes the gopher technology. Many browsers support the gopher protocol in delivering documents from gopher servers. You can find "The World of Gopher" manual at http://www.unidata.ucar.edu/projects/ieis/manual/manual/gopher.html.

Wide Area Information Server (WAIS)

The Wide Area Information Server (WAIS) represents an attempt to standardize access requests to databases on the Internet. Thinking Machines Corporation invented WAIS in 1988. WAIS is now owned by WAIS Inc. Although there are approximately 500 freely available WAIS databases on the Internet, the WAIS protocol is not widely used because of the much more popular Web and Internet search products that are available.

Mailto

Mailto is an Internet protocol for sending messages to an Internet user. Because e-mail is a popular Internet service, most browsers support an e-mail facility for users to send and receive mail that may include multimedia objects and URLs, without explicitly using the protocol. Figure 1.4 shows the mail service provided by a Netscape browser.

News (Usenet)

News or Network News Transfer Protocol (NTTP) is an Internet protocol enabling users to participate in user groups, bulletin board systems (BBSs), and forums, which are essentially public e-mail facilities, where you can share your opinion on a certain topic or seek advice from experts. Most browsers provide news support by enabling you to read messages from a news group, append your reply to a particular message, and post messages. See Figure 1.5 for an example of news group on DB2www/Net.Data.

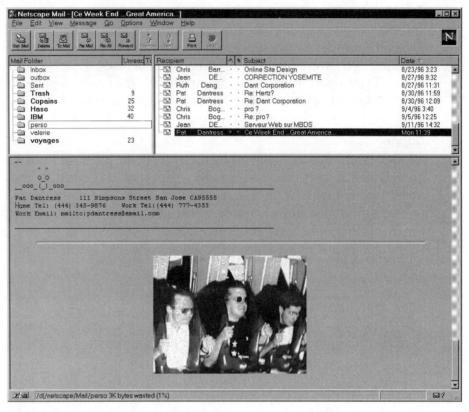

Figure 1.4 Mail support in a browser.

Database Retrieval

One of the most exciting attractions for users surfing the Web is the promise of finding the information they want. There are many content databases with search engines on the market. Most provide free query service; with a paid subscription, you can get your personalized news and clippings delivered to you daily. Some give you a summary of the documents that satisfy your search criteria. The quality of the search software depends primarily on its database coverage and index mechanism. Almost all Internet search software returns a different set of documents, even when the search criteria are the same. You have to explore each product to find the one that suits you best. Table 1.1 summarizes some of the Internet search software on the Internet today.

Introduction to the Internet and Intranet

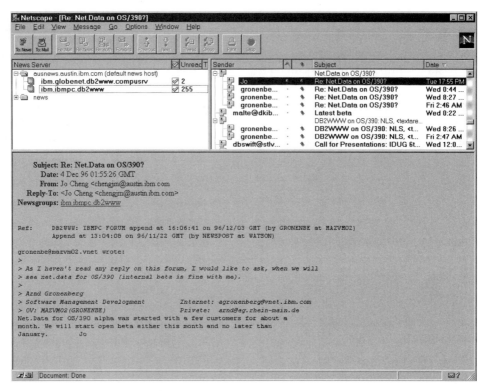

Figure 1.5 A news group on DB2www/Net.Data.

Web Use

The Graphic, Visualization and Usability Center (GVU) of Georgia Technical University has been conducting online surveys of Web use since 1994. According to the GVU's fifth World Wide Web User Survey of May 1996 (see Figure 1.6), more than 80 percent of the 11,700 respondents access the Web on a daily basis, and most use it for browsing and entertainment purposes. The survey found that one of the major issues of Web use is data privacy—respondents strongly believed that a user ought to be able to visit sites on the Internet anonymously. The major problem reported (80.9% of respondents) about Web use was, not surprisingly, speed.

A detailed report on Web use can be found on the GVU's World Wide Web User Surveys page, http://www.cc.gatech.edu/gvu/user_surveys.

Table 1.1 Internet Search Products

Name	URL	Database Coverage	Function
AltaVista	http://altavista.digital.com	30 million pages, 14,000 Usenets	Gives summary, URL
Excite	http://www.excite.com	Web, reviews, Usenet, advertisements	Gives rank Gives summary, URL
InfoMarket	http://www.infomarket.ibm.com	69 newswires, 300 newspapers, 798 newsletters, 6306 journals, 11 million companies	Queries by subject Gives summary Pays per views
Infoseek	http://www.infoseek.com	Web, Usenets, selected sites, within categories of selected sites	Enables query by field of interest Gives similar page
Lycos	http://www.lycos.com	3.5 million URLs, A2Z directory, reviews	Enables query by subject Gives rank, summary
Magellan	http://www.mckinley.com	Web, Magellan's ratings and abstracts	Enables query by site's rating Gives review, URL
Yahoo!	http://www.yahoo.com	Web	Enables query by field of interest Gives summary

INTRANET: CLIENT AND SERVER REVISITED

In the early 1980s, client and server technology was introduced to divide an application into two parts. One part (the client) interfaces with end users and uses the power of desktop computing. The other part (the server) interfaces with the enterprise where resources such as files, databases, larger memory, and more powerful processes are shared. Client and server technology provides many benefits: cleaner interfaces and better programming practices to separate the end-user interface from the application logic; the ability to use desktop computing while at the same time sharing resources of a more powerful server; and more flexibility for client environments, than the traditional server programming. Therefore, many

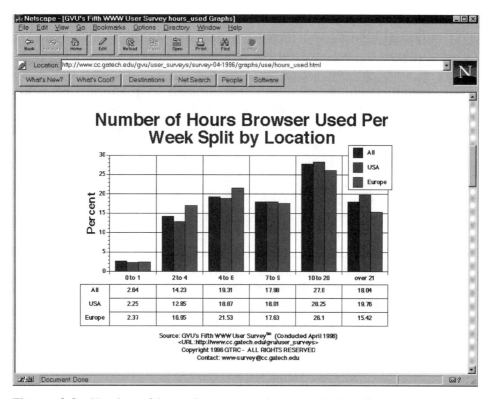

Figure 1.6 Number of hours browser used per week, http://www.cc.gatech.edu/gvu/user_surveys/survey-04-1996/graphs/use/hours_used.html.

information technology (IT) shops have deployed their enterprise applications, using the client and server model. However, the implementation of client and server technology becomes very expensive when the IT departments can no longer control the client environments and platforms. For example, one department may choose to use the UNIX platform, while another group may want to use Windows desktops. When the client environment becomes more diverse, porting a client application from one platform (for example, Intel PC) to another (for example, Macintosh) becomes difficult and complicated. Moreover, the distribution of client applications to the clients (end-user machines) is a challenge when the clients are not necessarily stationary.

The Intranet, the Internet inside your company, is the implementation of Internet technologies within a corporation over the enterprise network inside a firewall. Web technologies use a client and server model. The graphical browser is the client, and it communicates with the server through HTTP. The browser, being ubiquitous (that is, you can find a browser on any hardware or software platform), facilitates the distribution of client software. It is also the preferred end-user interface because it enables users to link multiple documents by pointing and clicking, work with multiple data types (text, image, audio, video, and animation), and enable plug-in viewers for customized data sources such as video movies and Cryptolope documents. On the server side, the HTTP server links to the server application through the CGI program or dynamic link library (DLL) exit. Many gateway tools have been developed to ease the linking of existing applications to the Web.

Web technologies are solving many of the challenges that IT shops have faced in the past decade to deploy their client and server applications. With the Intranet, one can enjoy the benefits of Web technologies without ever going outside the company's network. Intranets have become the focus of the next stage of client and server implementation. Packaged software companies, such as Dun & Bradstreet, SAP, and PeopleSoft, are developing their software packages to be used on the Intranet. It is expected that many applications will be run on Intranets in the next few years.

PRESENT AND FUTURE INTERNET TRENDS

Other Internet technologies are trying to achieve as great an impact as Web technologies. In this section we look at Sun Microsystems' Java technology, Netscape's JavaScript, Microsoft's Visual Basic Script (VBScript), the Virtual Reality Modeling Language (VRML), network computers, and Internet phone. Finally, we hypothesize what will happen in the Internet area over the next 10 to 20 years.

Java

Sun Microsystems' Java is a new object-oriented programming language that has gained high visibility on the Internet. Java was originally designed in 1990 by James Gosling, who named the language *Oak* after the tree outside his office window. Oak was designed to be used for writing control software for microprocessors inside consumer appliances such as televisions and VCRs. It has a small footprint (compact code) and is a safe (crash-proof) language. Over the years, Oak went through several revisions. It did not become a popular programming language until Sun Microsystems renamed it Java (because Oak was a name trademarked by others) in 1995 and distributed it free of charge over the Internet.

Besides its small footprint, its object-oriented features, and its being a safe language without pointer references, Java's rise to fame is attributable primarily to its HotJava browser capability to download Java applets (small applications) to the client (browser) for execution. The browser contains the Java run-time, known as the Java Virtual Machine, executes the Java applets (Java byte codes). This mechanism allows data and programs to reside anywhere in the network and be accessible to your local computer. The HotJava browser transforms a dumb browser, where most of the work is done in the server, into an intelligent browser, where some of the customized logic can be executed in the client through Java applets. It is no wonder that Netscape Communications Corporation, which has the majority browser marketshare, is eager to incorporate the support of Java applets into its own browser to compete with others. The timing is also right—Internet use has exploded exponentially. Because Sun provides free licensing of the Java interpreter, many Java applets containing animation have been developed and shared among users. Therefore, Java has become so popular on the Internet that many companies have licensed the Java interpreter from Sun and promise to deliver a Java virtual machine in their operating systems. Suddenly, Java has become the universal client language.

Sun has also introduced JavaBeans, an architecture- and platform-neutral API for creating and using dynamic Java components. JavaBeans is Sun's strategy to follow the object-oriented programming paradigm to establish reusable software components for the construction of customized applications. If, indeed, one can build customized applications easily with the JavaBeans components, Java will have an extraordinary impact on software development.

Although popular, Java presents its own challenges. Its byte codes are interpreted language. It is still slower than some of the native platform languages, despite many just-in-time (JIT) compilers that report more than a 20-fold improvement over the Java interpreter. Tools for Java application development are still in their infancy. According to the GVU's fifth World Wide Web User Survey of May 1996, only 17.3 percent of respondents who have authored on the Web have programmed in Java. Programming in Java requires more skills than publishing documents in HTML. Furthermore, Java is not without competition. Microsoft, which dominates the PC operating system platform market, is introducing ActiveX controls for the Internet. The success of Java is yet to be proven.

JavaScript and VBScript

JavaScript is an object-based, interpretive scripting language invented by Netscape Communications Corporation. Although Netscape named the language JavaScript, it is not the same language as Java. JavaScript statements are embedded in HTML documents; they describe links between events such as clicking on a button. JavaScript enables flexible definition of dialogs between users and applets. One of the features of JavaScript is that it allows user input to be validated at the client side. JavaScript is supported by the Netscape browser and Netscape servers. On the server side, it can be used to access data from files and databases. Microsoft has announced its intent to support JavaScript in its Internet Explorer.

Microsoft is promoting Visual Basic Script (VBScript), a subset of Visual Basic that works with ActiveX controls, as the standard interactive environment on the Web. VBScript is supported by Microsoft Internet Explorer Version 3.0 and higher. Microsoft is making the VBScript runtime code free of license charge to encourage software vendors to develop applications using VBScript.

Both JavaScript and VBScript are evolving. They are both simple, object-based, event-driven scripting languages that provide interactive elements in HTML documents. JavaScript has a head start over VBScript; but VBScript, as a subset of Visual Basic, has its appeal to the large installation base of Visual Basic users.

Virtual Reality Modeling Language (VRML)

Virtual Reality Modeling Language (VRML) is a scene description language for describing three-dimensional (3D) graphics and their environments on the Web. It is a file syntax for defining nodes, or 3D objects, and their behaviors (see the example below). VRML was first developed by Mark Pesce and Tony Parisi in late 1993. It was presented to the First International Conference on the World Wide Web in Geneva, where the name VRML was introduced. A group was formed to work on a VRML specification immediately after the conference. A subset of the Inventor File Format and other extensions from Silicon Graphics Inc. form the basis of VRML. The following is an example of a VRML program.

VRML has been used for art galleries, environmental sciences, entertainment and games, and scientific modeling. Figure 1.7 shows an example of using VRML to model a virtual city, which you can explore by "walking"

> **Example of VRML Syntax Defining a Red Shape**
>
> ```
> #VRM; V2.0 utf8
> Transform
>   children [
>     DirectionalLight {
>       direction 0 0-1 # Light shining into scene
>     },
>
> Transform    { #The red sphere
>   translation 3 0 1
>     children [
>       Shape {
>         geometry Sphere {radius 2.3}
>         appearance Appearance [
>           material Material {diffuseColor 1 0 0}]#Red
>         }
>       ]
>     },
>            ....
> ]
> ```

around it. Most of these hot spots are hyperlinked to other information Web sites.

The use of VRML greatly enhances the visualization capability of the Internet. Many projects are under way to place museums or libraries (e.g., the U.S. Holocaust Museum, Vatican Library, and U.S. Library of Congress) online, model a city (virtual Los Angeles project) before roads and houses are built, and build virtual malls. VRML technology provides us with more educational opportunities, promotes art appreciation, and enables simulation at a relatively low cost.

Network Computers

Network computers are also known as *thin clients, Internet appliances, Java stations, Java machines, net boxes, bare metal,* and *hollow PCs.* Essentially, a network computer is a relatively inexpensive computer (under $1,000) that supports Internet access through a browser with a Java virtual machine for running Java-based applications. The objective of network computers is to create a new desktop computer that can introduce new network comput-

Figure 1.7 Virtual San Francisco, http://www.planet9.com/worlds/vrsf.wrl.

ing applications and user interface technologies to customers with a dramatically reduced total cost of PC ownership.

Today, most network computers are targeting businesses, not consumers, to replace the estimated 30 million dumb terminals in service. Potential users include data processors, airline ticket reservation personnel, and people who take customer orders. IBM, Oracle, and many other companies have described their strategy of network computers. Network computers will have a major impact on the community when consumer can use them.

Internet Phone

Internet phone is software that enables you to communicate verbally with others over the Internet. You can conduct long distance or even international conversations through Internet phone for the cost of a local Internet connection. You can make calls to Internet phone users from within a Web browser to hold private conversations or participate in a public online forum. Using Internet phone is simple—just click on a hypertext link to a Web forum that supports Internet phone, and the browser will automatically connect you with the forum. With the latest Digital Simultaneous Voice Data (DSVD) modems, you can even send data and talk at the same time. Intel markets an application that enables you to share photos while you talk to your family and friends over the Internet. Many companies are using Internet phone for online technical support.

To enhance the utility of the Internet phone, the JavaTel initiative developed by Sun and other companies such as Lucent Technologies, IBM, Intel, Northern Telecom, and Novell, provides a uniform interface for computer telephony applications in the Java environment through the Java telephony application interface (JTAPI). JTAPI defines basic telephony functions such as call, disconnect, and hold, as well as advanced functions such as call transfer and conference calls. Applications supporting JTAPI can run on Java-compatible devices such as network computers and telephones. With the uniform API, users can choose components from different communications hardware and software vendors.

Many Internet phone providers, are adding features such as audio compression for improved audio quality, video compression for transmitting live pictures, and online phone directories. IBM DirectTalkMail provides a phone mail service on the Internet that users can use when they are not available to answer the phone. IBM, Intel, and Vocaltec are some of the Internet phone providers.

What's Next?

Every two years or so, the computer industry champions a new technology. In the recent past, we have seen client/server technology, object-oriented design and programming, object-oriented databases, and multimedia technology. Remember the interactive TV that promised to deliver movies at home on demand? Is the Internet just another passing fancy? In this section, we share with you consultants' predictions and hypothesize about what to expect next from the Internet.

The number of users accessing the Internet will grow to 200 million by the year 2000. The number of Web pages that will be connected to the Internet will grow exponentially, doubling every year. Having your personal home pages connected to the Web will be commonplace. The majority of desktop computers will have one or more Websites, with their own HTTP servers residing on the desktop. A significant increase in the amount of network data will create tremendous opportunities for the software and hardware and services industries. There will be a breakthrough in information gathering and filtering technology, which will handle trillions of bytes of data.

Forester Research indicates that three-quarters of the companies surveyed expect to offer online transactions through the Internet by 1997. There are now 23 million workers using corporate Intranets worldwide. By 2000, there will be 180 million, according to the IDC consulting company. Both Java and ActiveX will become popular. As a result, third-party vendors will continue to develop applications and tools for both the Microsoft and non-Microsoft worlds.

The biggest impact of the Internet is the way in which it facilitates interaction and improves communication. Today, its biggest limitation is speed due to network bandwidth requirements for multi-media content. Ten to 20 years from now, network providers will complete the installation of high-speed lines to every household. Every home could have an Internet address, analogous to the 95 percent of U.S. households that are wired for cable. Personal and network computers will become household appliances, just like television sets, which will also be networked. Furthermore, they will be used for multiple purposes, serving as a home's central repository for phone mail, e-mail, faxes, files, and databases. Interaction with people remotely will be enhanced with Internet videoconferencing, greatly reducing the need to travel in order to communicate. As a result, virtual communities, virtual workplaces, virtual universities, and virtual malls will be very common. Children with special interests and talents will be able to meet via an Internet conference room for their special education, creating the virtual classroom.

With people working at home over the Internet, children attending virtual schools, and people shopping in virtual malls, there might be less traffic on the nation's highways, but there will be more demand on the information superhighway! With improvements in technology, more competition, and government deregulation, all of these scenarios could occur in the foreseeable future.

CHAPTER **2**

Business Applications on the Web

Can you make money on the Internet? Is the Internet ready for real-time transactions? In this chapter, you will see how the Internet can be used as a communication tool to reduce time to market, as an information-sharing tool to raise product quality, and as a business management tool to reduce overhead costs. First, we look at the many reasons why you should go online and the different models for doing business on the Internet. Next we describe the different kinds of Internet and Intranet business applications, giving examples of each. Many of these applications use database management systems to store and retrieve pertinent information as well as transaction management systems to support large numbers of online transactions. Of the examples described, most were built using techniques and Web gateway tools described in this book. We conclude the chapter by listing the points you must consider to ensure a successful Internet or Intranet application.

WHY GO ONLINE?

The reasons for moving your business applications to the Intranet or Internet are endless, but consider these:

1. *Improve customer service.* The Internet provides easy access to the most up-to-date company or customer order information. When customers, partners, and suppliers can retrieve the information they need when they need it, their satisfaction is bound to improve. One reason why United Parcel Service (UPS) customers are so satisfied, for example, is that they can obtain online, up-to-date information on the status of their overnight packages.

2. *Exploit low entry cost.* Setting up a Website is fairly easy and inexpensive. You can use Web server freeware, or you can buy a Web server with service support at a relatively low cost. Many TCP/IP providers offer a flat monthly fee for Internet connection. The cost of communication is even cheaper than an 800 number or fax. Indeed, the cost of setting up a Website is so inexpensive that many individuals have their own Websites.

3. *Reduce costs of services rendered.* Services provided on the Internet save on labor costs by eliminating human intervention. In addition, the Internet's nonstop service, 24 hours a day and seven days a week, eliminates having to pay overtime to anyone.

4. *Improve corporate image.* The Internet is the hottest technology going. Any company that has anything to do with the Internet is automatically perceived as a technology leader. Moving applications online greatly improves the corporate image.

5. *Reach a common, global market place.* The Internet reaches your existing and potential customers worldwide, thereby increasing sales opportunities, without an enormous sales force and marketing infrastructure.

6. *Conduct paperless transactions.* You can enter a contest, purchase an opera ticket, and submit a travel expense for your manager's signature through the Internet or Intranet without any paper transaction. Furthermore, publishing can be done online without killing one tree. Internet applications eliminate not only paperwork but also the potential for human error in handling the paper transaction.

7. *Develop alternative distribution channel.* Instead of the traditional product packaging on a CD-ROM, some companies are using the Internet to distribute software. Because of the low bandwidth of the Internet for most consumers without Integrated Services Digital Network (ISDN) or T1 connections, however, distribution of soft-

ware through the Internet is effective only for relatively small software.

8. *Create new business opportunities.* The Internet creates many new business opportunities, such as virtual stores, virtual education centers, electronic commerce, and on-demand entertainment. It also creates different models for doing business online, as discussed in the next section.

9. *Increase productivity.* The browser is so intuitive that everyone can learn how to use it within minutes and link together pertinent data to obtain more background information about related topics. With such in-depth information readily at hand, users can easily increase their productivity.

10. *Enhance internal operations.* Like Internet applications, Intranet applications rapidly disseminate information and thus improve the efficiency of internal operations.

Downside of Business on the Internet

Before rushing to put your applications on the Web, be aware that Web technology for commercial use is still in its infancy. A lot of the benefits of the Internet and Intranet are intangible. The results are sometimes difficult to measure because there is no easy way of accounting for sales made in a shop advertised on the Internet or from a previous visit to a home page. Performance is a challenge because it is hard to predict the number of concurrent users at any given time, and the response time of retrieving a home page depends on multiple factors, such as the speed and bandwidth of the communication line, the number of concurrent users, and the power of the server. More often than not, the server is down and the document cannot be delivered. In the worst case, slow response time or unavailability of the Web page may create a negative impression among your customers. Although both the Internet and Intranet has low entry costs, using them could become very expensive if you consider the costs of hiring a top graphic designer to design your home page and acquiring more hardware and software to manage your expanding Internet activities. Both Internet and Intranet applications do improve productivity, but employees may have a tendency to goof off and browse non-business-related information on company time.

SO YOU WANT TO MAKE MONEY ONLINE?

The Internet opens up many business opportunities. To make money, you can choose from among four Internet business models:

1. *Selling products or services online.* Many retail companies such as L.L. Bean have put their merchandise catalogs online. Many consulting companies provide services to set up your applications online, with a revenue-sharing option that benefits both you and the provider.
2. *Leasing advertising space.* Many companies lease advertising space to promote their products. Every time you visit the Yahoo! Web page, you are bombarded by advertisements ranging from automobiles to magazine subscriptions.
3. *Charging content fee.* You have to subscribe or pay before you can view the content. This model is used for many adults-only pages.
4. *Providing Internet connection services.* All of the major telephone companies provide some form of connection services. You are charged a monthly fee or by connection time.

The success of selling products and services and charging a content fee on the Internet depends heavily on the degree of security of the secure payment mechanisms that the electronic commerce systems provide. Many people feel uncomfortable supplying their credit card information for small transactions, such as paying a dollar to obtain an interesting article or a quarter to play an Internet game. As an alternative to using your credit card for purchases, CyberCash, Inc. offers CyberCoin, electronic money to be used for Internet shopping. You can buy CyberCoin for your electronic wallet using your credit card through a secure transaction. From then on, you can spend the CyberCoin money you have.

WHICH APPLICATIONS BELONG ONLINE?

In addition to creating opportunities to make money on the Internet, many Internet or Intranet applications reduce the cost of running a business. In this section we discuss applications that are well-adapted to the Internet, namely:

- Advertising and marketing
- Publishing (information retrieval)

- Market research
- Services and maintenance
- Education and training
- Sales
- Electronic commerce
- Chat and collaboration

Advertising and Marketing

Every big enterprise, including the U.S. Government, has a Website. The low entry cost and ease of use of the Web enable many small companies and individuals to have their customized Web pages too. According to GVU's Fifth World Wide Web User Survey conducted in May 1996, users surf primarily for product information from company home pages. Users can quickly learn about new product announcements from the Web without having to deal with marketing representatives or salespeople. As a result, more sales can be made sooner. Companies enjoy the built-in and "free" advertising and marketing infrastructure provided by the Web.

Because the Internet can be reached by a large audience, it is an ideal place for advertisements. Many newspapers make their advertising sections freely available online, and more than a dozen newspapers across the United States share a Website for recruitment advertising, as shown in Figure 2.1. Rather than reading the employment opportunities in a newspaper, Internet users can specify search criteria to locate jobs that are of interest to them. Posting job opportunities on the Internet greatly enhances the job-searching process both for people who are looking for a career move within the same city or for those who want to relocate to another city. The Pathfinder Research Group's survey on job recruiting on the Internet (see http://www.ak.com/summary.htm) showed that two-thirds (67%) of the respondents considered the Internet more cost effective than any other method of job searching.

To attract people to visit their sites, many companies provide free gifts or free trial offers of their products. For example, Supermarket Online gives out coupons at http://www.SuperMarkets.com. PointCast Network (http://www.pointcast.com) provides a free subscription to monitor the weather in cities of your choice and the prices of your selected stocks. Of course, you also get whatever advertisements are "broadcast." In return, PointCast Network is making money by selling advertising space to other companies.

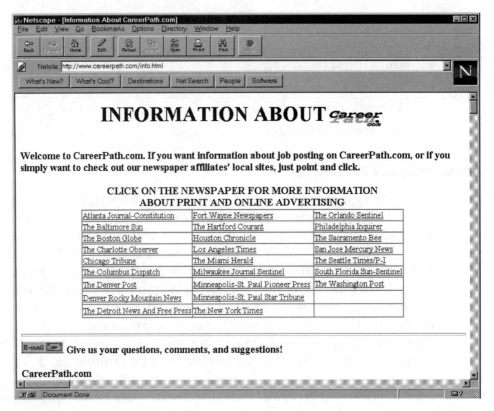

Figure 2.1 Pathfinder.careerpath for advertisement on job openings, http://www.careerpath.com/info.html.

Publishing (Information Retrieval)

With the proliferation of user-friendly Web authoring tools, publishing a document on the Internet is as easy as point-and-click. As a result, a lot of organizations are publishing many new and existing documents on the Internet. They also take full advantage of the hyperlink capability to reference other documents and the hypermedia capability to include multimedia objects such as image, audio, animation, and video. The tremendous increase of available documents on the Internet also brings a multitude of Internet search services (for example, Yahoo!, Infoseek, and AltaVista) to help people find the information they want quickly and easily.

The Internet is a boon to the publishing industry itself. Many publishers have put entire copies of magazines, newspapers, and books on the Internet (see Figure 2.2). Many also keep previous issues of magazines

Business Applications on the Web

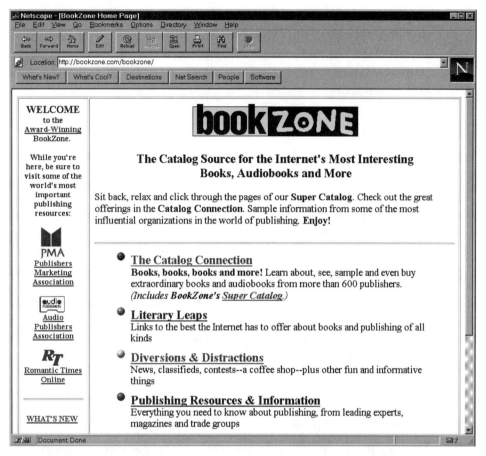

Figure 2.2 Bookzone: online catalog, http://bookzone.com/bookzone.

online to attract visitors to their Websites. One of the goals is, of course, to induce net surfers to subscribe to their magazines and newspapers or buy their books. National bookstore chains are also getting in on the action by including reviews, excerpts, and even the tables of contents of the books they carry. Publishers' Websites also feature promotional events such as author appearances.

Some companies simply use Internet publishing as a cost-effective way of disseminating information. For example, State Farm Insurance (http://www.statefarm.com/) enables its clients to locate an agent in their own neighborhoods. Mount Holyoke College puts the campus directory on the Internet so that professors and students can be located easily. Most companies on the New York Stock Exchange have a Web page that contains detailed information on the company and its stock. The Children's Hospital Medical Center in Cincinnati provides a physicians' referral guide, patient education programs, and library resources for parents at http://www.chmcc.org.

Market Research

The Internet is a great place for conducting surveys. You can easily get a large number of respondents in a short time. The GVU's Fifth World Wide Web User Survey received more than 17,000 responses over a one-month period. Because the Internet reaches audiences worldwide, survey results cut across geographical boundaries. Most important of all, an Internet survey is extremely inexpensive and more effective than asking respondents to dial a 900 number. As a result, many news media, which often conduct public opinion surveys on current issues, are turning to the Internet survey as an alternative to a 900 call. Many marketing research and consulting firms are also moving their survey applications online. Internet surveys can also be used by businesses to obtain direct feedback from existing customers (see Figure 2.3) or requirements from potential new customers.

Services and Maintenance

Because the Internet can be used to readily distribute information worldwide, service and maintenance representatives as well as customers can get the most up-to-date information from the Web. For example, IBM has all DB2 publications and recent updates on the Web so that customers and service representatives can look up debugging tips online when they encounter a problem (see Figure 2.4). Through the Web they can search books, readme files, and technical notes on fixes and frequently asked questions any time, anywhere.

Education and Training

The Internet can also be used for online education and training (see Figure 2.5). Training at your desktop enables you to save travel time, and learn new skills at your own convenience, with minimal impact on your regular work schedule. Companies enjoy the effectiveness of Internet training as

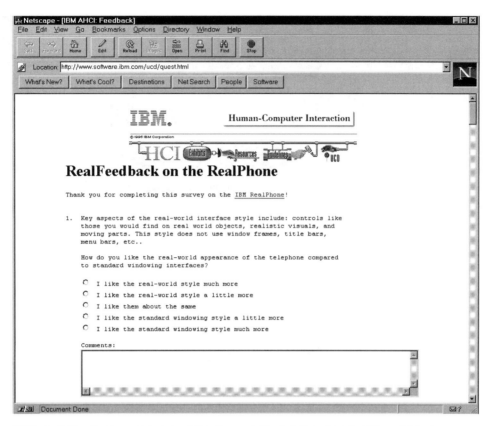

Figure 2.3 Customer survey, http://www.software.ibm.com/ucd/quest.html.

well as the cost savings in employees' education travel. As more and more companies put education and training online, users will have more choices, and the quality of the training materials will improve.

Sales

Once the Internet was no longer perceived as associated only with academic and research institutions, individuals and companies started viewing it as a virtual gold mine and rushing their products to sale on the Internet. There are more Internet flower shops than U.S. local florists. You can order a pizza to be delivered to your home at http://www.waiter.com/roundtable, purchase wine directly from Italy at http://www.newtech.it, and book a hotel reservation for your Hawaii vacation at

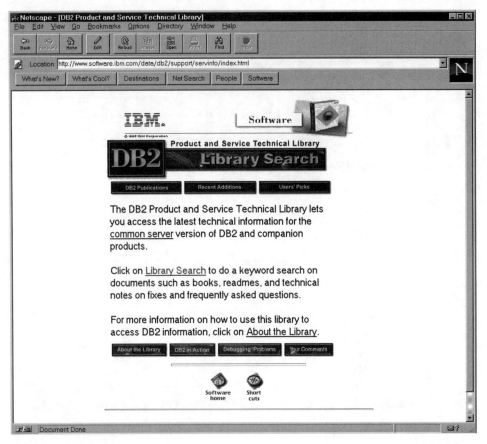

Figure 2.4 DB2 product and service technical library, http://www.software.ibm.com/data/db2/support/servinfo/index.html.

http://www.corretti.com. As Figure 2.6 shows, you can even purchase art work and "attend" weekly art sales at http://www.canyonart.com.

Are surfers buying via the Internet? According to the GVU's Fifth World Wide Web User Survey, only one-third of the respondents bought anything over the Internet, and more men than women have used the Web for shopping. Figure 2.7 shows the frequency of online shopping from the survey. IBM put up the Olympic Games Ticket Server to sell tickets online for the 1996 Olympic Games, expecting to sell 10,000 tickets during the entire period. To its surprise, 100,000 tickets and many souvenirs were sold through the IBM system, and more than $5 million was raised for the Olympics!

Figure 2.5 The JavaScript tutorial, http://gmccomb.com/javascript/index2.html.

Those who benefit most from selling through the Internet seem to be smaller companies, the so-called *cyberpreneurs*. These companies often do not have a physical storefront and enjoy the global market of the Internet. Large corporations that have their own marketing and sales network often use the Internet as a niche market, and enjoy the publicity and attention that they get from being on it.

Electronic Commerce

The electronic mall, also called the virtual mall, or the Web warehouse, is a form of electronic or Internet commerce. It is a collection of shops on the Internet selling goods and services (see Figure 2.8). An electronic mall is virtual one-stop shopping. It enables you to purchase everything you need in one place. There are many providers of electronic malls, all

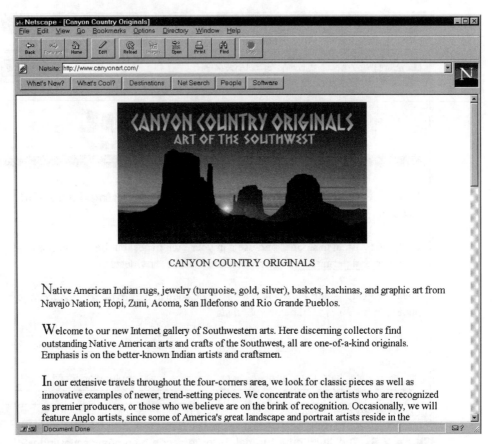

Figure 2.6 Canyon Country Originals, http://www.canyonart.com (website design by Web Exporium).

offering virtual space for lease and providing common services such as secure transactions, credit card authentication, and a Website. Some also provide services to create the contents catalog and graphic design of your storefront (home page). An electronic mall can be a good, economical alternative for someone who wants to do business online. IBM, Open Market, and Netscape provide products that support electronic commerce.

There are other forms of electronic commerce, such as Bank of America's Home Banking, where, besides transferring money from one account to another, you can pay your bills online (see Figure 2.9), and the American Airlines Interactive Travel Network, where you can find

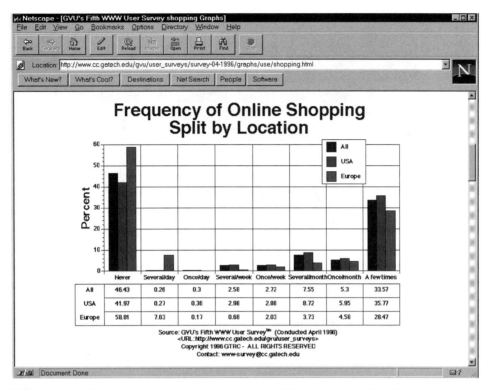

Figure 2.7 Frequency of online shopping split by location, http://www.cc.gatech.edu/gvu/user_surveys/survey-04-1996/graphs/use/shopping.html.

flights, purchase tickets, select seats, and change or cancel your travel plans.

Chat and Collaboration

The Internet breaks geographic boundaries and facilitates online interactions among people all over the world. Many browsers support a chat plug-in (for example, Quarterdeck Corporation's Global Chat) to integrate chat capability directly so that you can participate in real-time, ongoing chat sessions (also called forums). You can chat by sending and receiving messages, or you can chat verbally (see http//www.talk.com). The International Network of Women in Technology (WITI) Campus (http://www.witi.com) offers live chats and interaction with a wide variety of professional experts. Figure 2.10 shows an example of a virtual design studio

Figure 2.8 World Avenue, http://mer.shop.ibm.com/shopping.

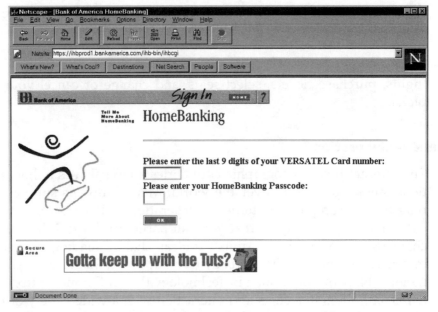

Figure 2.9 Bank of America's Home Banking, http://www.bankamerica.com.

Business Applications on the Web

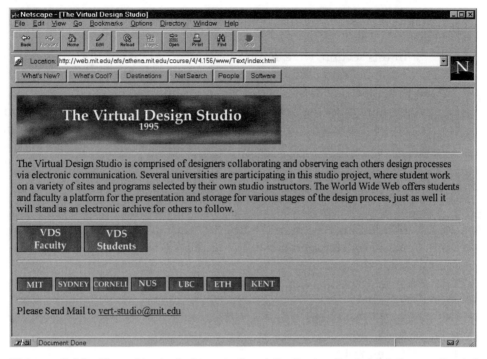

Figure 2.10 The virtual design studio, http://web.mit.edu/afs/athena.mit.edu/course44.156/www/Text/index.html (Imagery courtesy of the School of Architecture and Planning, MIT.).

where designers from different universities across multiple continents collaborate through the Web chat facility. Although videoconferencing is feasible through the Web, the high bandwidth requirement for acceptable performance prevents it from being viable for most users today.

EXAMPLES OF INTRANET APPLICATIONS

Intranet applications enjoy the same benefits as Internet applications. In addition, Intranet applications, which are accessed only from within an enterprise, do not have to have the same security exposure as Internet applications. Furthermore, an enterprise network is much more reliable and controllable than the Internet, which consists of many public networks. Accessing Intranet applications within the enterprise network through a local area network (LAN) is much faster than accessing Internet applications through a modem or an ISDN line typically associated with home access. Therefore, Web technologies are well suited for Intranet applications.

In this section, we examine five categories of enterprise applications for the Intranet: office, human resources, communications, information sources, and product development. Chapter 9 introduces the Lotus Domino Server, which integrates the Lotus Notes Server and the Web server into a single server so that users can access Notes documents from a browser and Web documents from a Notes Client. Many of the Intranet applications described below can easily exploit Lotus Notes capabilities and enjoy Web functions in the Notes environment.

1. *Office.* With today's reduced cost structure, many organizations are eliminating secretarial support and depending on automation for many office functions. Some of the office functions that can be moved to the Intranet are:
   - Conference room scheduling
   - Employee phone directory
   - Calendar
   - e-mail
   - Phone mail

2. *Human resources.* Many human resources (HR) functions have become automated in an enterprise system. Operations manuals for employees and managers are published online, and you can submit forms and obtain your manager's signature online. Some of the HR functions that can be readily accessed through a browser from the Intranet are:
   - Employee record updates
   - Forms
   - Job postings
   - Salary planning
   - Operations manuals
   - Contacts
   - Education and training

3. *Communications.* With the wide geographical spread of company branches, laboratories, headquarters, and sales and marketing units, good communication with employees is crucial for tying a company together. Some of the communication functions that can be moved to the Intranet are:

- Strategic planning
- Newsletters
- Forums
- Event calendars
- Organizational charts

4. *Information sources.* Making the most up-to-date information available to employees improves their productivity. Examples of information sources that can be made available over the Intranet are:
   - Computer services
   - Business conduct guidelines
   - Employee events and awards
   - Libraries
   - Manuals

5. *Product development.* Development organizations can use the Intranet to publish information to be shared among the team—developers, testers, information developers, and quality assurance engineers. In addition, to reach a wide variety of users, the browser is becoming the preferred user interface for your products. For example, the DB2 administration tool provides its interface through a browser enable system administer to manage DB2 remotely. Some of the product development functions that can be moved to the Intranet are:
   - Development team directory lookup
   - Development process
   - Product documentation
   - Project status tracking
   - Product user interface
   - Product requirements
   - Defects tracking

Figure 2.11 illustrates how the IBM Software Division makes use of the Intranet. On its Software Marketplace Network page, employees can learn about corporate strategy and news, the competition, and customers; find resources; participate in a discussion forum on topics of interest; and access information related to the marketplace, partners, and channels.

Figure 2.11 IBM Internal Software Marketplace Network home page.

PLANNING YOUR APPLICATIONS ON THE WEB

There are many ways of launching your applications on the Web. As mentioned earlier in this chapter, you can purchase electronic commerce products and tailor them to your business needs, or you can lease space in an electronic mall. For example, World Avenue, developed by IBM Distribution Industry, is an online shopping environment that offers retailers and other businesses a new, secure way to sell their goods and services over the Internet to millions of consumers. To exploit the cyber-retailing opportunity fully, merchants can use sophisticated search tools, advanced security features, intelligent agents, and data-mining (analysis of data for correlations and segmentation) tools to take full advantage of electronic commerce—with low startup costs and a shared-revenue model. Should you not be in a position to purchase electronic commerce products, you can develop them yourself. This book takes the do-it-yourself approach by introducing Web application techniques and numerous Web gateway tools for deploying your applications.

To ensure the successful deployment of your business applications on the Web, be sure to consider these items in your planning activities:

1. *IP address.* If this is your first external Internet presence, ask your Internet service provider for an IP address (or a range of addresses). Depending on the type of service provider you are using, you may find that you have to ask your Internet service provider's provider for an IP address. When you have your IP address, ask the InterNIC organization to register your domain name, such as *newcompany.com,* so that your users have a relatively friendly way of accessing your home page (for example, *www.newcompany.com*) or sending you e-mail (for example, *myname@newcompany.com*). For more information about registration procedures, including how to register your domain name if you are outside the United States, look at the InterNIC home page at http://ds2.internic.net/.

2. *Proof-of-concept projects.* When embarking on a venture to deploy your existing business applications from the Intranet or Internet, it is advisable to begin with one or two small proof-of-concept (prototype) projects, such as putting an employee phone directory online, to complete within a short period, say, two to six weeks. Such projects will help you identify areas that will require special attention when you move on to the next project. Although your ultimate goal may be putting your business applications on the Internet, you may want to begin with some Intranet prototypes.

3. *Skills.* Consider allocating personnel with a variety of skills, such as TCP/IP and Web expertise, mainframe experience, and Internet security knowledge, to work on your initial projects. Some of the people may serve as advisors only and not be completely involved in the project; nevertheless you will need a variety of experts. Debugging problems can be difficult when you use unfamiliar software components.

4. *Hardware and software.* For your initial proof-of-concept projects, you are unlikely to require significant amounts of hardware or expensive software. Small systems usually suffice for running such projects and enable you to gain experience before launching the major project. A lot of free software is available on the Internet—but, of course, you must adhere to the license agreements. After launching and monitoring your prototype projects, you will be in a better position to assess the size and types of systems you will require for the next stages. There

are situations where you may consider providing more powerful systems than usual for your prototype developers. For example, many of the graphics tools that you are likely to require run more effectively on a fast processor with more memory and disk space than a system devoted to word processing would need.

Existing and new business applications can be implemented in many ways from the Web. This book outlines a number of approaches. Different approaches require different software. Select the approach that best suits your applications. Factors that will affect your decision include the types of data being accessed, whether or not the data will be updated, the anticipated number of users, and the skills you have or want to acquire.

5. *Configuration and performance.* The configuration of your initial prototype project may be quite different from your final goal. However, configure your prototype project in such a way that you can predict potential bottlenecks in the next stage of your project. For example, try to evaluate the maximum number of concurrent users and the maximum throughput supported in each component of your solution. If you are planning a major project, ensure that the solution is scalable and that, when you reach a bottleneck, you can solve it without significantly redesigning your application. If you have many (30 or more) internal users of the Web (on either the Intranet or Internet), consider installing a proxy cache system to improve performance. The proxy locally stores the most recently accessed items, such as images, programs, and Java applets, thus reducing data transmission on the network.

6. *Firewalls.* If you do not have a firewall, select an appropriate firewall configuration. (See Chapter 3 for the main configurations.) You will have to define your firewall policy. For example, inbound traffic could be restricted to e-mail, with all external Web servers placed outside the firewall, possibly behind a router in a kind of "no-man's land." If Web server gateways are accessing existing systems that have to remain behind the firewall, however, you will have to configure the firewall to enable requests to flow between the appropriate machines inside and outside the firewall. You may also want to consider applying restrictions on outbound traffic. Note that a firewall can inhibit performance and become a bottleneck because all communication between your Intranet and the Internet flows through the firewall. Thus, exercise care when configuring a firewall. A large or international company may have multiple firewalls at different locations.

7. *Encryption.* If you are planning to transmit sensitive data such as credit card numbers over the Internet, select software that provides the appropriate degree of encryption. (See Chapter 3 for information about encryption.) You may also consider encryption within your Intranet, for example, when you are processing personal information.

8. *TCP/IP support.* If you are planning to access data and applications on the mainframe from the Internet, assess whether you should use TCP/IP on the mainframe or set up a separate TCP/IP gateway system that accesses the mainframe through Systems Network Architecture (SNA). This is a major decision for mainframe users, as mainframes have traditionally supported SNA applications. A number of TCP/IP implementations and software products on the mainframe support TCP/IP.

9. *New users.* If new users will access your Internet application systems, you may have to consider revising your security scheme for authentication and access control. Checking the identity of five employees in a company who run a particular application is very different from ensuring that 10,000 users see only the data that is relevant to them.

10. *End-user interfaces.* To meet the needs of your new users, consider radically revising the end-user interface for your application instead of using an existing interface. User interfaces in a variety of languages may also be appropriate, depending on the type of application you are building. A number of design principles can help guarantee that your customers' and/or employees' use of your application will be both enjoyable and productive. The principles include ensuring that the volume of data transmitted is appropriate for your users—for example, large graphics files are unsuitable for people accessing the system from a telephone line. Your Website should follow a logical structure. (Chapter 4 includes some general design guidelines.)

11. *Keeping your site up-to-date.* Do not underestimate the effort required to keep a Website up-to-date and interesting. Your applications will not be used if they are not beneficial, efficient, and pleasant to deal with. You must ensure that the information on your pages is accurate. Your users will be reassured if your pages include a date or some indication that they are maintained regularly or created dynamically in response to their requests. The main IBM home page (http://www.ibm.com) used to have a different theme each month. It now has a different set of headlines each day.

12. *Testing your site.* Test your production Website frequently, say, every week or so, to check that your Web pages and associated applications are accurate, operating correctly, and responsive. For example, if you provide an e-mail address on your Web page, check that the e-mail address has a real human being who replies to queries. If you want to reduce the number of unsolicited questions, create and maintain appropriate frequently asked questions (FAQ) pages based on the questions received.

13. *Making your site discoverable.* Irrespective of whether your application is for the Internet or Intranet, with the enormous increase in data and applications on the network, you must ensure that your users can easily find your site and navigate and search portions as appropriate to your application. Pay particular attention to data that resides on a database or file that the standard crawlers cannot find. (Crawlers are programs that access and index part of an Intranet or Internet). You can place the keywords that you want the crawlers to index in the appropriate HTML META tags. As part of your regular tests, use the Internet search tools to monitor how easily users can find your site with appropriate keywords. You can also find out what sites are saying about your company and correct any inaccuracies. (Remember that other companies will be checking the information you publish in the same way.) Refer to Chapter 1 for a list of the search engines on the Internet.

14. *System availability.* If you are building a worldwide Internet application, you must consider the various time zones and make your system available at the appropriate times. Thus, you may have to consider extending support for your systems and applications for startup and recovery in case of system failure.

15. *Legal issues.* As is often the case with new technologies, the law is playing catch up with regard to activities on the Web. What governmental authority has jurisdiction for activities on the Web? What countries' law controls when people worldwide can simultaneously view material located on a server in one country? Who should be responsible for defamatory materials displayed on a Website? The owner of the server? The "owner" or creator of the Website? Or the person who placed the material on a forum on which anyone is free to post materials? What if material posted infringes someones copyright? Who should be liable? What privacy rights can be violated by posting information on the Web?

Intellectual property laws, export laws, privacy laws, jurisdictional issues and many more legal concerns are only now beginning to be looked at with regard to how they apply or may need to be revised to deal with the unique characteristics of the Web. While answers to some questions may be clear, many others will only become clear over time. Anyone interested in doing commerce over the Web, or simply looking to provide a Website to allow the free exchange of ideas in an open forum, would be well advised to seek competent legal guidance before doing so.

CHAPTER **3**

Internet and Web Security

Network security, though complex, is important for enterprise users who want to put their applications in a networked environment. In this chapter, you will learn about several important security concepts, including security requirements, cryptography, symmetric and asymmetric key encryption systems, digital signature, digital certificate, authentication, access control, and firewall. You will find concrete examples of how to use two popular security protocols, SSL and SHTTP, to achieve certain security requirements, and examine three firewall mechanisms, namely, the packet filter, socks server, and proxy server. To illustrate how to use these mechanisms to protect networked assets, we discuss firewall configurations for Net.Data.

You will learn how to protect your assets (data and computer systems) against unauthorized access and evil security attacks, and how to provide useful information to authorized users through the network. There are various measures that can make your system more secure. Readers interested in a comprehensive discussion can read the books by Denning, Garfinkel, Russell, and Cheswick listed in the For Further Reference section at the end of the book for more information.

This chapter is merely an introduction to network security. We also provide examples of firewall configurations for Net.Data. However, security issues particular to a specific topic, such as Lotus Notes, CICS, and electronic commerce, are discussed in the relevant chapters of this book.

Security must be of primary concern to you when you plan to put your enterprise data online. Internetworking poses additional technical challenges in terms of security: sensitive data is no longer stored in a secured location accessible only to a few authorized personnel. Instead, people throughout the world can access your machine through the public network, using a variety of services such as the World Wide Web, File Transfer Protocol (FTP), finger, and remote login (telnet or rlogin). Some of these services may seem harmless at first. However, a hacker can take advantage of the security holes in the services and cause you a lot of trouble.

Security Risk Example

To illustrate the vulnerability of security in a networked environment, let us use the example of *finger*, a simple Internet service. The Internet finger service provides a convenient way of finding detailed information about networked users, such as their full name, login status, and telephone number. It can also be used to find out information about all users who are currently logged on in a networked computer. Here are two examples of using finger.

Finger Example 1: Getting Information about a Networked User

```
> finger young@cs.purdue.edu

  [young@discus.cs.purdue.edu]
  Login name: young                In real life: Michal Young
  Office: CS-220, 49-46023         Home phone: 497-2704
  Directory: /homes/young          Shell: /bin/csh
  Since Jan 20 18:40:45 on pts/2 (36 minutes 54 seconds idle)
  Since Jan 20 18:40:56 on pts/3 (2 hours 9 minutes idle)
  Unread mail since Fri Jan 26 13:43:58 1996
  Project: Arcadia-research in software engineering environments
  CATS: Concurrency Analysis Tool Suite
```

(continued)

```
Plan:
Position: associate professor
voice: (317) 494-6023 (office)
fax: (317) 494-0739
http://www.cs.purdue.edu/people/young
```

Finger Example 2:
Find Out the Users Currently Logged On in a Networked Computer

```
> finger @apple.cs.garden.edu

    Login   Name            TTY    Idle    When
    smith   John Smith      p0     5:07    Tue 10:35    xds9
    smith   John Smith      p2     4:59    Tue 10:35    xds9
    shen    A Shen          p1     5       Tue 09:22    nimitz
    taylor  Keith Taylor    p4     3d      Sat 12:31    lukasz
    bs      Brian Stevens   p3             Tue 16:09    arges:0.0
```

Because finger does not modify any data in the server machine, it seems rather innocuous. If you are currently connected to the Internet, however, try to finger one of your friends working in a computer company. Most likely, your request will be rejected, and you will get the following message: "finger: Can't connect to port 79: Connection refused." Why, then, do many companies disable this useful service?

A closer look at finger reveals two potential problems. First, a potential intruder can use finger to get a list of the user names of your system, as we did in the second example above. Getting this list can dramatically increase the intruder's chance of breaking into your system because now he or she has only to guess the password or a user identifier (User ID), instead of guessing both. The second problem can be more serious. Because a finger server has to provide the personal information about any user in a system, the server, called *fingerd* in UNIX, usually runs with superuser (or root) privileges. Therefore, any compromise of the fingerd server can cause grave consequences to your system. Indeed, the now-famous 1988 Internet worm by Robert Morris was based on the above concept. He took advantage of an implementation flaw in the UNIX fingerd server and broke down tens of thousands of computers on the Internet. In the original fingerd program, the runtime machine stack will overflow if the finger request contains more than 512 bytes of data. In normal situations, a user will not supply such a long string of data to the fingerd program. However, Morris used this security hole to cause the stack to overrun. Moreover, he developed code that caused the now ill-behaved fingerd server to execute a shell that has the superuser privilege! Fortunately, his program only multiplied itself by using the shell, instead of erasing data stored in

(continued)

the system, which would have caused far more serious problems for the Internet community.

Our story is just an example of how a service as simple and benign as finger can cause a serious security breakdown. Now compare the complexity of the services you are going to offer with finger! Although we do not want to use the story to scare you away from getting online, we do want to remind you that while you enjoy the benefits of open networks, you have to be very cautious—and deal carefully with threats to security.

SECURITY BASICS

Security is a broad topic. The *American Heritage Dictionary* defines "secure" as:

- Free from danger or attack
- Free from risk of loss; safe
- Free from the risk of being intercepted or listened to by unauthorized persons
- Free from fear, anxiety, or doubt
- Reliable, dependable
- Assured, certain

The above definition covers what we generally regard as secure in our daily lives. Intuitively, you will feel secure as defined above if the following five goals for a secure computer system are met:

1. *Secrecy and confidentiality:* Information must not be disclosed to unauthorized users.
2. *Accuracy and integrity:* Information must remain intact. It must not be altered by either accidental or malicious changes.
3. *Accountability:* The sender and receiver cannot deny that an information exchange has taken place.
4. *Authenticity:* The parties involved can identify themselves to one another.
5. *Availability:* The system can provide information services under various conditions and is not prone to attacks such as network virus.

Several aspects of security must be addressed. Security should include physical security, which prevents your machine, including diskettes, tape, and printout, from being stolen or damaged by such acts as theft, vandalism, natural disasters, and carelessness of operation personnel. It should also include computer security from the traditional operating system perspective, which controls who can access what kind of information in a computer system. In addition, security should address such network security issues as how to protect information and computing systems in a networked environment.

The emphasis in this chapter is on network security, although we also discuss some fundamentals of traditional computer security. We first introduce several important security concepts, including symmetric and asymmetric encryption systems, digital signature and certificate, authentication, access control, and firewall. We then discuss two popular Web security protocols, the Secure Sockets Layer (SSL) and Secure HyperText Transport Protocol (SHTTP), that help achieve the security goals of secrecy and confidentiality, accuracy and integrity, and accountability. Finally, we present an example of how to achieve the availability goal by using various firewall mechanisms.

Security Concepts

First let us discuss several important security concepts that we will use throughout this section.

Cryptography

Cryptography is a way of scrambling a message such that it is unintelligible to those who do not have the associated key. The original message is often called *plaintext,* and the resulting scrambled message is called *ciphertext*. Cryptography forms the basis for authentication and communication secrecy. It can also be used for message accuracy and integrity. As illustrated in Figure 3.1, a cryptography system consists of two components: *encryption* and *decryption*. The encryption process takes as input an encryption key from a user and scrambles a message, using an encryption algorithm. The decryption process reverses the encryption. It takes as input a decryption key from the user and recovers the original message from the scrambled message. Usually, the algorithm used in encryption and decryption is not a secret. Therefore, the only way to recover a message is to know the decryption key for the message.

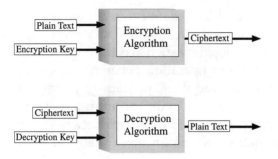

Figure 3.1 Encryption and decryption.

Modern encryption systems can be classified as symmetric (also called private) key encryption systems and asymmetric (also called public) key encryption systems. The symmetric key encryption system uses only one key for both encryption and decryption. The asymmetric key encryption system uses a pair of keys: one key for encryption and one for decryption. Given only one key, it should be computationally very hard to find the other key. Using modern, conventional computers, it would take a long time, perhaps hundreds or even thousands of years, to compute the other key.

If we use Encrypt(Msg, K) and Decrypt(Msg, K) to denote that key K is used to encrypt and decrypt a message, Msg, symmetric and asymmetric key encryption systems are best illustrated by the following two formulas:

- For a symmetric key encryption system: Decrypt(Encrypt(Msg, K), K) = Msg
- For an asymmetric key encryption system: Decrypt(Encrypt(Msg, K1), K2) = Msg

Compared with the asymmetric key encryption system, the symmetric key encryption system is more efficient. Its major disadvantage, however, is the difficulty in managing keys. Obviously, the encryption and decryption key used in the symmetric system must be kept secret, because only one key is involved in both encrypting and decrypting the message. How can the parties involved exchange this secret key securely? In addition, should the encryption party trust the receiving side with its private key? Does one have to create a private key for each communication party involved? If so, how can these keys be managed? The above issues are resolved by the asymmetric key encryption system.

In an asymmetric key encryption system, each party has two keys, one for encryption and one for decryption. Only the decryption key (usually called the private key) has to be kept private, and the encryption key (usually called the public key) should be accessible to the general public. To send a secret message to someone, one need only get the other party's public key and encrypt it by using the key. In this way, only the party who has the private key can to recover the encrypted message.

Currently there are many symmetric key encryption algorithms. The best known is Data Encryption Standard (DES), which was originally developed by IBM. DES has four modes of operation: Electronic Codebook (ECB), Cipher Block Chaining(CBC), Cipher Feedback(CFB), and Output Feedback (OFB). CBC and CFB use the concept of chaining for encryption and therefore can also be used for checking the integrity of messages. This method can conceptually replace the traditional method of using checksum to verify the message integrity. In other words, if a message is encrypted in CBC or CFB mode, and if it can be decrypted by using the original key, the receiver can rest assured that the message is the original message. Of course, this is based on the assumption that the secret key used in the encryption is not compromised.

The most popular asymmetric key encryption system is RSA, named after its three inventors, Rivest, Shamir, and Adleman. The security of RSA is based on the computational difficulty in factoring large numbers. To be safe, one has to pick very large keys, which are awkward to store and transmit. In addition, the encryption and decryption process is much slower than that of a symmetric key encryption system. To solve the storage and transmission problem of large keys, a lot of the software that uses the asymmetric key encryption system, including IBM's secure Web products, provides an easy-to-use interface to help you store, retrieve, and transmit the public keys. To solve the efficiency problem, usually you can use the asymmetric key encryption system to establish a secure connection while using the symmetric key encryption system for subsequent data encryption. We will discuss this technique in more detail later in this section.

A nice property of RSA is that you can decrypt a plaintext message, using a public key, and get a scrambled ciphertext. You can subsequently recover the original plaintext by encrypting the ciphertext, using the private key. This can be summarized by the following formula:

```
Encrypt(Decrypt(msg, public(K)), private(K)) = msg
```

From another perspective, the encryption and decryption process is functionally symmetric. Both processes can be used to encrypt and decrypt a message given the right key. This property can be used to support the concept of digital signature, as discussed later.

Figure 3.2 shows how to use RSA to establish a secure communication channel between two parties. Let us assume that user A wants to send private message M to user B. User A would first decrypt M, using his private key, which results in ciphertext C1. A would then encrypt C1 using B's public key and send the resulting ciphertext C2 over to B. Because C2 is "sealed" with B's public key, B, and only B, can recover C1 by decrypting C2, using his private key. Therefore, both parties can rest assured that no one else can recover the original message. Now B can encrypt C2, using A's public key, and get the original message. Because C2 is sealed with A's private key, B can be sure that the message indeed comes from A.

To overcome the inefficiency associated with asymmetric key encryption systems, you can use both asymmetric and symmetric key systems to communicate with each other. Specifically, you can use the asymmetric key system to establish an initial secure communication channel and negotiate a private key used for the session. Because this process involves only a small amount of data, the expense associated with asymmetric key encryption is kept to a minimum. You can then use the symmetric key system to encrypt and decrypt all the subsequent data, using the session key.

Digital Signature

A *digital signature* is a digital fingerprint. It is a message encrypted by using the sender's private key. The receiver can use the public key of the sender

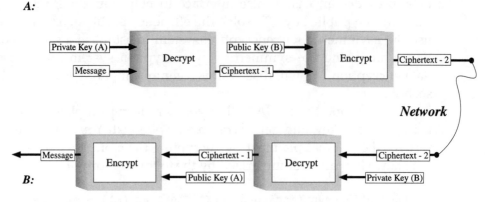

Figure 3.2 Using RSA for two-way secure communication.

to decrypt the message and make sure that it really comes from the sender. With RSA, the initial encryption process actually uses the decryption algorithm, and the receiver uses the encryption algorithm to recover the message. The effect is the same, however. Once you put your signature on a message, the receiving party can be sure that the message really comes from you.

Digital Certificate

The digital signature relies on the assumption that the receiver can safely get your public key. In a networked environment, the public key is generally fetched through the network. It is therefore possible that the public key can be tampered with or forged. This problem is resolved by the use of a *digital certificate*.

A digital certificate contains information about a person that is sealed with the signature of a trusted authority called a certification authority (CA). The role of a certification authority is similar to the authority that issues driver licenses. To issue a license, the Department of Motor Vehicles (DMV) first obtains personal information from the applicant and validates that information. It then puts the information on the license itself, along with the official DMV seal. If one has a driver license that bears the DMV seal, the information on the license is regarded as trustworthy because people trust the DMV (to some extent, at least). Similarly, if one trusts a CA, one should also trust the certificate issued by the CA. Moreover, one should be able to get the authentic public key of the CA securely. From a certificate issued by the CA, one can recover a person's public key, name and address (usually referred to as the *distinguished name*), and the issue date and expiration date. Because the certificate is sealed with a trusted party's signature, the information itself can be regarded as authentic.

Authentication

Authentication is the process of establishing that the party you are talking to is really the party he or she claims to be. The digital signature and digital certificate form the basis for authentication. Typically, in a client/server environment, authentication must involve both the client and server part:

1. *Client authentication.* How can the information provider (the server) know for sure that users (clients) are really who they claim to be? This is important, for instance, if the information the server provides is available to a specific group of users, say, registered users only.

2. *Server authentication.* How can the clients ensure that they are really talking to the right server? For instance, customers of an online bank certainly want to ensure that they are really talking to the server of their bank before they give out their account information.

Access Control

Access control regulates who (subject) has what kind of access right to which objects or services. Access control is usually classified as discretionary or mandatory. Discretionary access control is a means of restricting access to objects according to the identity of a user. For example, an owner of a document may want to impose the restriction that only users in a particular network can read his document. Mandatory access control is a means of restricting access to objects according to the sensitivity of the information in the objects and the formal authorization (clearance) of subjects to access information of such sensitivity. For example, you may want to specify that "Unclassified personnel cannot read data at confidential levels." Although both discretionary access control and mandatory access control are useful for users with different security needs, most systems, including the existing Web products, support only discretionary access control.

Access definitions are often stored in an access control list (ACL), a list of (subject, access right) pairs associated with each object. An alternative way of storing access definitions is to associate each subject with a list of (object, access right) pairs, which are called *capabilities*. Current secure Web products use ACLs as a means of storing access definitions.

Access control and authentication are different, but they are both integral components of a secure system. Access control depends on effective user authentication to identify the user.

Firewall

A *firewall* is a barrier that sits between your private network and a public network such as the Internet. It regulates the kind of traffic that can flow between two networks, thereby protecting your private network from attacks from the public network.

SECURE SOCKETS LAYER AND SECURE HYPERTEXT TRANSPORT PROTOCOL

SSL and SHTTP are two important protocols that support Web security. Both help you to achieve communication secrecy, accuracy, accountability, and authenticity.

Internet and Web Security

SSL: Secure Sockets Layer

SSL is a protocol developed by Netscape Communications Corporation and supported in Netscape and the Web products of some other vendors, including IBM's secure Web products. SSL directly supports server authentication and the establishment of secure communication channels. For SSL to operate, the server must have a certificate that is issued by a CA trusted by the client Web browser. After the client authenticates the server through the server's certificate, both the client and server can negotiate a key to use for encrypting and decrypting subsequent messages in the session and thereby establish a secure communication channel. Using the channel, the server can further authenticate the client by requesting the client to supply additional information.

To use SSL, your Web browser must be SSL-enabled; that is, it must support a client-side SSL protocol. Netscape and IBM's secure Web browser are SSL-enabled. To access a document protected by SSL, the URL must begin with https://.

On the server side, the most important step in using SSL is to get a certificate from a trusted CA. A well-known CA is Verisign. For a nominal fee and through the appropriate procedure, you can get a certificate from Verisign that most of the secure Web products recognize. You can also create certificates for your own organization. Many secure Web products come with tools to help you request and store certificates. IBM's secure Web server, for example, enables you to use a graphic user interface to request and store certificates from Verisign or create certificates for your own organization.

The following is an example of a certificate issued by a local CA using IBM's secure Web server.

A Certificate Example

```
MIIBxTCCAU8CBCAhT4gwDQYJKoZIhvcNAQECBQAwPjELMAkGA1UEBhMCVVMxGDAW
BgNVBAoTD01CTSBDb3Jwb3JhdGlvbjEtVMBMGA1UEAxMMQW5uZSBPbnltb3VzMBoX
Czk1MDgzMTIwNTRaFws5NjA4MzAyMDU0WjB+MQswCQYDVQQGEwJ1czETMBEGA1UE
CBMKQ2FsaWZvcm5pYTERMA8GA1UEBxMIU2FuIEpvc2UxDDAKBgNVBAoTA2libTEM
MAoGA1UECxMDc3RsMRswGQYDVQQDExJ2aXNobnUuc3RsLmlibS5jb20xDjAMBgNV
BBETBTk1MTQxMFwwDQYJKoZIhvcNAQEBBQADSwAwSAJBAK35YdV1hFE6rGUVC7Ur
X+EdM1FKE1Nkkw67Vkcr1z07V5iBskpjhRep2vI9jcfvvtu7QS7/jUjJ06/8HUhn
rScCAwEAATANBgkqhkiG9w0BAQIFAANhACJicmIhNL4aIgDBjSyA53C79VrXi1iJ
BYyEMK0xznXTLtHgZoS5JE9uLvjs8jIv6MjQ3hNmGuyLXyKZMl1prdT3/O/afvuk
ZGKqv1eMsRnHkpNrcbLBVMtYyopHYDuMgg=
```

Secure HyperText Transport Protocol

SHTTP is a security enhancement to the HTTP protocol. It was developed by Enterprise Integration Technologies (EIT) and is supported in Mosaic and some vendor-supplied Web products, including IBM's secure Web products. It directly supports both client and server authentication. In addition, it enables service providers to have a fine-grained security specification over the data.

To use SHTTP protection, you must carry out two major steps:

1. Code an HTML document for SHTTP.
2. Code server protection setup and ACL files.

Step 1 notifies the client of the SHTTP security and supplies the client with the server's certificate. It also provides crypto options that the client must follow to establish secure connections with the server. For example, it can specify that, to fetch a document, the client must sign and encrypt the message.

Step 2 is used on the server side to ensure that security is enforced when the referenced document is served. It allows the service provider to have a fine-grained access control mechanism over the document to be served. Specifically, you can define that only requests coming from specific sources can perform certain operations, such as delete or get, on a specific document. The source can be flexibly specified: It can be a specific subnetwork, a specific machine, a particular user from a specific machine, or certain users that can supply a valid User ID and password. In addition, you can specify whether the message exchange between the requester and the server has to be signed and/or encrypted.

Using SHTTP is more complex than using SSL. A mistake in specifying the security options can create a security hazard. However, SHTTP does give you additional control over the security options you want to impose. In the discussion that follows, we use IBM's secure Web server to illustrate how to use SHTTP security. We give many examples to illustrate the most important features of SHTTP.

Code an HTML Document for SHTTP

The purpose of coding an HTML document for SHTTP is to supply the client with the security-related information of a document referenced in a Web link (anchor), including the server's certificate and the security options of the document.

Internet and Web Security

Server's Certificate. The server's certificate is used for server authentication and to establish a secure communication channel between the client and the server. The following is an example of how to include a server's certificate in the header of an HTML document. The 10 lines between the `<CERTS FMT=pem>` and `</CERTS>` represent the digital certificate of the server.

An Example of Including a Server Certificate in an HTML Document

```
<head>
<CERTS FM=pem>
MIIBxTCCAU8CBCAhT4gwDQYJKoZIhvcNAQECBQAwPjELMAkGA1UEBhMCVVMxGDAW
BgNVBAoTDO1CTSBDb3Jwb3JhdGlvbjEVMBMGA1UEAxMMQW5uZSBPbnltb3VzMBoX
Czk1MDgzMTIwNTRaFws5NjA4MzAyMDUOWjB+MQswCQYDVQQGEwJ1czETMBEGA1UE
CBMKQ2FsaWZvcm5pYTERMA8GA1UEBxMIU2FuIEpvc2UxDDAKBgNVBAoTA21ibTEM
MAoGA1UECxMDc3RsMRswGQYDVQQDExJ2aXNobnUuc3RsLmlibS5jb20xDjAMBgNV
BBETBTk1MTQxMFwwDQYJKoZIhvcNAQEBBQADSwAwSAJBAK35YdV1hFE6rGUVC7Ur
X+EdM1FKE1Nkkw67Vkcr1zO7V5iBskpjhRep2vI9jcfvvtu7QS7/jUjJO6/8HUhn
rScCAwEAATANBgkqhkiG9w0BAQIFAANhACJicmIhNL4aIgDBjSyA53C79VrXiliJ
BYyEMKOxznXTLtHgZoS5JE9uLvjs8jIv6MjQ3hNmGuyLXyKZM11prdT3/O/afvuk
ZGKqv1eMsRnHkpNrcbLBVMtYyopHYDuMgg==
</CERTS>
</head>
```

Another way of including a server certificate in an HTML document is to use the notion of *certificate imbed* (also referred to as *server-side include*). Instead of putting the certificate directly in a document, you can store the certificate somewhere else and label it. In the document, you use the label to refer to the corresponding certificate. The Web server fetches the certificate for you and sends it to the requesting client at runtime. This technique adds much flexibility and enables you to easily manage multiple certificates. Moreover, if one certificate expires, you do not have to update all of the documents whose headers use the certificate. Instead, you can simply update the certificate that is associated with the original label. The server will start using the new certificate when it references it from the label. Some products, such as IBM's secure Web server, also provide an easy-to-use graphical user interface to help you establish a certificate imbed.

The following is a simple example of using certificate imbed in an HTML document. The "mycert1" label is associated with the long certificate in the previous example.

```
<head>
<!--#certs name="mycert1"-->
</head>
```

Document Security Specification. The security specification for an HTML document referenced in an anchor includes SHTTP security transport mode, and, optionally, the distinguished name (DN) associated with the server's certificate, and crypto options.

The specification of SHTTP security transport mode in an HTML document anchor notifies the client of SHTTP security. It is pretty straightforward to add this specification to the anchor of an HTML document, as the following example shows:

```
<a href= "shttp://www.vishnu.stl.ibm.com/db2www.html">
sample SHTTP link to DB2 </a>
```

The DN of the server certificate gives a client additional information about the server. The client uses the server DN to uniquely identify the public key of the server, which is needed if the server wants the client to encrypt messages. The DN of a server follows the syntax of the X.500 standard. It has several parts, including the common name (CN), organizational unit (OU), organization (O), and country (C). It is simple to add the DN of the server's certificate to an anchor, as illustrated in this example:

```
<a href="shttp://www.vishnu.stl.ibm.com/db2www.html"
DN="CN=DB2, OU=stl, O=IBM, C=SanJose, ST=CA, C=US">
sample SHTTP link to DB2 </a>
```

You can use DN security imbed to ease the specification process; that is, you can label the DN of a certificate and use the label in the HTML document to denote the DN. A Web server will send the associated DN at runtime when it references the label. The following is an example of using DN security imbed for the specification:

```
<a href="shttp://www.vishnu.stl.ibm.com/db2www.html"
DN=<!--#dn name="db2cert"-->>
sample SHTTP link to DB2 </a>
```

To specify crypto options for a document, you add the CRYPTOPTS elements to the header of an HTML document. CRYPTOPTS specifies the security information of the document referenced in an anchor. It enables you to specify the format for an encrypted message, which can be Public Key Cryptography Standard 7 (PKCS7) or Internet Privacy-Enhanced Mail (PEM). It also enables you to specify the security you want, that is, whether to encrypt and/or sign the messages, as well as a number of other options, including key exchange algorithms and signature algorithms.

Here is an example of specifying a CRYPTOPTS:

```
CRYPTOPTS=
"SHTTP-Privacy-Enhancements: orig-optional=encrypt,sign;
   recv-optional=encrypt,sign"
```

Seven crypto options are available in IBM's secure Web server. Because you can use most of the default settings for these options, we do not discuss the details of the options here. For details consult the relevant user's manual.

There is, however, one important option that you must deal with carefully: the SHTTP-Privacy-Enhancements option, which specifies whether the server and the client will sign and/or encrypt messages. Depending on your security needs, you may not want to use its default setting, which is the example we gave earlier:

```
CRYPTOPTS=
"SHTTP-Privacy-Enhancements: orig-optional=encrypt,sign;
   recv-optional=encrypt,sign"
```

This default option specifies that the server can send the client signed, encrypted, or both signed and encrypted messages. However, the server is not required to sign or encrypt the message if the client does not require it. Furthermore, the server can accept messages from the client that are signed, encrypted, or both signed and encrypted. However, the client is not required to encrypt or sign messages.

Obviously, the default setting for the SHTTP-Privacy-Enhancements option may not reflect the security needs of your application if you want a more restrictive setting.

Here is an example of a restrictive SHTTP-Privacy-Enhancements option that you may want to use:

```
CRYPTOPTS=
"SHTTP-Privacy-Enhancements: orig-required=encrypt,sign;
   recv-required=encrypt,sign"
```

This more restrictive option tells a client that:

- The server will send the client signed and encrypted responses for the document referenced in the anchor.
- The client must encrypt and sign the request for the document referenced in this anchor.

Code Server Protection Setup and ACL Files

Coding server protection setup and ACL files provides the server-specific information about how to enforce security when the document is served.

The major step in setting up server protection is to specify the kinds of protection that certain requests require. Let us illustrate using the following specification:

```
Protect /db2/* {
DeleteMask @9.112.12.181
MASK Anybody@9.112.*.*
}
```

This specification indicates that all requests starting with /db2 will activate protection. Furthermore, all delete requests must come from a machine with an IP address of 9.112.12.181. To use any other HTTP method, such as POST or GET, the request must come from a machine that is in subnet 9.112.*.*.

Our sample specification demonstrates how to base the protection on the Internet address of the requester. Another useful way of protecting your resources is to base the protection on user name and password. Such protection allows specific access to your resources from only those users who can correctly supply the User ID and password information you define in the server machine.

To use protection based on user name and password, you have to create a set of (UserID, password) pairs and store them in a password file. You should also specify which kinds of requests are valid for which User IDs.

When the requester accesses the resources in certain mode (for example, POST, GET), it will be prompted for the user name and password information. If the information does not match what you specified in the password file, the request will be rejected.

The following protection specification example is based on user name and password:

```
Protect /db2/* {
....
PasswdFile /etc/dbti.pwd
PutMask admin, u1
}
```

The example specifies that, to put files, the requester must enter userid admin or u1, and the associated password defined in the /etc/dbti.pwd file.

To further limit access to specific files in an already protected directory, you can create an ACL file, and place it as .www_acl in the directory. For example, .www_acl of a directory may contain this entry:

```
limit.html: GET,POST :hhs@vishnu.stl.ibm.com
```

which specifies that only user hhs from vishnu.stl.ibm.com can GET and POST the limit.html file.

In order for SHTTP protection to work, you should also add the CRYPTOPTS elements in the protection setup. When a server receives a request, it only knows the CRYPTOPTS options that the client uses. Therefore, the server depends on the server-side setup to know what the original CRYPTOPTS setup is in the anchor.

This example specifies CRYPTOPTS for the server:

```
Protect /db2/* {
....
PasswdFile /etc/dbti.pwd
GetCrypt SHTTP-Privacy-Enhancements: recv-required=sign,encrypt
GetCrypt SHTTP-Privacy-Enhancements: orig-required=sign,encrypt
GetMask All
}
```

The example indicates that the requester must supply a User ID and password defined in the /etc/dbti.pwd file. In addition, all message exchanges between the requester and the server are signed and encrypted, as defined by the SHTTP-Privacy-Enhancements option.

Finally, you have to specify the kind of requests that the server should accept and how to map the requests to actual directories and files on the server. For instance, the following specification tells the server that, for requests beginning with /db2/, the server should go to the /usr/lpp/Internet/server_root/pub/db2/ directory to find the file, and for other requests, the server should go to the /usr/lpp/Internet/server_root/pub/ directory to find the file:

```
Pass /db2/* /usr/lpp/Internet/server_root/pub/db2/*
Pass /* /usr/lpp/Internet/server_root/pub/*
```

To further simplify the specification process, you can define user groups and use them in place of multiple user names in the protection setup. You can also define a protection template so that you can reuse a protection setup.

So far, we have discussed the protection setup for HTML documents. The protection setup for CGI programs is very similar. You can find details on how to set up protection for CGI programs by consulting your user's manual.

Differences between Secure Sockets Layer and Secure HyperText Transport Protocol

There are several differences between SSL and SHTTP. SSL operates on top of the TCP/IP transport layer but below the HTTP layer, whereas SHTTP is an enhancement to the HTTP protocol and operates on the application layer. SSL directly supports server-side authentication only, whereas SHTTP directly supports both client and server authentication. Compared with SSL, SHTTP is more flexible in that it allows you to specify security options for the data in an HTML file. SSL is much easier to use, however, for two reasons. First, a client does not have to have a digital certificate to access a service. Second, service developers do not have to code various security options. Both protocols are not mutually exclusive. You can use them for different documents in the same server.

FIREWALL

As mentioned earlier, a firewall is a barrier that sits between your internal, "safe" network, such as a corporate network, and a public, "unsafe" network, such as the Internet. A firewall serves two purposes: It regulates your internal users' information exchange with the outside network and prevents outside users from attacking your private network (Figure 3.3).

Three firewall mechanisms are popular today: the packet filter, which often comes with your Internet router product; the application level gateway, also referred to as a proxy server; and the circuit level gateway, the most popular and widely used being the socks server. These three firewall mechanisms are not mutually exclusive and are actually often used together. In the discussion that follows, we use IBM's NetSP to illustrate how to configure and use firewall packages. Other commercial firewall packages support all three mechanisms and can be used similarly.

Be forewarned that a firewall mechanism is not a panacea for all security concerns your company might have. For example, many companies have a security policy that does not allow company data to be transported to outside networks. Although you can configure your firewall to prevent direct file transfer to outside networks, it is easy for an "insider" to put the data on a floppy disk or magnetic tape and take it out of the company. Firewall mechanisms are also not designed to prevent virus invasions through

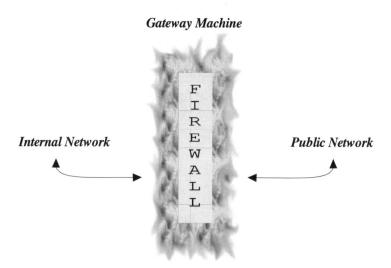

Figure 3.3 Firewall: A barrier between private and public networks.

channels outside their control. For instance, some viruses can sneak into a corporate machine indirectly if someone executes a program that is copied from a borrowed disk, downloaded from an Internet newsgroup, or received from e-mail. These attacks must be addressed from an entirely different perspective than a firewall.

Packet Filter

A *packet filter* provides the least expensive, most primitive, yet effective form of defense against outside attacks. To understand the packet filter, you must have a basic understanding of the underlying TCP/IP technology. First, IP forms the basis of the TCP/IP suite (Figure 3.4). All higher-level protocols, including TCP, FTP, telnet, and HTTP, depend on IP to deliver data. Therefore, security established at the IP level would be simple and generic. Second, TCP/IP uses the concept of packet switching to deliver data. Instead of establishing a dedicated link for a connection (circuit switching as used in a telephone network), TCP/IP cuts a large chunk of data into many small pieces called packets and sends them one by one to the destination through network gateways. The packets are reassembled in their original form at the destination node. In addition to carrying portions of the data of the original message, packets contain their source and destination information, and information about which higher-level protocol is going to use them. Therefore, for instance, it is possible to identify that 9.112.12.181 is the destination of an IP packet, and FTP is the high-level protocol that will be used to reassemble the message carried in the packet.

A packet filter controls the flow of IP packets between the internal and external networks. Basically, all incoming and outgoing IP packets must go through a gateway that is responsible for passing over all IP packets. By installing a packet filter in the gateway, you can control the kind of IP pack-

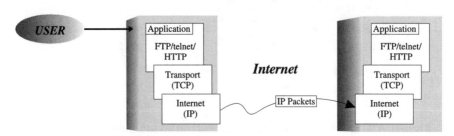

Figure 3.4 Internet protocol layer.

ets that are allowed to come in or go out. For instance, you may want to let your internal users access external machines through telnet. However, you may not want to allow outside users to use telnet to tamper with the machines in your internal network. To realize the above security policy, you can specify the following filtering rules for your packet filters:

- Reject all IP packets from outside that are destined to port 23 (telnet port) of any machine in my internal network.
- Allow all IP packets that originated from my internal network and are destined for port 23 of any machine outside my internal network.
- Allow all IP packets from outside the network that are acknowledgments to a telnet session.

Although packet filters seem simple conceptually, their use is not trivial. You must have a deep understanding of TCP/IP before you specify filter rules and run a thorough test to verify that your filter setting is correct. Otherwise, you risk exposing your entire private network to outside attacks.

Because packet filters operate at the IP level, they cannot control what is happening at the application level. For instance, it is not possible to use a packet filter to specify that only some users in a private network be allowed to exchange files with the public network. Therefore, a packet filter is often used along with a proxy server and a socks server.

Proxy Server

A proxy server provides a way of protecting your private network at a higher level than a packet filter. It is also more flexible as it allows fine-tuning of your protection setting at the application level. Conceptually, a proxy server running in a gateway acts as a liaison between your application and the external network. To access services outside the firewall, a user first uses a client such as FTP or telnet to access the gateway. Usually, to use the proxy server, a user must first be authorized by supplying a User ID and password to the gateway. After successful authorization, the proxy server connects the user to the outside network, just as if the user were talking directly with the outside server. In reality, the proxy server creates another link to the outside server, and exchanges the information on behalf of the client. The proxy server also maintains the link with the internal client and exchanges information with the client on behalf of the outside server. In its role as liaison, the proxy server can control the kind of traffic that flows through it.

Let us illustrate our discussion by using a concrete example of an FTP proxy server. The FTP proxy server helps a user in a private network get files from a machine in the public network by using a conventional FTP client. To use an FTP proxy server, a user first uses a conventional FTP client to access the FTP proxy server in the gateway. After entering a legitimate User ID and password, the user can enter the destination site he or she wants to access. The proxy server then creates a link to the destination on behalf of the user. Any subsequent FTP commands the user enters are passed along by the proxy server to the remote machine. The remote machine executes the command and sends the result back to the proxy server, which in turn passes it back to the client.

The script of an FTP session with an FTP proxy server is displayed below. In the session, a user who has an account, *hhs*, in the proxy server machine named *tollbooth* fetches an rfc/rfc 1579.txt file from a ds.internic.net machine outside his or her private network.

An FTP Session Using a Proxy Server

```
>ftp tollbooth
Name: hhs
331 Password required for hhs.
Password:********
200 Specify Remote Destination with SITE command
ftp> site ds.internic.net
220-            ******************************
220-
220 ds0.internic.net FTP server ready.
ftp> user anonymous hhs@vnet.ibm.com
331 Guest login ok, send ident as password.
230 Guest login ok, access restrictions apply.
ftp> cd rfc
250 CWD command successful.
ftp> get rfc1579.txt
200 PORT command successful.
150 Opening ASCII mode data connection for rfc 1579.txt (8806 bytes).
226 Transfer complete.
9032 bytes received in 0.3954 seconds (22.31 Kbytes/s)
local: rfc 1579.txt remote: rfc1579.txt
ftp> quit
221 Goodbye.
```

Theoretically, the proxy server should also work if users from a public network want to access a machine in your private network, provided that they have a valid User ID and password. However, you must remember that the communication channel between the proxy server and users in a public network is not secure. Therefore your User ID and password could be stolen while in transmission. More sophisticated authentication mechanisms, such as a onetime password, should be used to solve this problem.

Proxy servers that support common network services such as telnet and FTP are widely available. IBM's NetSP firewall package, for instance, comes with the telnet and FTP proxy server. Proxy servers are generally easy to install and configure. Moreover, you do not have to change any client code to use a proxy server. In our sample script of an FTP session, the FTP program we use at the client side is the standard FTP client program that comes with a conventional TCP/IP package.

There are, however, three major drawbacks to using the proxy server. First, a proxy server is specialized for a specific set of services such as FTP, telnet, and finger. If you want to add a new service, the proxy server must be changed or rewritten. Second, accessing services outside a network through a proxy server involves two connections: one between the client and the proxy server, and one between the proxy server and the target server outside. Performance may therefore be compromised. Third, every time internal users want to access the outside network, they have to enter a User ID and password, which could be inconvenient and annoying.

Socks Server

A *socks server* is designed to address the three drawbacks to using a proxy server. First, a socks server is generic for all services, and the coding effort involved in accommodating a new service is much less than the effort involved in creating a new proxy server. Second, a socks server does not require users to enter their User IDs and passwords each time they want to access an outside network and is therefore more convenient to use than a proxy server. Third, a socks server creates a virtual pipe for the connection between the client inside the firewall and the server outside the firewall and is therefore more efficient.

To be more specific, when an authorized client makes a connection request to a host outside the firewall, the request is first directed to the socks server running in the firewall machine. The socks server checks the origin of the request. If the request comes from an authorized source, it is granted, and the socks server creates a pipe that connects the requesting machine to the outside server. All subsequent interactions between the client and the outside server flow through the pipe without further interference from the socks server.

For a client to connect to a socks server before it can establish connections with an outside machine, the client code must be changed slightly. This is called "socksifying" a client. Conceptually, all you have to do to socksify a client is add the appropriate socks function calls in your program, recompile it, and link it with the appropriate socks library. Generally, it is much easier to socksify a client than to write a proxy server for each new service. The simplicity of socksifying a client enhances security because you are less likely to introduce a security hole in the code than you are in writing a new proxy server. Remember the fingerd example, which demonstrates that a single line of misbehaving code can cause a serious security hole. Many popular socksified clients are available, including rftp, rtelnet, and rfinger, and Web browsers such as Mosaic and Netscape. As a result, the socks server is gaining more and more popularity among users who want to control access to services outside a private network.

Let us illustrate the above discussion using a concrete example. Assume a user wants to use a socks server to fetch an rfc/rfc1579.txt file from a ds.internic.net machine outside his or her private network. To achieve the task, the user can use *rftp*, a socksified FTP client, to have an FTP session with the remote host. rftp first connects to the socks server running in the gateway. The socks server, after verifying that the connection comes from an authorized source, creates a pipe that connects the client to the remote host. From now on, the FTP session is between the client and the remote host. To the user, the existence of the socks server is transparent. Here is the script of the session:

An FTP Session Using a Socks Server

```
> rftp ds.internic.net
Connected to ds.internic.net.
220-        *******************************
220-
220 ds0.internic.net FTP server ready.
Name (ds.internic.net:shen): anonymous
331 Guest login ok, send ident as password.
Password: hhs@vnet.ibm.com
230 Guest login ok, access restrictions apply.
```
(continued)

```
ftp> cd rfc
250 CWD command successful.
ftp> get rfc1579.txt
200 PORT command successful.
150 Opening ASCII mode data connection for rfc 1579.txt (8806 bytes).
226 Transfer complete.
9032 bytes received in 0.62 seconds (14 Kbytes/s)
ftp> quit
221 Goodbye.
```

To use the service of a socks server, a user must have a socksified client, such as rftp or rtelnet. In addition, the user must set up the environment so that the socksfied client knows the address of the socks server and other related information. Many socksified clients such as rftp and rtelnet use special environment variables to get the required information. In UNIX, for instance, you have to set the SOCKS_SERVER and SOCKS_NS environment variables, which specify the address of the socks server and socks name server, respectively. Some other clients, such as socksified Web browsers, have a built-in facility that enables the user to specify the information through a graphical user interface.

On the socks server side, a firewall administrator must specify a set of rules according to his or her security policy. The rules are stored in a special file, which the socks server uses to check whether a particular client request should be granted or rejected. Some firewall products, such as IBM's NetSP package, also come with a graphical user interface to assist system administrators to generate the rules. Using such products, you do not have to be concerned about the detailed syntax of the socks server configuration rules.

A socks server differs from a proxy server in several ways. Unlike a proxy server, a socks server does not exert any control over the messages that are exchanged between the internal and external machine once the pipe is created. In other words, the socks server is merely a message gateway. A proxy server, however, must run the actual requested service in the gateway machine and can control the message exchange if so desired. In addition, the socks server checks the origin of the initial request of a client by two means. First, it examines the header of the requesting IP packet and finds the source machine address. Second, it uses an identification protocol to ask the source machine whether a User ID is valid. Therefore, users are not required to supply a User ID and password, which are needed in the case of a proxy server.

This convenience for users, however, is not free; it has security implications. First, the user identification protocol is not supported in all TCP/IP implementations, and a hacker can subvert the User ID checking. Therefore, it is safer to assume that a socks server can control only those connections based on the address of the requesting machine. In other words, it is not always possible to have finer-level control over who can access the outside service. If your organization has a security policy based on user identity, and some of your client machine TCP/IP implementations do not include the identification protocol, you may want to choose a proxy server instead. Second, although an IP packet header can tell from which machine and subnet the request comes, it is still possible for a hacker to change the IP packet header so that it looks as if it comes from a particular network. This activity is called *IP spoofing* in networking terminology. Therefore, the socks server is seldom used as a means to control external access to services inside the internal network because the external network cannot be trusted, and IP spoofing can occur.

A Firewall Configuration Example

In this example, we use an Internet firewall setup for DB2 World Wide Web Connection or Net.Data to illustrate how to protect an internal network by using firewall.

DB2 World Wide Web Connection and Net.Data are IBM products that provide a gateway to access DB2 and other databases through the Web. For a detailed description of Net.Data, see Chapter 8. Below we discuss solutions to protect the DB2 World Wide Web Connection or Net.Data gateway products and internal network from external network attacks.

Security Policy

The configuration of a firewall depends on the security policies of the organization. In this example we describe a possible configuration that conforms to a particular security policy. Assume that before inbound Net.Data service is supported, the security policies of the organization are these (Figure 3.5):

- Policy 1: Most incoming Internet connections are rejected.
- Policy 2: Most outgoing connections are allowed, so that users inside can use FTP, telnet, or other protocols to access outside services.

Internet and Web Security

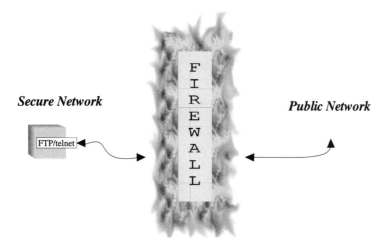

Figure 3.5 Original firewall configuration before providing Net.Data service.

These policies can be easily implemented with a combination of a packet filter, socks server, and proxy server with a commercial firewall product, such as IBM's NetSP.

The following security policies are added after Net.Data is installed (Figure 3.6):

- Policy 3: HTTP requests initialized from the public Internet should be allowed to go to the host that runs Net.Data.
- Policy 4: By allowing policy 3, the Net.Data machine may not be secure. Therefore we want the Net.Data host to be isolated from the rest of the secured network, except that it can still access DB2 inside the secured network through a DB2 client enabler. In addition, to facilitate application development, FTP and telnet access are allowed from the secured network to the Net.Data machine.

Firewall Configuration

Figure 3.6 illustrates one way of realizing our sample security policy. In the figure, another subnet is created that contains only the Net.Data machine. The net is placed inside the firewall but is isolated from other corporate networks. Here is the detailed configuration of the firewall:

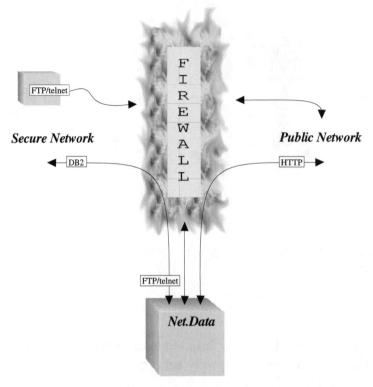

Figure 3.6 A firewall configuration that provides inbound Net.Data service without compromising security.

- Configuration Rule 1: In the packet filtering configuration file, add the following additional filtering rules:
    - Permit incoming TCP packets originating from any host to port 80 (httpd port) of the Net.Data host.
    - Permit outgoing TCP acknowledgment packets from the Net.Data host to any host.
- Configuration Rule 2: Install a socks server in the firewall. In the socks server configuration file, add the following entry to allow FTP and telnet access to the Net.Data machine from the secured network:
    - Permit any host in the secured network to connect to the FTP or telnet port of the Net.Data host.

Users inside the secured network who want to telnet or FTP to the Net.Data machine should edit their /etc/socks.conf file appropriately so that such requests go through the socks server.

- Configuration Rule 3: To allow Net.Data to access the DB2 databases inside the secure network, define packet filtering rules such that only DB2 traffic can go through the firewall between Net.Data and the secure network.

Discussion

Other configurations are possible depending on the security policy of the organization. Figure 3.7 illustrates a simpler, "less secure" configuration where Net.Data is put outside the firewall. Because Net.Data is put outside of firewall, it is prone to attacks, and therefore we recommend that Net.Data not access the database inside the firewall. Additional firewall rules do not have to be added in this case. If you feel insecure having your databases outside the firewall you can choose to use the solution outlined in Figure 3.6. Alternatively, you can put your database inside the firewall

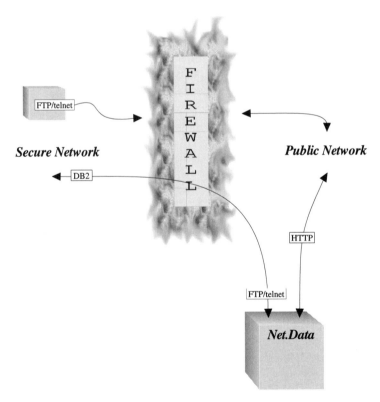

Figure 3.7 Another possible firewall configuration: putting the Net.Data host outside the firewall.

and reconfigure the packet filter so that DB2 traffic is allowed to go through the firewall between Net.Data and the DB2 server. Remember that in such cases, it is not a good idea to use a socksified DB2 client in the Net.Data machine to access the databases inside the firewall because the socks server is not designed for controlling traffic inbound to a private network. However, if you have a DB2 proxy server that controls accesses from DB2 clients residing outside the firewall to DB2 databases inside the firewall, you can use it to support the configuration outlined in Figure 3.7.

SECTION 2

Application Development

CHAPTER 4

Integrating Your Applications with the Web

A number of methods have evolved for integrating traditional applications and data with Web applications and enabling easy access through Web browsers. The methods include Web server gateways (server-side programming), Java clients and gateways (client-side programming), and integrated HTTP support. Each of these methods has its advantages; however, HTTP plays a considerable role in all of them.

Irrespective of the integration method you select, the success of your Web applications depends on pleasant and straightforward user interfaces, easy-to-understand functions and structures, and acceptable response times. You also have to allocate resources for maintaining your Website and applications, even if you do not plan to make major changes after the initial implementation.

After reading this chapter, you will be able to distinguish the methods for accessing applications and data from the Internet and identify software tools in each category. You will also become aware of the basic principles that make a heterogeneous Website successful and the significance of an agreeable user interface for your applications. (A heterogeneous Website consists of a variety of resources such as static and dynamic HTML pages and collections of gateways and applications.) For information on creating new applications, please see Chapter 7.

HTTP OVERVIEW

Web servers and applications usually communicate with Web browsers through HTTP. Before you can appreciate the functions in Web gateways that access database and application servers, you must have some understanding of HTTP.

HTTP consists of requests from clients to servers and the corresponding replies from servers to clients. A request or a reply consists of a series of header lines followed by a blank line (CRLF—carriage return line feed) and an optional message body. A request is a method on a resource where the resource is a logical entity expressed as a URL. HTTP allows an open-ended set of methods on diverse resource types. HTTP methods issued from browsers to servers include:

- *GET* to download various objects from Web servers such as HTML pages and images. GET often retrieves a *static HTML page* created before the GET request is issued and held in the Web server file directories.
- *POST* to send user input, usually typed into an HTML form, from a browser for processing by a program, such as a Web gateway running alongside the Web server. POST results in the server program creating a *dynamic HTML page* at the time the POST request is issued and which is returned to the browser.
- *PUT* to send updated objects from a browser to a server, enabling updates of items such as static HTML pages in the directories managed by the Web server. Many browsers and servers do not yet support PUT.

URL consists of a *protocol type* (such as http) and an *instance of an object*, such as www3.hursley.ibm.com. It is a tribute to the flexibility of the URL naming convention and HTTP that both have been able to absorb many more object types and protocols since their introduction in 1990, having been originally intended for downloading hypertext documents to browsers that process text only. One reason for the versatility is that type and instance information are clearly separated in both the object names used and the protocol itself, making it possible to incorporate additional object types and protocols easily. The additional object types included multimedia, such as images, sound, and video, which were introduced in 1993 along with the Mosaic browser. Programs such as Java applets were downloaded across the Internet through HTTP when the applet HTML tag was introduced in 1995. Portions of state information such as Netscape cookies, see Chapter 6, are also transmitted through HTTP.

Here are some examples of HTTP methods issued by a client to a server when the client makes contact with server:

- *GET/index.html HTTP/1.0* issued on URL http://www.ibm.com using the HTTP 1.0 format. This is a request from a client to retrieve the default page, index.html, in the top-level document directory managed by the Web server running at TCP/IP port 80 on the system called www.ibm.com.
- *GET/pub/WWW/TheProject.html HTTP/1.0* issued on URL http://www.w3.org using the HTTP 1.0 format. This is a request to retrieve the TheProject.html file in the /pub/WWW directory managed by the Web server running on port 80 at the W3C Website.

In a *GET* request, the client also lists the Multipurpose Internet Mail Extension (MIME) types, in other words, the data types that it supports, using an *ACCEPT* line (e.g., text/plain, text/html, audio). The client also identifies itself using a *USER-AGENT* line (e.g., Mozilla 2.03b) for a particular release of the Netscape browser. Here is an example of a complete client request to retrieve a page:

```
GET /ruth.html HTTP/1.0

Accept: text/plain

Accept: text/html

Accept: audio/*

User-Agent: NCSA Mosaic

CRLF
```

The HTTP response from the server consists of a series of header lines followed by a blank line (CRLF) followed by the body of the response:

> *Status-Line*, HTTP-Version Status-Code Reason-Phrase
>
> *Date-Line*, Date and time in Greenwich Mean Time
>
> *Server-Identification*, Server type, version, and name
>
> *MIME version* (e.g., 1.0)
>
> *MIME content type* (e.g., text/html)
>
> *CRLF*
>
> *MIME content*, such as the static or dynamic HTML page or an image

These are the types of status codes that can be returned:

- 1xx: Informational—Reserved for future use.
- 2xx: Success—The action was successfully received, understood, and accepted.
- 3xx: Redirection—Further action must be taken in order to complete the request.
- 4xx: Client Error—The request contains bad syntax or cannot be fulfilled.
- 5xx: Server Error—The server failed to complete an apparently valid request.

Many Web users are familiar with response code "404 Not Found." If you are a software supplier yourself, you may want to ensure that you do not run your competitor's Web server on your public systems. It is relatively easy for users of the Web to discover the identity of your server software, because the identity is placed in the HTTP response header and browsers often display it when an error response such as "404 Not Found," occurs. Indeed, there are Websites that tell you about the server software that any Internet Website of your choice uses by sending a request to its server, displaying the contents of the response header, and providing hyperlinks to the supplier of the server software.

The browser can use the MIME type in the response header to determine whether it should use a helper application or offer the user the option of selecting such an application to view the downloaded file, if the browser does not know how to display or process it.

HTML pages often refer to images (e.g., by using the <IMG SRC= image-name> HTML tag) and other items that are displayed as part of the page. When a browser retrieves an HTML page by using the HTTP GET request, it checks the references and issues separate GET requests for each of the relevant items. Typically many HTTP GET requests are required to construct and display a single page.

In a business or academic environment very often an HTTP request goes through a proxy server that is typically located near a group of clients before it reaches its target server system (see Figure 4.1). The proxy server is responsible for passing the request on to the target server, possibly after modifying it, and for returning the reply back to the client. Thus, proxies act as both clients and servers in their use of the HTTP protocol. Some proxies simulate functions that are not supported in the clients. As shown in Figure 4.1, they may also cache frequently accessed pages and associated files, such as images, to improve response times for the users. The HTTP protocol includes explicit provision for proxies.

HTTP is *stateless;* that is, in a subsequent request from a particular client to a particular server, there is no indication that an earlier request between that same client and server has occurred. Resources (e.g., data areas in memory and communication connections) associated with an individual

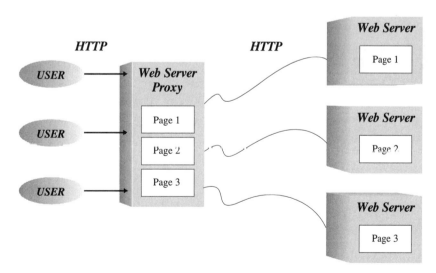

Figure 4.1 HTTP requests through a proxy server.

request-reply pair are usually dismantled when the response is returned to the client. In a *stateful* protocol, such as telnet, a communication connection is maintained over multiple requests, and system tokens are usually transmitted to show the relationship between the requests.

Statelessness is ideal for surfing the Web, that is, when a user clicks on a hypertext link to retrieve a page from a server. The user then clicks on another link in the retrieved page to access another page, often from a different server (see Figure 4.2). If HTTP were stateful and resources such as memory were maintained in all of the systems through which a user navigates, more powerful computers would be required to run Web servers. The additional computing capacity would be required to keep track of the trail of memory and operating system resources a user would generate.

Techniques have become available to provide session state across HTTP requests, as many Web applications that access existing systems require some kind of state mechanism to avoid asking users to repeatedly retype the same information. Thus, Web gateway tools are very much concerned with managing state.

HTTP 1.1 includes extensions to assist with efficient proxy caching and refreshing the contents of the proxy cache at appropriate times. A variation of HTTP called *HTTP New Generation* (HTTP-NG) has been proposed to support stateful HTTP sessions. It is not upwardly compatible with HTTP, however, and it is not a standard.

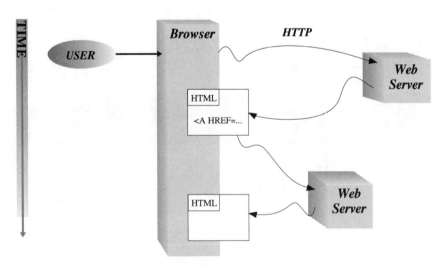

Figure 4.2 Surfing the Web through hypertext links.

ACCESSING EXISTING APPLICATIONS AND DATA

Web gateways provide access to application and database servers from Web servers that support HTTP. In this section we discuss three gateway approaches.

Server-side Programming: The Basic Web Gateway Approach

The basic Web gateway approach (Figure 4.3) is the most common way of accessing application and database servers in the Web. Typically a CGI application (which constitutes part of the gateway) translates between the language of the Web (CGI parameters inbound and HTML outbound) and the language of the target data or application source (e.g., SQL—Structured Query Language—and ODBC—Open Database Connectivity). The gateway code usually resides on the same machine as the Web server and has to deal with multiple users concurrently accessing the target data by using HTML forms. Some gateways use various Web server APIs, such as NSAPI, instead of the CGI, for improved performance. Another trend is for Web servers to provide an object-oriented programming environment, such as the Java Jigsaw server from CERN.

Gateways differ in the amount of system and application programmer involvement for their installation and setup. For example, a 3270 or 5250 gateway may not require any application programming, because the gateway can perform a complete translation unaided. (3270 and 5250 are IBM screen display protocols.) Other gateways require some configuration and programming to provide customization.

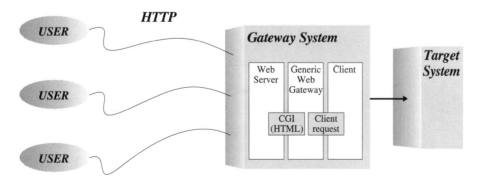

Figure 4.3 The basic generic Web gateway approach.

It is also possible to write an application-specific gateway between a Web server and a target application, and there are many examples of this approach (see Figure 4.4). For an example of application-specific code used in conjunction with CICS, see Chapter 11.

Net.Data, described in Chapter 8, combines the flexibility of an application-specific gateway by enabling considerable customization, with a generic runtime element to process the Net.Data requests. In addition, the Net.Data system provides an effective location for accessing and integrating diverse data types in a variety of servers onto a single Web page. Java and JavaScript, for example, can be used in conjunction with Net.Data to improve the user interface.

We discuss aspects of building and using basic Web gateways in Chapter 5.

Client-side Programming: Using Java Clients and Gateways

When Java clients and gateways are used to access database and application servers, a Web server downloads the Java classes required to access the target data and applications directly (see Figure 4.5). In this case the Web server is the source of the appropriate Java client, and the Web is the distribution mechanism for the client software. The Web server does not have to be on the access path between the Java classes and the target system. The communication protocol used between the Java client and target system can be specific to the target system, although there are advantages if the protocols are based on standard Internet protocols such as HTTP, for example, to ease outbound navigation through firewalls.

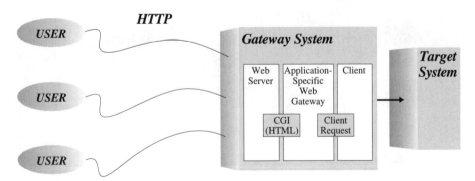

Figure 4.4 Application-specific gateway.

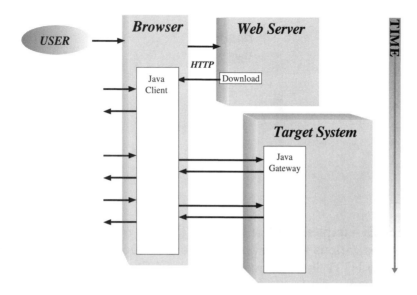

Figure 4.5 Java client and gateway approach.

The Java client and gateway approach is similar to traditional client/server programming, and related design issues apply with one major exception: The Java download mechanism ensures that the most recent level of client software is being used. (At present, the latest versions of the appropriate Java classes are downloaded the first time the relevant page is accessed from an instance of a browser.)

Using Java clients and gateways provides a more flexible user interface than just a Web browser. In addition, the Java code on both the client and server is portable. This approach is likely to perform better than the Web gateway approach because it does not use a Web server on the path between the client and the target system.

HTTP Protocol Support: Web Integration

In this approach (Figure 4.6), the target system implements HTTP itself and maps it onto the constructs appropriate to the system. An example is the Lotus Domino server's mapping of Lotus Notes elements to Web constructs. This mapping enables relatively easy access to Lotus documents and interactive applications from Web browsers without requiring a separate Web server and gateway or Lotus Notes clients. Another example is

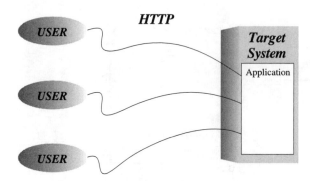

Figure 4.6 HTTP protocol integration.

the CICS/ESA implementation of HTTP, known as the CICS Web Interface, which maps various Web server interface constructs to the CICS API.

Because HTTP is a relatively simple and flexible protocol, it is likely that many more application and database server systems will integrate HTTP support directly and it is usually quite straightforward to map HTTP constructs to elements in existing systems.

Significant performance benefits on server systems, as well as a simple configuration, can be achieved by direct HTTP support. This approach is difficult for users to implement, however. The official supplier of the system software for the target system usually has to implement it.

GUIDELINES FOR THE USER INTERFACE

In traditional database and transaction processing system environments, it is generally assumed that responsible people are in control of defining long-lasting user interface and application development standards. In contrast, Websites are often created and maintained with few people in overall control. Indeed, the fact it is possible to create Websites without much initial administration or control is one of the essential ingredients that led to the Web's rapid adoption and contributes to the high rate of change in many aspects of the Web, especially the user interface. Conventions from both the traditional database environment and the rapidly changing Web environment are required to create and maintain a heterogeneous Website successfully. In particular, when you build a Web gateway application, it is important to understand the technical aspects, diversity, and frequent shifts in the Web user interface.

The quality of the user interface is extremely important for the success of your Web applications, irrespective of whether you use static or dynamic HTML, forms, multimedia, Java, JavaScript, or some combination of techniques. The user interface should reflect the requirements and expectations of your users.

In this section we describe some guidelines for designing pages, structuring your Website, integrating your Web applications' dynamic HTML pages with your static HTML pages, and maintaining the quality of your site. It is essential that your gateway applications conform to flexible guidelines that are reviewed frequently.

HTML and Page Design

Many tools, including word processors, produce static HTML. We recommend that you use one of these tools, and that you consult a book such as Ian Graham's *The HTML Sourcebook* (see the For Further Reference section at the end of this book).

If you are producing HTML pages from your existing applications and data, in order to integrate them with the Web you must familiarize yourself with the guidelines for good Web page design. Your application is more likely to be successful if it adheres to the accepted practices of the Web, rather than to the mainframe user interface, for example.

Individual Web page structure has evolved through stages:

- *Text only*
- *Three-part page* (header, body, footer)
- *Image maps*
- *Frames* where multiple HTML pages are displayed concurrently within one browser window

Often the individual page structure on a corporate Website reflects the time the site was first created. In keeping with traditional practice, the design guidelines for the page are not subsequently revised. In other words, corporate Websites often show their age!

Here are some general Web page design guidelines:

- *Concentrate on content and applications.* The content and function of your pages and applications are the most important elements of your Website. If they do not satisfy your users' requirements, your site will not be used irrespective of how entertaining and well structured it is. Most users can override the options you specify in the HTML, such as switch images off or modify the font size, so you have limited control over how your pages look. Nevertheless, a site with excellent applications will not be used if the applications cannot be found because of poor structure, navigation, and search options.

- *Be concise.* Reading speeds from computer screens are more than 25 percent slower than reading speeds from paper. Avoid welcome messages and introductory paragraphs. Concentrate on providing facts. Users usually look for hyperlinks and rarely scroll down a page unless it has attracted their attention.
- *Consider how the information will be used.* If you expect your users to print some of the information on your pages to review later at their leisure, make it straightforward for them to print a suitable collection, by providing a Postscript file consisting of a group of pages, for example. Most browsers support printing only one HTML page at a time.
- *Use standard HTML tags.* Some browsers support extensions that are not in the HTML standard. For example, JavaScript is not included in HTML 3.2. Consider carefully how much to deviate from the standards and rely on browser-specific extensions.
- *Use standard image formats.* There are a number of formats for images. The main formats supported by most browsers are CompuServe Graphics Interchange Format (GIF) and Joint Photographic Experts Group (JPEG). The file extension for GIFs is GIF, and for JPEGs it is JPG. JPEGs are recommended for photographs and continuous-tone images. In early 1995, transparent GIFs became popular. The pixels (dots of color) in the image background were removed so that the central item in the image seems as though it is part of the page on which it appears, instead of having a border. The background color of the page shows through instead of the image background. Tools such as Corel Draw and Photo Shop produce transparent GIFs. In the summer of 1996 a new GIF format, called animated GIF, became popular. Sometimes, users assume that an animated GIF is a Java program animation, but in fact it is a single GIF file containing a series of images along with information about how the images should be animated over time. Software packages are becoming available to create animated GIFs. They appear as a single static image on a browser that does not support animated GIFs.

- *Keep image and page sizes small.* The usual recommendation is to ensure that the total size of an HTML page and inline images is about 30 to 50 KB or less, particularly if your users are at the end of a 14.4 baud telephone line. One very small image, even if repeated on the page, is preferable to a single large image. Most browsers detect that the same image is required multiple times on a page, and they just retrieve the image once. Use interlaced images where possible, so the user sees portions of the image sooner.

- *Keep down the number of different images in a page.* Each unique image in a page generates a separate HTTP GET request and corresponding reply, which implies a separate communication connection. The overhead of each connection will slow down the display of the page. Most browsers issue separate GET requests even if all the images reside on the same server, although they may issue up to four GET requests concurrently for a page. HTTP 1.1 makes *persistent connections* the default behavior, enabling multiple GET requests to use the same communication connection.

- *Create your own material.* Create your own images using graphics packages. Many presentation tools, such as Lotus Freelance, will also create GIFs from slides. If you use images from other sources, make sure you get permission from the real owner. It easy to copy and display images on the Internet and thus to inadvertently imply ownership.

- *Use image maps with care.* You can design an image such that when the user clicks on a particular portion of the image, another HTML page is displayed, thus providing an alternative to clicking on hypertext links. Such an image is called an *image map*. Unfortunately, image maps are usually large in order to convey clearly the appropriate portion of the image that has to be clicked. Hypertext links typically change color when they have been clicked previously, giving the user feedback, whereas portions of an image map do not change color when the linked-to pages have been visited, unless the image map is enhanced, for example, with Java or JavaScript. If you use image maps you must provide a textual alternative. Avoid using a large image map for your initial page that introduces your Website.

- *Use color with care.* Colors are displayed very differently on various systems. Pages that look appealing on your system may appear strange on other systems. Plain backgrounds such as pastel colors or white are recommended for pages that contain a lot of text. Become familiar with the red, green, blue (RGB) notation that is widely used on the Web. For example, in HTML you can use tags with values in RGB notation to define the color of text, hyperlinks, and backgrounds. Colors are represented in RGB as hexadecimal numbers, where #FF0000 is red, #00FF00 is green, and #0000FF is blue. Combinations can be used too, such as #000000 for black and #FFFFFF for white. The following color names, originally the standard Video Graphics Adapter (VGA) colors, can be used in HTML tags as alternatives to RGB: aqua, black, blue, fuchsia, gray, green, lime, maroon, navy, olive, purple, red, silver, teal, white, and yellow.

- *Use backgrounds with care.* Instead of specifying a background color, you can specify a background image which the browser places like kitchen wall tiles throughout the page. Although a background image can be quite small (e.g., less than 5 KB) and thus network transmission time is low, tiling and displaying the image can slow down the browser.

- *Test your Website using different browsers.* Surveys show that an individual may use two or three different browsers daily at home and at work. Many tools, such as Lotus Notes, incorporate their own browser. Some browsers, such as mainframe browsers, do not display graphics. Make sure you provide text in the IMG ALT HTML tag to display some text as an alternative to the image. Test using different browsers, and also test different releases of the same browser. The way in which a browser displays and prints an HTML page can vary considerably across releases.

- *Provide options for user feedback.* Make it is easy for your users to contact you by e-mail, for example, by using the HTML MAILTO option. Ensure that the e-mail user name you specify is monitored frequently. Webmasters, the creators of static HTML pages, and Web authors sometimes forget about alternative forms of communication. Do include telephone and fax numbers and addresses for your organization and employees.

- *Monitor changes in general styles.* Pages on the Web can look out of date if their appearance remains unchanged for a few months. Review the images, fonts, and backgrounds used by your applications at least once every six months, and preferably more frequently. Examples of features that came into general use during 1995 are colored backgrounds and text, background GIFs, and HTML tables. HTML tables in particular are used to control the layout of text and images as well as for expressing tabular information precisely. Since 1996, animated GIFs, Java,

JavaScript, and frames are often used to make pages easier to follow. Frames are also used to provide tables of contents for large quantities of text and to assist when navigating through complex structures and presentations.

Website Structure Guidelines

The type, quantity, and regularity of the hyperlink navigation controls you provide affects your users' experiences of your Website and applications. In this section we discuss the navigational elements of your Website. Finding the same information again at a Website a few hours or days after first locating it is an important test. Even the *authors* of poorly organized Websites find it difficult to recall where to find their own applications and data!

It is essential to have a simple and stable initial URL, such as http://www.company.com, for your site even though you cannot prevent people from recording other URLs at your site, using them as their main point of entry and bypassing the initial URL. Use a Web server running on port 80 as your primary point of entry, to avoid decorating your initial URL with a port number. Use hyperlinks to reach pages on servers running on other port numbers. When navigating through hyperlinks, avid Web users notice changes in server name and will attempt to access the default initial page for that server (e.g., http://www.company.com:8001/) in an attempt to discover other items on that server. Be sure to provide a sensible default initial page (often index.html) for all your secondary Web servers. The default initial page for your servers may also be accessed by *crawlers* (programs that navigate across the Internet retrieving pages, usually to index them).

Consider devising a naming convention that encompasses both static pages and dynamic pages created by gateways. Gateway applications often use an initial static page as their entry point, and thereafter refer either to the name of the gateway CGI program or some logical name that represents the gateway. You may want to consider providing intermediate static pages should you require your users to return to particular points within your gateway application.

Most users of the Web maintain bookmarks (lists of favorite URLs), in either their individual browsers or their personal Web pages. Avoid making frequent changes to your important URLs, as it may annoy your users, particularly those who have saved your URLs in their bookmark files. When you must change your URLs, consider using the HTTP redirection option, which enables a server to notify a client that the page the client just requested has moved. The server also returns the URL for the new location, making it possible for the client to issue a request through the new URL, without the user realizing that a redirection has occurred.

There are a number of possible navigational structures for a Website. Your goal should be to enable your users to reach the information or applications they require in the minimum number of hyperlink clicks. A common approach is to use a hierarchical structure, and place as much information as possible in the form of hyperlinks near the top of the hierarchy. Here are some typical Website structures:

- *Sequential*—Linear with forward and backward hyperlinks
- *Hierarchical*—Menus with hyperlinks up and down the hierarchy (no links between siblings)
- *Flexible*—Weblike with hyperlinks from any page to any other page
- *Composite*—Some combination of structures

Figure 4.7 illustrates a composite scheme, with a shallow hierarchy leading to a sequence that provides an intermediate static page within the two parts of a gateway application. The first part of the gateway application could be for new users, and the second part could be for both new and

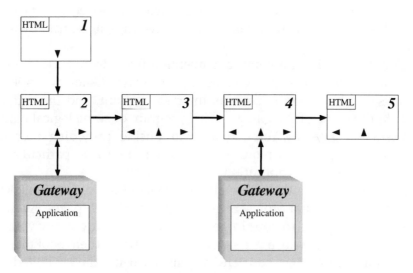

Figure 4.7 A composite user interface structure for a Web application.

existing users. For existing users, the initial menu could provide direct access through a hyperlink to the second part of the sequence.

Be aware that your users may start navigating from any point in your Website, perhaps because the page was retrieved earlier and kept in a bookmark file or was found by a Web search tool. So your users may never see explanatory material or important news items on your initial page. Irrespective of the structure you choose, select a consistent navigation style. For example, you could include a standard page footer that always refers back to your main initial menu page.

Consider whether some portion of your Website and application should be executable on a single computer in standalone mode when the network is inaccessible. Using standalone mode, that is, placing both the client and server on a single computer, is often required when running a demonstration or giving a presentation so as to reduce dependence on phone lines and unfamiliar network configurations. Running a standalone Web application can also be useful for data collection systems, where new and modified data is transmitted to a shared server only when connecting to a network. Many personal Web servers are available for use on standalone systems in TCP/IP loop back mode when the client and server software communicate with each other over TCP/IP within the same computer. Personal servers can also be used as regular shared servers, as well as for testing Web applications locally.

Integrating Your Static and Dynamic Pages

Webmasters and Web authors often adopt a different presentation style from the programmers who design the dynamic pages, as with the pages generated from accessing IMS, Encina, DB2, or CICS. Users should not have to adapt or be surprised by a new set of navigation styles when accessing what appears to be a single application.

- *Use hyperlinks in your dynamic pages.* Hyperlinks are widely used in static pages but are often neglected in dynamic pages. Using hyperlinks between your dynamic and static pages is a good way of integrating your site, from a user's point of view. Hyperlinks can also be used to provide integration among data items displayed on your Web pages generated from your gateway applications. For example, you can link key fields (both primary and foreign keys) from your databases in your dynamic Web pages by specifying URLs in the generated HTML that incorporate query strings (see Chapter 6).

- *Include multimedia in your dynamic pages.* It is straightforward to embed images in dynamic pages generated from your gateway applications, even if your applications are running on mainframes. Using common multimedia items and navigation controls in both your dynamic and static pages improves integration.
- *Personalize your pages.* If at some stage you ask your user to type in personal information, and you create your pages dynamically, consider including appropriate personal information on subsequent pages during that user's session. For example, you could include text that says "This order was prepared for Susan Malaika," or if you prefer a more informal approach you could say "Would you like to visit any more departments in our store, Susan?" You should be aware that modes of address vary considerably around the world; for example, in some countries a concatenation of the names of male ancestors is used to qualify a person instead of a family name.
- *Time stamp your pages.* Include dates and times in your dynamic pages. It shows your users that the information is fresh. Time stamps can be included in your static pages by using Server-side Includes, which many Web servers support.

Maintaining the Quality of Your Site

In traditional computer systems, tests usually are not run after an application moves into production status. Further tests are conducted only when modifications are made in the application itself or in the hardware or underlying software that the application uses.

To maintain quality in networked systems, you must conduct tests periodically (e.g., weekly), even when no changes have been made to your application. Changes in the organization, network, related software, and other Websites can adversely affect your system. Here are some examples of tests you should run regularly:

- *E-mail tests.* Send e-mail to all users listed as recipients of queries on your Websites and ensure that you receive a response within a reasonable length of time. Some e-mail addresses, such as those specified in the HTML MAILTO option, on Web pages are no longer associated with anyone who responds to questions. The lack of replies is often attributable to a change in organization or a job change by the person who was originally responsible for answering queries.

- *Hyperlink tests.* Check all hyperlinks in your static and dynamic pages and ensure that they are still valid. Changes in the structure of other sites may cause your hyperlinks to fail. A number of hyperlink checkers for static pages are available. However, it is usually important that a human being also review the content of the linked-to page to ensure its appropriateness and relevance, and not just that the linked-to page still exists.

- *Browser, screen, and print tests.* Check that all current browsers your users are likely to have continue to provide pleasing and easy-to-understand results when your pages are viewed. Check your pages on different screen types. Screen size can have a dramatic effect on the appearance of your pages. Check your pages with the *images off* option on the browser to ensure that the pages and applications can still be used, particularly if you have users accessing your pages across slow communication lines. Review what your pages look like when they are printed. A page's appearance can differ significantly across releases of the same browser.

- *Performance tests.* Check that the application response time is acceptable. Additional applications on the same server system or on the same communication line to the Internet may affect the performance of your application.

- *Search tool tests.* If your Website is on the Internet, periodically check the most popular search tools to ensure that your pages and applications are found when you type in the appropriate keywords. If they are not retrieved, investigate the scheme the search tool is using, and adapt your pages, for example, by adding keywords to the HTML META tags. Watch your users trying to find your pages and attempting to navigate between them. Periodically use the search tools to determine the sites that are linking to yours. For example, with Digital's AltaVista (http://www.altavista.digital.com/) you can use the link and host options to search on external hyperlinks to your site. For example:

```
link:http://www.mycompany.com -host:http://www.mycompany.com
```

Make frequent visible minor changes to your site (e.g., weekly) to ensure that your users feel there are responsive people behind the scenes. Making changes, perhaps by adding time-stamped questions and answers in the FAQ section on your site, also reduces the amount of e-mail your users send you. Be sure to remove out-of-date information, including *new* and *updated* markers that are no longer recent.

Avoid repeated major structural changes as they will confuse your existing users. When you do make an important structural change, be sure to test the new design with both existing and new users. Avoid frequent URL name changes, particularly for significant pages.

It is important to provide consistent and straightforward user interfaces on the Web. Software and interfaces of poor quality are less likely to succeed on the Internet and Intranet today than ever before because of the choices users now have. Bulletin boards and news groups enable users to share their views, identify the interesting and useful sites and applications quickly, and communicate their experiences when they encounter software of poor quality. The speed at which programmers and universities throughout the world adopted the Java programming language in 1995 when it was applied to the Internet in late 1994 with the HotJava browser is an example of the dramatic effect the Internet can have on useful software. The Java programming language and the Java Virtual Machine were nearly five years old at the time.

Searching and Being Found

Provide a way of searching your Website or collection of Websites, particularly on the Intranet. The value of Web information is greatly enhanced if it can be located across your company.

If you want your external Internet Websites to be found on the Internet, you may want to register your site with some of the well-known search tools, instead of waiting for the crawlers to visit your site. Understand that some search tools, such as Yahoo!, do not have crawlers and will only find your Website if you register it.

Search tools usually include the following components:

- *Crawler* (needed if multiple Websites are included within the scope of the search facility)
- *Indexer*
- *Search engine and user interface*

The search tools vary in what they index (e.g., all the words on a page or just the words in the title lines and major headings).

Digital's AltaVista indexes a considerable portion of the Internet and provides a search option by domain, so, for example, you can type the following keywords:

- "Lou Gerstner" host:ibm.com
- "Tim Berners-Lee" host:www.w3.org

The host option restricts the scope of the search to the appropriate servers.

Consider how your existing data and applications can be integrated into the standard search mechanisms of the Web. One way is to create some HTML pages containing significant keywords that the search tool would use in its indexes, such as *opera, tickets, tenor, soprano, Verdi,* for an opera tickets Web application. The pages would also include hyperlinks to the gateway applications that provide access to the relevant data. There are a number of projects that attempt to provide integrated mechanisms for searching heterogeneous structured data, held in existing databases and files, from the Web. These projects include Harvest, Harness, and Nescape's Catalog Server. Standards are emerging to enable a non-HTML-based site to advertise its contents in such a way that it can be indexed.

CONCLUSION

HTTP, along with URLs, HTML, and hyperlinks, is the basis for the success and versatility of the Web. HTTP is also the basis for accessing application and database servers from the Web. To review, three main approaches are available for accessing application and database servers:

1. *Web gateway* (generic and application specific). Net.Data and the MQSeries Internet Gateway and CICS Internet Gateway.
2. *Java client and gateway.* The CICS Gateway for Java and some JDBC implementations.
3. *HTTP protocol integration.* Such as the Lotus Domino server and the CICS Web Interface

Designers of gateway applications should take into account the importance of the user interface on the Web. Do not underestimate the effort required to maintain your Website and preserve its quality. Even if you make no modifications, the network environment around your site is constantly changing.

CHAPTER 5

Server-side Programming Techniques

In this chapter we describe techniques for accessing database and transaction processing systems from the Web with custom-built software that runs on the server. We cover the important aspects of HTML forms and the CGI, which are the most widely used techniques for accessing Web server applications. We also discuss ways for server application programmers to manage concurrent users and browser sessions that consist of a sequence of requests from a particular user. We explain the integration of browser sessions with legacy systems that have their own conversation management.

This chapter presents some of the methods used in Net.Data, the CICS Internet Gateway, the CICS Web Interface, and the MQSeries Internet Gateway, all of which incorporate some degree of server-side programming involving a Web server or HTTP. Some of the topics covered in this chapter are illustrated in practical examples in Chapter 14.

After reading this chapter, you will understand the essential methods for writing your own software to run on a server system that accesses existing and new data and applications.

INTRODUCTION

Many users typically access a database or transaction processing system concurrently, which means that server-side software is multiuser. Concurrent access brings with it a number of issues, for example, distinguishing one user from another and dealing with security. Conserving resource usage consumption, such as memory, disk, and processing power is particularly important, as it is the limiting factor in determining the maximum number of concurrent users and maximum throughput. Insufficient resources can be of concern on the Internet where it is difficult to predict the number of users in advance. Therefore, your server-side solution must be *scalable* so that it will support an increase in both the number of users and throughput without major redesign.

WEB FORMS PROGRAMMING

Web forms enable users to type data onto a Web page. When the user clicks on the submit button on a Web page that includes a form, the input data is sent to a Web server through HTTP, where an application program, often known as a *script,* processes the input (see Figure 5.1). The application program can access databases, files, and other applications. Eventually, the program creates an HTML page, which can include variable data retrieved from files and databases, to send back to the user through HTTP. The output page can itself include more Web forms, enabling further user interaction (see Figure 5.2 and 5.3)

The creation of Web pages dynamically by a program as a result of user interaction is known as *dynamic HTML*. Pages that are predefined and held in Web server directories are known as *static HTML*.

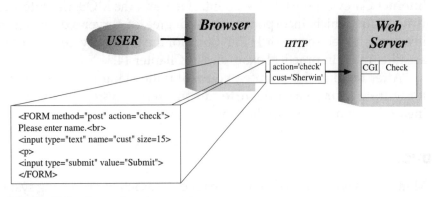

Figure 5.1 Forms input example.

Server-side Programming Techniques

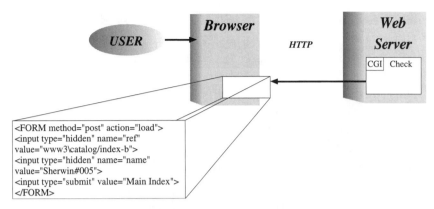

Figure 5.2 Forms output example.

The FORM ACTION and METHOD Options

An HTML page can contain a number of forms. A form is delimited by the <FORM> and </FORM> tags. The FORM has an ACTION option: <FORM ACTION="URL">. The URL determines the name of the server program that will process any user input for that form. Thus, the creator of an HTML form (a human or program) decides which program will be invoked to process any input. In Figure 5.1, the name of the server program is *check*. Another important option on the FORM tag is the <FORM METHOD="http_method">, which determines the mechanism used to pass the input data between the browser and the server.

The *default method is GET,* where the browser passes the input data onto the Web server by appending it to the URL in the HTTP header. The Web server places the input data in an environment variable called QUERY_STRING for the server application to process. There are limits on the lengths of environment variables and hence limits on the maximum length of the input data using the GET method. Here is a query string produced by the Alta Vista search form:

```
http://www.altavista.digital.com/
cgi-bin/query?pg=q&what=web&fmt=.&q=%22tim+berners-lee%22
```

A query string consists of a series of variable name and value pairs separated by ampersands. So in the example above, the *pg* variable is set to value *q*, the *what* variable is set to value *web,* and so on.

Figure 5.3 Display corresponding to figure 5.1.

It is possible to refer to a URL containing a query string in a hyperlink to avoid asking users to click on a submit button. Instead users just click on a hyperlink as usual, but in this case a server program is run and a dynamic HTML page is generated. Here is an example from AltaVista where a query string is included in the hyperlink URL:

Server-side Programming Techniques

```
<a href="/cgi-bin/query?pg=tmpl&v=about.html">
<IMG   src="/av/pix/default/av-logo.gif"   alt="[   AltaVista]"
BORDER=0 ALIGN=middle HEIGHT=73 WIDTH=204></a>
```

Note that in this case the hyperlink appears as an image (IMG src = . . .) not as text.

In the *POST method*, data is passed in the HTTP message body, as in this example:

```
MIME content type: application/x-www-form-urlencoded
MIME content length: 43
pg=q&what=web&fmt=.&q=%22tim+berners-lee%22
```

The server program receives the POST input parameter through *standard input*.

The <INPUT . . . > tag is used to define fields that the user can type into or click on within a form, such as:

- INPUT TYPE=TYPE—For text input
- INPUT TYPE=PASSWORD—For nondisplay input
- INPUT TYPE=HIDDEN—For sending nondisplay fields that will be sent to the server when the user submits the form
- INPUT TYPE=CHECKBOX—For multiple-choice data entry
- INPUT TYPE=RADIO—For selecting one item from a list
- INPUT TYPE=IMAGE—For a submit button that is represented by an image or for an image map
- INPUT TYPE=SUBMIT—For a regular submit button containing text
- INPUT TYPE=RESET—For clearing all input fields to their default values

Here is an extract of a form that uses the GET method with a submit button:

```
<CENTER><FORM method=GET action="/cgi-bin/search">
<B> Search
<SELECT NAME=query.val>
<OPTION VALUE="." SELECTED> in Standard Form
<OPTION VALUE=c > in Compact Form
<OPTION VALUE=d> in Detailed Form
</SELECT></B><BR>

<INPUT NAME=q size=55 maxlength=200 VALUE="&quot;tim berners-
lee&quot;">

<INPUT TYPE=submit VALUE=" Submit">
</FORM></CENTER>

<li><ul><a href="http://www.bcs.org.uk/news/timbl.htm">
Tim Berners-Lee receives BCS Distinguished Fellowship</a><br>
British Computer Society honours creator of WWW<br>
<a href="http://www.bcs.org.uk/news/timbl.htm">
http://www.bcs.org.uk/news/timbl.htm</a>
<br>

<li><a    href="http://www.aec.at/prix/kunstler/Eberners.html">
Tim Berners-Lee</a><br>

Tim Berners-Lee scientist. Abstract. Founder of the World Wide
Web! Biography.
Tim Berners-Lee (GB) is a graduate of Oxford University.
```

Here is a form generated by the CICS Internet Gateway that uses the POST method:

```
<!doctype html public "-//IETF//DTD HTML 2.0//EN">
<html><head><META NAME="Copyright" CONTENT="(C)Copyright IBM
Corporation, All Rights Reserved">
<title>IBM CICS Internet Gateway.</title></head><body>
<BODY>
<img src="/cig/cigmast.gif" alt="IBM">
<HR ALIGN=center SIZE=4>                                  (continued)
```

```html
<br>
<FORM ACTION="/cig-bin/cigcgi/SendData" METHOD="POST">
<INPUT TYPE="hidden" NAME="CommData" VALUE="5">
<INPUT TYPE="hidden" NAME="SessionID" VALUE="7878">
<INPUT TYPE="hidden" NAME="SequenceNo" VALUE="1">
<PRE>
FAACESN                         <B>CICS Sign-on</B>
Type your userid and password:
Userid.........: <INPUT TYPE="text" NAME="Inp594L8" VALUE="" SIZE="8" MAXLENGTH="8">
Password.........:   <INPUT   TYPE="password"   NAME="Inp674L8" VALUE="" SIZE="8" MAXLENGTH="8">
New  password.......:  <INPUT  TYPE="password"  NAME="Inp914L8" VALUE="" SIZE="8" MAXLENGTH="8">
New  password.......:  <INPUT  TYPE="password"  NAME="Inp994L8" VALUE="" SIZE="8" MAXLENGTH="8">

Enter F1=Help F3=Exit
<HR ALIGN=center SIZE=4>
<INPUT TYPE="submit" NAME="FENTER" VALUE="Enter">
<INPUT TYPE="submit" NAME="FESC" VALUE="Clear">
<INPUT TYPE="submit" NAME="F1" VALUE="PF01" ALT="PF01">
<INPUT TYPE="submit" NAME="F2" VALUE="PF02" ALT="PF02">
<INPUT TYPE="submit" NAME="F3" VALUE="PF03" ALT="PF03">
<INPUT TYPE="submit" NAME="F4" VALUE="PF04" ALT="PF04">
<INPUT TYPE="submit" NAME="F5" VALUE="PF05" ALT="PF05">
<INPUT TYPE="submit" NAME="F6" VALUE="PF06" ALT="PF06">
<INPUT TYPE="submit" NAME="F7" VALUE="PF07" ALT="PF07">
<INPUT TYPE="submit" NAME="F8" VALUE="PF08" ALT="PF08">
<INPUT TYPE="submit" NAME="F9" VALUE="PF09" ALT="PF09">
<INPUT TYPE="submit" NAME="F10" VALUE="PF10" ALT="PF10">
<INPUT TYPE="submit" NAME="F11" VALUE="PF11" ALT="PF11">
<INPUT TYPE="submit" NAME="F12" VALUE="PF12" ALT="PF12">
</PRE>
</FORM>
</body></html>
```

The form generated by the CICS Internet Gateway is the usual user sign-on screen for CICS. It includes multiple submit buttons within a single form. The CICS Internet Gateway generates the HTML for the page and uses the submit button to simulate the program function keys in mainframe applications.

As illustrated in Figure 5.2, and in the form generated by the CICS Internet Gateway above, the server application has included various hidden fields. These hidden fields are used to maintain state across user requests (see Managing Browser Session State later in this chapter).

It is instructive to contrast the techniques used on the Web with those used in traditional systems, for example:

- In traditional systems, administrative and control information is typically held in separate and secure files. With the Web, you can place control information, such as the name of the next program to run, in Web pages.
- In traditional systems, application state information is usually stored in databases, files, or memory. With the Web, state information is often stored in the Web page as hidden fields. Alternatively, the URL can be adapted to hold state information as well as identify the program to be executed.
- In traditional systems, program instructions are usually kept in distinct files separate from data files. With the Web, you can include program instructions in Web pages, using JavaScript.

Thus, Web forms provide a variety of functions in a flexible way that does not require significant administrative overhead for small systems, but which could become complicated in a large system. For example, it is straightforward for an HTML form to refer to a server program in another Website. Because it is so simple to invoke server programs in other Websites, deciding which server programs are in general use can be quite difficult, and it may be necessary to consult the Web server's audit logs. Create separate directories for production HTML files and Web server programs to reduce confusion.

COMMON GATEWAY INTERFACE

The CGI defines an interface between a Web server and a program (see Figures 5.1 and 5.2). The CGI program's function is to process the input param-

Server-side Programming Techniques

eters and produce an HTML page as output. The Web server invokes the appropriate CGI program when a CGI program name is specified in a URL, for example:

```
<FORM METHOD="POST" ACTION="/cgi-bin/db2www.exe/example1.d2w/report">
```

to invoke the Net.Data gateway called db2www.exe.

The Web server passes the HTTP header data to the CGI program in environment variables. Any METHOD=GET input is passed to the CGI program in the QUERY_STRING environment variable. Any METHOD=PUT input is passed to the CGI program as *standard input*.

The server program must always return a response in *standard output*, even if it decides it cannot create an output HTML page. Here are the possible responses:

- *MIME content type: text/html* causes the server to return the dynamic HTML page to the client.
- *Location: URL* causes the server to perform a redirect, that is, to ask the client to retrieve the specified URL without notifying the user.
- *Status: Message-String* causes the server to return the status and message specified by the CGI program to the client.

Each invocation of a CGI program has to run in a separate process because environment variables are used to pass parameters to CGI server programs, and only one set of environment variables is permitted in an operating system process. Often the number of computer instructions required to start and terminate a process is significantly less than that required by the CGI server program itself to execute. Thus, the CGI has a performance overhead and is considered to be slow. Nevertheless, the CGI is fast enough for many simple applications.

Here are some common uses for the CGI:

- *Visitor page counts*. Often used to display the number of times a page has been visited within the page itself. You can use an IMG tag to define where the counter should be displayed on the page and name the CGI program that maintains the counter. Append a QUERY_STRING to identify the particular page, for example, <IMG SRC=/cgi-bin/

viscount.pl/pretty.counter?malaika.html ALIGN=MIDDLE>. The viscount program has individual counters for each of the pages it maintains, often held in separate files. The output from the viscount program is an image in GIF format, for example, that contains the appropriate counter. Thus, visitor count programs usually create images dynamically at runtime and use the HTTP content type header *MIME content type: image/gif.* Many visitor count programs and software to generate images dynamically are available on the Internet.

- *Server-side includes (SSI).* Make it possible for a Web server to insert variable items into static and dynamic Web pages at runtime. An SSI is useful for boilerplate information such as copyright notices and date of last modification. It is not necessary to use a CGI program with SSI, because the Web server itself acts on directives included in HTML just before transmitting a page to the server, for example:
  - You can insert an HTML file into the page:
    <!—#include file="disclaimer.html"—>.
  - You can also display CGI environment variables:
    <!—#echo var="REMOTE_HOST"—>.
  - You can also run a program, such as a CGI program, and insert its output into a page: <!—#exec cgi="/cgi-bin/viscount.pl"—>

  An SSI can be inefficient if you apply it to all of your pages and programs in all your directories, as your Web server will then parse all output pages.

- *Clickable image maps.* Allow a user to click on a portion of a displayed image, and cause an action to take place at a server, such as selecting another URL to be displayed. The IMG tag for the image map must include the ISMAP option and be surrounded by a hyperlink to a map file, such as: <A HREF="/cgi-bin/maps/malaika_face"><IMG SRC=malaika_face.gif" ISMAP></A>. The map file contains the mappings from the image coordinates to the URLs to be retrieved. The format of the map files varies from server to server. There are utilities to help generate map files. More sophisticated image maps are possible with Java or JavaScript running on the client side.

- *Gateways to existing systems.* A server program is used to translate between the CGI and the interface language, such as SQL, of an existing system to enable Web browser access to the existing system. Examples include Net.Data for accessing various file types and databases, the MQSeries Internet Gateway, and the CICS Internet Gateway.

CGI Alternatives

There are many alternatives to the CGI, such as NSAPI and ISAPI. One of the functions of these APIs is to provide an alternative to environment variables for passing parameters to server programs. You can use long-running server processes to avoid the operating system process initiation and termination overhead. The Java Jigsaw server from CERN is another alternative to CGI, and it enables the dynamic addition of Java-based functions for use by server programs.

MANAGING BROWSER SESSION STATE

The stateless HTTP protocol does not link consecutive server requests from a particular browser. Thus, Web server programs do not receive any indication when a user request is part of a sequence of requests. Therefore, a programmer developing a server application that requires more than one user interaction to complete its functions has to devise mechanisms for recognizing multiple requests from the same user. For example, when a user is asked to identify himself or herself, it would be most unfortunate if he or she were asked repeatedly to type in his or her identification just because the server application has no way of knowing that the subsequent requests are from the same user.

We use the term *browser session* to denote a series of related requests from a particular browser to a particular server application (see Figure 5.4). To manage a browser session, you must create or use a token that represents the session and is passed between the browser and the server application. We call the token a *browser session identifier*.

A session identifier can be transmitted between a browser and the appropriate server application as:

- *Part of the URL:* The server program places URLs with query strings or path extensions that include the browser session identifier, which a user then selects, causing the session identifier to be returned to the server in the PATH_INFO environment variable. (See the application server in Chapter 14 and the CICS Web Interface in Chapter 11.)
- *A hidden field in the form:* The server program places the browser session identifier in appropriate hidden fields in a form that causes it to be returned to the server. (See the CICS Internet Gateway and the CICS Web Interface in Chapter 11.)

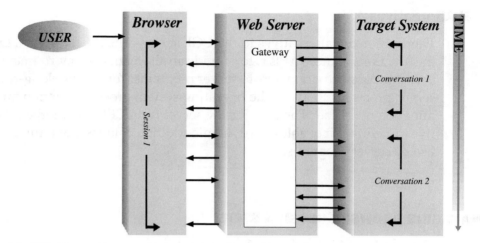

Figure 5.4 Integrating a browser session with a conversation.

- *Part of an authentication mechanism:* The server program uses the REMOTE_USER environment variable to represent the browser session. Once the user has typed in his or her user identifier and password, the browser continues to transmit the information to the server, enabling the server program to detect that the requests are part of the same browser session.
- *Netscape cookies:* Netscape cookies are data items that can include browser session identifiers. They can be defined in the server or the client, can be transmitted between the two, and are kept on the client in a file. They are described in the JavaScript section of Chapter 6, which covers client-side programming, although it is not essential that a client program be involved in manipulating the cookie. (See Net.Data use with Netscape cookies in Chapter 8.)
- *Part of a client/server protocol:* With Java on the client a private or public protocol can be used to transmit browser session identifiers. (See the CICS Gateway for Java in Chapter 11.)

The Web Environment

We highlight some aspects of the Web environment that affect the behavior of browser sessions and that affect how you manage them:

- *Web browser caching:* Most browsers have an option to keep local copies of pages, associated multimedia items, and applets retrieved from servers. The lifetime of the cached items varies from browser to browser. These browsers also include an option to page back and view earlier pages from the cache. Thus, a user who runs an application consisting of a sequence of interactions may confuse the server application by paging back to an earlier point in the application, and then resubmitting some input data using an earlier form. Web server applications can either disallow the use of the browser cache or include explicit support for the cache. The CICS Internet Gateway, which is a CGI application, recognizes when the browser cache has been used, and informs the user to return to the most recent page generated by the CICS Internet Gateway during that browser session. The CICS Internet Gateway cannot provide additional support for browser caches because it invokes CICS applications that usually require a particular execution path through the application's screens and do not support arbitrary navigation.
- *Web proxy caching:* Proxies hold copies of pages and retrieved multimedia items (see Figure 4.1). A server application that repeatedly generates a dynamic page (or image) with the same name must ensure it sets the appropriate HTTP header field when returning the page, causing the proxy to ignore any versions of the page (or image) held in the cache.
- *Web browser page refresh:* Many browsers support a page refresh or reload option. Browser page refresh enables a user to submit a request to a Web server, that retrieves a new version of the current Web page and all the multimedia elements it contains. If there is no new version, the current page is retrieved again. Page refresh also causes any copy of the page held in intervening proxy caches located between the user and target servers to be refreshed. Page refresh will not necessarily refresh all copies of the page held in the local browser cache. (Some browsers cache multiple copies of the same page and distinguish the access path to reach the page as well as the name of the page.) When a page contains a form, page refresh causes the user input to be retransmitted to the server. This retransmission can confuse a server program.
- *Using multiple browsers:* A user can abandon a browser session at any point, and then can attempt to return to it later from the same browser or from a different system altogether. Client-side state mechanisms, such as Netscape cookies, do not work in the latter case.

- *Bookmarks:* Also known as hotlists or quicklists, bookmarks are personal lists of URLs maintained by users and are supported by most browsers. (However, a browser from one supplier does not usually understand the bookmarks file generated by a browser from another supplier.) A user typically saves his or her favorite URLs in a bookmarks file held on his or her client computer. At any point during a browser session a user can select a URL from the bookmarks file that is unrelated to the current browser session. When a session identifier, is appended to the URL, the URL cannot be reused later. Changing or unstable URLs can cause frustration when a user saves the URL as a bookmark, as the page cannot usually be found again.
- *Surfing:* While stepping through a browser session a user can select an unrelated URL, for example, by typing it in or choosing it from the bookmarks file. That user may never complete the original browser session.

Managing Browser Sessions

To develop software that manages a browser session, consider the following:

- *Session initiation:* You must identify the event that causes your server application's session with the browser to begin. You also must decide whether it is your application code on the server that initiates the session, or, for example, your Java client application code.
- *Session identifier transmission:* You must select a mechanism such as hidden field and URL query string to transmit the session identifier between the browser and the server.
- *Storing session state:* You must decide whether you will store the session state information (such as your application variables) on the client or the server.
- *Session termination:* You must clearly identify the events that cause the browser session to terminate. Often there is more than one such event.
- *Handling unexpected errors:* You have to consider a variety of events, such as an incomplete browser session that has never terminated.

In Chapter 11 we discuss how the CICS gateways manage browser sessions and in Chapter 14 there are some practical examples of how you can manage browser sessions yourself.

After reading this section, you may decide that it would simpler to avoid maintaining session state. You can do so by placing all the data items you want to collect from your users in one HTML form. One form may not be friendly, but it may be adequate initially.

Integrating a Browser Session with a Conversation

Many systems have their own mechanisms for supporting consecutive related requests from an individual user. We refer to these mechanism generically as *conversations*. One of the functions of a server-side gateway is often to integrate browser sessions with the existing conversation structures (see Figure 5.4). Various mappings between browser sessions and conversations are possible:

1. *One Browser Session to One Conversation.*
   - Example: Net.Data where one browser session maps to one database connection (see Chapter 8) and the CICS Gateway for Java where one browser session maps to one unit of recovery (UOR) (see Chapter 11).
2. *One Browser Session to Many Conversations.*
   - Example: The CICS Internet Gateway where one browser sessions maps to multiple CICS pseudoconversations (see Chapter 11).
3. *Many Browser Sessions to One Conversation.*
   - Example: In a gateway that uses Netscape cookies, it is possible to interact with a long-running server application over a long period from multiple browser sessions.
4. *Many Browser Sessions to Many Conversations.*
   - Example: The CICS Web Interface could be used to combine a variety of CICS conversations with browser sessions of varying duration, although this is not recommended because of the complexity it would cause.

State Management Guidelines

In general, these are the options for managing state in Web-based and client/server applications:

- *Store state on the client only:* With forms-based applications, you can save all your state information on the client side by placing all state information in hidden fields. Alternatively, you can use Netscape cookies if the state information is less than 4KB. If you are using client-side programming, such as Java, then you can store the state information in Java variables. (Storing state on the client only was also adopted in traditional client/server applications—see Figure 5.5).

- *Store state on the server only:* With forms-based applications, you can transmit the identifier that represents the user (browser session) as a hidden field or as part of the URL, to enable the server program to detect who the user is, while maintaining the state information on the server. Alternatively, you could use an authentication mechanism or Netscape cookies (for managing the browser session identifier).

- *Store state on both the client and server:* With forms-based applications, you can transmit state information in hidden fields as well as session identifiers, enabling state information to be stored on both the client and server. You can store state information on both the client and server when using Netscape cookies and Java client programming. The drawback with this approach is that both parties (client and server) have to agree when it is time to clean up the browser session.

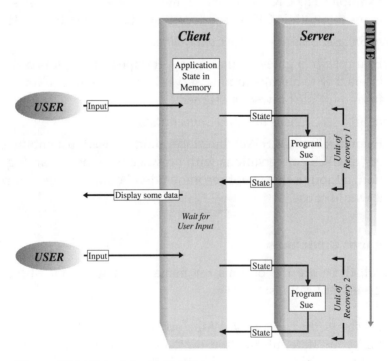

Figure 5.5 Using client-side state.

WHEN TO UPDATE DATABASES AND FILES

Applications that incorporate a series of user interactions and that update data in databases or files require special attention. With the appropriate software, a *unit of recovery* (UOR) can be used to ensure that updates conducted within a user interaction either all happen or don't happen, irrespective of failures in any component of the system. For example, in a shopping application, if a user buys items a, b, and c within a UOR, then either a, b, and c will *all* be bought and the database will be updated appropriately, or *none* of the items will be bought.

However, when an application consists of a number of related user interactions, you have to design the system to deal with partial updates. You must consider the following:

- *Removing the effects of partial updates:* Partial updates can occur because a user does not complete the sequence of required interactions. For example, a user buys a few items but then never confirms the order, thereby preventing others from acquiring the goods he or she has partially ordered.

- *Seeing the effects of another user's partial updates:* Problems arise if a user should see items for sale that have been ordered by another customer but have not yet been confirmed and paid for.

You can use one of two main approaches to correctly process applications that incorporate sequences of interactions and updates:

- *Perform updates on every interaction:* In this case, the server program updates the relevant data directly in the databases, remembering to set in-use flags to indicate that the data is in flight, for example, that an item has been ordered provisionally. Eventually, the server program asks the user to complete all of the updates, for example, by asking the user to confirm the shopping order. At that point the application completes the processing, which may involve resetting some of the flags if the user cancels part or all of the order. Periodically, a program should check for user timeouts, and if detected, the appropriate in-use flags should be reset. A side effect of this approach is that a lot of data may unnecessarily appear to be in-use for long periods.

- *Perform updates in the final interaction:* In this case, the server program records all updates in a temporary work area. Eventually, when the server program asks the user to confirm the updates, and the user agrees, the server program applies the updates to the database.

Updating in the final interaction provides more concurrency than updating on every interaction. It is also suitable when client-side programming is being used, as the client program does not have to contact the server program to perform updates on every user interaction. Updating in the last interaction does have an unpleasant side effect in that the server program may have to revalidate the user input on the final interaction because the database may have changed. The items that appeared to be available at the time the user asked for them could have been sold at the time of the final confirmation, as no in-use flags were set. If complex data structures are involved in the application, then updating on the final interaction can be more difficult to program than updating on every user interaction.

SECURITY

Firewall placement is one aspect of security using server-side programming as a way of accessing existing systems from the Web. An option shown in Figure 5.6 is to place the Web server and gateway outside the firewall and configure the firewall to permit certain requests to pass between the gateway and the existing system. For more information, see Chapter 3.

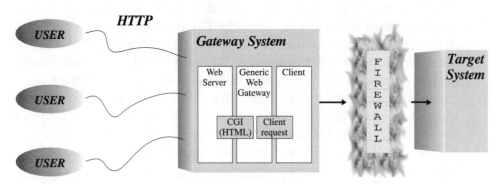

Figure 5.6 Firewall placement and Web gateways.

MULTIMEDIA

You may want to integrate multimedia objects in the Web pages generated from your system. The integration is quite straightforward, even if your target system does not support multimedia very well. You can choose to store the images, audio files, and video in the directories accessible by the same Web server that is running your CGI programs, or you can use another Web server on the same or a different machine. By using appropriately qualified names when referring to the object in the generated HTML, it is possible to embed objects from a variety of systems and to initiate CGI programs on various machines from a single HTML page.

CONCLUSION

HTML forms and CGI programs are among the main ways of running Web applications. You can use CGI programs as gateways for accessing existing systems such as DB2 and IMS from the Web. There are many ways of overcoming the statelessness of the Web; for example, you can use hidden fields in forms to transmit browser session identifiers to develop relatively sophisticated applications that consist of multiple steps. You can also integrate browser sessions with the conversation constructs that many existing systems support in order to manage state across user requests. Where updates are involved across a number of user interactions, you must take care to ensure that your users do not see partially updated data. Other aspects for you to consider when developing Web server applications include secure configurations and the use of multimedia.

CHAPTER **6**

Client-side Programming Techniques

In Chapter 4 we discuss the methods for accessing existing systems from the Web with software that runs on the server or the client and software that supports the HTTP protocol directly within the target system. In this chapter, we concentrate on the client software and how Sun Microsystems' Java affects the development of Web applications.

We describe some of the features of Java and review the issues to consider when you access applications from Web browsers with software that runs on the client. We explain how to use JavaScript to manage browser session state on the client. We also include a brief description of the Java-based NetRexx language and PointCast, a specialized non-Java client.

After reading this chapter, you will understand how to use Java gateways to access existing database and transaction processing systems across the Internet.

JAVA

Since late 1994, the Java programming language and the Java Virtual Machine (JVM) have rapidly gained popularity. Today, the Java language is taught in many universities and Java user group meetings attract thousands of participants. The main reason for Java's success has been its use on the Web, initially through the HotJava browser and later through Java support in other browsers such as Netscape. Java is widely used for programs that run on clients and increasingly for applications that run on servers.

Java is a general-purpose, object-oriented programming language with a syntax similar to C and C++. Sun Microsystems began the development of the Java language, formerly known as Oak, in 1991 to provide a language that would work well with electronic household devices. Thus, the language had to be compact and tolerant of frequent changes in underlying technology. Instead of compiling Java into the target system machine code, Java is compiled into a concise intermediate language known as *Java byte codes*. Java programs are then distributed in Java byte code form and processed by the JVM (sometimes known as the *Java interpreter*) at runtime on the target system. The JVM interprets and executes the Java byte codes and acts as the interface between the Java program and the target operating environment. A compiled Java program can run on any system, provided that the JVM exists on that system.

The major breakthrough in the Java project occurred in late 1994, when Sun built the HotJava browser, formerly known as WebRunner. Sun incorporated the JVM within the HotJava browser software, thereby enabling HotJava to run compiled Java programs (that is, in byte code form) known as *applets*. Sun introduced an additional HTML tag, <APPLET>, formerly <APP>, so that HotJava could retrieve applets across the Internet. Here is an example of an HTML page that includes an APPLET tag.

```
<HTML>
<HEAD><TITLE>Hello World JavaApplet</TITLE></HEAD>
<BODY>
<P>
Here is the output from my first JavaApplet:

<APPLET CODE="HelloWorldApplet.Class"
height=100 width=200>
We are sorry but you are not running a Java capable browser.
</APPLET>

</BODY>
</HTML>
```

Applets, like HTML pages and various multimedia items, are placed in directories on regular Web servers. When the HotJava browser sees the APPLET tag, it retrieves the HelloWorldApplet.Class file from the appropriate Web server directory using the usual HTTP GET request. In our example, the HelloWorldApplet will be retrieved from the same directory in which the HTML page that includes the APPLET tag resides. The height and width options identify the portion of the page that will be devoted to displaying the output from the HelloWorldApplet. As browsers ignore tags they do not understand, the apology in the text above is shown instead of the applet if the browser does not understand the APPLET tag.

The idea of downloading Java applets spread quickly during 1995, and late in 1995 Netscape included the JVM within the Netscape browser, making it possible for Java applets to run within the Netscape browser. Applets are useful because they enable the distribution of software, along with a Web page, without the user realizing that software is being downloaded. The JVM is also being incorporated into operating systems. IBM's AIX is one of the first systems to include the JVM.

Java applets run under the control of software, such as a Web browser or the applet viewer (a test tool to run applets), other than the operating system software. The following applet methods are invoked:

- *init()*—called once after the applet is loaded and should be used for the environmental setup
- *start()*—starts the applet (invoked each time the referencing Web page is viewed)
- *stop()*—stops the applet running (invoked once each time the referencing Web page is removed)
- *destroy()*—cleans up resources held by the applet
- *paint(Graphics G)*—paints a graphics object into the allocated view

Java applications run directly in the operating system. HotJava itself was one of the first major Java applications as it was written in Java, but it had to incorporate the JVM within itself, because the JVM was not then available in any operating system.

Here is the Hello World application in Java:

```java
// HelloWorld.java
// My first Java application
class HelloWorld
  {
  static public void main(String args[])
    {
    System.out.println("Hello, World!");
    }
  }
```

Here is the Hello World applet in Java:

```java
// HelloWorld.java
// My first Java applet
import java.applet.Applet;
import java.awt.Graphics;
public class HelloWorldApplet extends Applet
  {
  public void paint(Graphics gr)
    {
    gr.drawString("Hello, World!, 10, 100");
    }
  }
```

As illustrated in the import statements in the Hello World applet example, Java has class libraries that can be used in Java programs. The class libraries include the Abstract Windowing Toolkit (AWT), the language, utilities, I/O, and applet classes.

Figure 6.1 illustrates the steps required to make a Java applet available for execution. First you write, compile, and test your applet, using the applet viewer. Then you place your applet in the appropriate Web server directory, together with HTML pages that refer to the APPLET. You can then access your applet from a browser by retrieving the appropriate HTML page.

To program in Java, you need the Java Developer's Kit (JDK), which consists of the following:

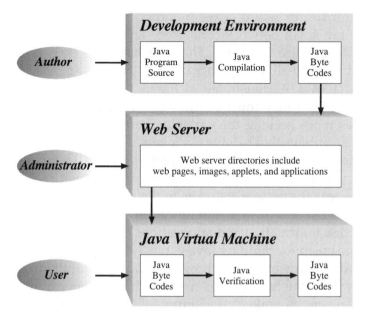

Figure 6.1 The Java programming environment.

- JVM
- Compiler
- Applet viewer
- Debugger
- Class file disassembler
- Header and stub file generator
- Documentation generator
- Applet demonstration
- API source code

You can obtain the JDK from the Sun or IBM Java home pages as listed in the For Further Reference section at the end of this book.

Java Security

The Java language and the JVM were developed with security in mind, as Sun's original intention was to download Java programs across a network, for example, for use in settop boxes to support shopping on television. (Settop boxes are small network-connected devices that enable users to interact with their television sets.) The Java language does not include pointers, so it is impossible for programmers to access memory beyond what the JVM allows. As illustrated in Figure 6.1, before a downloaded Java applet begins to run, it must go through a verification process. Verification includes type-checking the variable operations, thereby making it difficult to write applets that behave maliciously.

Another important constraint on applets prevents software viruses: Most browsers that support Java do not permit an applet that has been downloaded across the network to write to the hard disk.

Applets can use the Java communication classes to issue TCP/IP requests to access information and applications on other systems. Indeed, this is the mechanism for building Java gateways to existing database and application servers. However, most browsers allow the Java applet to communicate only with the host system running the Web server from which the Java applet was downloaded. Figure 6.2 illustrates this restriction, which is known as *applet host security level*.

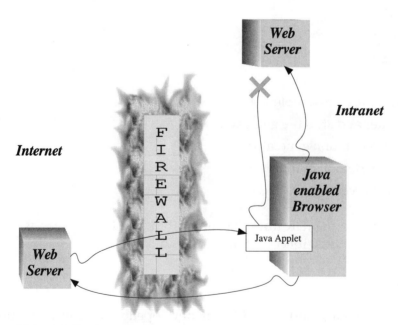

Figure 6.2 Java security.

As can be seen in Figure 6.2, if applet host security were not enforced, it would be possible for an applet that is downloaded from a system outside the corporate firewall to retrieve information from a server behind the firewall and then transmit it out through the firewall. Thus, when using a Java applet to access a Java gateway, which in turn communicates with an existing server system, you must place the Java gateway on the same machine as the Web server that contains the Java applet that plays the part of the client.

In the future, there will be sites on the Internet where users will be able to download trusted applets with more capabilities. For example, an applet that could write to the client hard disk would be useful for maintaining long-term session state for an application. Trusted applets need not be restricted to host applet security level. Currently, the Java applet viewer offers a number of communication security options that the user can select:

- *Unrestricted*, where an applet can communicate with any system
- *Firewall*, where an applet can communicate only with systems outside the firewall
- *Applet host*, where an applet can communicate with the server from which it was downloaded
- *None*, where an applet cannot communicate with any other system

Java Database Connectivity (JDBC)

JavaSoft, the group at Sun Microsystems that is now responsible for Java, has developed a standard structured query language (SQL) database interface called the Java Database Connectivity (JDBC), which provides access to a variety of databases using a variety of drivers. JDBC allows programmers to issue SQL requests to a local or remote relational database from Java applets and applications and receive and manipulate the results of the requests.

JDBC drivers can be classified in four categories:

1. *JDBC-ODBC bridge* provides JDBC access through most ODBC drivers. As illustrated in Figure 6.3, some ODBC binary code and database client code must be available on each client machine that uses this driver.
2. *JDBC native API driver* converts JDBC calls into calls for the client API for any database manager such as DB2, Oracle, Sybase, or Informix.

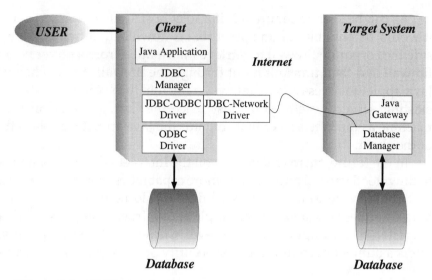

Figure 6.3 JDBC structure.

The JDBC native API driver is similar to the JDBC-ODBC bridge and also requires that some binary code be loaded on each client machine.

3. *JDBC all Java net protocol driver (applet)* translates JDBC calls into a database-independent network protocol, which is then translated to a database protocol by a Java server running alongside the database server. No specialized code is needed on the client system. This approach is very flexible as any communication protocol can be used and additional provision can be included to incorporate network security requirements and firewall navigation, for example.

4. *JDBC all Java net native protocol driver (applet)* converts JDBC calls into the network protocol that database managers use. Thus, there is no requirement for an additional Java server along with the database server. No specialized code is needed on the client system, but the communication protocol used has to be a protocol that the database server supports. This type of driver is generally provided by the database supplier.

For DB2 IBM provides JDBC native API drivers for Java applications accessing local or remote databases and JDBC all Java net protocol drivers for Java applets accessing remote databases. The structure of the CICS Gateway for Java is similar to the structure of the third category of JDBC drivers in the list above.

The JDBC URL structure is similar to regular URL:

```
jdbc:odbc://www3.hursley.ibm.com:400/suesdatabase
```

Java Remote Method Invocation

RMI permits Java objects to communicate with one another across JVMs, that is, across network connections. RMI is intended for a homogeneous Java environment, and not for use by non-Java programs, so, for example, Java remote objects are garbage collected as though they are running locally.

A Java program can call a remote object once it obtains a reference to the remote object. It can either look up the remote object in the RMI naming service or receive the reference as an argument or a return value.

The RMI communication protocol was not publicly documented at the time this book was written. It is clear however, that the RMI does not use HTTP. The RMI requests do not appear to traverse through firewalls that permit HTTP flows.

Java Interface Definition Language (IDL)

Java IDL enables Java objects to invoke remote server programs that may or may not be written in Java. IDL, defined by the Object Management Group (OMG), is used to describe interfaces between remote programs. The OMG also defines the Common Object Request Broker Architecture (CORBA) and the CORBA Internet Inter-ORB Protocol (IIOP). CORBA Object Request Broker (ORB) software provides interoperability between distributed objects that are possibly written in different languages. IIOP describes the communication protocol used between an ORB and an object, for example, to invoke remote objects whose interfaces are described in IDL.

Using the Java IDL support, you can write the description of an interface to a remote application in IDL, compile the IDL with the IDL stub generator, and produce Java client and server stubs. Using the appropriate stub, your Java client applets or applications can call Java or non-Java IDL server objects and your Java server applications can be invoked by IDL clients. The Java IDL system from Sun Microsystems uses the OMG's IIOP.

Managing State on the Browser

Running Java code on the client makes it possible to store state on the client as well as, or instead of, storing it on the server. Figure 6.4 shows a screen shot of a shopping demonstration application, where the buyer's purchases are stored in a virtual shopping basket on the client side.

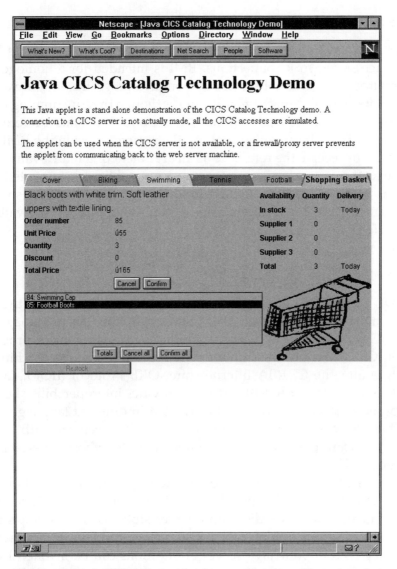

Figure 6.4 A CICS Gateway for Java application with a shopping basket.

Client-side Programming Techniques

Note that the Java applet whose output is shown in Figure 6.4 communicates directly with a CICS system and uses the Java AWT to create and manage its own windows.

Mixing Server-side and Client-side Programming

For many gateway applications, it is appropriate to mix some elements of client-side session management with server-side session management. As illustrated in Figure 6.5, once the appropriate client code, in the form of Java applets, has been downloaded to the browser, it initiates a session with the user to interact, collect, and validate data, without the overhead of contacting the server system. Eventually, the client code initiates a conversation with the target server system and transmits the user's input for processing on the server.

Using Java for Server Programming

A number of Web servers have been written in Java. The Java Jigsaw server from CERN is an example.

Such characteristics as scalability, performance, and throughput are significantly more important on server systems than on client systems, because servers are shared among a number of users. Studies show that

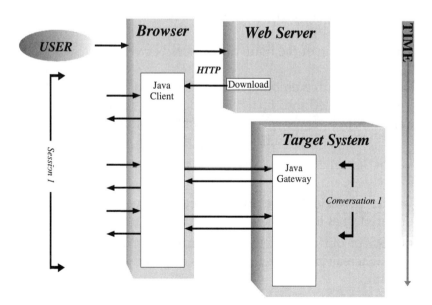

Figure 6.5 Java session with the user.

Java is about ten times faster to run than perl, and about ten times slower than C. Java's performance can be improved by compiling to the machine code of the target system, which, of course, means that the runtime code is not portable. For a server system, however, it may be more important to have high throughput than runtime portability.

Java's thread support is advantageous in a multiuser environment because it is possible to build efficient multithreaded Java gateways to access application and database servers. Performance measurements comparing the CICS Internet Gateway, which is a CGI application, with the CICS Gateway for Java on the same operating system show that the latter is more efficient. One of the reasons for better performance is that the CICS Gateway for Java does not incur the CGI program overhead caused by process initiation on every user request.

JAVASCRIPT

JavaScript is a scripting language from Netscape that can be used for client- and server-side programming. JavaScript does not originate from the Java language, so, for example, it does not include the same security features as Java. In this section, we concentrate on JavaScript as a client programming language.

JavaScript is popular among Web page authors and nonprogrammers partly because the JavaScript code is embedded in HTML pages and can be easily learned.

These are some of the main differences between JavaScript and Java:

- JavaScript source embedded in HTML is interpreted by the browser. Java is compiled into Java byte codes and is either downloaded as an applet from a server as a separate entity distinct from an HTML page, or it is executed as a standalone application.
- JavaScript does not support inheritance, whereas Java supports inheritance.
- JavaScript variables are not declared, whereas Java variables must be declared (that is, Java has strong typing).
- JavaScript objects are checked at runtime (known as dynamic binding), whereas Java object references are checked at compile time (static binding).

Both Java and JavaScript are case sensitive.

Be aware that JavaScript is not part of the HTML standard and there is no indication that JavaScript will become part of the HTML standard. However, the *W3C*, which is responsible for defining such Web standards as HTTP and HTML, has stated that frames will be supported in HTML, (see next section).

Here is the Hello World program in JavaScript:

```
<HTML>
<HEAD><TITLE>Hello World JavaScript</TITLE></HEAD>
<BODY>
<P>
This is my first JavaScript program.
Here is the output from the script:
<P>
<SCRIPT LANGUAGE="JavaScript">
document.write('Hello World')
</SCRIPT>
</BODY>
</HTML>
```

Frames

Frames are an important HTML feature; they help display complex data and information in a friendly way. With frames, an HTML author can display multiple HTML pages concurrently within a single browser window. Each HTML page is known as a FRAME, and the whole set of frames within the browser is known as a FRAMESET.

Frames are used, for example, to include ensuring that certain information, such as an index for a presentation or a table of contents for a document, is always visible to the user. Most users do not scroll down a page, so making crucial information visible is important. The CICS Internet Gateway simulates program function keys at the bottom of each page, which many inexperienced users do not notice. An alternative implementation would be to include the relevant program function keys in a frame near the top of the browser window. The following is a fragment of the HTML source to display the table of contents for an IBM manual in a frame (see Figure 6.6). The HTML that appears between the <FRAMES> and </NOFRAMES> tags appears when the page is accessed from a browser that does not support frames (see Figure 6.7). The HTML also includes a JavaScript application variable called STATE, which is used in subsequent HTML pages.

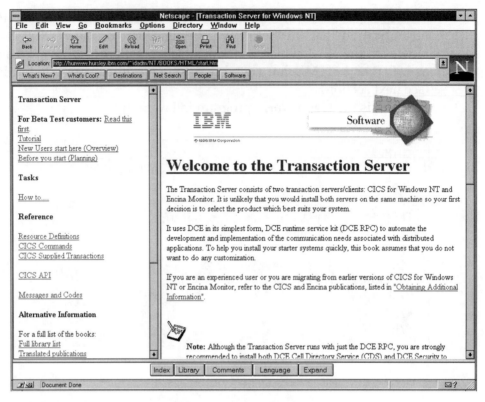

Figure 6.6 Using frames in IBM product manuals.

```
<HEAD>
<script language="JavaScript">
<!--Hide this from browsers that can't handle this
state = 1
// state=1: contents, state=2: no frame, state=3: index
//-->
</script>
</HEAD>
<FRAMESET ROWS="*,36">

<NOFRAMES>
```

(continued)

Client-side Programming Techniques

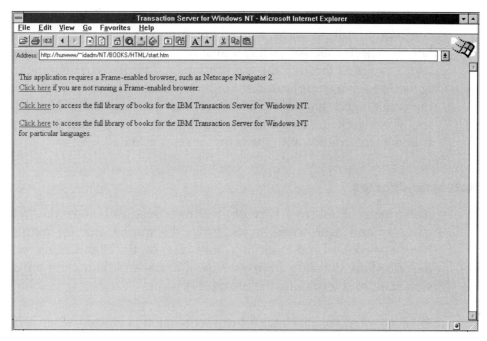

Figure 6.7 Alternative display using a browser that does not support frames.

```
<p>This application requires a Frame-enabled browser, such as
Netscape Navigator 2.
<BR><A href="atsfa600.htm">Click here</A>
if you are not running a Frame-enabled browser.
<P><A href="atsfa800.htm">Click here</A> to access the full
library of books for the IBM Transaction Server for Windows
NT.<BR>
<P><A href="atsfa700.htm">Click here</A> to access the full
library of books for the IBM Transaction Server for Windows
NT<BR> for particular languages.
</NOFRAMES>

<FRAME SRC=atsfa602.htm NAME="toc">
<FRAME SRC=atsfa601.htm NAME="navbar" SCROLLING="NO"
MARGINWIDTH="0"
MARGINHEIGHT="0">
</FRAMESET>
```

Frames can be helpful when you are running a Web application that consists of multiple steps, and where browser session state is being maintained. The JavaScript programmer could assign a frame to display the user's progress through the application, and perhaps to help the user navigate through a complicated set of instructions. The JavaScript running on the client could maintain the browser session state, using Netscape cookies. The JavaScript could also control what is displayed in the progress frame in accordance with the browser session state.

Netscape Cookies

Netscape cookies are a way of creating a session between a Web server gateway and a browser. JavaScript is the mechanism for manipulating Netscape cookies and associated state data on the client. Below we briefly describe how to create a browser session, transmit and store browser session state, and terminate the browser session.

1. *Browser session creation:* A browser session is created when a Netscape server application creates a Netscape cookie and sends it in through HTTP to the browser (see Figure 6.8). The syntax of the Netscape cookie creation request is:

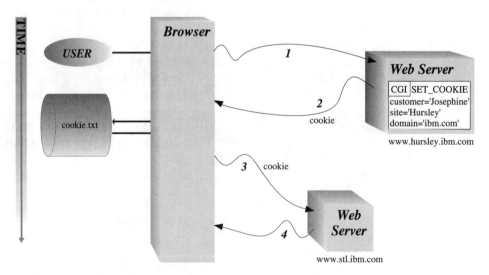

Figure 6.8 A Netscape cookie traversing between servers.

```
Set-Cookie:
  name=value
    [;EXPIRES=dateValue]
    [;DOMAIN=domainName]
    [;PATH=pathName]
    [;SECURE]
```

The name is the name of the cookie, and the value is the corresponding state information.

- The EXPIRES option determines when the cookie and associated state are deleted.
- The DOMAIN option defines the servers to which the browser sends the cookies. For example, DOMAIN = ibm.com would cause the cookie to be sent to www.stl.ibm.com, www.hursley.ibm.com, and www.ibm.com.
- The PATH option defines the URLs within the most general path. For example, PATH=/su would cause the cookie to be sent when www.stl.ibm.com/susan/index.html and www.hursley.ibm.com/sue/ are requested but not when www.ibm.com/leila/ is requested.
- The SECURE option indicates that the cookie is transmitted only when the HTTP connection between the browser and server is secure, that is, when the data transmitted is encrypted using SSL.
- JavaScript embedded within an HTML page and executing on the client can also create and manipulate Netscape cookies.

2. *Transmitting browser session state:* When a browser makes a request to retrieve a URL that matches both the DOMAIN and PATH options, the relevant cookies and their session state are transmitted in the HTTP request as follows:

```
Cookie: NAME1=STRING1, NAME2=STRING2...
```

The server can reset cookies in the HTTP response by reissuing the Set-Cookie request.

3. *Storing browser session state:* Up to 4 KB of browser session state information can be transmitted along with the Netscape cookie from the server to the browser where it is stored in the Netscape cookie.txt file.

4. *Terminating the browser session:* The browser session is terminated with respect to a particular cookie when:
    - The date specified on the Set-Cookie request is reached.
    - The date specified on the Set-Cookie request is in the past.
    - The browser is terminated and a Set-Cookie request was specified that did not include an EXPIRES option.

   When the browser session terminates with respect to a particular cookie, the browser no longer sends the cookie and associated state to any servers, and it deletes all relevant information for that cookie in the cookie.txt file.

The main advantage of Netscape cookies over some of the other browser session management methods is that most aspects of cleanup and termination of the browser session can be left to Netscape. Browser session cleanup routines can be quite troublesome to program correctly, especially when trying to deal with unexpected errors.

Another advantage of Netscape cookies is that they can be used to include servers other than the initiating server in the same browser session (see Figure 6.8). Care must be taken in this case to determine which server application is responsible for terminating the cookie, unless of course, the termination is processed when the EXPIRES value specified on first Set-Cookie request is reached.

The disadvantages of Netscape cookies are similar to the disadvantages of using hidden fields in HTML; for example, transmitting state data back and forth across the network may be inefficient. The state data itself can be stored on the server, with just the token passed back and forth between the server application and the browser. You then revert back to having to code the management and cleanup routines on the server for the state data, thus eliminating the main advantage of Netscape cookies.

Another disadvantage of Netscape cookies is that the cookie is specific to a particular computer and cannot be used to maintain a session across client machines. Consider an application that creates and manages personal pages on a server for each user. The server application uses Netscape cookies to differentiate the users. Unfortunately, however, the server application can only distinguish the client machines being used, or, to be more precise, the cookie.txt files on the client machines. Thus, when a user tries to access his or her personal page from a computer other than the computer he or she generally uses, either no page is retrieved, or the page belonging to the user who usually uses that machine is retrieved.

In addition to the disadvantages discussed above, Netscape cookies are unsuitable for integrating a long-lasting legacy system conversation with the Web when building a customized Web gateway. Note also that not all browsers support Netscape cookies. In Chapter 8 we illustrate the use of Netscape cookies with Net.Data.

NETREXX

NetRexx is an IBM programming language that is an extension of REXX and incorporates some features of Java. REXX, developed by IBM in the early 1980s with the goal of making programming easier, is often used as a scripting language. REXX has many useful text-processor functions, such as, parse, strip, substr, translate, verify, word, and wordpos. These functions make REXX suitable for processing HTML forms input and creating dynamic HTML pages, that is, writing CGI programs.

NetRexx programming is simpler than Java programming in a number of ways: Punctuation is not required, the language is not case sensitive, and variables do not have to be declared.

Here is the Hello World program in NetRexx:

```
/* Here is my first NetRexx program */
say 'Hello World!'
```

The NetRexx compiler takes NetRexx source and produces a Java class file that can execute wherever there is a JVM. Thus, NetRexx is suitable for writing applets as well as applications. Just-in-time Java compilers can be used with NetRexx generated classes to reduce execution time. Java classes can be called from NetRexx programs, so, for example, the Java AWT class library can be used in conjunction with NetRexx.

SPECIALIZED NON-JAVA CLIENTS

Some specialized non-Java clients have been very successful on the Internet. Examples include Netscape helper applications and various Internet Relay Chat (IRC) clients. One of the most well-known non-Java clients is PointCast, which delivers news at regular intervals or on request. The user interface includes many elements, such as buttons, lists of news items in a variety of categories, the full text for the news items, ticker tapes, and simple graphics for advertising. PointCast provides an example of the use of client-side programming with an HTTP gateway to access existing and new data and applications. Its success may encourage owners of legacy data to adopt a similar approach.

A new PointCast user downloads the client from the PointCast Website and performs a simple installation. The user then tailors the client to deliver news according to personal tastes. No customization is needed for the PointCast client to begin working, other than specifying a Web server proxy if one is in use locally. Initially, PointCast uses defaults for each of its news categories; for example, the client delivers information about the weather in certain major U.S. cities, but it is possible to define options to deliver weather information about cities around the world. The PointCast client also behaves as an entertaining and informative screen saver. When a connection to the network is unavailable, PointCast runs very successfully in standalone mode by displaying the most recently retrieved news items.

The PointCast client communicates with the PointCast servers through HTTP, although it is not a traditional browser. Because PointCast uses HTTP, customization of firewall software is not necessary to enable employees within corporations who already have Web access to use PointCast. Most of the news items PointCast displays are stored in HTML. When the user clicks on the constantly changing advertising material, a browser session is initiated to access the relevant advertiser's home page. Some advertisers create Web pages specifically for PointCast users.

PointCast, in common with Web browser software generally, confirms the fact that when software offers significant functions, users will take the time to download and install it.

CONCLUSION

Although the Web's initial success was due to the widespread adoption of a simple and universal client, the Web browser, more sophisticated client software for the Web is emerging. For example, application-specific clients are now in use, and it has become possible to use client-side programs to manage session state. Some of the reasons for the change are:

- The user requirement to include more than just the functions of a browser in Internet applications
- The technical requirement, motivated, for example, by a desire for improved performance, to communicate directly between a client and a server and bypass an intermediate Web server
- The ease of software download and installation for experienced computer users across the Internet

Another crucial factor in the adoption of application-specific clients is the availability of Java and Java applets. The characteristics of Java applets (e.g., that they are downloaded with a Web page), and the way in which they are supported have these effects:

- Inexperienced computer users are unaware that they are downloading software.
- The latest version of the software is always downloaded, eliminating release management problems, but incurring a performance overhead.
- The downloaded software can be assumed to be relatively secure.

Java also offers programmers many functions and such desirable characteristics as object orientation and portability. The use of existing Java applets appeals to HTML authors, as does the use of JavaScript, because it is easier for nonprogrammers to learn than Java. NetRexx combines the simplicity that is appropriate for HTML authors and Webmasters with the security and portability of Java.

The use of Java in client-side programming has affected the construction of gateways to database and transaction processing systems. Examples include the various JDBC drivers for relational database access and the CICS Gateway for Java.

CHAPTER 7

Visual Programming for the Web

A Web application can be characterized as a special type of client/server application because of the similarities between the two. In particular, both Web and client/server applications have server components containing business logic that communicate with client components and back-end resources such as databases and transactions. Furthermore, both Web and client/server applications rely on graphical user interfaces. The differences between Web and client/server applications tend to be associated with the client component. For example, a Web application has a Web browser for a client, but a client/server application has a custom-developed client. Furthermore, the user interface of a Web application is defined in terms of HTML rather than program calls to graphic functions. Given the similarities between Web applications and client/server applications, it should come as no surprise that the genre of visual programming environments that has proven so useful for developing client/server applications is also well suited for building Web applications.

In a typical visual programming environment, the developer of a client/server application authors the application's user interface by assembling sets of prebuilt visual parts (also known as *components*) and the application's logic by writing procedural code. The visual parts represent objects such as windows, scrolling lists, and buttons that the developer assembles into the application user interface by dragging and dropping them from a palette onto an electronic canvas. In some environments, there are also nonvisual parts that represent objects such as databases and transactions and even fragments of application logic. In these environments, the developer can author some amount of application logic by dragging and dropping nonvisual parts onto the electronic canvas.

You can extend an existing visual programming environment to cover Web application development by adding functions that enable application logic to read and write data to a Web server and visual parts that generate HTML. Figure 7.1 shows the basic configuration and operation of a Web application developed by using an extended visual programming environment. The Web browser sends a request to the Web application. The request travels across the network, and a Web server delivers it to the Web application. The Web application receives the request through a link function that formats the data in the request before passing the request to the application logic. The application logic can access back-end resources, and it can pass data to the visual parts. The visual parts generate HTML tags, which are sent back to the link function. The link function sends the HTML tags to the Web server, which in turn sends them to the Web browser for display to the end user.

The use of a visual programming environment to develop Web applications has several advantages compared with other approaches:

- *Single environment.* Developers create many Web applications by using multiple tools. For example, they use a Web page editor to create the HTML for a Web application, and they merge the HTML into applica-

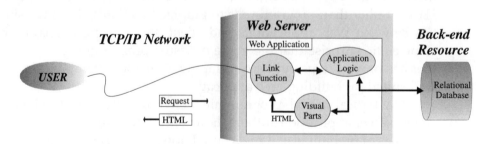

Figure 7.1 Configuration and operation of Web browser, Web server, and Web application.

tion logic that they create with a programming tool. A visual programming environment obviates the need for multiple tools.
- *Back-end connectivity.* Components that provide connectivity to back-end resources such as databases and transactions are typically available for visual programming environments. An important requirement for Web applications is that they interact with back-end resources; thus a visual programming environment is an attractive tool for developing Web applications.
- *Familiarity.* A developer requires time and effort to learn any programming environment (visual and otherwise). When a familiar client/server development tool is extended to develop Web applications, the amount of time and effort that a developer requires to learn how to develop Web applications is minimized.
- *Hidden plumbing.* A visual programming environment presents the developer with a "black-box" view of components in the environment. In other words, the low-level programming details of how components accomplish their functions are hidden from the developer. When the components in a Web-application-enabled environment generate HTML and communicate with the CGI, the developer does not have to learn the details of HTML and CGI to build a Web application.
- *Visual editor.* Visual programming environments have visual editors that enable developers to create application user interfaces in an environment that also shows how the user interface will appear to an end user. In a Web-enabled visual programming environment, the visual editor shows how the user interface will appear in a Web browser.

Several visual programming environments, such as IBM's VisualAge with Web Connection parts and ParcPlace-Digitalk's VisualWave, have been extended to develop Web applications. One of the differences between the VisualAge and VisualWave approaches is the nature of the parts that generate HTML. VisualAge has special-purpose parts to generate HTML, whereas VisualWave generates HTML from preexisting parts. The advantage of special-purpose parts is that the developer has fine control over the appearance of the user interface as it appears in the browser. The disadvantage of special-purpose parts is that, to enable an existing application to run as a Web application, the developer must replace the existing visual parts with special-purpose parts. In comparison, the VisualWave approach of reusing existing parts has the advantage that the developer can enable existing applications to run as Web applications by upgrading existing parts but without replacing any parts. The disadvantage of this approach is that VisualWave interprets the existing parts to generate the HTML, but this interpretation may be different from the developer's. Therefore, the developer may require additional work to make the user interface appear as desired in the browser. Despite this difference, overall VisualAge and VisualWave probably share more similarities than differences.

In the remainder of this chapter you will learn how to build a Web application, using the Smalltalk version of IBM's VisualAge extended with Web Connection parts. You do not have to be familiar with Smalltalk, however, because the sample Web application is built almost entirely visually, simply by dragging and dropping and connecting prebuilt parts.

THE PIZZA SCENARIO

To illustrate visual Web programming and its advantages, we use the venerable Pizza application that enables you to order pizza over the Web. From a customer's point of view, two Web pages are associated with ordering pizza: a page containing an order form and a confirmation page. We start by describing these pages from a customer's point of view, and in the next section we describe how to build the Web application that is responsible for creating these pages.

Suppose that our customer, Helen, wants to order pizza from Lou's Cyber Pizza. To start, she opens the URL for the pizza shop, and an order form appears in her Web browser. As you can see in Figure 7.2, the order form contains controls that Helen can use to enter the particulars of the pizza she wants to order. There is a text field where she has entered her name, a selection list for selecting the pizza size, and a selection list for selecting a pizza topping. The order form also contains a button to submit her order, and some fancy images. If you are familiar with HTML, you can see that the HTML tags for the page (Table 7.1) are quite standard. The HTML tags also specify an HTML form that is used for directing the pizza order back to Lou's Cyber Pizza.

Helen is hungry, so she has selected a large pizza, plus a mushroom topping. After making her selections, she clicks on the Send My Order! button, which sends her order to the pizza shop where they start making her pizza. A short time later, Helen receives a phone call to verify payment and

Visual Programming for the Web

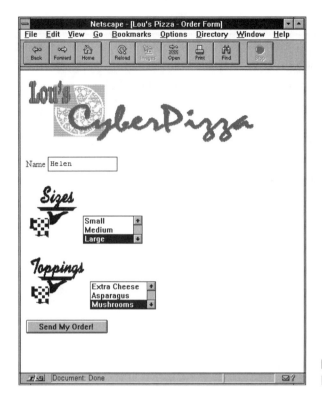

Figure 7.2 Order form page in browser.

delivery details. In the meantime, the pizza shop sends a confirmation to Helen, as shown in Figure 7.3. The confirmation is addressed to Helen and provides her with a breakdown of the pizzas she has ordered recently. The fact that this page displays a history of Helen's account is a clue that the Web pizza application is storing data. In fact, the application is using a relational database to maintain the pizza shop's customer accounts.

THE PIZZA APPLICATION

Now that you have seen how a customer interacts with the pizza application, and how the application appears in the Web browser, let us look at how a developer sees the application. The Web application developer authors an application whose "body" runs at a Web server, and whose "head," or user interface, runs at a Web browser. The user interface is transmitted as an HTML file from the application, through the Web server, to the

Table 7.1 HTML for Pizza Order Form

```
<!DOCTYPE HTML PUBLIC "-//IETF/DTD HTML 2.0/EN">
<!-- generated by VisualAge Web Connection on 07-07-96 at 5:22:13 PM -->
<html><head><title>Lou's Pizza - Order Form</title></head>
<body bgcolor="#FFFFFF">
<img src="/pizalogo.gif">
<p>
<form method="POST" action="ConfirmAPizza">
Name
<input type="text" name="CustomerName" size="15" value="" >
<p><img src="/sizes.gif">
<select size="3" name="PizzaSize" >
<option>Small
<option>Medium
<option>Large
<option>Extra Large
</select>
<p><img src="/toppings.gif">
<select size="3" name="PizzaTopping" >
<option>Extra Cheese
<option>Asparagus
<option>Mushrooms
<option>Olives
<option>Spinach
<option>Anchovies
</select>
<p>
<input type="submit" name="Html Push Button1" value="Send My Order!" >
<input type="hidden" name="_ABT_FROM_PAGE" value="OrderAPizza">
<input type="hidden" name="_ABT_SESSION_KEY"
value="305F3A82858DB8507361BD3B1A7824F7">
</form>
</body>
</html>
```

Web browser, as shown in Figure 7.1. Fortunately, the VisualAge environment hides many of the details of this transmission from the developer, who can author most of the application as if its head and body are collocated. Figures 7.2 and 7.3 show how the order and confirmation forms generated by the pizza application appear in the Web browser at runtime.

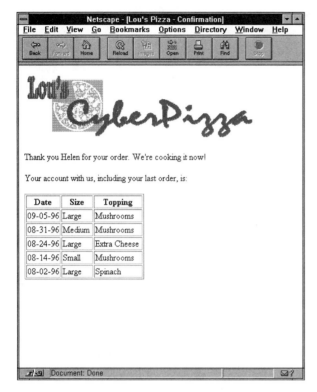

Figure 7.3 Confirmation page in browser.

Now let us see how they appear in the VisualAge environment during development.

The Application Part: LPizza

You can think of the pizza application as a hierarchy of parts (a *part* is a VisualAge term that is generally interchangeable with the term *object*.) At the top of the hierarchy is a pizza application part called *LPizza*. This application (part) contains two Web Connection parts that appear in the next layer of the hierarchy, one of which is called *OrderAPizza*, and the other, *ConfirmAPizza*. As shown in Figure 7.4, the two layers of the part hierarchy are represented graphically in the Organizer window of VisualAge.

The OrderAPizza and ConfirmAPizza parts are responsible for the details of the Web pages that appear in the Web browser. OrderAPizza and ConfirmAPizza each contain a type of part called an *Html Page,* and these Page parts contain a variety of other parts that appear in the Web browser,

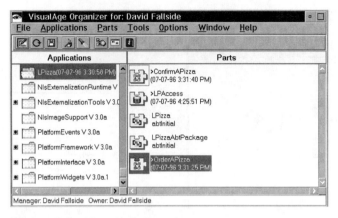

Figure 7.4 VisualAge Organizer.

for example, snippets of text, images, and push buttons.[1] In addition to an Html Page, ConfirmAPizza also contains parts that interact with the relational database.

When Helen enters the URL for the pizza shop, the OrderAPizza part of the pizza application is executed, and the Html Page that is a part of OrderAPizza generates the HTML that Helen sees in her Web browser as the order form. When Helen clicks on the Send My Order! button on the order form, her pizza selections are sent to the pizza application, and the ConfirmAPizza part runs. The database-related parts interact with the Html Page that is a part of ConfirmAPizza, and the Page generates the HTML that is Helen's confirmation.

The Order Form: OrderAPizza

Figure 7.5 shows OrderAPizza in the context of the Composition Editor that the developer uses to build this part of the application. On the left side of the Editor window there is a palette of parts. The items in the left column of the palette are folders containing different categories of parts. The right

---

1. Note that an *Html Page* is a part (object) within the programming environment, whereas an HTML page is a file containing HTML tags that is displayed by a browser. In the course of the chapter we sometimes abbreviate the names of parts. For example, we refer to the *Page* instead of the lengthier *Html Page* part. Similarly, we refer to a Paragraph rather than to an *Html Paragraph* part.

Visual Programming for the Web 153

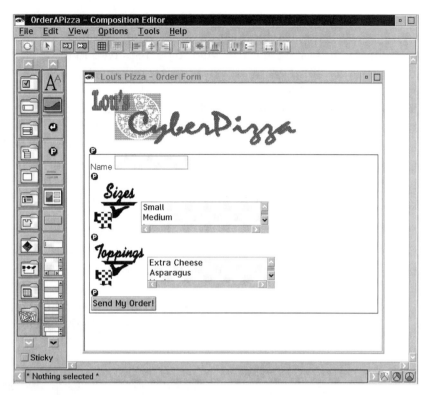

Figure 7.5 OrderAPizza in Composition Editor.

column displays the contents of the currently opened folder, the Web Connection folder in our figure. To the right of the palette there is an Html Page entitled "Lou's Pizza—Order Form." This Page has been built by dragging and dropping parts from the palette onto its surface. The 13 parts it contains are, from top to bottom and from left to right, an Html Image, an Html Paragraph (appears as a P), an Html Form, an Html Text, an Html Entry Field, an Html Paragraph (P), an Html Image, an Html List, an Html Paragraph (P), an Html Image, an Html List, an Html Paragraph (P), and an Html Push Button.

The Html Page and its 13 parts determine the details of the HTML that is generated when OrderAPizza runs. Many of the parts have attributes that the developer can alter once the part has been placed on the Page, and the attributes specify how the parts will appear in the Web browser. To take some examples, an Html Page part has settings that determine its title and the color of the background; Html Text has a bold font attribute; and Html Image has attributes for the locations of two image files, one to be displayed during authoring and the other to be displayed in the Web browser. To set the title and background color of an Html Page, the developer opens the Page's settings notebook. Figures 7.6a and 7.6b show the two sections of the settings notebook where a developer has set the title and background color attributes of the Html Page in OrderAPizza.

To set the Page's title, the developer has entered the phrase "Lou's Pizza—Order Form" into the Title entry field. To make the background appear white, the developer has unchecked the Use default color checkbox and maximized the Red, Green, and Blue color values. The effects of these settings are apparent in the browser at runtime: The Page part generates HTML that includes the fragments bgcolor=#FFFFFF and <title>Lou's Pizza - Order Form</title> (see Table 7.1), and the browser displays the background color and title of the order form accordingly, as shown in Figure 7.2.

Attributes such as background color and title determine the appearance of a page in the Web browser, and in our example the developer sets

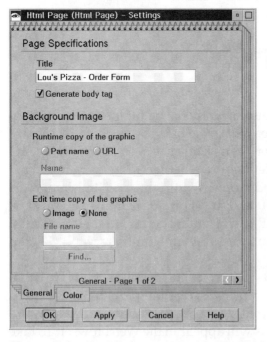
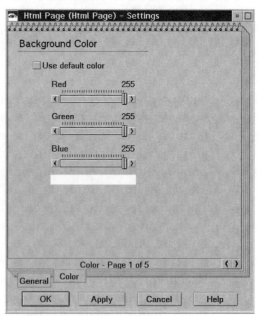

Figure 7.6 Html Page settings: (a) title, (b) background color.

the value of these attributes only once during development. In later sections of this chapter, we describe part attributes that determine the *behaviors* of elements in a Web page and part attributes whose values are set *at runtime*, but first, let us see how the Composition Editor mimics the appearance of pages in the Web browser.

The appearance of a Web page as it is displayed by the editor in a visual programming environment may more or less accurately reflect the appearance of the page as it is displayed by a Web browser. The more accurate an editor is, the better it is for the developer because he or she must spend less time manipulating parts in the editor so that they appear as intended in the browser. The appearance of a page can be characterized in terms of its *visual* properties (e.g., the color of a page), and its *spatial* properties (e.g., the location of a word on a particular line). We have already described how the Composition Editor displays some visual properties, and now we describe how it displays the spatial properties of a page.

As the developer adds parts to an Html Page, VisualAge automatically arranges them to mimic the arrangement of the page as it will appear in the Web browser. For example, after the developer added the Html List part to the right of the Sizes image, both parts appeared on the same line. But when the developer added the Toppings image to the right of the Html Paragraph part (represented as a blank line in a Web browser), the Image part appeared on the next line, just as it would in the browser: Compare the order page in the Web browser in Figure 7.2 with OrderAPizza in Figure 7.5.

The extent to which the Composition Editor can mimic a page's appearance in the browser is somewhat limited. In general, as the developer adds parts to an Html Page, the Composition Editor arranges them in a line from left to right until the line is filled, and then it starts at the beginning of the next line (assuming that there are no Paragraph or Line Break parts). This scheme is quite successful because Web browsers do exactly the same thing. One problem, especially with long lines, is that the browser places an element on a line according to the width of the browser window. Because the width is set by the user and is completely independent of the width of the Html Page (set by the developer), the location of an element cannot be guaranteed. Despite this limitation, however, the Composition Editor quite accurately represents both the visual and spatial properties of a Web page.

An important function of the pizza application, and any other application, is to make data entered in the browser available to the application. In the case of the pizza application, the Html Form in OrderAPizza determines where the browser sends customers' pizza order data, and several parts located within the Form determine which data the browser can send. The Html Form has an address attribute that specifies where the browser should send form data. This address can be specified in terms of a VisualAge part or a fully qualified URL. If the Form address is specified as a VisualAge part, it is assumed to be a Web Connection part located within the same VisualAge application as the Html Form itself. In LPizza, the Form in OrderAPizza references ConfirmAPizza. To set the address attribute to this reference, the developer opens the Form's settings notebook, selects *Part Name* for the URL of the query server, and enters ConfirmAPizza in the Name field, as shown in Figure 7.7.

Interestingly, the address in the Html Form can refer to the same Web Connection part that contains the Html Form. This makes for easy development of Web applications where data is input on a page at the browser, and an application uses the submitted data to update some facet of the same page. Alternatively, the Form address can be specified as a fully qualified URL, such as http://lou.icecream.com/cgi-bin/abtcgil.exe/OrderOne, in which case the browser will send the data to another application. This option is useful for passing data and control to another Web application.

The Html Entry Field and the two Html Lists enable Helen to enter her name and select the size and topping of her pizza. Note that because these parts are valid only in the context of an Html Form, the Composition Editor does not permit them (and similarly restricted parts) to be placed anywhere *except* inside an Html Form. Each Html List enables the customer to

Figure 7.7 Html Form settings.

select one item (a size, or a topping) from a predefined list of items. In LPizza, the developer enters the lists of items (Small, Medium, Large, and Extra Large; Extra Cheese, Asparagus, Mushrooms, Olives, Spinach, and Anchovies) into an attribute, called *Initial list of items,* of the appropriate part.

To make use of the order data that the customer enters at the browser, the developer must be able to identify the data that is obtained from the entry field and each of the selection lists. In the VisualAge environment, data that is returned from a browser is identified by the names of the parts that represent the data entry elements in the browser. In LPizza, these parts are the Html Entry Field and the two Html Lists. Hence, the developer should give these parts meaningful names such as CustomerName, Pizza-Size, and PizzaTopping for easy recognition when developing other parts of the application. The developer can set the name of a part in its settings notebook. In the next section, "The Confirmation: ConfirmAPizza," we describe in detail how to read the data represented by CustomerName, PizzaSize, and PizzaTopping.

A Web application created in the VisualAge environment is referenced by a URL of the form http://your.web.server/cgi-bin/abtcgil.exe/Part. In this URL, your.web.server is the domain name of the Web server that processes the requests for the Web application, abtcgil.exe is the name of a small program that communicates between the Web server and the Web application, and Part is the name of the part in the application to be referenced. So, the URL that Helen entered to reference the order form (Figure 7.2) would have been something like http://lou.pizza.com/cgi-bin/abtcgil.exe/OrderAPizza.

URLs to Web applications created with VisualAge reference the abtcgil.exe executable rather than the LPizza application. The position of this program in the URL string indicates that the Web server launches abtcgil.exe, rather than the Web application. The exact chain of events is that the browser sends its request to the Web server, and the Web server launches abtcgil.exe (short for CGI Link), which passes the request to a process called the CGI Link Server running in a VisualAge image. The particular CGI Link Server that the abtcgil.exe contacts is determined by preset parameters in the CGI Link Server and abtcgil.exe. Finally, the CGI Link Server passes the request to the appropriate part in the application. Note that the VisualAge application runs continuously, and only the abtcgil.exe executable is launched on every request. This configuration is adopted because it is far quicker to bring up the tiny abtcgil.exe with every request than it is to bring up the VisualAge application with every request. Moreover, because the application is running all the time, it is possible to store state information between requests. But more about that later.

The Confirmation: ConfirmAPizza

The confirmation page tells customers which pizzas they ordered and displays a statement of their pizza account. To provide a simple demonstration of how to incorporate other systems into a Web application and dynamically create page content, the pizza application uses a relational database to store Lou's pizza orders and provide content. When a customer sends a pizza order to Lou from an order page, the details of the order are first stored in the database. The database is then queried to find all of that particular customer's orders, and the results of the query are included in the confirmation page that is returned to the customer.

Figure 7.8 shows the completed ConfirmAPizza part in the Composition Editor. In addition to the Html Page and the parts it contains, a number of parts appear off the Page and are connected to the Page parts. These

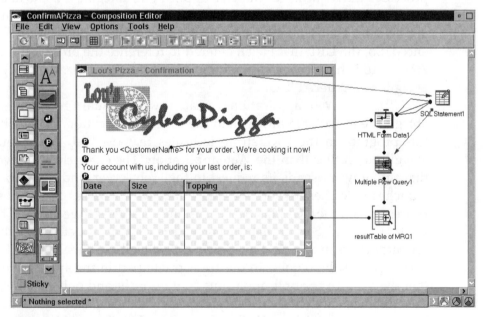

Figure 7.8 ConfirmAPizza in Composition Editor.

nonvisual parts receive input from the Web browser, interact with the database, and provide the data that is incorporated into the confirmation page at runtime. In particular, an Html Form Data part is responsible for passing data from a browser, an SQL Statement stores pizza orders in the database, a Multiple Row Query queries the database for a customer's pizza account, and a resultTable contains the query results. As you can probably infer from some of the connections between the parts shown in the figure, the Html Form Data part provides the customer's name that is displayed in the confirmation page, and the resultTable provides the details of the pizza account that are displayed in a three-column table as part of the confirmation page (see Figure 7.3).

Dynamic Content and Form Data

Lou likes to call his customers by name, and so the greeting text on a confirmation page should read something like "Thank you Helen for your order." To substitute the appropriate customer name in this sentence, the application must have access to the name that the customer enters in the order form and include a part for displaying the text of the name in the confirmation page. Customers enter their names in an entry field contained in an HTML form, both of which are defined in OrderAPizza. Access to any data that is obtained through a form defined in VisualAge can be made through an Html Form Data part, and so ConfirmAPizza contains such a part. The greeting text is created by using a combination of three separate Html Text parts: One displays the words "Thank you," a second displays the customer's name, and a third displays "for your order." (For clarification, during development the second Text part displays the text string <CustomerName>.) At runtime, the text string displayed by the second Text part is simply set to the customer's name obtained from the Form Data part, and the resulting concatenation of the text strings from all three parts creates the appropriate greeting text.

A Form Data part can access data defined within any one of an application's Web Connection parts. To enable the developer to specify a particular Web Connection part, the Form Data part has an attribute whose value the developer can set to be the desired Web Connection part. The developer of the Form Data part in ConfirmAPizza sets the value of this attribute to *OrderAPizza*, and as a result VisualAge creates several new attributes for the ConfirmAPizza Form Data part. The names of the new attributes are CustomerName, PizzaSize, and PizzaTopping, and the values of the new attributes (available at runtime) are the data values obtained from the order form page. To specify that the customer name obtained through the Form Data part must be passed to the Text part, the developer uses a feature of the Composition Editor that enables him or her to program this data transfer by visually connecting the CustomerName attribute of the Form Data part to the string attribute of the Text part. The completed connection is represented as a line between the two parts, as shown in Figure 7.8.

The Html Form Data part is a smart part that saves the developer from having to deal with a lot of low-level programming. Consider what the developer must program and what happens under the covers. To use the Html Form Data part, the developer need only specify the name of a Connection part, and subsequently the values of the appropriate data entry parts appear as attribute values that can be used in the rest of the application. Surfacing the data entry parts and the data as attributes and attribute values hides two secrets. The first secret is that the apparently direct linkage between the values of the data entry parts and the attributes of the Html Form Data part is actually a very indirect linkage. The values entered by a user into the data entry parts are actually entered into HTML data entry parts managed by the Web browser, and the browser sends the values across the network, through the Web server, and back into the application. The second secret is that the orderly data presented as attributes of the Html Form Data part must be thoroughly massaged to appear that way. The actual values that the browser sends to the application are formatted as long strings that look something like this:

```
CustomerName="Helen"&PizzaSize="Large"&PizzaTopping="Extra"%20
"Cheese"
```

Fortunately, the developer does not have to deal with the raw strings! In short, the Html Form Data part enables the developer to develop applications that read HTML form data without having to deal with the fact that it is actually entered into a Web browser.

Database Access

The pizza account data is stored in a relational database, and ConfirmAPizza has two database queries that insert individual customer orders into the database and retrieve all of a customer's orders from the database for display by the Html Table. The SQL Statement and Multiple

Row Query parts that handle the two queries are standard parts within the VisualAge environment providing access to DB2 and other databases. To simplify the description of database access in ConfirmAPizza, we describe the parts and their connections in approximately the same order as they are invoked when the application runs.

The SQL Statement part inserts a customer's order into the database. For this insertion, it requires information about the database in which the orders are stored, a query specifying how to insert an order, and the order data itself. The database information includes the type of database, for example, IBM Database 2, and the name of a particular database. This information is specified in the attributes of a database access set and a connection alias, although the details of these parts are beyond the scope of this chapter. VisualAge provides the developer with an easy-to-use visual interface for building queries; Figure 7.9 shows one of the windows from this interface that is used to build the insert.query.

A customer order consists of the customer's name, the order date, the size of the pizza, and the topping on the pizza. The query responsible for inserting each order is shown under construction in Figure 7.9. The query is called InsertOrder, and it will insert order data into the CUST_NAME, ORDER_DATE, PIZZA_SIZE, and PIZZA_TOPPINGS columns of the ORDERS table. The figure shows that the value to be inserted in the CUST_NAME column is :CUST_NAME. This value represents a host variable (indicated by the colon), and so it can be set as an attribute of the SQL Statement part. In other words, the value can be set by another part in the application. Although not indicated in Figure 7.9, the values of the

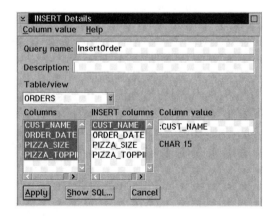

Figure 7.9 Insert Details window.

PIZZA_SIZE and PIZZA_TOPPINGS columns are also set through host variables, and the value of the ORDER_DATE column is set by the operating system. Once the developer has completed the SQL Statement part, he or she can make the data supplied by the Form Data part available to it. To do this, the developer makes three separate connections from the Form Data part to the SQL Statement part. Each connection links a different pair of attributes, namely: CustomerName and CUST_NAME, PizzaSize and PIZZA_SIZE, and PizzaToppings and PIZZA_TOPPINGS. The completed connections appear as the three lines between the two parts shown in Figure 7.8.

The purpose of the Multiple Row Query is to return from the database all pizza orders belonging to a particular customer. To do this, it requires information about the database, a query specifying which data to return, and the name of the customer. The database information (as specified in the connection alias and the database access set) used by the Multiple Row Query and the SQL Statement is the same because both parts access the same database.

The Html Table displays three fields from every pizza order: the order date, the pizza size, and the pizza topping. Because every pizza order stored in the database contains at least one other field (customer name), the developer must indicate which fields the Multiple Row Query must return. The developer indicates the field names by using a window similar to the INSERT Details window (see Figure 7.9). In particular, the developer selects the ORDER_DATE, PIZZA_SIZE, and PIZZA_TOPPINGS fields.

The Multiple Row Query must return records for a particular customer. Hence, the developer creates a WHERE clause to limit the query results to those records in which the customer name field is equal to the customer name that is supplied from the Html Form Data part. The developer defines the query's WHERE clause in the window shown in Figure 7.10. Here, the developer has selected the customer name field (ORDERS.CUST_NAME) from the Left operand column and the equal-to operator from the list of operators and entered the host variable name :CNAME in the Right operand column. The host variable name directs VisualAge to create a new attribute called CNAME. Hence, the developer can create a connection between the CNAME attribute of the Multiple Row Query and the CustomerName attribute of the Html Form Data part to pass the customer's name into the query.

To ensure that the customer's current order appears at the beginning of the pizza account, the orders returned by the Multiple Row Query must be

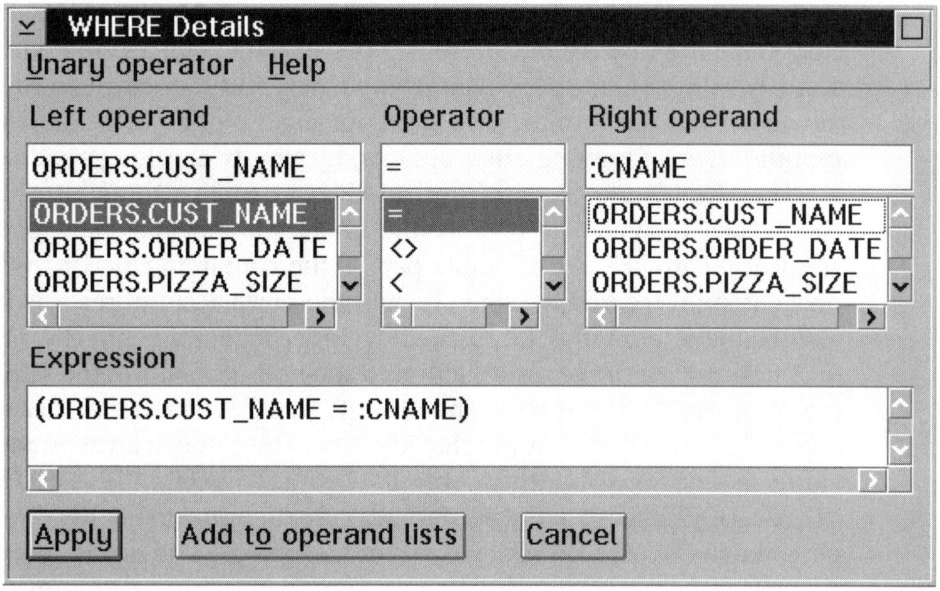

Figure 7.10 WHERE Details window.

ordered by date. To do this, the developer adds an ORDER BY clause to the query and indicates that the order of the records returned by the query be determined by the values in the ORDER_DATE column. Moreover, the developer specifies that the values in this column be ordered by descending date.

The Multiple Row Query part represents the query definition rather than the query results. The results themselves are available in a resultTable that the developer creates by selecting a special type of Multiple Row Query attribute. VisualAge then automatically generates the resultTable and connects it to the Multiple Row Query, as shown in Figure 7.8.

Dynamic Content in a Table
The developer can conveniently display tabular data, such as the date, size, and toppings of a pizza account, by using an Html Table and a few Html Column parts. However, the data in these records is returned from the database in some format that may be more or less suitable for display in the confirmation page. For example, although the preferred display format may be the European format, day-month-year, the date may be returned in the American format, month-day-year. To help the developer display data

in the most appropriate format, VisualAge provides the ability to easily customize the display of different types of data such as zip codes, social security numbers, numeric character strings, and monetary amounts. The developer can customize date data, for example, as day-month-year or month-day-year (among other options) by simply checking a radio button.

The Html Table part in ConfirmAPizza contains three Html Column parts, each of which is responsible for displaying one field of a pizza account record. The Html Table part is the containing part to which the pizza account records are sent. To pass the pizza account records from the resultTable to the Html Table, the developer makes a connection between the *rows attribute* of the resultTable and the *items attribute* of the Html Table; the completed connection is shown in Figure 7.8. The developer also sets one attribute for each column that identifies the name of an attribute whose value is displayed in the column (ORDER_DATE, PIZZA_SIZE, and PIZZA_TOPPINGS), and a second attribute to indicate the heading to display above the column (Date, Size, and Topping). The developer can also customize the display of the data in a column by setting a column attribute.

Sequence of Events

The confirmation page contains two queries, one that will insert new pizza orders into the database and one that will select orders from the database. For the application to work properly, the queries must be executed in a particular sequence. If the insert query runs before the select query, the table will display the new order. If the select query runs before the insert query, the table will not display the new order until a customer makes his or her next order. Clearly we would like the insert query to run first (and be completed) so that a customer can see his or her order. Therefore, the VisualAge parts generate a variety of events that can be used to signal parts to take actions in a desired sequence. For our purposes, the relevant events and actions are that the Html Page part generates an event before it causes any HTML to be generated, and both queries can be directed to start execution as well as signal when they have completed execution. By connecting the appropriate part events and actions, the developer can ensure that the pizza order is inserted into the database before the database is queried for a customer's account. Both of those database actions (and the subsequent population of the Html Table from the ResultTable) will be completed before the Html Page generates any HTML.

To ensure that the queries execute in the desired sequence before any HTML is generated, the developer makes two connections. To ensure that the SQL Statement part starts first, the developer makes a connection from the aboutToGenerateHtml event of the Html Page part to the executeQuery action of the SQL Statement part. To ensure that the Multiple Row Query part starts only after the SQL Statement part has completed, the developer also makes a connection from the queryExecuted event of the SQL Statement part to the executeQuery action of the Multiple Row Query part.

The timing of the aboutToGenerateHtml event provides a glimpse at the underlying sequence of events between the time that the CGI Link Server receives a request and the time it returns a stream of HTML to abtcgil.exe. The CGI Link Server is a process that runs continuously within a Web application. The URL that is sent to the CGI Link Server with each request includes the name of a Web Connection part, for example, ConfirmAPizza. The CGI Link Server creates a new instance of the part and, if the part contains an Html Form Data part, passes along any data suitable for that part. After creating the new part and passing it any data, the CGI Link Server signals the generateHTML action of the Html Page that is contained by the Web Connection part. On receiving this signal, the Page tells each of its parts to generate its own HTML. The Page packages up all returned HTML tags in the correct order and returns the package to the CGI Link Server. Because nonvisual parts such as database queries are not part of the Html Page, the Page has no way of knowing that they must be executed. Therefore, the Html Page part provides an aboutToGenerateHtml event so that the execution of nonvisual parts can be forced.

The completed pizza application is set up as a continuously running process that is accessed by a Web server through the abtcgil.exe program that is launched with every browser request. The first reference to the application is through a URL such as http://lou.pizza.com/cgi-bin/abtcgil.exe/OrderAPizza. An instance of the OrderAPizza part is created, including an Html Page part, which in turn directs each of its subparts to convert themselves to HTML. The Page part packages the HTML tags, and they are returned by the application, the abtcgil.exe program, and the Web server to the browser where they are displayed as the order form page. The customer enters the details of his or her order and clicks on the "Send My Order!" button. The browser transmits the order data according to an HTML form that is part of the order page. This form references the ConfirmAPizza part of the application, http://lou.pizza.com/cgi-bin/abtcgil.exe/ConfirmAPizza, and the data is sent to this URL. An instance of the ConfirmAPizza part is created, and the data is massaged and made available to the Form Data part. This data is used to fill in the customer's name in ConfirmAPizza's Html Page, and it is passed to the query that inserts the order into the database. The second query subsequently finds all of the customer's orders, and these are used to populate the Html Table. When the subparts of the Page have been updated, the Page directs all of them to convert themselves to HTML. The HTML tags are returned to the browser, where they are displayed as the confirmation page.

ADVANCED APPLICATIONS

The pizza application is a relatively simple demonstration of a particular type of Web application. It illustrates how a visual development environment can be used to develop Web applications and highlights some of the strengths of that environment, such as the seamless integration of an external function—a relational database—into a Web application. However, visual programming environments like VisualAge were designed for developing more sophisticated applications than our pizza example. Furthermore, there are additional Web Connection parts that support the development of more sophisticated Web applications. In this section we discuss some advanced application examples involving those Web Connection parts. In addition, we briefly discuss the fact that visual programming environments can be used to develop different types of Web applications.

Other Web Applications

Not all visual programming environments are used to develop the same type of Web application that is the focus of this chapter. Some visual programming environments are used to develop Web applications in which the user interface at the client machine is not defined in terms of HTML, although the client component of the application is uploaded by a Web browser. Two well-known examples are Java applets and ActiveX controls. In the case of Java applets, a visual programming environment such as Symantec's Visual Cafe enables the developer to visually construct an application's user interface as a Java applet that is later uploaded by a Web browser. Similarly, in the case of ActiveX controls, a visual programming environment such as Microsoft's Visual Basic enables the developer to visually develop an ActiveX control for later upload. In both cases, the uploaded applet or control is launched by the browser, and it can provide a user interface for an application that executes at a remote server. The Java applet or ActiveX control approach to developing Web applications has many of the advantages of the visual programming environment approach. A disadvantage of the Java applet and ActiveX approach is that it requires more resources at the client machine than a strict HTML approach, and ActiveX controls are (today) largely restricted to client machines running a Windows operating system.

Elsewhere in this book, we describe a number of gateways that are located in the same position behind the Web server as the Web application shown in Figure 7.1. These gateways effectively provide an HTML interface to a resource such as a relational database, CICS, or Lotus Notes. In contrast, the Web application we focus on in this chapter is not limited to any particular resource; indeed it can be enabled to zero or any number of resources. Furthermore, our Web application can contain any arbitrary logic that is necessary for a particular application's needs.

Maintaining State

One of the major differences between a client/server application and a Web application such as LPizza is that the client and the server maintain a connection across multiple client requests, but a Web browser and a Web server maintain a connection only for the duration of a single browser request. The practical effect of such a limited connection is that Web applications often do not maintain any state between requests and treat every request as an independent event. The pizza application is simple enough that it does not have to deal with state. However, if LPizza is extended by adding an account payment page, *PayForPizza*, for example, that is referenced from the confirmation page, the application would need some way of associating Helen's name with the request for PayForPizza (assuming we do not want her to enter her name in a field in the confirmation page). The Session Data part can be used to do this. It effectively provides Web Connection parts such as ConfirmAPizza and PayForPizza with a variable whose value persists across multiple browser requests. Four basic steps would be required to extend LPizza by using a Session Data part:

1. Create a Session Data part to store the customer's name.
2. Modify ConfirmAPizza so the value of the customer name obtained through the Html Form Data part is copied into the Session Data part.
3. Add an Html Form to the Html Page in ConfirmAPizza. Set the address attribute of the Form to PayForPizza, and add an "I Want to Pay My Bill!" push button to the Form.

4. Create a Web Connection part called PayForPizza. and within it access the Session Data part to obtain the customer name for querying the database and other functions.

After making these modifications, when Helen submits her pizza order to ConfirmAPizza, her name is stored in the Session Data part, and she is sent the confirmation page. Then, if she decides to pay her bill by clicking on the payment button, the URL references the PayForPizza part. When this part runs, the customer name made available to PayForPizza through the Session Data part is "Helen." Note that if Thomas orders a pizza at the same time as Helen and decides to pay his bill at the same time as Helen, the customer name accessed by the instance of PayForPizza associated with his request is "Thomas."

When the HTML tags for a Page containing a Form are generated, a hidden field is added to the HTML that contains a unique identifier called a *session key*. For example, the tags shown in Table 7.1 contain the hidden field definition, <input type="hidden" name="_ABT_SESSION_KEY" value="305F3A82858DB8507361BD3B1A7824F7">. If any data is added to a Session Data part by the same process (Web Connection part) that creates this session key, the data is associated with the key. When the browser transmits the data, it includes the session key in the transmission so that when the CGI Link Server creates a new instance of a Web Connection part that includes a Session Data part, it can make the appropriate data available. The Session Data part has attributes that enable a developer to specify a lifespan for the stored data such that the CGI Link Server discards any data that has not been accessed within a specified period of time.

In sum, the Session Data part enables the development of Web applications that can store data between browser requests and maintain data for a particular user.

Java Applets

The pizza application relies on the application running behind the Web server to do all of the work. In many cases this will be an adequate balance of work, but ultimately it will be desirable to move work to the browser. Java applets provide a way of moving work to the browser. For example, suppose the page created by PayForPizza asks customers to enter a telephone number or zip code. With the current pizza application, if a customer enters an invalid telephone number or zip code, it must be transmitted across the network to the Web application before the error can be caught. Clearly this is a poor use of the network's bandwidth, and it would be better to catch and rectify the error at the browser. Currently, applets are developed in their own development environments, which are typically different from those used to develop Web applications. Once built, a reference to the applet can be embedded into the PayForPizza Page by using an Applet part. When the application is run, the HTML tags sent to the browser include a URL that references the applet executable (byte code), and the browser dereferences the URL to upload the applet. Once loaded into the browser, the applet can check the validity of the phone number and zip code before they are sent to the Web application.

Multiple User Interfaces

The pizza application has only one user interface—the order form and confirmation pages—and it is used by customers. A pizza application in real life would need additional user interfaces, for example, to display incoming pizza orders so that Lou knows what to cook. Such an interface is not well suited to an HTML page because the changes to the contents of the page are driven by events that are unrelated to the page itself. One solution is to augment an HTML page with a Java applet that would be responsible for displaying the incoming orders. A second, hybrid solution takes advantage of the existing development environment although it does not rely exclusively on HTML. Specifically, the user interface for Lou can be added to the existing LPizza application as one or more Visual parts (a type of part that is not Web enabled) that contain Window parts (the equivalent of Html Page parts) and logic to integrate these parts with the existing Web application. For example, a Window might contain a selectable list of pizza orders and a button for Lou to indicate when a particular order has finished cooking. The list would be updated from the database through a query, and the button would also update the database through another query. The new Window would be displayed on Lou's screen continuously (remember that the Web application runs continuously) and operate in parallel with the Web-related parts of the application.

Using Other Parts

The pizza application uses visual Web Connection parts, that is, parts that appear on an Html Page and subsequently in the browser, and it uses some nonvisual parts that are not from the Web Connection. The visual parts in a Web application must be Web Connection parts (unless they are used on Window parts as described above); however, the nonvisual parts can be any nonvisual parts. The pizza application uses a nonvisual part to access a back-end relational database. Many other parts provide a great variety of access to back-end systems including parts that access IMS, MQSeries, CICS, and Lotus Notes. In short, Web applications can act as middleware that provides a Web-based interface to back-end enterprise systems.

CONCLUSION

The visual programming approach to building Web applications described in this chapter represents a first step in an evolutionary process. The advantages of the approach are that it uses a single and familiar tool that leverages the visual construction by parts methodology to hide many of the lower-level details of the implementation, provides visual editing, and eases the development of applications that can access enterprise systems. In the short term, the visual programming approach is likely to evolve by incorporating recent improvements in Web technology, such as the NSAPI, which provides better performance than the CGI, and by improvements learned from the development of the programming environments themselves. The desire to develop Web applications seems to represent a swing of the pendulum where development has moved from client/server applications whose functions are distributed between the client and the server toward Web applications whose functions are concentrated at the server. However, the pendulum is already swinging back; Java applets represent application function moving back to the client. To the extent that visual programming environments keep pace with this pendulum, we would expect to see them provide more capabilities for building massively networked applications in which function can be distributed at will between the client and server, and the language for implementing function can be manipulated according to location.

WEB CONNECTION PARTS

The parts made available in the first release of Web Connection appear on the palette in the Composition Editor, and they are all visual parts except where otherwise noted. The full name for each part listed below is Html followed by the name given in the text, for example, Html Page.

- *Page.* Basic building block for Web applications. The subparts on a Page are converted to HTML at runtime. Remember to set the title of each Page! Only visual Web Connection parts can be dropped onto a Page.
- *Page Wrapper.* Enables you to refer to one Web Connection part from inside another. You can build a "switch" into your web application by connecting a CGI Link Request to some conditional logic and each condition to a different Page Wrapper. This is a nonvisual part.
- *Composite.* A Composite part can be placed onto an Html Page to provide the Page with standardized elements such as a logo and a navigation bar.
- *Text.* Use the Text part for putting text onto a Web page. The attributes of Text parts control heading level, font style, and the like. Also, use the built-in converters to format data such as dates and currency.
- *Image.* Image parts make images appear in Web application pages. GIF and bitmap (BMP) types of images can be displayed during development.
- *Table.* The Table part is a container for Table Column parts.
- *Table Column.* Each column displays rows of data having a certain format, for example, European date format. Use the built-in converters to specify the formatting required.
- *Rule.* A horizontal line.
- *Paragraph.* Put one of these on a Page (or in a Form) to tell the Web browser to insert a paragraph break (usually one blank line) between the parts appearing immediately before and after the Paragraph.
- *Line Break.* Like Paragraph, the next part is displayed on the next line.
- *Form.* If you want to pass data between Pages, you have to put a Form on at least one Page.
- *Form Data.* Use a Form Data part to access the data that users input to data entry parts within a Form. This is a nonvisual part.
- *List.* Textual lists of items. Can take several forms such as enumerated and bulletted.
- *Drop Down List.* Enables users to select one item from a drop-down list. Can only be used inside a Form.

- *Multiple Select List.* Enables users to select one or more items in a list. Can only be used inside a Form.
- *Entry Field.* Enables users to enter text on a single line. Can only be used inside a Form.
- *Multiple Line Entry Field.* Enables users to enter text on multiple lines. Can only be used inside a Form.
- *Push Button.* Comes in two flavors, Submit and Reset. You can name your buttons whatever you want. Submit buttons cause the contents of data entry fields in a Form (plus the name and the value of the Submit button) to be sent by the browser to the destination specified in the Form. Reset buttons simply reset all data entry parts to their initial values. It is possible to have zero, one, or more Submit buttons in a Form. (It does not make sense to have more than one Reset button.) The browser should accept a Return keystroke in lieu of no Push Buttons. Can only be used inside a Form.
- *Checkbox.* Enables users to select an option. Can only be used inside a Form.
- *Radio Button Set.* Enables users to make one selection from several possible choices. Can only be used inside a Form.
- *Applet.* Put one of these parts on an Html Page if you want a Java applet to run at the browser. The height and width of this part as it appears on a Page are used to specify the height and width of the area that is set aside in the browser window to run the applet.
- *Embed.* Similar to an Applet part but mainly used for browser plug-ins.
- *CGI Link Request.* Use this part to access parameters supplied by the Web server, such as the IP address of the Web browser, or if you want to intercept requests to your application rather than letting them be automatically routed to the appropriate Connection parts. This is a nonvisual part.
- *CGI Link Session Data.* This part provides a means for storing data between requests. It is stored on a per-application per-user basis. This is a nonvisual part.

SECTION 3

Integrating Database Applications on the Web

CHAPTER **8**

Using Net.Data to Access Databases and Files

Any useful computer application on the Web must be able to create, access, and manipulate data that is stored persistently in a database management system (DBMS) or a file in the computer's file system. Therefore, building a new application on the Web almost always requires the ability to access data stored in one or more DBMS and file systems. Furthermore, because the Web's success is largely based on its standard presentation of results, businesses are typically not developing brand new applications but merely trying to make their existing applications accessible from the Internet or, in the case of large organizations, a companywide Intranet built using Internet standards.

In this chapter, you will learn how to build new Internet (or Intranet) applications that access data from DBMSs and/or files. Our discussion is based on an IBM product called *Net.Data,* which provides powerful capabilities for accessing data from relational DBMSs (DB2, Oracle, Sybase, SQL server), nonrelational DBMSs (IMS, Lotus Notes, object-oriented DBMSs), operating system files (UNIX and PC files), and applications written in programming languages such as Perl, REXX, C, C++, Java, and COBOL. In conjunction with another IBM product, *DataJoiner,* Net.Data provides the ability to build Web applications that can access all of the data that is distributed throughout an enterprise and stored in various DBMSs and file systems. We first provide an overview of the problems encountered while building database applications for the Web and compare standalone solutions for these problems with general-purpose solutions offered by products such as Net.Data. We then demonstrate (using several examples) how to build Net.Data applications, from the relatively simple to the fairly complex. We conclude by discussing other products that enable applications to access an enterprise's data from the Web.

Also in this chapter, we will discuss examples that are specific to Net.Data. However, many of the building Web applications concepts that access data are similar to concepts present in other products, such as Allaire Cold Fusion and Sybase web.sql. Overall, the Net.Data's layout approach to building Web applications require less programming than most of the other products.

DYNAMIC WEB PAGES

As you can see in Figure 8.1, Net.Data enables Web application developers to extend the capabilities of a Web server, thus providing an extremely pow-

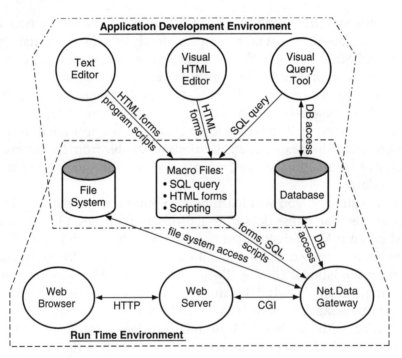

Figure 8.1 Net.Data system overview.

Using Net.Data to Access Databases and Files

erful method of creating *dynamic* Web pages. The Web page that results from a user's request is dynamically generated according to such factors as input provided by the user, the user's identity, and the current state of the database.

To set the stage for our discussion in this chapter, we first describe a basic scenario involving a dynamic Web application:

1. An HTML fill-in form (an *input* form) is required to obtain input from users. An input form may be stored as a static HTML-based Web page on the Web server, or it may be generated dynamically by a Web application (see box below). Many Net.Data installations generate the input form dynamically. Figure 8.2 is a sample HTML input form viewed in a Web browser.

2. On viewing the input form at a Web browser, the user makes selections on the form and then submits the form. In Figure 8.2, the user can submit the form by clicking on the *Submit Query* button. The selections on the input form translate to variables (Name=Value pairs) that are transmitted to the Web server when the user submits input form. The HTML

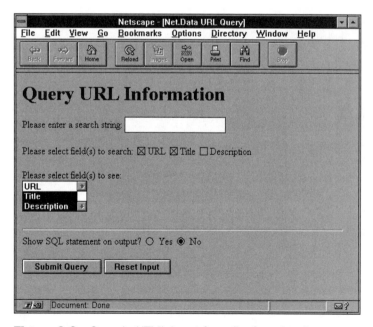

Figure 8.2 Sample HTML input form (inpform.html).

HTML Source for Input Form in Figure 8.2 (inpform.html)

```
1.  <TITLE>Net.Data URL Query</TITLE>
2.  <H1>Query URL Information</H1>
3.
4.
5.  <FORM METHOD="post"
6.        ACTION="/cgi-bin/db2www.exe/urlquery.d2w/report">
7.  Please enter a search string:
8.  <INPUT TYPE="text" NAME="SEARCH" SIZE=20>
9.  <p>
10.
11. Please select field(s) to search:
12.
13. <INPUT TYPE="checkbox" NAME="USE_URL"
14.        VALUE="yes" CHECKED>URL
15. <INPUT TYPE="checkbox" NAME="USE_TITLE"
16.        VALUE="yes" CHECKED>Title
17. <INPUT TYPE="checkbox" NAME="USE_DESC"
18.        VALUE="yes">Description
19. <p>
20. Please select field(s) to see:
21. <br>
22. <SELECT NAME="DBFIELD" SIZE=3 MULTIPLE>
23. <OPTION VALUE="url">URL
24. <OPTION VALUE="title" SELECTED>Title
25. <OPTION VALUE="desc">Description
26. </SELECT>
27. <p><HR>
28. Show SQL statement on output?
29. <INPUT TYPE="radio"
30.        NAME="SHOWSQL" VALUE="YES"> Yes
31. <INPUT TYPE="radio"
32.        NAME="SHOWSQL" VALUE="" CHECKED> No
33. <P>
34. <INPUT TYPE="submit" VALUE="Submit Query">
35. <INPUT TYPE="reset" VALUE="Reset Input">
36. </FORM>
```

source for the form in Figure 8.2 (see box below) illustrates the variables underlying an input form. Note that the search string maps to a variable of name *SEARCH* (line 8). The three check boxes map to three variables, *USE_URL* (line 13), *USE_TITLE* (line 15), and *USE_DESC* (line 17), respectively. The select box maps to the *DBFIELD* variable (line 22), which can have multiple values to reflect the fact that multiple fields can be selected from the select box. The radio button is attached to the *SHOWSQL* variable (line 32), whose value determines whether to show the SQL statement used in a subsequent result form. The variable values that will be set for the selections that the user has made in Figure 8.2 are shown in the Variable Values box. Note how the *DBFIELD* variable has multiple values reflecting the multiple selections indicated by the user.

Variable Values Set for Selections in Figure 8.2

```
SEARCH = ""         USE_URL = "yes"    USE_TITLE = "yes"   USE_DESC = ""
DBFIELD = "title"   DBFIELD = "desc"   SHOWSQL = ""
```

---

3. When a form is submitted to the Web server, the Web server executes the action defined in the form and returns a new Web page containing the result of the action to the Web browser for display. The action for the form illustrated in Figure 8.2 is indicated in the *ACTION* clause of the equivalent HTML source (line 6) and involves accessing the /cgi-bin/db2www.exe/urlquery.d2w/report URL. The browser provides this URL to the Web server along with the user input variables and their values, that is, the information in the Variable Values box. The Web server interprets the URL and executes the db2www .exe program (The Net.Data executable is called db2www.exe for backward compatibility with applications written with Net.Data's predecessor, DB2 World Wide Web Connection.) The Web server subsequently collects the output from the Net.Data program and returns it as the response Web page to the Web browser for display.

In our example, it is possible to call any program in place of the Net.Data executable *db2www.exe*. Before generic application development solutions like Net.Data were available, sites that wanted to generate dynamic Web pages used standalone applications written in popular scripting languages like Perl and REXX or standard programming languages such as C and C++.

In fact, many Websites still use such standalone solutions, mostly for performance reasons. Unfortunately, there are some real problems with using standalone solutions, as we discuss below.

1. Developing a CGI script with Perl or REXX requires complex code development skills, and the application programmer has to handle both the CGI as well as the interfaces to the DBMS or file system. This kind of procedural programming is far removed from the declarative nature of HTML, the dominant language of the Web, as well as SQL, the most popular language for accessing data. Besides, this approach cannot be used with existing visual building tools for HTML, such as HotMetal and NetObjects Fusion, or SQL, such as Lotus Approach and Microsoft Access.

2. In standalone scripts, invariably the application logic is intermixed with the reporting, and it becomes extremely hard to adapt applications to newer versions of HTML. Features and extensions to HTML (such as Applet, JavaScript, or ActiveX support) are added every few months in a typical browser. As a result, the look and feel of a Website can change frequently to reflect organizational changes as well as the necessity to use the latest features of HTML to create "cool" sites that people would like to revisit often. Standalone applications are not amenable to frequent changes and hence are ill suited for building applications for a dynamically changing Website.

3. Standalone scripts provide very good performance. However, generic application development solutions have improved considerably, thus making their performance disadvantage less significant. For instance, Net.Data takes advantage of the performance enhancement features of Web servers like Netscape's NSAPI, Microsoft's ISAPI, and IBM's ICAPI.

4. In general, standalone solutions are less portable. For example, a Perl program is only portable to a different platform if a Perl interpreter exists on that platform and supports all of the Perl features used in the application. A large part of the applications developed with Net.Data do not need to be ported because the HTML/SQL macro files are platform independent and the Net.Data runtime engine is available on multiple platforms. Furthermore, generic Web application development platforms like Net.Data can shield the application from porting problems arising out of supporting the Web server APIs mentioned above.

It is clear that a general-purpose solution to develop dynamic Web data applications must have the following characteristics: First and foremost, applications must be easy to build. Preferably, programming should not be required to build a large class of simple applications. It should be possible to build dynamic Web page applications with a what-you-see-is-what-you-get (WYSIWYG) interface, or, at the least, the solution should work well with existing visual HTML editors and visual database query tools. In addition to being easy to build, applications must be portable across operating systems and Web servers with minimal changes (preferably no changes at all). Dynamic Web applications must have complete access to current (and future) HTML capabilities, and it should be possible to change the presentation of applications by using the latest and greatest HTML features. In addition to providing complete HTML support on the Web side, the application platform must provide complete freedom in accessing any form of data from a DBMS or file system. In particular, rich support for dynamically generating SQL queries is a must. Because the report generated by getting data from a DBMS should be dependent on the application as well as the look and feel of the Website, it should be highly customizable by a user. (Standard reports are virtually uninteresting.) Finally, it must be possible to escape to user-driven processing to ensure that everything that can be done with a standalone application can also be done with the Web application builder. In the rest of this chapter we show how Net.Data satisfies many of the requirements of a generic application development solution.

BUILDING A SIMPLE DATABASE APPLICATION

We begin our discussion with a simple phone book application and take you through the steps of building it with Net.Data. Assume that the data for the phone book is stored in a relational database called *celdial* in a table named *customer* whose schema is shown in Table 8.1. The columns of the *customer* table that are relevant to the phone book application are *contact*, which contains the contact person's name; *con_phone*, which contains the contact's phone number; and the *custname*, which contains the contact's company name.

The input form of our phone book application should have a text input field where users can type in the name of the person whose phone number they require. In addition, users should be able to choose the information they want to see in the result (possible choices are name, phone number,

Table 8.1 Database Schema of Customer Table

Column Name	Description
CUSTNO	A unique customer identification number
CUSTNAME	The company name
CONTACT	Name of the contact person
CON_PHONE	Phone of the contact person
CON_FAX	Fax number of the contact person
CON_ADDR	Address of the contact person

and company). The report form generated in response to a phone book request should have a table containing the information requested by the user and a link to the input form in order to make further queries.

Figure 8.3 shows the format of the desired input form of this application as realized in a Web browser. To create the report, the user types in *Smythe* and then clicks on the search button. Figure 8.4 shows the report form that is returned from the search.

The Web phone book application is contained in the Net.Data example1.d2w macro file (see box below). Let us examine this macro file to see how easy it is to build Web-based applications for accessing databases. To reiterate, the phone book application creates two distinct elements: the

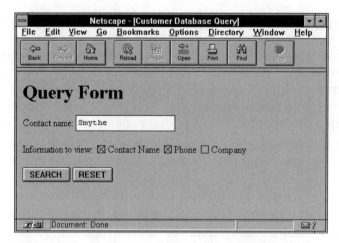

Figure 8.3 Phone book input form (example1.d2w).

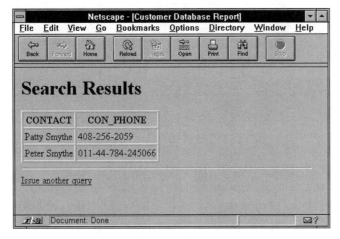

Figure 8.4 Phone book report form (example1.d2w).

input form, and the report form that it creates from the user input on the input form. (Figure 8.5 illustrates the flow of control during the creation of the input form and the report form). Note that the application does not need database access to create the input form, but it must access the database to create the report form.

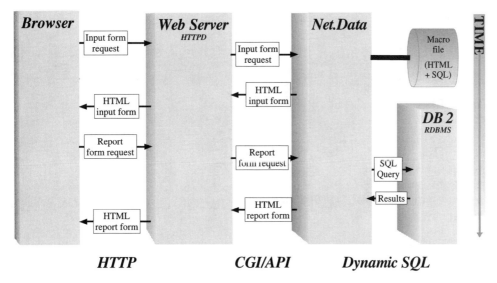

Figure 8.5 Runtime flow control.

Macro for the Phone Book Application (example1.d2w)

```
1.  %{------------------ Phone Book Input Form ------------------ %}
2.
3.  %HTML(input){
4.  <TITLE>Customer Database Query</TITLE>
5.
6.  <H1>Query Form</H1>
7.   <FORM   METHOD="POST"   ACTION="/cgi-bin/db2www.exe/example1.d2w/report">
8.  Contact name: <INPUT TYPE="text" NAME="CONTNAME">
9.  <p>
10. Information to view:
11.  <INPUT TYPE="checkbox" NAME="COLNAME" VALUE="contact" CHECKED>Contact Name
12. <INPUT TYPE="checkbox" NAME="COLNAME" VALUE="con_phone"
13. CHECKED>Phone
14. <INPUT TYPE="checkbox" NAME="COLNAME" VALUE="custname">Company
15. <p>
16. <INPUT TYPE="submit" VALUE="SEARCH"> <INPUT TYPE="reset"
17. VALUE="RESET">
18. </FORM>
19. %}
20.
21. %{------------------ Phone Book Report Form ------------------ %}
22.
23. %DEFINE DATABASE="celdial"
24.
25. %DEFINE {
26. LOGIN = "USERID"
27. PASSWORD = "PASSWORD"
28. DTW_HTML_TABLE = "YES"
29. %}
30.
31. %FUNCTION (DTW_SQL) get_phone_no () {
32. select $(COLNAME)
33. from customer
34. where contact like '%$(CONTNAME)%'
35. order by contact
36. % }
37.
38. %HTML(report){
```

(continued)

```
39. <TITLE>Customer Database Report</TITLE>
40.
41. <H1>Search Results </H1>
42. @get_phone_no()
43. <HR>
44.  <A  HREF="/cgi-bin/db2www.exe/example1.d2w/input">Issue  another
query</A>
45. %}
```

URLs to Access Net.Data Applications

To implement the phone book application, you store the example1.d2w macro at a Website and then access the macro, using an URL. Below we discuss two ways of accessing the macro: using the standard CGI protocol (supported by virtually all Web servers), and using the NSAPI protocol.

The http://cherry/cgi-bin/db2www/example1.d2w/input URL informs the Web server listening on port number 80 (the default HTTP port) of the *orion* machine that the Net.Data *db2www* executable is a CGI program that should be executed using the parameters in the rest of the URL. On receiving the URL, the Web server looks up its configuration to perform any name and path translations. Typically, *cgi-bin* in the path indicates that the rest of the URL should be processed by executing the *db2www* program, which is sometimes referred to as the CGI *script*. Note that each request in the CGI protocol results in the creation of a *separate* process to execute the request.

In the http://kiwi:8081/example1.d2w/input URL, the Web server listening on port number 8081 of the *gryphon* machine is a Web server that supports the NSAPI protocol. For this URL to work, the *d2w* suffix must be mapped to a service function (corresponding to the Net.Data entry function) in the configuration information of the Netscape Web server. In addition, the Web server must be configured with the location of the Dynamic Link Library (DLL) containing the Net.Data entry function so that the Web server can load the Net.Data DLL when it starts up. Subsequently, the Web server will process any URL request that contains the *d2w* suffix by executing the Net.Data entry function in the Web server's address space. All of the parameters needed to process the service request are provided to the Net.Data entry function, which then proceeds to execute the request by accessing the macro. Unlike the CGI protocol, where a separate *process* is spawned per URL request, in the NSAPI protocol each request is processed by a *thread* in the Web server. Creating and managing threads have substantially smaller overhead than creating and managing processes. In addition, the DLL-based execution of Net.Data enables common activities such as reading the Net.Data configuration file to occur once at server initialization time rather than once per request. As well as having performance advantages, the NSAPI provides tighter integration between the security mechanisms of the database and the Web server. For detailed information about how Net.Data can be used with the NSAPI, see the *"Net.Data Programming Guide"* available from http://www.software.ibm.com/data/net.data/docs.

A typical Net.Data macro like *example1.d2w* has several sections. Typically, there are three kinds of sections in a macro, namely, HTML sections, variable definition sections, and function definition sections. Comments can appear anywhere within a macro. Each section is tagged with a keyword: HTML sections are tagged with the *%HTML* keyword, variable definition sections are tagged with the *%DEFINE* keyword, and function definitions are tagged with the *%FUNCTION* keyword. Each section can also have subsections, as we explain later in the chapter. Let us first try and understand how the example1.d2w macro implements our phone book application. We discuss this in two parts: the input form and the report form.

The Input Form

The macro begins with a comment that describes the section (line 1); comments are enclosed between %{ and %} and can cross line boundaries. The first section in the macro (lines 3–19) is an HTML section called *input* (enclosed between the tags *%HTML(input){* and *%}*). The HTML sections can have arbitrary names; the only restriction is that there be no two HTML sections in the same macro with the same name. As you have probably have guessed by now, the *input* HTML section implements the entire input form for our phone book application. The contents of the *input* section are pure HTML, and you could very well have generated them by using your favorite HTML editor! In fact, like any good macro processor, Net.Data processes only the macro language directives and is unaffected by the specific syntax of HTML (or any other language that can be used in the macro, such as SQL, Perl, or REXX). Therefore, applications written with Net.Data (and its predecessor, DB2 World Wide Web Connection) can use any flavor of HTML, including those that support VRML, Java Script, Java applets, and Navigator's "LiveConnect" features.

The *input* section of the phone book application macro contains a simple header followed by an HTML form. This form (see Figure 8.3) defines two HTML input variables: the *CONTNAME* variable (line 8), whose value is used to look up the phone number in the database, and the *COLNAME* variable (lines 11–14), which is used to pass the names of the columns needed in the report. The *COLNAME* variable can have multiple values, which we refer to as *list* variables.

Let us assume that we store the *example1.d2w* macro file in the *ilex* machine and use the CGI version of Net.Data. In this case, we can invoke the input form in our phone book application macro by using the http://ilex/cgi-bin/db2www.exe/example1.d2w/input URL. When we access this URL, using a Web browser, the browser contacts the Web server on ilex, and it invokes the Net.Data program with two arguments: the name of the macro, *example1.d2w,* and the name of the macro section to be processed, that is, *input*.

Net.Data processes the request by first locating the macro in a directory on the server. The possible locations where Net.Data will search for the macro are provided through the *MACRO_PATH* variable in Net.Data's configuration file. (The configuration file is discussed in detail in the "Net.Data Programming Guide.") After locating the *example1.d2w* macro file, Net.Data opens the file, reads it, and processes the macro, searching for the section named *input*. First, Net.Data encounters the comment at the beginning of the file and skips it entirely. It then encounters the HTML section named *input,* which matches the section named *input* in our URL. Having successfully located the HTML input section, Net.Data now proceeds to process the text in that HTML section.

Processing the *input* HTML section in our phone book application merely involves returning all of the text in the HTML section (excluding the opening tag %HTML(input){ and the closing tag %}, in other words, lines 4 through 18 of the macro). To comply with the HTTP protocol, however, the output from Net.Data has to be prefixed with a header that indicates the MIME type of the result (in this case, the result is HTML). In our example, Net.Data automatically prefixes a header to the text in the *input* HTML section, thereby indicating that the type of the result is HTML. In practice, this header consists of the Content-Type: text/html string followed by a blank line. We explain later how you can direct Net.Data to return customized headers for other types of data such as postscript, images, and Netscape cookies.

After Net.Data processes the required HTML section (in this case, the *input* section), it terminates without processing the rest of the macro. In other words, Net.Data processes exactly one HTML section during every URL request. As a result of the above processing the input form shown on Figure 8.3 appears in the browser.

The Report Form

After viewing the input form on the browser, you can now fill in the form and submit it for processing. As shown in Figure 8.3, the user is looking for the phone number of a person named Smythe. The user also wants to see the list of contact names and phone numbers in the report. After selecting the information to view, let us suppose that the user clicks on the *SEARCH* button to submit the query. Note that the action for the form, as indicated by the *ACTION* clause for this form (line 7 of the example1.d2w macro), is to execute the /cgi-bin/db2www.exe/example1.d2w/ report URL. Recall that the original input form was requested from the host machine called *ilex*. Clicking on the SEARCH button, therefore, results in a request for the http://ilex/cgi-bin/db2www.exe/example1.d2w/report URL. This request is sent to the Web server at ilex where the Net.Data CGI script is invoked with the macro file name *example1.d2w* and the section name *report*. In addition, the following variable values corresponding to the user's selections on the input form are sent to the server:

```
CONTNAME = Smythe  COLNAME = contact   COLNAME = con_phone
```

Unlike the input form case, where there were no input variables, these variable values are passed to Net.Data using the CGI protocol. Net.Data processes these variables and adds them to its symbol table. Based on the above input variables, the CONTNAME variable's value is set to the Smythe string. The COLNAME variable is a list variable because it has multiple values, and the default delimiter of a list variable is the comma. Therefore, the value of COLNAME in the macro will be set to the custname,con_phone string. As we explain soon, the COLNAME variable is used to set the list of columns in a SELECT clause of an SQL statement; therefore, the comma is the appropriate delimiter here.

After processing the HTML input variables, Net.Data processes the example1.d2w macro file just as in the input form case. It skips the comment at the beginning of the file (line 1), and it then skips the HTML input section (lines 3–19) because the current section name, *report*, does not match this section's name. Net.Data continues processing until it encounters two variable definition sections (tagged by the *%DEFINE* keyword). The first variable definition section is a line statement (line 23) that defines a DATABASE variable and sets its value to be the *celdial* string. (Note that a line statement can be used only to define a single variable.) The second variable definition section is a block statement (delimited by { and %}, lines 25–29) that is used to set the LOGIN, PASSWORD, and DTW_HTML_TABLE variables to the *USERID, PASSWORD,* and *YES* values, respectively. The LOGIN and PASSWORD variables are used to set the User ID and password required to access the *celdial* database. The DTW_HTML_TABLE variable is used to indicate to Net.Data that any default report generated should use the HTML table format.

Net.Data processes the variable definition sections by initializing the values of the DATABASE, LOGIN, PASSWORD, and DTW_HTML_TABLE variables in its symbol table, where the values can be later accessed as needed. Net.Data processes these variables at the server only, and they are never communicated to the browser. By restricting these variables to the server, Net.Data offers a level of security not available with pure HTML forms, where the variables are embedded (as hidden fields) in the HTML that is sent to the browser. In addition, the Net.Data symbol table stores both the variables in the HTML input (e.g., COLNAME) and the variables in the macro (e.g., DATABASE). Therefore, Net.Data unifies the name space of the HTML variables with the name space of the macro variables defined in the variable definition sections. If the variable present in the HTML input is also defined in the macro, the value passed from the input form takes precedence over the value in the macro. In other words, the macro definitions can be thought of as default definitions that can be overridden by user input from the form.

After processing the variable definition sections, Net.Data encounters a function definition section that defines a function called *get_phone_no()* (lines 31–36). The get_phone_no function contains an SQL string to be executed every time it is called. The DTW_SQL name in the function definition identifies the language environment in the Net.Data configuration file that will be used to execute this function. Net.Data processes the function definition section by creating an entry in a function symbol table for the get_phone_no function and stores an internal representation of the function that enables later execution when the function is actually called. The SQL string in the function definition contains references to the COLNAME (line 32) and CONTNAME (line 34) variables; variable references are enclosed by $(and). The variables referenced in the SQL string are not evaluated just yet as Net.Data evaluates variables in a *lazy* manner, in other words, as late as possible in the execution cycle.

After processing the function definition section, Net.Data encounters the HTML *report* section (line 38) whose name matches the section name in the URL request. Net.Data proceeds to process the HTML section in much the same way as it processed the HTML input form. It first prints out the MIME header indicating that the result is HTML, followed by the HTML text in the section, up to but not including line 42; in other words lines 39, 40, and 41 are copied to the output. Line 42 contains the @get_phone_no() pattern, which is interpreted to be a call to the get_phone_no function defined in line 31. (A function call is specified in the macro file by the @ character followed by the function name and the list of function arguments enclosed within parentheses.) As part of processing the *report* HTML section, Net.Data now executes the get_phone_no function. The SQL in the body of the function (lines 32–35) includes several variable references that must be replaced by actual variable values before the SQL and the function can be executed. In the example, the variable references $(COLNAME) and $(CONTNAME) are replaced by contact,con_phone and Smythe, respectively. The resulting SQL string is:

```
select contact,con_phone
from customer
where contact like '%Smythe%'
order by contact
```

Net.Data invokes the DTW_SQL language environment to process the SQL statement. The results of this processing are two rows from the customer table. Each row contains two columns: the name (from the column called contact), and phone number (from the column called con_phone). During the evaluation of the query, the DATABASE variable is used to determine the database where the customer table resides, and the LOGIN and PASSWORD variables are used to authenticate with the database.

The built-in report-generating facility in Net.Data prints the resulting rows. Because the DTW_HTML_TABLE variable is set to YES, an HTML table formatted report is automatically generated to replace the @get_phone_no() string in the output. Note that the *where* clause in the SQL statement ensures that the names returned match the user input string *Smythe*. Note also that the rows in the report are sorted alphabetically as directed by the *order by* clause in the SQL statement. After processing the function call, Net.Data appends the rest of the HTML section (lines 43 and 44) to the output.

Net.Data's completed processing of the HTML report section is displayed by the Web browser, as shown in Figure 8.4. The user can click on the Issue another query text to return to the input form (Figure 8.3) and perform another phone book lookup.

CUSTOMIZING REPORTS

The default report form (Figure 8.4) uses the column names from the database schema (*CONTACT* and *CON_PHONE*) to print the title of the report. These names are not very meaningful to the user, and the report would be more understandable if it used the same tags (Contact Name and Phone) as the check boxes of the input form in Figure 8.3. Net.Data provides a report section (tagged by the %REPORT keyword) that you can use inside function definition sections to customize the reports generated from function results.

The example2.d2w macro (see box below) shows how to use a report section to customize the printing of a report. Figure 8.6 shows a sample report generated with the new macro. (All three check boxes in the input form of Figure 8.3 have to be checked to generate this report). The column names in the report are now more meaningful and correspond to the strings attached to the check boxes in the input form of Figure 8.3. Also, the contact name returned is a hyperlink to another Net.Data URL request to obtain more information about the contact person. Let us now see how to achieve this change in formatting by using the report section. First, note

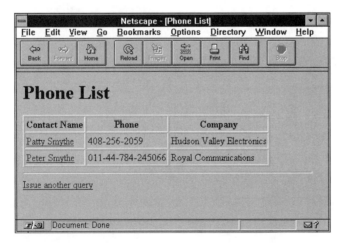

Figure 8.6 Customized report form (example2.d2w).

example2.d2w Macro: Customizing Reports and Drill Down

```
1.  %{ ------------------ Phone Book Query Form ------------------ %}
2.
3.  %HTML(input) {
4.  <TITLE>Customer Database Query</TITLE>
5.
6.  <H1>Query Form</H1>
7.  <FORM METHOD="POST" ACTION="/cgi-bin/db2www.exe/example2.d2w/report">
8.  Contact name: <INPUT TYPE="text" NAME="CONTNAME">
9.  <p>
10. Information to view:
11. <INPUT TYPE="checkbox" NAME="COLNAME" VALUE="contact" CHECKED>
Contact Name
12. <INPUT TYPE="checkbox" NAME="COLNAME" VALUE="con_phone"
13. CHECKED>Phone
14. <INPUT TYPE="checkbox" NAME="COLNAME" VALUE="custname">Company
15. <p>
16. <INPUT TYPE="submit" VALUE="SEARCH"> <INPUT TYPE="reset"
17. VALUE="RESET">
18. </FORM>
19. %}
20.
21. %{ -------------- Phone Book Report Form -------------------- %}
22.
23. %define DATABASE = "celdial"
24. %define DTW_HTML_TABLE = "YES"
25.
26. %FUNCTION(DTW_SQL) get_phone_no() {
27. select custno, $(COLNAME) from customer
28. where contact like '%$(CONTNAME)%'
29. order by contact
30. %REPORT {
31. <TABLE BORDER CELLPADDING=2>
32. <TR><TH>Contact Name</TH><TH>Phone</TH><TH>Company</TH></TR>
33. %ROW{
34. <TR><TD><A HREF="/cgi-bin/db2www.exe/example2.d2w/cust_info?
CUSTNO=$(V_custno)">
35. $(V_contact)</A></TD>
36. <TD>$(V_con_phone)</TD>
37. <TD>$(V_custname)</TD>
38. %}
```

(continued)

```
39. </TABLE>
40. %}
41. %}
42.
43. %HTML(report) {
44. <TITLE> Phone List</TITLE>
45.
46. <H1>Phone List</H1>
47. @get_phone_no()
48. <BR>
49. <A HREF="/cgi-bin/db2www.exe/example2.d2w/input">Issue another query</A>
50. %}
51.
52. %{ -------------- Customer Information Report ----------------- %}
53.
54. %FUNCTION(DTW_SQL) get_more_info() {
55. select custname, contact, con_addr, con_phone, con_fax from customer
56. where custno = '$(CUSTNO)'
57. order by custname
58. %REPORT {
59. <PRE>
60. %ROW{
61. Company: $(V_custname)
62. Contact: $(V_contact)
63. Address: $(V_con_addr)
64. Phone: $(V_con_phone) Fax: $(V_con_fax)
65. %}
66. </PRE>
67. %}
68. %}
69.
70. %HTML(cust_info) {
71. <TITLE>Customer Phone List</TITLE>
72. <H1>Customer Info</H1>
73. @get_more_info()
74. <br>
75. <A HREF="/cgi-bin/db2www.exe/example2.d2w/input">Issue another query</A>
76. %}
```

that the HTML sections named *input* (lines 3–19) and *report* (lines 43–50) of the example2.d2w macro are functionally identical to the corresponding sections in the example1.d2w macro (lines 3–19 and lines 38–45).

A major difference between the two macros is in the definition of the get_phone_no() function (lines 26–41). Specifically, the new definition of this function differs in two ways: (1) the SELECT clause of the SQL string has been changed to retrieve one additional column, namely *custno* (line 27), and (2) a report section has been added (lines 30–40). The first change, to retrieve the custno column, enables us to drill down to find more information about the contact person using a second query. Let us first concentrate on the second difference, that is, the report section.

The report section consists of three parts: a report header (lines 31 and 32) processed once at the beginning of the processing of the report section; a row section (lines 33–38) delimited by the tags *%ROW{* and *%}* that is processed for each row reported; and a footer that is processed at the end of the processing of the report section. The report section itself is processed as the last part of executing the get_phone_no() function call in the HTML report section (line 47). The input to the processing of the report is the table that results from executing the evaluated SQL query string (lines 27–29).

Here is how the HTML table in the customized report form (Figure 8.6) is generated by using the report section of the get_phone_no() function in the example2.d2w macro. First, the header is generated by evaluating the header text (lines 31 and 32) and outputting the result. As there are no variables in this header, it is printed as is and appears as the title row in the report (Figure 8.6). After the header, there is the row section (lines 33–38), which is processed for each row in the result table (for the search string Smythe in our example, there are two rows). Processing the row section involves evaluating the string in the row section (lines 34–37) and then appending the result to the report. This string contains four special variables, namely, V_custno, V_contact, V_con_phone, and V_custname. These special variables are system-generated variables that are valid only within the row section. (For a complete list of special report variables, see the Special Variables box). For each row that is processed by using the row section, the value of each V_variable corresponds to the value of the corresponding column in the row. Hence, V_custno has the value of the *custno* column, V_contact has the value of the *contact* column, and so forth. Because two rows are generated in the example, the row section is processed twice to generate HTML that corresponds to the two rows in the HTML table in the result form (Figure 8.6). The final step is to process the footer, which in this case involves merely appending the footer text (line 39) to the output, thereby terminating the HTML block for the HTML table declaration.

Special Variables in the Report	
The following variables are active in the entire report section:	
Ni	—Name of the ith column of the table being printed
N_*name*	—Name of the *name* column. Note that the value of this variable is the *name* string. The variable can be used to detect whether the column exists in the row.
NLIST	—List of the names of all the columns in the row, concatenated
NUM_COLUMNS	—Number of columns in the table being printed
The following variables are active only in the row section of a report section:	
Vi	—Value of the ith column of the current row
V_*name*	—Value of the *name* column
VLIST	—List of the values of all columns in the current row, concatenated
ROW_NUM	—Number of the current row in the table being printed

Drill-Down Report

Apart from the customization of the headers, the customized report in Figure 8.6 also generates each contact name retrieved as a hyperlink. Each of the hyperlinks is generated by using the template URL string "... / example2.d2w/cust_info?CUSTNO=$(V_custno)" (line 34). A different URL is generated for each row, and the URL for a row has the value of the custno column of that row embedded in it. Custno is the primary key column of the customer table, and its value is used to retrieve the customer row in the get_more_info() function. In the report for our example (Figure 8.6), two URLs are generated, one for Patty Smythe and another for Peter Smythe. When a user clicks the hyperlink named Patty Smythe in the form of Figure 8.6, the browser makes the underlying URL request, and Net.Data is called to process the request with three parameters: (1) the macro name, example2.d2w, (2) the section name cust_info, and (3) the HTML input variable, CUSTNO, set to the value of the custno column of the row in the customer table that contains the entry Patty Smythe. Net.Data executes this

URL request by processing the cust_info HTML section defined in lines 70–76 of the example2.d2w macro file. Processing of the cust_info HTML section involves calling the get_more_info() function (this function is defined in lines 54–68 and is called from line 73). The get_more_info() function retrieves a single row from the customer table, using the value of the CUSTNO variable (see the *where* clause in line 56). The report section used to print this row is defined in the get_more_info function (lines 58–67). Figure 8.7 shows the report printed as a result of this execution.

In our discussion of the example2.d2w macro, we have assumed that the user always checks all of the check boxes in the input form. However, if the user does not check one or more check boxes in the input form of Figure 8.3, the report will contain one or more blank columns. For example, consider the case where a user submits an input form but does not check the company check box. The report section in the get_phone_no() function (lines 31–32) will print a table with three columns, one each for the contact name, phone, and company, but the cells in the company column will be empty. (The value of $(V_custname) is null because custname was not selected.) This problem can be avoided by further customizing the report section with Net.Data's conditional logic statements.

Conditional Logic

If the report section in the Customizing box replaced the original report section of the get_phone_no() function in the example2.d2w macro, the report

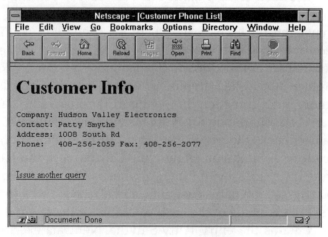

Figure 8.7 Drill-down report (example2.d2w).

printed would print only the columns that the user selects in the input form. The conditional logic checks whether each named column exists in the row that is returned. If a particular column exists, the logic adds HTML tags and variables to the report section so that the column with a header and rows will be printed as part of the report. Note how the logic checks for the existence of the N_ variables in both the header portion (lines 4–12 of box below) and the body of the row section (lines 16–26 of box below) to ensure that a column header is always printed when the column's rows are printed.

Customizing the Report Section with Conditional Logic

```
1.  %REPORT {
2.  <TABLE BORDER CELLPADDING=2>
3.  <TR>
4.  %if (N_contact)
5.  <TH>Contact Name</TH>
6.  %endif
7.  %if (N_con_phone)
8.  <TH>Phone</TH>
9.  %endif
10. %if (N_custname)
11. <TH>Company</TH>
12. %endif
13. </TR>
14. %ROW{
15. <TR>
16. %if (N_contact)
17. <TD>
18. <A HREF="/cgi-bin/db2www.exe/example2.d2w/
    cust_info?CUSTNO=$(V_custno)">
19. $(V_contact)</A></TD>
20. %endif
21. %if (N_con_phone)
22. <TD>$(V_con_phone)</TD>
23. %endif
24. %if (N_custname)
25. <TD>$(V_custname)</TD>
26. %endif
27. %}
28. </TABLE>
29. %}
```

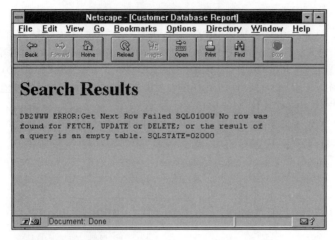

Figure 8.8 Default error message for a failed search (example1.d2w).

Customized Error Handling

A critical requirement of any application is good error handling. Consider, for example, that we want to query the name *Jones,* using the input form in Figure 8.3. If the database does not contain a record for Jones, then executing such a query results in the default error message shown in Figure 8.8. The standard error message (passed through from DB2 in this case) is hard for an end user to understand. When such an error occurs, it would be much better to display a simple customized message with a hyperlink that lets the user proceed farther. To enable customization of error handling, Net.Data macros support message sections that can be embedded inside function definition sections much like report sections. The example3.d2w macro (see box below) is a modified version of the example1.d2w macro and illustrates (among other things) the use of a message section.

---

example3.d2w Macro: Error Handling

```
1. %{ ------------------- Phone Book Query ------------------- %}
2. %HTML(query) {
3. <TITLE>Customer Database Query</TITLE>
4.
5. <H1>Query Form</H1>
```

(continued)

Using Net.Data to Access Databases and Files

```
6.  <FORM METHOD="POST" ACTION="/cgi-bin/db2www.exe/example3.d2w/
    phone_list">
7.  Contact name: <INPUT TYPE="text" NAME="CONTNAME">
8.  <BR>
9.  Information to view:
10. <INPUT TYPE="checkbox" NAME="COLNAME" VALUE="con_fax" CHECKED>Fax
11. <INPUT TYPE="checkbox" NAME="COLNAME" VALUE="custname">Company
12.
13. <INPUT TYPE="submit" VALUE="SEARCH"> <INPUT TYPE="reset"
    VALUE="RESET">
14. </FORM>
15. %}
16. %{ -------------------- Phone List Report -------------------- %}
17. %define DATABASE = "celdial"
18. %define DTW_HTML_TABLE = "YES"
19. %define {
20. %LIST "," COLNAME
21. COLNAME = "contact"
22. COLNAME = "con_phone"
23. COLNAME = "custno"
24. %}
25.
26. %FUNCTION(DTW_SQL) get_phone_no() {
27. select $(COLNAME) from customer
28. where contact like '%$(CONTNAME)%'
29. order by contact
30.
31. %MESSAGE {
32. 100 : "No record matched the name '$(CONTNAME)'" : continue
33. %}
34. %}
35.
36. %HTML(phone_list) {
37. <TITLE>Customer Phone List</TITLE>
38. <H1>Phone List</H1>
39. @get_phone_no()
40. <br>
41. <A HREF="/cgi-bin/db2www.exe/example3.d2w/query">Issue another
    query</A>
42. %}
```

The message section (enclosed between the %MESSAGE and %} tags) in the get_phone_no() function (lines 31–34) defines a message handler. A message section is a table of one or more rows, each row containing three columns separated by a colon (:). The first column is the message code and is a positive or negative integer (the value *default* here can be used to refer to all error codes not explicitly handled). The second column is a piece of text within double quotes or enclosed within the separators { and %}. An optional third column is a directive (*exit* or *continue*) that tells Net.Data whether to continue processing or exit. The message section in the example3.d2w macro contains a single entry for the error message code 100 because that is the code indicated by the SQL0100W string in the error message on the form in Figure 8.8. Figure 8.9 shows the output generated by executing the query *Jones* with the example3.d2w macro. While Net.Data is executing the get_phone_no() function (line 26) in the HTML *phone list* section, the database returns the SQL0100W error message because it does not have a Jones record. Net.Data processes this error code, using the entry for the code in the message section associated with this function (line 32). Net.Data evaluates the message text for variable values and prints it as part of the output (Figure 8.9). Notice how the string in the message section uses the current value of the CONTNAME variable (the Jones string) to print an appropriate message. Also, because the message entry for error code 100 is tagged with the *continue* token, Net.Data continues to process the HTML phone_list section and puts out the hyperlink at the bottom of the form (Figure 8.9) that enables the user to issue another query.

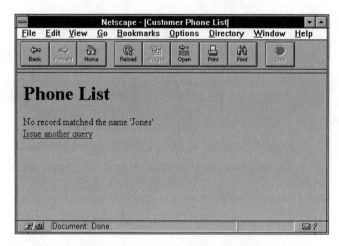

Figure 8.9 Customized error message for failed search (example3.d2w).

List and Conditional Variables

A common problem that occurs in building dynamic applications is that simple variable substitution sometimes does not work well with dynamic SQL statement generation. For example, if no columns are selected in the input form of the example1.d2w macro, the SELECT clause will have no parameters (the COLNAME variable is the null string). Thus, a statement of the form "select from customer . . ." is created and results in a syntax error message from the database. Net.Data provides a number of ways to solve this problem, and we discuss one solution here.

To solve the syntax error problem, you can use explicitly defined list variables in the macro file. In the example1.d2w macro, Net.Data treats COLNAME as a list variable because users can set its value by selecting zero or more check boxes. In the example3.d2w macro, the COLNAME variable is explicitly defined as a list variable (*%LIST* tag) with the comma as a delimiter. Lines 21–23 initialize COLNAME to three values: contact, con_phone, and custno. The input form of the example3.d2w macro (the HTML query section in lines 2–15) does not contain the column names used in the definitions in lines 21–23. Instead, it contains an option to include the con_fax (Fax) and custname (Company) columns in the report. The SELECT clause of the SQL string in the get_phone_no() function (line 27) therefore always has the components of the COLNAME list variable that are defined in the macro. Because any extra values selected by the user in the input form are appended to the COLNAME variable, and so the user report can have a maximum of five columns in this example. If the user does not select any columns from the input form, the report is printed with the three columns defined in the macro.

In addition to list variables, Net.Data also supports conditional variables that are useful for constructing syntactically correct SQL statements (see the Error Case box below). For the error_case() function, when the CUSTNO variable is NULL, the where clause in the SQL string evaluates to the string WHERE custno =. This *where* clause causes a syntax error in the SQL parser.

Error Case When CUSTNO Is NULL

```
%FUNCTION (DTW_SQL) error_case() {
SELECT contact, con_phone
FROM customer
WHERE custno ="$(CUSTNO)"
%}
```

You can easily fix this problem, however, by using a conditional variable to create the where clause that is evaluated by the SQL parser. The Conditional Variable box (below) shows the correct_one() function where a conditional variable called where_clause (defined using a C-like syntax) is used to create the where clause. In this case, if the value of CUSTNO is NULL, the where_clause variable is defined to be NULL, thus creating an SQL query that will retrieve all rows in the customer table. The "Net.Data Programming Guide" has more information about conditional variables and how they can be combined with list variables to easily generate syntactically correct SQL statements.

> **Conditional Variable for Creating Syntactically Correct SQL**
>
> ```
> %define where_clause = CUSTNO ? "WHERE custno = '$(CUSTNO)'" :""
>
> %FUNCTION (DTW_SQL) correct_one() {
> SELECT contact, con_phone
> FROM customer
> $(where_clause)
> %}
> ```

Sharing Macros among Applications

Net.Data provides an include facility for sharing macro files among applications. It supports the inclusion of files (the %INCLUDE tag followed by a quoted string) as well as URLs (the %INCLUDE_URL tag followed by a quoted string). The include facility is typically used for sharing pieces of HTML among several macro files. It can also be used to share function definitions for functions that have to be accessed in many Net.Data macros.

A particularly interesting use of the include facility is for reducing the size of a macro by including only the functions for the section that is being called. Let us demonstrate two different ways of including only the functions for the section being called. Assume that we have a macro that has two sections, called *first* and *second,* and that the include sections needed for these sections are in the first_fns.inc and second_fns.inc files, respectively. Further assume that the section name is passed by an input variable called SECTION. The Include box shows two different ways of selectively including only the functions for the section being called. The first example uses conditional logic to include the appropriate file according to the section name, and the second example uses variables in the include string to achieve the same result (see box below).

Include with Conditional Logic

```
%if ("$(SECTION)" == "first")
%include "first_fns.inc"
%elif ("$(SECTION)" == "second")
%include "second_fns.inc"
%endif
```

Include with Variables

```
%include "$(SECTION)_fns.inc"
```

Net.Data processes an include statement in two steps. First it replaces any variables with their runtime values. In the Include with Variables example, Net.Data replaces the $(SECTION) variable with the *first* or *second* string. The resulting string, for example, first_fns.inc, is the file (or URL) name to include. Net.Data searches for the file name in the path specified in the *MACRO_PATH* environment variable of the Net.Data configuration file. Including URLs works in much the same way as including a file, except that the data for a URL is dynamically obtained by accessing the Web server referenced in the URL.

Including files and URLs in macros enables better Website management. By including files and URLs, many Web pages can reference common items such as headers and hyperlinks. When one of these items is changed, the new version is automatically referenced by all of the Web pages. Thus, a Website administrator can easily update many Web pages by changing only one copy of each item.

POSTPROCESSING OF DATA

One of the major requirements of building dynamic Web pages is the ability to transform the data retrieved from a database or a file to produce a desired output. The Net.Data report section provides a certain level of postprocessing ability for simple applications. More often than not, however, postprocessing requires that the data retrieved be stored in a temporary table so that it can be processed further. Net.Data supports postprocessing with a special type of variable called the *table* variable, whose value is a table like the table returned in the example1.d2w and example2.d2w macros. The DTW_SAVE_TABLE_IN variable can be used to specify the name of the

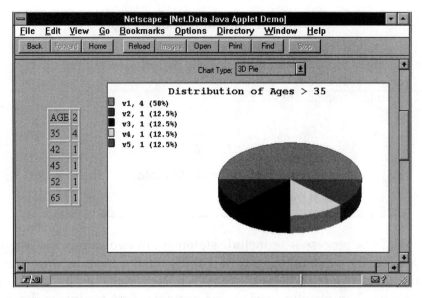

Figure 8.10 Postprocessing with a Java applet (example4.d2w).

table variable into which the result of an SQL query must be stored. Such a table might then be passed as a parameter to other macro functions for postprocessing. We illustrate postprocessing with a Java applet that builds a pie chart using data retrieved from a DB2 database. You can run this application on any Java-enabled browser from the Net.Data Website at http://www.software.ibm.com/data/net.data. The macro file used by this application is shown in example4.d2w (Figure 8.10).

---

example4.d2w Macro: Postprocessing with a Java Applet

```
1.  %define DATABASE="celdial"
2.  %define DTW_SAVE_TABLE_IN = "careertable"
3.  %define MACRO = "/cgi-bin/db2www/"
4.  %define SHOWSQL = "YES"
5.
6.  %INCLUDE "netdata.inc"
7.
8.  %{Define variable for Chart %}
9.  %define ChartUI2.width = "400"
10. %define ChartUI2.height = "250"
11. %define ChartType = "3D Pie"
12. %define name = "$(N2)"
```

(continued)

```
13. %define numrow = "$(ROW_NUM)"
14. %define field = "35"
15. %define ChartUI2.codebase="http://testcase.boulder.ibm.com"
16. %{ // end of Chart define %}
17.
18. %function (DTW_APPLET) ChartUI2();
19.
20. %FUNCTION (DTW_SQL) java_print_report() {
21. select age, count(age) AS Guests from guests where age >= $(field)
    group by age
22. %REPORT{
23. <table border=2 cellspacing=40 cellpadding=0>
24. <tr> <th colspan=2 bgcolor='a7a7ff'>Percentage of Guests by Age
25. <tr> <th bgcolor='ffaacc'>Raw Data (from DB2) <th
    bgcolor='ffaacc'> Java Applet
26. <tr>
27. <td align=center>
28. <table border=1 >
29. <tr><td>AGE</td> <td># of Guests</td>
30. %ROW{
31. <tr><td>$(V1)</td> <td align=center>$(V2)</td>
32. %}
33. </table>
34. <td>
35. </table>
36. @ChartUI2(ChartUI2.codebase,ChartUI2.width, ChartUI2.
    height,ChartType, numrow, careertable, name)
37. %}
38. %}
39.
40. %HTML(report){
41. <TITLE>Net.Data Java Applet Demo</TITLE>
42.
43. <form method="post" action="$(MACRO)showmacro.d2w/report">
44. <img src="/images/hcad1.gif">
45. <input TYPE="hidden" name="filename" value="example4.d2w">
46. <input TYPE=SUBMIT value="View this macro's source">
47. </form>
48.
49. The following are the results of your query.
50. @java_print_report()
51.
52. $(footer)
53. %}
```

Java Applet

Figure 8.10 shows the report generated when the example4.d2w macro is invoked with the section named *report* (see box below).

The table on the left of Figure 8.10 and the pie chart on the right are both printed by using the report section of the java_print_report() function that is defined in lines 20–38. The query in line 21 of the function retrieves the number of guests grouped by their age. The report section portion in lines 23–35 prints the HTML table with the two columns that appear on the left in Figure 8.10. This part is quite similar to the customized report in the example2.d2w macro. The difference in the report processing here is that the result of the query is stored in the table variable called *careertable* because the DTW_SAVE_TABLE_IN variable is set to the value "careertable" (line 2). The last line of the report (line 36) contains a call to the ChartUI2 function, which is a macro function that is executed by using the DTW_APPLET language environment (see line 18 for this definition). Several variables are passed to the ChartUI2 function that provide the DTW_APPLET language environment with information needed to generate the HTML required for running the applet. The ChartUI2.codebase variable (line 15) points to the machine where the applet code file (ChartUI2.class) is stored. The ChartUI2.width (line 9) and ChartUI2.height (line 10) variables are used to set the height and width of the applet display area in the browser window. The ChartType variable (value "3D Pie" from line 11) tells the ChartUI2 applet to print a three-dimensional pie chart. The numrow variable (line 13) informs the applet about the number of rows in the table, the variable careertable contains the result of the SQL query, and the name variable (line 12) contains the name of the column in the careertable variable for building the pie chart. Note that all of this input from the macro variables is converted into parameters of the Java applet by using the <param> tag. The ChartUI2 applet, when invoked on the browser, reads the input parameters, using the applet.getParameter() function, and builds the pie chart. Figure 8.10 shows the report form that is generated on the browser by running this application.

In addition to supporting client-side postprocessing with Java applets, Net.Data supports server-side postprocessing with interpreted languages Perl and REXX. Perl and REXX functions can be written in the macro by using a syntax similar to the syntax we have been using for writing SQL functions, except that the SQL strings will be replaced by Perl or REXX code. The Net.Data package comes with Perl and REXX language environment DLLs that can be used to execute the Perl and REXX code included in the macro file. Macro variables (including table variables) that are passed to these functions are accessible in the Perl or REXX code. In the case of Perl functions, these variables are available through named pipes whose names are available from the environment, and in the case of the REXX functions they are available as bona fide REXX variables. Note that variable values can be changed and passed back from a Perl or REXX function, and the new values will be used in subsequent macro processing. The Postprocessing box shows part of a macro file containing a REXX function called rexx_print_report that is used to postprocess a table variable passed as input.

REXX Function

Let us assume that the HTML report section is called in the same way as in the example2.d2w macro, that is, all three check boxes are selected in the input form of Figure 8.3, and the search string is Smythe. When Net.Data processes the report section (see box below), it calls the get_phone_no() function (line 29).

Postprocessing with a REXX Function

```
1.  %define DTW_SAVE_TABLE_IN = "saved_table"
2.
3.  %FUNCTION (DTW_REXX) rexx_print_report(IN table){
4.  say "<TABLE BORDER CELLPADDING=2>"
5.  say "<TR><TH>Contact Name</TH><TH>Phone</TH><TH>Company</TH></TR>"
6.  Do i = 1 to table_rows
7.  say "<TR>"
8.  say "<TD>"table_V.i.1"</TD>"
9.  say "<TD>"table_V.i.2"</TD>"
10. say "<TD>"table_V.i.3"</TD>"
11. say "</TR>"
12. End
13. say "</TABLE>"
14. %}
15.
16. %FUNCTION(DTW_SQL) get_phone_no() {
17. select $(COLNAME) from customer
18. where contact like '%$(CONTNAME)%'
19. order by contact
20. %REPORT {
21. @rexx_print_report(saved_table)
```

(continued)

```
22. %}
23. %}
24.
25. %HTML(report) {
26. <TITLE> Phone List</TITLE>
27.
28. <H1><img src="/images/suilogo.gif"> Phone List</H1>
29. @get_phone_no()
30. <BR>
31. <A HREF="/cgi-bin/db2www.exe/example2.d2w/input">Issue another
    query</A>
32. %}
```

Evaluating this function causes the results of the SQL query (lines 17–19) to be saved in a table variable called saved_table (DTW_SAVE_TABLE_IN is defined in line 1). Note that the report section has no row section and is therefore treated as a report section with only a footer. Net.Data processes the entire query and saves the query results in the saved_table table variable. The results are the two rows seen in Figure 8.6 (without the hyperlinks). Net.Data then processes the report footer text (line 21) by calling the rexx_print_report() function and passing to it the saved_table table variable. This function is defined in lines 3–14. Of particular importance is the way in which the values of the columns of the rows are retrieved (lines 8–10). The table_V.i.j variable refers to the value of the jth column of the ith row of the table variable named *table*. Also, the REXX variable called table_rows contains the number of rows in the table and is used to control the loop execution (line 6). Executing the rexx_print_report() function results in a report much like the report in Figure 8.6.

As the postprocessing example shows, Net.Data macro variables are accessible as native REXX variables because the REXX language environment implementation has special code to transfer the macro variable state from the macro processor to the REXX interpreter and vice versa. REXX native variables like the table variable (table_V.i.j) can have their values changed in the REXX code, and the new values will appear in the macro variable after the function execution is completed. (The returned values are incorporated only for variables declared with the OUT or INOUT tags.)

Perl Function

Using Perl in a macro works in much the same way as REXX, except that the variables are communicated back and forth through a named pipe whose name is defined in the DTWPIPE environment variable; the variables are communicated as Name=Value pairs with this pipe (see box below). In the Perl example, when the today() function is executed, the Perl interpreter is called to run the Perl code given in the definition of this function. The Perl language environment and the Perl program communicate through the named pipe. The Perl code in the function computes the date and passes the value of the result variable through the pipe. The DTW_PERL language environment reads this value and sets the return value of the function to be the value of the *result* variable that is sent through the named pipe.

Passing Variables Back from a Perl Program

```
%FUNCTION (DTW_PERL) today () RETURNS (result) {
  $date = 'date';
  chop $date;
  open (DTW, "> $ENV{DTWPIPE}") || die "could not open: $!";
  print DTW "result = \"$date\"\n";
%}

%HTML(input){
Today's Date = @today()
%}
```

Built-in Functions

While writing macros, it sometimes becomes necessary to transform the value of an HTML input variable before using the value to access a database or file. We describe one interesting case where a user types in something that causes an unexpected, catastrophic application error. A common example is when a user is searching for a name that contains an apostrophe, for example, O'Hara. This string will cause an SQL syntax error if Net.Data creates a where clause that contains the single quote character (see line 34 of the example1 macro). To circumvent this problem, Net.Data provides a built-in function called *dtw_raddquote()*. Here is the improved where clause that incorporates dtw_raddquote():

```
"where contact like '%@dtw_raddquote(CONTNAME)%' "
```

When the SQL string with this where clause is evaluated, the dtw_raddquote function adds an extra quote so that the actual *where* clause generated is:

```
"where contact like '%O''Hara%'
```

This *where* clause is syntactically correct, and the SQL statement executes as intended. In addition to the built-in function for fixing up a single quote, Net.Data provides dozens of other built-in functions for performing operations that are required for building practical applications. Net.Data provides built-in functions for changing case from upper to lower and vice versa, math, URL encoding and decoding, a file library for reading the contents of files, implementing a Web registry based on a lightweight object database, and many other operations. All of the built-in functions are implemented efficiently in C and C++. To further illustrate Net.Data's built-in functions, let us look at the support available in Net.Data for accessing files.

Calling User Functions and Applications from a Macro

Despite the rich variety of Net.Data's built-in functions, you may need to write a special-purpose function and call it from Net.Data. You can write special-purpose functions in Perl and REXX, as we have shown, but such implementations of complex functions may not perform acceptably. To enable the building of sophisticated industrial-strength applications, Net.Data provides a facility for users to call their own functions written in a programming language like C or COBOL by using the same function call syntax that we have used to call SQL functions like get_phone_no() and built-in functions like dtw_addquote(). To enable a user function to be called from Net.Data, you must build a DLL that contains the function code and make the DLL known to Net.Data through its configuration file. Net.Data processes a function call by loading the appropriate DLL specified in the configuration file and then calling the entry point in the loaded DLL to execute the function.

To make it easy for users to develop customized functions, Net.Data provides a standard application developer's kit for building DLLs. The developer's kit comes with a library of functions that can be used to manipulate table variables and read configuration information available in the Net.Data configuration file. These functions are extremely useful for performing sophisticated reporting and postprocessing on data that has been accessed from a database or file. The interface for building Net.Data-compatible DLLs whose functions can be called from a macro is discussed in the *Net.Data Programming Guide*.

Net.Data provides a special language environment called SYSTEM that enables a Net.Data macro to execute other applications and incorporate their output into the macro result. In addition, there is a simple way of escaping from Net.Data by using the execute variable (the %EXEC tag). In both the SYSTEM language environment approach and the execute variable approach, applications run as separate processes. The Execute Variable box (below) shows how the operating system *date* program can be executed from a Net.Data macro using these approaches. Note that the execute variable approach works only with the CGI version of Net.Data, whereas the language environment approach works with all versions of Net.Data, including those that support NSAPI, ISAPI, and ICAPI.

Execute Variable

```
%define date = %exec "date"

%HTML(report){
Today's Date = $(date)
%}
```

Language Environment

```
%FUNCTION (DTW_SYSTEM) date () {
  %exec date
%}

%HTML(report){
Today's Date = @date()
%}
```

Some Notes on Function Parameters

Net.Data function definitions can have parameters passed to them. The parameters can be either input-only (the IN tag), default, output-only (the OUT tag), or input and output (the INOUT tag). An input parameter to a function can be read inside a function, but any changes in its value will not propagate to the calling place. Function calls cannot be nested in an unlimited manner. Typically, one level of nesting works well, but more than one level is not supported. Remember that Net.Data macros are intended to contain simple, easy-to-use constructs and are not meant for heavy-duty programming. If a complex program is needed, you can write in Perl or REXX or even build your own DLL, using a C program that Net.Data can load and call at runtime. You can completely bypass the function-passing mechanism for input by simply using the Net.Data syntax to substitute the interpreted string (as is done for the SQL strings of the get_phone_no() functions in the example1.d2w and example2.d2w macros).

When there are output parameters to be passed or when the parameters have to be passed to a stored procedure that will be executed in a database, the simple variable substitution of the interpretable code is not sufficient. To drive home this point, let us look at how to access a DB2 stored procedure with Net.Data (see box below). Note how we must specify the SQL types of the columns, for example, CHAR(40), because that information is not available from the database catalog although it is required to execute the stored procedure! Also note that the interpretable statement is expected to be the *call* string followed by the name of the stored procedure in the database.

Stored Procedure Example

```
%FUNCTION (DTW_SQL)
stored_proc(IN CHAR(40) tablename, OUT FLOAT(7,2) number) RETURNS
(RESULT) {
call stored_proc_name_in_database
%}

%HTML(store_ex){
@stored_proc(tablename, number)
%}
```

ACCESSING FILES

To understand how you can use Net.Data's built-in file support to access data from files, consider the case where our phone list (used in the example1.d2w macro) is stored in a file instead of a database. Also assume that each stored entry is delimited by semicolons. For the macro to generate a report like that in Figure 8.4, see the Phone Book Lookup box (below).

Phone Book Lookup with Files

```
%define{
result_table     = %TABLE
search_string    = "$(CONTNAME)"
file_name        = "phone_list"
mode             = "r"
file_type        = "DELIMITED"
delimiter        = ";"
%}

%HTML(phone_list){
@dtwf_open(file_name, mode)
@dtwf_search(file_name, file_type, delimiter, result_table,
search_string)
@rexx_print_table(result_table)
@dtwf_close(file_name)
%}
```

The phone book query is implemented by the HTML phone_list section. Let us assume again that the CONTNAME variable is set to Smythe. The file containing the phone book is first opened by using the DTWF_OPEN function. A table variable called result_table is defined and passed to the DTWF_SEARCH function, which searches the phone book file for an occurrence of the Smythe search string. The function stores any matching rows in the table variable. The table resulting from the search is output by using the rexx_print_table function that we used to illustrate customized reporting of tables. Finally, the file is closed by using the DTWF_CLOSE function. In addition to providing the function for searching files, Net.Data provides a number of functions for other types of file manipulation such as inserts, deletes, and appends. For a complete list of functions available for accessing files, see the Net.Data Built-in Functions box (below).

Net.Data Built-in Functions for Accessing Files

DTWF_APPEND —Appends the contents of a table variable to the end of a file
DTWF_CLOSE —Closes a file that was opened earlier using DTWF_OPEN
DTWF_DELETE —Deletes records from a file but does not delete the file

(continued)

DTWF_INSERT	—Inserts records from a table variable into a file at a specified position
DTWF_OPEN	—Opens a file for reading, writing, or appending
DTWF_READ	—Reads records from a file into a table variable
DTWF_REMOVE	—Deletes a file
DTWF_SEARCH	—Retrieves records from a file that match a search string into a table variable
DTWF_UPDATE	—Replaces existing records in a file starting from a specified position from a table variable
DTWF_WRITE	—Writes records to a file from a table variable

ACCESSING NON-HTML DATA

Before we wrap up our discussion of application building, let us illustrate how you can use Net.Data to return non-HTML data from an HTML section. Recall that Net.Data assumes that the content of the HTML sections in a macro is pure HTML and therefore automatically prefixes the appropriate MIME header (the string "Content-Type: text/html") to the output. This does not work if applications need to provide non-HTML data such as postscript or images, or users want to return data in a proprietary format that the browser can process by using a plug-in that understands the proprietary format. Net.Data supports such customization by providing a facility for you to disable the Net.Data standard header and append your own headers. Let us look at Net.Data's support for customizing headers, using an example that generates HTTP cookies.

First you have to understand how cookies work. Cookies are Name-Value pairs that a Web application typically returns when a browser visits the Website where the application resides. The browser keeps track of the cookies it receives from different Websites, and it may discard cookies that have expired or are taking up too much space. When a browser revisits a site, it returns to the server any cookies that are applicable to the URL being accessed. The server makes any received cookies available to Web applications by means of the HTTP_COOKIE environment variable. More information about the Netscape cookie specification is located at http://www.netscape.com/newsref/std/cookie_spec.html. Let us now see how you can use cookies in a Net.Data macro (see box below).

Generating a Cookie

```
%define{
DTW_PRINT_HEADER = "NO"
HTTP_COOKIE = %ENVVAR
%}

%HTML(cookies){
Set-Cookie: CustomerId=@get_customer_id(HTTP_COOKIE)
expires=@gen_expiry_time()
Content-Type: text/html
. . .
%}
```

To disable Net.Data's standard header for an HTML section, the DTW_PRINT_HEADER variable is set to "NO." In the first line of the HTML cookies section, a cookie called CustomerId is created by using the Set-Cookie directive of the header. In particular, a get_customer_id function is called to generate the cookie's value and a gen_expiry_time function is called to generate the cookie's expiry date. The HTTP_COOKIE environment variable is passed to the function by the server and contains all of the cookies passed from the browser for this request. (Environment variables can be accessed in a Net.Data macro by using the %ENVVAR directive.) The get_customer_id function (whose definition is not shown here) processes the HTTP_COOKIE to find out whether the cookie value already contains a customer ID. If it is set, the function returns the old customer ID. If it is not set, perhaps because the user making this request did not visit the site earlier, or the cookie from the earlier visit has expired, the get_customer_id function generates a new customer ID. After the cookie value and expiring date have been generated, the MIME header Content-Type is printed, and any remaining HTML processing is completed. Notice how in our example the full power of processing a Net.Data macro can be used to manipulate cookies. This capability enables Net.Data to take full advantage of the persistent state offered by cookies.

ACCESS CONTROL BY THE DATABASE

Most databases provide support for multilevel access control to the data. These levels are typically called system administrator, database administrator, and database user. Each user has a logon-password pair and different capabilities according to his or her level of authorization. A Net.Data application can access the database with either a default logon-password pair defined in the macro file or a user-specified logon-password pair from an HTML form. For example, the getdata.d2w macro file contains the line:

```
%DEFINE { LOGIN = "team" PASSWORD = "go4it" %}
```

When the macro file is processed, the Net.Data runtime engine logs on to the database as user "team" with password "go4it" and then issues the SQL command. This would be the default logon-password pair. Alternatively, the user could be presented with input fields for logon and password in an HTML form:

```
<FORM ACTION="/cgi-bin/db2www/getdata.d2w/;d3">
<br>Login:<INPUT TYPE="text" NAME= "LOGIN">
<br>Password:<INPUT TYPE="password" NAME= "PASSWORD">
<INPUT TYPE="submit" VALUE="Submit">
....
</FORM>
```

When the user clicks on the Submit button, the browser sends the user's entries in the LOGIN and PASSWORD fields to the Web server, which makes them available to the Net.Data runtime engine when Net.Data processes the getdata.d2w macro. The values of LOGIN and PASSWORD are used by Net.Data to log on to the database.

RELATED WORK

Early efforts in providing Web access to databases originated in universities and government agencies that had to provide searchable and well-managed data beyond the capabilities of plain HTML pages. These efforts looked to automate or simplify the application development process, shielding the database application developer from detailed knowledge of the CGI protocol. The commercial database vendors and tool providers quickly followed with their own methods based on the early work of these Web pioneers. In this section, we discuss current product offerings for accessing databases from the Web.

Sybase web.sql

Sybase web.sql enables development of Web applications for the Sybase database. It is quite similar to Net.Data in that it follows a page layout paradigm for building HTML templates or macro files, called HyperText Sybase (HTS) files, with embedded SQL commands. A closer look reveals two important differences between Net.Data and web.sql:

- web.sql requires more extensive programming for building Web applications. It supports only the default table report with the embedded SQL tag <SYB TYPE=SQL>. For customized reports, you must write Perl code inside the <SYB TYPE=PERL> tag, and it must make direct calls to the database and print out the reports. In contrast, Net.Data's %SQL_REPORT format allows customized report layout in HTML without any programming.
- web.sql supports only the Perl language, whereas Net.Data supports a number of scripting languages, including Perl, REXX, and Java.

web.sql's tight integration with Perl provides a programming advantage for using the Perl language with the Perl library's ability to access the Sybase database directly. On the other hand, Net.Data is coupled more loosely with Perl and contains a number of built-in functions for string processing and file access. The loose coupling provides a more generic cross-language variable substitution approach and allows Net.Data support other scripting languages such as REXX. The built-in functions are supported by the Net.Data runtime engine, and thus are not dependent on the existence of the scripting language, such as Perl or REXX, on the various platforms.

Informix Webkits

Informix Webkits are library routines to help database application developers write CGI programs. Informix provides a set of library routines for each of the programming languages that can be used with Informix databases, including Informix-4GL, Informix-ESQL/C, and Informix New Era. Each library includes functions that access environment variables and form values passed from HTML forms through the CGI and print results to output documents. Each library also includes utility routines for URL string encoding and decoding and for setting environment variables. In contrast to the approach taken by Net.Data and web.sql, the application developer must write full custom code to develop Web input and output forms.

Web Oracle Web (WOW)

To enable Web access to Oracle databases, Oracle provides the WOW toolkit, which contains extensions to Oracle's PL/SQL language for developing CGI applications. PL/SQL is Oracle's procedural extension to SQL for the Oracle relational database. Application developers typically use PL/SQL to build stored procedures, which are executed inside the database. For Web applications, a set of library routines is provided for building HTML input and report forms. Application programmers write Web applications in PL/SQL and call the library routines to create the forms. A new mechanism is provided to send HTML output from a PL/SQL stored procedure to a Web server's CGI output stream.

The key advantage of WOW is that, for programmers who are already familiar with PL/SQL, the new library routines provide a simple way of outputting results into HTML pages. The disadvantage is that building a Web application requires extensive PL/SQL programming, and the PL/SQL language is limited to Oracle databases.

Allaire's Cold Fusion

Cold Fusion from Allaire is quite similar to Net.Data in overall conceptual design. It supports a page layout approach to Web page development that uses HTML with embedded SQL queries. The Cold Fusion templates are quite similar to Net.Data macros and contain a number of new tags such as <DBSET>, <DBQUERY>, and <DBOUTPUT> that set variables, formulate SQL queries, and lay out HTML reports. The Cold Fusion runtime engine is a CGI program that can access a number of databases through the standard ODBC interface.

For laying out input and report forms, the Cold Fusion templates are quite comparable to Net.Data macro files. However, Cold Fusion cannot embed a variety of languages such as Perl, REXX, and Java as can Net.Data, and it does not exist on as many operating system platforms as Net.Data.

CONCLUSION

Net.Data is an enabling tool for developing Web-based applications that access database and file systems. It supports a page layout approach that requires no procedural language programming, and it makes use of standard HTML and SQL for development of Web applications. The use of the macro file and cross language variable substitution is a simple but powerful method of building Web-based applications. Although the basic components of Net.Data are sufficient for data access and report layout without programming, Net.Data also supports multiple language plug-in modules for Java, REXX, and Perl to enable more complex processing to be done. Finally, Net.Data is available on all major operating system platforms and supports a wide variety of international languages. It can be downloaded across the Internet from http://www.software.ibm.com/data/net.data.

CHAPTER **9**

Lotus Internet Applications

Lotus Notes is an environment for rapidly building and deploying business solutions. Notes has expanded beyond its beginnings as an intraorganizational communications tool—the application that defined groupware for the enterprise. The communications needs of business have grown beyond the traditional corporate limits: Companies are rushing to improve internal channels of communication and build public information systems that reach their customers. To support those companies, Lotus has created a new architecture on which to provide the applications that let businesses take advantage of new and existing Intranet and Internet technologies.

The Internet is reshaping computing for organizations. It has brought demands for standards-based solutions and for simplifying the user experience. As the standards of the Internet—TCP/IP, HTTP servers, and HTML documents—move to the center of enterprise computing, Lotus is adopting them. The Lotus Domino Server delivers the contents of a Notes application database to both Notes clients and Web browsers and provides the platform for the Lotus Internet Applications software enabling the deployment of Internet and Intranet technology in organizations.

Lotus Internet Applications build on the strengths of the Domino environment—its client/server architecture, security, easily administered replication of data, and support for multiple operating systems—to integrate legacy systems, provide the platform for authoring and approval workflows required to create content, and manage the interactive communications. The discussions, surveys, and transaction-processing applications make this new world of standards-based communicating so exciting.

The first group of Lotus Internet Applications will provide platforms for basic business processes:

1. *Domino.Action* provides the platform and tools for designing, creating, and maintaining an electronic presence on either the public Internet or private Intranet. Domino.Action provides templates for creating an Internet or Intranet presence quickly and effectively: For the Internet, this might mean a home page, information about the company, job postings, and databases of product specifications and press releases; for the Intranet, the templates would quickly yield graphically appealing job postings, policies and procedures manuals, and suggestion-box discussions. Domino.Action provides the management tools that let an organization grow its site from dozens of pages to thousands. The other Lotus Internet Applications are built on the SiteCreator and AppAssembler foundations of Domino.Action.

2. *Lotus Internet Publishing Solutions* provide delivery vehicles and storage for content over the Web. Domino.Broadcast for PointCast is an information delivery system based on the Lotus Domino Server technology, the Lotus Notes application engine, and the Internet broadcast technologies developed by PointCast Inc. It is an authoring, communication, and information delivery platform for Intranets that combines external news with internal communications. It is the second in a series of technologies that extend the Lotus architecture to Internet publishing, the first being the Lotus Notes:Newsstand on the Web product, available at http://www.newsstand.lotus.com/.

3. *Domino.Merchant* supports marketing and sales on the Internet, from activities as simple as registering prospects and distributing product literature all the way to accepting a credit card, processing a payment, and delivering a digital product. Domino.Merchant provides the facilities for collecting information about a given audience, its interests, and its use of the content. On the Internet, the process begins by supplying templates for catalogs and support for online selling activities—selecting items, placing orders, processing approvals, and authorizing payments. On the Intranet, this means surveys and questionnaires, and processes

for purchase requisitions and order approval. With its links to IBM's Net.Commerce Merchant system, Domino.Merchant can provide your organization with a growth path as the transaction volume grows.

4. *Lotus Internet Customer Service* takes advantage of the universal availability of the Internet to keep you in touch with your customers. A Customer Service application from Lotus, to be built around currently evolving Internet telephony technologies, will enable you to extend your 800 number to the Internet. This application will permit you to build a relationship with your customer: provide capabilities for downloading software, publicize product updates, and collect feedback in discussions and e-mail. On the Intranet, Lotus Internet Customer Service solutions will help take the pressure off internal hotlines and help desks; provide links to back-end database reporting processes, knowledge bases, and documentation libraries; and automate departmental approval processes.

This chapter introduces you to the Domino Server, which enables you to build your custom applications and other Lotus Internet Applications. Four Lotus Internet Applications—Domino.Action, Lotus Internet Publishing, Domino.Merchant, and Lotus Internet Customer Service—are described in detail. We include hands-on examples to customize the Domino Server for the World Wide Web. We conclude the chapter with a discussion of the strategic direction for Lotus Internet Applications.

LOTUS EXTENSIONS TO THE CLASSIC WEB SERVER

While discussion of standards-based computing has tended to focus on the thick client–thin client debate, far less attention has been paid to the capabilities of HTTP servers. The Web represents a tremendous opportunity for Notes as a server. The Domino Server raises the bar for Web servers by providing interactive communication, structured collaboration, and workflow coordination. The Domino server:

- Provides access to legacy data through a mature set of data-exchange tools and drivers.
- Eliminates the need to write CGI applications and scripts to collect data.

- Makes it easy to turn responses and e-mail into fielded data that can be reformatted and reused.
- Builds in integrated data indexing and text search capability.
- Supports applications that can automate the workflow necessary to create and manage a serious Website.
- Does not require new knowledge sets in your IS organization: You do not have to add Perl programmers or CGI scripting expertise or take on a new operating system platform—but you can maintain your existing investment by taking advantage of Domino's support for common Web server interfaces!

The back-end capabilities of the Domino server support robust information management, including an advanced multidocument database architecture, data replication, server-to-server communication, and multi-server management. In addition, Domino includes a toolkit for connecting to legacy systems, an API, and scripting tools that support a range of application development options that the current generation of Web servers do not support.

The advantages of Domino are just what an enterprise needs: flexible security for controlling access to sites and applications; templates for establishing enforceable presentation standards where HTML provides none; replication to enable distributed authoring of content; and workflow modeling to build the review and approval processes that are not present in the Web.

Domino makes it possible to create applications that live both in Notes and on the Internet in synchronization, enabling organizations to make their own decisions about the best security architecture and user interface for any application. Business applications can take full advantage of Notes' back-end strengths—its easy connectivity to legacy data, its unique semi-structured data store—without having to build the complete Notes infrastructure on the desktop.

The Lotus Internet Applications are designed for easy extension by anyone familiar with Lotus Notes. The next section describes how to create your own custom applications for use with the Domino Server. Many of the concepts described can also be used to extend the applications that Lotus provides to enable more complex Internet technologies, such as Internet commerce (Domino.Merchant) and Internet publishing, for use in your company.

EXTENDING THE DOMINO SERVER WITH LOTUS INTERNET APPLICATIONS

The Lotus Internet Applications extend the Domino Server with solutions geared toward standard business processes: facilitating commerce, electronic publishing, content creation, and customer service over the Internet. These applications are intended for customers who use Notes as well as customers who, while not yet using Notes on daily basis, want a way of solving real business problems through the Web.

For those organizations that already use Notes, Lotus Internet Applications offer the following benefits:

- Companies that use Notes for central business processes can implement these processes on the Internet to reach new users. Customers and suppliers can be brought into discussions and decision-making processes online. Prospects can tap applications that deliver customized information on demand.
- Internet applications can be developed and managed in the familiar environment of Notes. The learning curve is shortened, and the delivery time is reduced.
- Familiar workflows for production and approval can be used as the basis for managing the site and its contents: The company does not have to be reinvented to take advantage of the Internet.

Because the Lotus Domino Server and Lotus Internet Applications provide content-creation and site-management capabilities that go beyond existing Web tools, they also have much to offer companies that have no existing Notes infrastructure:

- Lotus Internet Applications create a maximum Internet presence with minimum effort. The SiteCreator that comes with each Internet application is designed to provide a quick and effective implementation path, without extraordinary effort or cost. Yet the immediate usefulness of Lotus Internet Applications does not imply any reduction in Notes' longstanding emphasis on end-user development. The Lotus Internet applications have been designed to encourage customization.
- The Lotus Domino Server combined with Lotus Internet Applications enables developers to use whatever Internet design and content-creation tools they want: graphics packages for high-impact pages that set a visual identity for a site; HTML editors for unique pages. Domino

adds programmable workflow and security, replication support for distributed authoring, threaded discussion support, and the ability to process intelligent forms and store the results in a database, rather than just as text.

- Because organizations can develop applications that reach both the Notes client and the Web browser, they can choose the best delivery solution for the applications and audience.

DOMINO.ACTION

Lotus Internet Applications provide an architecture that enables developers to create applications that express the business practices of companies and industries—as well as activities that cut across industry boundaries. The foundation for the Lotus Internet applications is embodied in the first application to ship from Lotus: *Domino.Action*. The starting point for any organization is the establishment of an electronic presence. It may be as simple as a single home page or a virtual business card. It will quickly become more complex, with the addition of information about the company, press releases, job postings, feedback forms, and more. It is the job of Domino.Action to make this startup as quick and easy as possible—and to make the growth process an orderly and manageable one.

Domino.Action and the Domino server are available with the shipment of Notes Release 4.5, and Domino.Action contains additional software and tools, including:

- SiteCreator, for selecting and configuring the main elements of the site: home page; about-the-company; press release library; job postings; customer feedback; policies and procedures manuals; discussions; visitor registration
- Editorial production tools: Rich Text Format (RTF) and ASCII-to-Notes/HTML translation, a version of the tools used by publishers on Lotus Notes:Newsstand

Turning Electronic Publishing into a Business Activity

Distributing information is an increasingly important business function—either in support of a line of business or as a product in its own right. For organizations doing electronic publishing to support other lines of business, Domino.Action provides the editorial tools to treat the creation of electronic presence as a business activity, using Notes to provide a platform for an ever-changing, content-rich Internet site. Where publishing is a product, the Lotus Internet Publishing solutions support traditional publishers moving into the electronic environment, giving them the design and management tools they need to create and deliver products.

Command and Control for the Internet

Domino's environment for application development provides a flexible structure for electronic publishing that solves an enormous problem of creating content on the Internet: The design of an electronic publication or a Website can be separated from the creation and management of its contents. Domino.Action supports the design of content applications that can be displayed in both the Notes client and a Web browser. Documents are saved by application and displayed in the proper form when retrieved. Therefore:

- Content-creation privileges can be set within the application, and authorship of the application's content can be distributed through the Internet. Domino administers security and controls access, and Notes replication can be used at any point in the process, from collecting text and images for editing to placing finished documents on the server.

- Design standards can be established and enforced. No longer is the look and feel of the page or the site at the mercy of the last person who edited the HTML page. Authors and editors no longer have to be experts at CGI scripting or system administration. Any user who can create e-mail can create content for an Internet site. Yet a company can maintain control over its appearance on open networks while granting access to information providers and authors who contribute the regularly updated information that is the lifeblood of a site.

- Management of the content can be as simple or as sophisticated as the organization requires. Workflow tools are available for the creation of editing and approval processes, audit trails, and signoffs. The management inherent in Notes provides a growth path for a Website: It is not hard to manage a site with a few dozen pages. A site with a few thousand pages is another matter. The database structure provided by Notes, with its text indexing and categorization, and aging, is the kind of tool that is required for a large site.

Built-in Interactivity

Domino.Action supports the creation of interactive applications as well. Its discussion templates bring threaded discussions to the Internet, thus enabling users to read and contribute to discussions as well as send letters to the editor, complete questionnaires and surveys, and participate in two-way information processes.

The architecture of Domino.Action comprises the foundation for solutions to typical business problems: from Internet and Intranet publishing to Internet commerce and customer service solutions. In the sections that follow, we focus on the extensions to the Domino.Action foundation product and the need for these new technologies in your business.

LOTUS INTERNET PUBLISHING

The Web is causing major changes in consumer information businesses. Publishers (using the term in its broadest sense to include the owners of media properties, whatever the medium) are finding it difficult to effectively promote their existing products on the Internet and to protect their traditional franchises from a flood of nontraditional competitors.

The Web has separated the three primary delivery models—broadcasting, subscription, and single-copy sales—from their traditional media channels (respectively, TV and radio, magazines and newspapers, and book publishing). The bad news for publishers is that no single delivery model is a clear path to profitability on the Web. The good news is that this new understanding of delivery models can be applied to other content sources. Even better news is the fact that the new technology of the Internet is yielding new tools for mixing and matching the traditional publishing models.

As publishers are pushed out of their traditional niches, they face the challenge of adapting the models to their marketplaces, and their products to these models. It is clear that electronic publishing on the Web must play a major role, and a successful strategy will have to be cross-media. These changes will create new demands on the processes of creating and revising content for electronic publishing, providing access to it, and storing and managing it. Lotus is moving to bring together the three electronic publishing models into a unified architecture for electronic publishing that provides publishers with a flexible solution.

The Need for a Framework

As the amount of content that is created for electronic distribution grows, so do the requirements for managing that information resource: the physical locations of the data; the relationships among the elements of the content, often described by complex taxonomies; the collaboration processes necessary for individuals to create and edit the content; and the management of document storage and aging. These problems can be classified into (1) storage, (2) relationship, (3) creation, and (4) retention.

The Web provides a technology for storing and retrieving data, but no context: Information is stored on static pages. Web pages are indexed by complex search engines, but even a search agent or service can only index the content that has been placed in these static pages. It cannot provide a clear understanding of the context in which the information was gathered. Indeed, because information is ephemeral, much of a search engine's index becomes quickly outdated, serving up links to information that no longer exists or has been moved to a different physical storage location.

The explosion of ideas and information made possible by the technology of the Web will only be tamed by technology: technology to organize the storage of the existing content; technology to establish relationships, taxonomies, and indexes of different types of content; technology to provide workflow processes for content creation; technology to apply intelligent methods to retention.

Lotus Internet Publishing Solutions

The Lotus Internet Publishing architecture brings together implementations of three models—broadcast, subscription, and single-copy sale—that have proven track records in electronic publishing: For broadcast products, Lotus is allied with PointCast Inc. to join Lotus data-management technology to PointCast's client/server broadcast technology in the product Domino.Broadcast for PointCast. For subscriptions, Lotus's own Lotus Notes:Newsstand on the Web is a subscription and publishing environment for the World Wide Web based on the Notes server engine. For single-copy sales, Lotus is using the Cryptolope technology for secure storage and distribution of pay-per-view information products.

By combining the strengths of all three Internet publishing models, Lotus provides an integrated tool set that a publisher can use to create an electronic publishing business on the Web as complex as its business in print. This new business can take advantage of the native strengths of the Web to build products that work as well in electronic form as their traditional products work in print. The structured technologies of Lotus Internet Publishing Solutions provide a publisher with the means of controlling access and preserving revenue opportunities, while publicizing and promoting those revenue opportunities with the Web tools and services for easy linkage, free access, and addressed delivery of information.

Single-Copy Sales

IBM's InfoMarket technology provides an electronic equivalent of the sale of a single copy of a print product (a book or newspaper) or other media—CDs, cassettes, videotapes—that are selected by the consumer one at a time. The Cryptolope (derived from Encrypted Envelope) is a mechanism for charging for electronic data on a per-item-delivered basis. Instead of sending the data directly to the consumer, a link to the data is provided, which must be viewed by using a viewer equipped to decrypt the contents of the Cryptolope. This viewer decrypts the media only after it receives information from a central server that a payment has been processed for the media.

Although the Internet holds great promise as a single-copy sales medium, it raises many problems, the chief one being the ease with which multiple copies of a work can be produced and distributed. It is difficult to produce a copy of a book, less so to copy a sound recording, and in any case most copies are limited to personal use. But it is easy to copy digital data, and "personal use" tends to mean the redistribution of the data to others and potential loss of revenue to the data's owner. Less damaging financially, perhaps, but equally vexing to publishers, is the problem of selection—helping users cope with the process of finding the data they want and are willing to pay for. The technology embodied in Cryptolopes is the answer for overcoming these limitations on single-copy sales in an electronic environment.

Broadcast

PointCast's broadcast technology is a client/server system comprised of two primary components: PointCast Network (PCN) client software, and the IServer. The PCN client combines the SmartScreen screensaver and the ability to receive broadcast channels from a central source. When the system running the PCN client is idle, a dynamically updating screensaver opens to display the latest news organized by channel or topic area. The

PCN currently provides six channels of information to registered users. (To register and download the SmartScreen software, visit PointCast's Website at http://www.pointcast.com/.)

PCN conforms to the classic broadcast business model, providing editorial content of value, calculated in content and style to appeal to and define a target audience, and earning its revenue from the sale of advertising. The PointCast technology differs from traditional radio and television broadcasting in one critical respect: Unlike a radio transmitter, the IServer knows the addresses of its receivers. The client SmartScreens are registered with their server and updated with data in "channels" or categories the user has selected. (This has implications for the business model: Although PCN is a free service, the technology provides for the possibility of charging the user for the delivery of the selected categories of information, either per channel on a subscription model much like premium channels on cable TV, or single-copy sale.)

The IServer technology that provides the mechanism for organizing and distributing the data to its hundreds of SmartScreens is one of the more revolutionary solutions to the problem of creating a broadcast business model over the Internet. But making the IServer technology into a scalable model creates challenges of information content storage, relationship, and retention. How long should the information be kept at the client? How is the information organized? How can relevant information be provided to the individual user? How can the load on network bandwidth be minimized while maximizing the relevance of the information?

Subscription

Lotus Notes:Newsstand on the Web is a system for delivering subscribed information products and managing those subscriptions in a way that suits the needs of the corporate environment. (Visit the Lotus Notes:Newsstand on the Website and sign up for a sample publication at http://www.newsstand.lotus.com/.)

At the heart of Newsstand is a cluster of Notes servers, which perform several functions:

- *Warehouse,* serving as a central repository for electronic publications from the participating publishers
- *Circulation manager,* managing the registration of subscribers and payments for the subscribed content and the record-keeping for subscription terms and expiration dates

- *Librarian,* controlling access to the publications and ensuring that the customers' use of the products conforms to the terms of their subscriptions
- *Production manager,* coordinating the transfer of content from the publishers and the availability of individual issues of their publications

Publishers manage the design and content of their products on their own servers and update the central server through replication. Lotus Notes:Newsstand on the Web acts as an agent or distributor for those products, providing the marketing facilities in the electronic environment, and retaining a portion of the subscription fee.

The success of the subscription model in print rests on the traditional reliability of the distribution system—the U.S. Postal Service. But "delivery" means something different in cyberspace, and as a result the subscription model is only an approximate fit with the Web: One of the challenges of a successful subscription model on the Web is the difficulty of requiring subscribers to visit an information source on a regular basis without prompting. Success on the Web also means finding avenues for successfully reaching prospects for the electronic product—revenues depend on sales. Finally, the subscription model by itself is different from the browsing style that typifies Web users—subscriptions imply delivery of a fixed-price package with no way of charging on a per-article basis, whereas the Web is by nature a pay-by-the-piece medium.

Benefits for Publishers and Media Companies

In traditional media, subscription is the most evolved of the publishing models in both distribution and revenue. The simplest subscription model involves only one audience, one product, one revenue stream, and one means of distribution: a newsletter, for example, or season tickets to the symphony. More typically, however, the price of a subscription is used primarily as a tool to qualify the subscriber, and the bulk of the product's revenue comes from advertising, sales of goods and services to the subscribers, and the management of the subscriber base as an information asset, mixed in ways that create an almost infinite number of revenue models.

The significance of Lotus Internet Publishing Solutions is that they provide the tools for mixing and matching products and business models with the strengths of electronic delivery, for example, to enable a publisher to build single-copy sales into an electronic catalog marketing business.

The partner technologies of Lotus Internet Publishing Solutions provide a framework for Internet publishing, overcoming the limitations of the individual technologies for single-copy, broadcast, and subscription. PointCast provides the mechanism for driving volume past a site subscription managed by Lotus Notes:Newsstand on the Web. Lotus Notes:Newsstand on the Web provides the mechanism for creating content and for managing and providing a new channel for Pointcast's IServer. The Cryptolope technology provides information organized by user profile and ensures that a user does not have to purchase an entire subscription to buy a single article. And all combine to provide a framework that is completely media-nonspecific—not just text articles, but audio, video, and software can be distributed through the framework.

Lotus Internet Publishing Solutions are designed to satisfy pragmatists, providing an end-to-end infrastructure for disseminating information to a worldwide marketplace while maintaining management and organizational structure around the storage of the media. These solutions provide vehicles for broadcasting information to the widest possible audience; methods for building understanding of the customer base and their needs; provisions for document or broadcast channel subscription coupled with the ability to sell a single copy of a report.

DOMINO.MERCHANT—LOTUS INTERNET COMMERCE SOLUTION

Companies that want to do marketing and sales on the Internet will use the Lotus Internet Commerce package, Domino.Merchant, to add these functions to the Domino Server and Domino.Action package:

- SiteCreator for creating catalogs; requests for information; surveys and questionnaires; lead capture; collateral library (including page templates for brochures, white papers, press releases, specification sheets, price lists); event scheduler and signup
- Production and workflow tool
- Marketing tools
  - Mailing list manager and lead manager
  - Catalog builder
  - Order processing and shopping basket manager
  - Payment processing

Domino.Merchant builds on the content management features of Domino.Action to support on-demand delivery of information to prospects and customers. It takes advantage of the server's interactive features as well, providing templates for forms and questionnaires that let an organization gather information about a given audience and its stated interests and deposit it in Notes or relational databases for aggregation and analysis.

- *Automated information distribution.* The most immediate benefit provided by Domino.Merchant is in the improvements it brings to the fulfillment of prospect and customer requests for publications such as product brochures and information, account status updates, and technical specifications and documentation. Electronic publishing makes these materials available on demand 24 hours a day, 7 days a week. The version delivered is always the current one. The cost of fulfillment can be greatly reduced, and the volume of material available can be increased.

- *Qualifying the audience.* Domino.Merchant architecture enables publishers to qualify prospects as well. Forms-based surveys can collect information from prospects, and Notes applications on the server can turn that data into immediately actionable information. Inquiries can be routed to the proper salespeople, and electronic dialogs initiated. Statistics can be generated to track interest in particular product lines, and feedback can be collected. Completion of screening questionnaires can be used as triggers for granting access to sites and discussions.

- *Proactive marketing and advertising.* The Lotus Domino Server provides a capable platform for sophisticated targeted marketing and advertising applications based on content usage analysis, whether third-party applications or developed in Notes. And where the product is appropriate, Domino.Merchant handles ordering, payment, and delivery, so that the entire marketing and sales cycle can be implemented in the Internet environment.

- *Building a catalog or store.* Notes databases provide the foundation for creating and managing a selling environment (a catalog or a "store"). Domino.Merchant adds tools and templates for the easy creation of widely used applications, such as document libraries, catalogs, and electronic brochures. The catalog can be managed as a distributed application with controlled access and integrated approval workflow. Documents or other electronic products can be published or updated quickly. The fact that the user's access and membership in groups are controlled through the server name-and-address book, factors such as prices and discount percentages can be treated as variable data.

- *Processing the order.* Domino.Merchant supports a shopping cart metaphor that lets a user browse the available items, accumulate selections for purchase, place an order for the items, and, if appropriate, manage the delivery or route the order through an approval process. Because information can include a specification of the payment rendered as well as the product sold (a user might complete a questionnaire on purchase plans to receive a product description, for example), the solution makes use of Notes applications for securely storing and communicating customer information in much the same way as the Internet Customer Service solutions.

- *Handling payments.* Domino.Merchant includes all elements required to accept payment information from the customer and validate the transaction with a clearing agent in a secure environment, and in real time. Thus a user can enter a credit card number to "buy a subscription" to an information product and have immediate access to the product. In its first version, Lotus will provide access to a payment processing switch. When the Secure Electronic Transaction (SET) protocols sponsored by MasterCard, VISA, IBM, and Netscape, among other companies, are finalized, they will be supported as well.

- *Requirement for scalability.* Domino.Merchant is aimed at the needs of organizations that want payment capabilities to close the loop of their online marketing activities, such as selling and delivering research reports and technical documents online, or accepting payment for a conference registration. But there are no inherent limits to the tools, and a growth path exists for any catalog built with the Domino.Merchant from the integrated Notes/HTTP server to other IBM solutions, such as IBM's Net.Commerce system.

LOTUS INTERNET CUSTOMER SERVICE

The Lotus Internet Customer Service solution builds on the Domino Server and Domino.Action with:

- SiteCreator for creating problem reporting; problem routing; a knowledge base with query capability; catalogs; a documentation library (product updates, Frequently Asked Questions and Responses (FAQs) and/or tips and techniques); and digital download

- Link toolkit (to give users with Web browsers views into transaction and/or order processing systems)
- Service tools: reporting and analysis tools (to generate statistics on visitor registrations and/or unique IDs, number of logged messages, for what products, how long to close, and the like)

One of the most critical applications for many organizations is customer service and support. Many companies have devoted extensive resources to building service applications on the workflow and knowledgebase capabilities of Notes, and Lotus Internet Customer Service solutions enable them to bring their customers directly into the system through a Web connection. Lotus Internet Customer Service supports applications that can collect information in forms and questionnaires, then act on it, directing the users to information sources and routing problem reports to customer-service providers within the organization.

For organizations that do not yet use Notes, doing customer service on the Web may be the application they have been waiting for. There is a sizable installed base of applications that use Notes workflow for call tracking and its document management to control knowledgebases, and a vast amount of expertise exists among the Notes Business Partners who created these applications.

As Internet phone software moves telephony onto the Web, the Lotus Internet Customer Service solutions will provide the management tools to integrate this new technology into a high-quality customer-care system. With these tools, Lotus Internet Customer Service can be used to create a managed escalation path that guides the customer toward an answer and creates a record of the process. The path can begin with databases of FAQs and technical notes, move through product updates and timely information, and, if necessary, generate e-mail requests that bring the customer into direct contact with an employee, with built-in status reporting all along the way until the problem is resolved.

CUSTOMIZING THE DOMINO SERVER FOR THE WORLD WIDE WEB

Setting up a Lotus Notes database so that it can be accessed through the Web using the Domino Server is a powerful way to enable your customers to access your corporate information. Similarly, using the Domino Server in your corporation enables any employee anywhere in the world to collaborate with employees in your corporation through the use of a standard Web browser.

Enabling your organization to take advantage of the Domino Server by giving instruction on how to install and configure the server, how to control Web access to databases through the easy access control extensions provided by the Domino Server, and how to manage the users who have access to various areas of your Website is the focus of this section.

First of all, the Domino Server functions as a complete Web server, allowing access to standard HTML or static files, CGI programs or Java applets, as well as more complex database (or dynamic) Web server functions, facilitating access to dynamic data through extensions built into a Lotus Notes engine.

Introduction to the Domino Server

If you have some information, such as a set of documents or a database, that you want external audiences to view, you can make it available through the Web. Ordinarily, this would require that you rewrite the documents or database using HTML. The Domino Server, however, enables you to take documents or any sort of data created in just about any environment or with just about any tool, store them in a document within a Notes database, and then automatically translate the contents into HTML upon request by any Web browser. Using Domino, Web users can access dynamic data directly from a Notes database itself.

The Domino Server extends Lotus Notes to the Web, using server gateway functions. It automatically transforms Lotus Notes into an Internet application server by using the following Internet standards:

- HTTP—Domino uses HTTP to serve Notes data as well as HTML documents in the file system.
- HTML—Domino translates each object in a Notes database into HTML as requested by the Web client.
- URL syntax—Domino supports direct addressing of objects stored in a Notes database as well as file system–based URLs.
- CGI—Domino contains full support for the CGI.

- Multipurpose Internet mail extensions (MIME) encoding—Domino supports the configuration of MIME-type mapping of data and file objects stored on the server.
- SSL—Domino currently supports SSL Version 2.

Using the Domino Server, you can build applications that provide access control to databases, views, forms, or fields. Thus, you can present information or commands differently to different users, using a single database as the source. You can control whether users can have read or write access to your databases, and the type of write access you want them to have. You can set up different access levels for various types of databases, such as for administering discussion groups, for gathering customer information, for taking product orders, or for problem reporting.

With the addition of Domino to the widely accepted Notes environment, any changes you make to your Notes database will be dynamically accessible from a Web client, so your Website will always contain "live" data. Alternatively, you can use the replication features of the Notes client to enable offline manipulation of data, and when you reconnect to the Web, the Notes database will automatically be updated for the display of the current data over the Web.

How Domino Works

The Domino HTTP Server component is the part of the Domino Server that understands HTTP requests from Web clients, enabling them to communicate transparently with the Notes server. The Domino Server examines the URL of an incoming request and determines whether it is for an item in a Notes database or simply for an HTML file held in the file system. If the request is for an item in a Notes database, the Domino Server interacts with the Notes database either to get information out to the Web client or to put information from the Web client into the Notes database. If the request is for an HTML file, the Domino Server simply serves it up to the Web client just like any other HTTP server. Figure 9.1 shows the Domino Server architecture.

The Domino Server translates Notes constructs such as navigators, views, documents, and hotspots into HTML for display by the Web client. The Notes constructs enable your databases to provide all the things you expect to see in a Web application. The Domino Server translates all of

Lotus Internet Applications

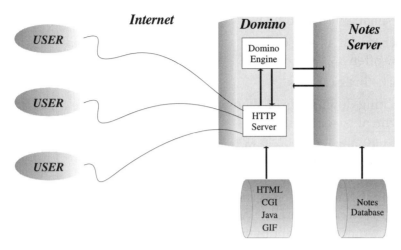

Figure 9.1 Domino Server architecture.

Notes constructs to HTML on the fly when the application is requested from the Web, as well as generating all necessary URLs for any links such as action buttons, hotspots, or navigators in the application. Thus, you can create your entire Website in Notes, without having to use any HTML tags whatsoever. All of your hypertext links are automatically maintained, so that checking your Website for disconnected links or links to deleted data is no longer required. You use Domino to translate and configure the application for use on the Web.

A Sample Registration Application

One way you can use the Domino Server and Lotus Notes together for a business solution is as a registration application to store registration information in the Notes database. You may want Web users to register themselves, entering details such as their name, e-mail address, and the company they work for, before they view dynamic, Web-enabled Notes documents. Once registered, each user can be assigned his or her own unique access, or part of a group access, to contribute to a discussion, submit a problem, order goods or software, or download software, for example. Many Website owners require you to register before you participate in any of those activities. They do this mainly for security reasons (allowing only registered users access to the data held on the site). They also use the registration information to carry out activities such as:

- Personalizing welcome messages
- User tracking—to see how many different people access the site and how often
- Marketing exercises
- Tracking downloads of shareware, so that they can be followed up for payment or registration
- Individualizing content and/or informing users of any changes made since they last visited the site

Alternatively, you can set up your database so that users have only to register to see certain areas, with anonymous access for others. For example, you would allow anonymous users to access the home page (otherwise, how will they know what they are registering for?) and possibly other read-only pages, but you would require them to register to download software or join in a discussion.

The Domino Website provides a sample registration application that you can download and configure to use on your own Website. The URL for the Domino Website is http://domino.lotus.com.

How the Application Works

You have to register to download the sample. The application asks you to enter details such as your name, username, and e-mail address and assigns you a random password, which you can change. The application then takes the information and, using a Notes agent, puts it into the Notes Public Address Book. (The application is already set up to do this, so you do not have to change it when you download it.) The next time you want to access any protected information, you are prompted to enter your username and password. Once you have entered them, the application checks whether the details match those stored in the Public Address Book. If the details match, you are allowed access. If they do not match, an *Authorization failed* panel appears, and you are asked to try again.

The registration application uses the Notes Default Value, Input Translation, and Input Validation field events. The Default Value event is used for creating a password in the password field. The Input Translation event is used to detect invalid input and, when used together with an @Failure formula, can generate a message if invalid input is detected. The Input Validation event is used together with @Failure and @Success formulas and a field called *$$Return,* which control the responses you get when you submit the registration form. You can see the full formulas when you look at the registration example.

You could run a custom CGI program when a user submits a form to further process the input data, as the Domino Server supports CGI. However, the Domino Server eliminates the need for many types of CGI programs that are required with a typical HTTP server, as you can set up field events and formulas in Notes, so you may find that you do not have to use CGI scripts with the Domino Server.

Installing the Domino Server

To install the Domino Server you need:

- Lotus Notes Version 4 or later running on Windows NT or Solaris. (Plans are underway to extend Domino to other platforms.) Lotus Notes 4.5 will have Domino as an integrated part of the server.
- A connection to a company LAN or Intranet that uses TCP/IP as a protocol.
- TCP/IP on the Notes server where the Domino Server resides.

If you plan to use Domino to manage an external Website, you will need an Internet connection through a leased-line or dialup connection to an Internet Service Provider. We also recommend that you have at least the following: 1GB disk drive; 64MB of RAM. Before you install the Domino Server, ensure that neither the Notes server nor Notes client is running.

You can currently download a trial version of the Domino Server free from the Domino Website (at http://domino.lotus.com). The software is distributed in a self-extracting executable file called DOMINO.EXE. When you run DOMINO.EXE, it extracts all installation files to a temporary directory and runs the setup program. All you have to do during the installation is confirm the location of both the Notes server directory and the Notes data directory.

Setting Up the Notes Application to Use the Domino Server

The Domino Server configuration settings are contained in a subform called *$HTTPServerFormSubform*. The Domino Server install program adds this subform to the Public Address Book (NAMES.NSF) and its associated template file (PUBNAMES.NTF). First you have to add a reference to this subform in your Server form in PUBNAMES.NTF:

1. Open PUBNAMES.NTF and select Design—Forms.
2. Double-click on the Server/Server form.
3. Move to the area where you want to insert the $HTTPServerFormSubform subform.
4. Select Create—Insert Subform.
5. Select the $HTTPServerFormSubform in the Insert Subform dialog box.
6. Save the form, then close it.

Next, add the HTTP Password field to the Person form:

1. Select File—Database Open and type HTTPCNF.NTF in the Open Database dialog box and add the icon to the workspace.
2. In HTTPCNF.NTF, go to the Design panel and select Design—Forms.
3. Highlight the HTTP Password field and select Edit—Copy.
4. Close HTTPCNF.NTF and remove it from the workspace (by selecting the icon on the workspace, and then either selecting Delete or clicking the right mouse button).
5. Open PUBNAMES.NTF and select Design—Forms.
6. Open the Person form, move to the Names section, and select the area where you want to paste the field.
7. Select Edit—Paste to paste the HTTP Password field into the form.
8. Add text to label the field.
9. Save the form, then close it.
10. Close PUBNAMES.NTF and remove it from the workspace.

To refresh the design of the Public Address Book:

1. Open the Public Address Book (NAMES.NSF).
2. Select File—Database—Refresh Design. In the dialog box, click on OK.
3. In the confirmation dialog, click on Yes.

Finally, edit and save the server document so that the new subform is recognized:

1. Open the Public Address Book (NAMES.NSF).
2. Open the server document.
3. Press CTRL-E to edit the document and move to the HTTP Server setting section.
4. If necessary, change any settings in the section. You will probably have to change the Hostname and the Home URL. The default Home URL opens an index (or view) of the Notes databases on your server. If you have a home page on the server, leave this field blank, and in the Welcome field, enter the file name of your home page (the URL will look something like dbasename.nsf?OpenDatabase).
5. Save the server document and close it.
6. Close the Public Address Book.

Note that if you want to create a home page, it should be an About page or a navigator, and you should create it in its own separate database. (The reasons for this are explained in the Access Control Lists subsection, below).

Initializing the Domino Server

You can either start the Domino Server manually or set it to start automatically when you start the Notes server. To start it manually, start the Notes server, and type *load http*. You will have to do this every time you restart the Notes server.

To start Domino automatically whenever the Notes server is started:

1. Using a text editor, open the NOTES.INI file.
2. Move to the ServerTasks= line and add the command *http*.
3. Save the file, then close it.

The next time you start the Notes server, and any time after that, Domino will start automatically.

If for any reason you want to stop the Domino Server, on the Notes server screen type *tell http quit*. If you are making changes to the HTTP ServerSubform in Notes while the Domino Server is running, you will have to stop and restart the Domino Server for it to take on these changes. Otherwise, you should not have to stop the Domino Server at all.

If you want to test that the Domino Server started successfully, start up a Web client and in the Location box enter the hostname of the machine that you specified in the server record (probably your machine). The Web client will bring up an index of all of the databases available through your Domino Server. If you have a home page that you want to be displayed when a Web user first accesses the database:

1. Open your home page, and open the Database properties box.
2. Select the Launch option.
3. In the On Database Open field, select the About document or navigator that you created as your home page. This selection will make your home page launch automatically when the database is opened.
4. Close the Database properties box.
5. Save the database and close it.
6. Open the server document and, if you have not done so previously, enter the name of the database containing your home page in the Home URL field of the HTTPServerSubform of the server document (in the Public Address Book).

Go back to your Web client and type in the hostname again. This time you should see your home page displayed first. If you already have the Domino Server running, you will have to stop it (by typing *tell http quit* on the Notes server command line) and then start it up again (by typing *load http*) for the changes to take effect.

Accessing Your HTML Files through Domino

As the Domino Server is a fully functional Web server, you can use Domino to display static HTML files to a Web client.

When you install the Domino Server, a folder is created in your Notes\Data directory called *Domino,* and within this directory is a subfolder called *html.* Put any HTML files that you want to be displayed on your Web client in this html folder. Domino can also interpret Java and Javascript files, so you should place any files containing Java or Javascript in this html folder.

If you open the HTTPServerSubform within your Public Address Book server form, in the Mapping section you will see an entry for HTML directory that points to this html folder. If Domino receives a request for an HTML document from a Web client, Domino looks for it in the html folder.

Domino does not impose any naming conventions on HTML files. The only conventions you have to be concerned with are those imposed by your operating system.

Domino does not convert HTML documents into Notes documents. For this conversion, you need a different Notes add-on called the *InterNotes Web navigator*, which can translate standard Web HTML 3.0 documents including forms, tables, photographs, graphics, hyperlinks, and URLs into Notes for management in Notes. (For more information about this particular add-on, see the Lotus Website at http://www.lotus.com/corpcomm/264e.htm.)

Note that you cannot use the Domino Server as an independent Web server without Notes, as it makes extensive use of the Notes server for performance and dynamic information storage.

Security and Access Control

The Domino Server enables you to open your Notes system to Web users while still protecting the information in a number of ways.

Registering Web Users

One way of protecting your information is to make Web users register themselves before they are allowed access to your database. To set up user authentication at the server, create Person documents in the Public Address Book and add HTTP passwords for all Web users who are allowed to access the Domino server. The Domino Website provides a sample registration application you can use. A registration form should at least include a username and a password. To connect the registration form to your home page, create a hotspot on your home page and add the following action to the hotspot: @Command([Compose];"formname") (replacing formname with the real name of the form). You do not have to design a Submit button, as the Domino Server automatically provides one for you on all forms. Be sure to put the registration application in its own database.

Once you have the registration application running, you can use it to register users, instead of going into the Public Address Book and creating

Person documents for them. Web users can then also use the application to register themselves from their Web client.

To transfer the information from the registration form to the Public Address Book, create a Notes agent. (An agent is already created for you in the Domino Server sample.) You can set the agent to run either manually, by selecting *Manually from actions menu,* or automatically, by selecting *If documents have been created or modified.* If you set the agent to run manually, when you want to run the agent, from a View of the Requests database, select Action-Handle requests, and the agent will run. Setting the agent to run manually enables you to view users' applications for registration before you accept them. If you set the agent to run automatically, users are registered more quickly, but you do not get to "screen" them before they are accepted; you can only delete them afterwards. The agent processes each request by adding the new name to the Public Address Book.

Once users have an entry in the Public Address Book, they will be prompted to enter their username and password when they attempt to access your database. If the username and password match the entry in the Public Address Book, users will be given access to the database. Users who are not in the Public Address Book will have to register before they can go any further.

Access Control Lists

You can control the type of access a Web user can have to your Notes database by setting up a Notes access control list. (You have to set up a list for each database on your server.) The types of access you can allocate are:

1. No Access—Users cannot access the database.
2. Depositor—Users can create documents, but they cannot see any documents in the database, even those they create.
3. Reader—Users can read documents but cannot create or edit them.
4. Author—Users can create documents and edit only the documents they create.
5. Editor—Users can create documents and edit all documents, including those created by others.
6. Manager—Users can perform all tasks for other access levels and modify access control list settings. You must give yourself Manager access. Notes requires at least one Manager for any database.

To make your database widely available to unregistered Web users, create an *Anonymous* entry in the database's access control list and assign the appropriate access. (For example, for your registration application, set Anonymous access to Author, so that the user can enter text into the fields; and for the home page, set Anonymous access to Reader.) To protect the database from anonymous users, set Anonymous to *No Access*. Remember that there is only one access control list per database. Therefore, to give users a different access level to your home page and the registration application, these applications must each be created in separate databases.

Secure Sockets Layer

To make your Website even more secure, add optional encryption to HTTP transactions by activating the SSL at the server. SSL administration must be carried out while working in Notes, at the Domino Web Server machine. When you install Domino, the install program adds a database called *Domino SSL Administration* to your server. Open up this database and follow the steps there to set up SSL on your Website.

Tailoring a Notes Database for Use on the Web

This section shows how to make a Notes Database function as a typical Website.

Home Pages

The first thing you must think about when putting your database up on the Web is having a home page. If you do not have a home page, the Web user will automatically be presented with a list of all databases on your server, which is not a viable alternative. For one, it is a particularly unattractive page from which to start, and you may not want users to see all the databases on your server. Users may need some sort of explanation as to what is in each database, and a home page is a good place to put this information. Create your home page as the About page of a database, or as a navigator, as these are the only parts of a database that you can choose to launch as the Welcome page.

When you design your home page, consider including a link to your registration application, as well as a direct link to your database (which may well be password protected).

Be aware that the Domino Server handles only one button per page. If you have more than one button on a single page, the Domino Server activates only the first button and ignores all of the others. Use hotspots or action bars to provide extra links on your page. Use forms to create documents with data input fields, and navigators to create image maps. All of these can be created by using the Notes Design Client.

Navigators

Navigators can be very user-friendly and attractive constructs to use on a Website. When creating graphics-based navigators for use on the Web, you must create a background bitmap. The Domino Server does not recognize other navigator drawing elements. To create a background bitmap:

1. Create a bitmap image in a graphics package that contains all of the visual elements you want to include.
2. Copy this image onto the clipboard.
3. Open a new navigator.
4. Select Create—Graphic Background.
5. Paste the image into the navigator.

You can then create hotspots on the image, and the Domino Server will be able to translate them.

Links between Pages

The Domino Server provides most index pages (the equivalent of Notes views) with *next* and *previous* links (along with *expand* and *collapse* options), but you have to provide your own links from database pages back to the menu pages or your home page. You may also want to provide links to associated entries, as the Domino Server does not provide them. You can create all of your links with hotspots and action bars within Notes.

A key benefit of Notes links is that they are based on the unique identifier of the object of the link. Ordinary HTML links are file based, so, if a file is renamed or moved, the link is broken. However, Notes links work even if you move the object to a different database, so they are much more stable.

External Links

With the Domino Server, you can include links from a Notes database to an external offsite link:

1. Open the page in your database where you want the link to appear.
2. Select the text or graphic that you want to act as the anchor for the link.
3. Select Create—Hotspot—Action Hotspot.
4. In the Definition panel, highlight the formula field.
5. Click on the Fields & Functions button and from within the panel select the @URLOpen() function.
6. Insert the URL of the page to which you want to link inside the parentheses, enclosing the URL in inverted commas.

The User Interface

When your Notes application is displayed in a Web client, its layout is very similar to, but not exactly the same as, when you view it directly in Notes. Provided that the Web user has not configured the font, type size, and other properties of the browser, the typefaces and graphics are the same (taking monitor size and resolution into account). When the Domino Server converts the information in a Notes database to HTML, it cannot preserve formatting features that HTML cannot display. Therefore, when you access the database from a Web client, features such as indentation, interline spacing, and tabs are different.

One of the biggest problems you may find is that different Web browsers treat pages differently. For example, when we tested our database on WebExplorer, the headings that appeared red in Notes (and in Netscape) appeared black, and all of the background colors were different. On one occasion, running the same browser on two different machines created different colored backgrounds! Forms are also displayed quite differently in different browsers from how they are displayed in Notes. If possible, test your application on many different Web browsers to see how each browser displays your documents. You will have to be very careful about the use of color.

Customizing Content

Underlying all Notes applications are formulas that can define the contents of documents and views and determine how data is displayed. You can tailor your Notes database to customize some of the content according to such factors as user identity, client type (that is, Notes or Web), and time, by using hide formulas. To base the content on user identity, the Web username and password must be authenticated, and you must create an entry for Anonymous in the access control list and assign *No access*. You specify hide formulas from within a Notes database in the Action properties box.

You can see an example of hide formulas in use in the Domino discussion database on the Domino Website (you can also download a sample of this application). The discussion database allows the authors of discussion topics to edit or delete their own entries, and the hide formulas hide the edit and delete options from any user who is not the author.

This type of tailoring is inherent in Notes. You should refer to your Notes manual for a more detailed description.

Text Searching

The Domino Server automatically creates a full text search facility for your database. For the text search facility to work properly, you have to ensure that your database has an index and that the index is up to date. The Domino Server cannot find recent entries that have not been indexed. Once you have created an index, you should be able to set up your database to update the index automatically. To update your index manually:

1. Open your database.
2. Select File—Database—Properties.
3. Click on the Full Text tab.
4. Click on Update index.

As the search facility is based on a database's index, it only searches the database you are viewing.

Using the Domino Server: Conclusion

Using the Domino Server and Notes together to create a Website has many advantages. The main advantage is that the information obtained from Notes through the Domino Server is dynamic. Another significant benefit is that you do not have to learn HTML to create a Website, nor do you have to know how to create a text search facility, as the Domino Server creates one automatically. Image maps are particularly simple to create by using Notes navigators and can be more attractive tools for navigating a Website than lots of buttons or text-based hotlinks. Perhaps the most important property of the Domino Server and Notes combination is that it enables you to allocate different types of access to different users for each individual database, thereby ensuring that security can be provided where required.

For more technical details about the Domino Server, visit the Domino Website at http://domino.lotus.com.

THE STRATEGIC DIRECTION FOR LOTUS INTERNET APPLICATIONS

Lotus will continue to build on the Domino platform, using the integrated server model to enhance the ability of Domino to address the broadest possible base of clients, and to give those clients maximum access to the server—including future versions of the Notes client.

Other Lotus Internet Applications will build on providing access from a Web browser to the Domino Server's application-creation functions, which will let independent solution providers offer point-and-click Website creation to their customers, as just one example. Domino and the Lotus Internet Applications are the starting point for a development path that will tie the functions and architectural strengths of Notes to the protocols and implementations of the Internet as quickly as identifiable standards emerge.

SECTION 4

Integrating Transaction Systems with the Internet

CHAPTER **10**

Transaction Processing Systems and the Internet

The principles of transaction processing software form the basis of major computer systems that run tasks on behalf of many users concurrently. Supporting many concurrent users is also one of the goals of commercial Internet and Intranet systems. In this chapter, we examine transaction processing software and compare it with the constructs of the Web. We also outline the general issues of integrating transaction processing systems with the Internet. In Chapters 11 and 12, we describe the products that can be used to access existing and new transaction processing applications from the Internet. The ideas in this chapter are assumed in Chapter 13, which examines electronic commerce on the Internet and compares it with traditional systems.

After reading this chapter, you will understand the main transaction processing principles and their role in building commercial computer systems for the Internet.

TRANSACTION PROCESSING BACKGROUND

Transaction processing software first appeared in the late 1960s and early 1970s to provide good environments for running interactive applications that support many users performing short, repetitive tasks with some degree of predictability and regular response time. These tasks typically read and occasionally update shared data. The same characteristics occur when building commercial software on the Internet. The way transaction processing software evolved over 30 years to provide an efficient programming runtime environment is similar to the way commercial Web-based systems have evolved over the last three years.

The first transaction processing applications included billing systems for public utilities, managing the components for spaceships, organizing the ingredients of hair shampoo and soft drinks, and payroll, banking, and insurance applications. Later the applications became even more diverse and included providing immediate access to the results of major sporting events, such as the Olympics, tracking parcels and trains, making airline reservations, recording lending library information, and managing patient and medication records in hospitals. Some of these systems are already available on the Internet.

In general, operating systems are not well suited for short, repetitive tasks. For example, the number of computer instructions required to initiate and terminate an operating system process that performs one of these short tasks is orders of magnitude greater than the number of computer instructions required to perform the task itself. Keeping the numbers of instructions low when executing applications on behalf of many users that access shared resources (files and databases) was one of the motivations for developing specialized transaction processing software that behaves like an operating system. The way transaction processing software creates its own operating environment within an operating system is analogous to the way that the Windows system runs within DOS. (However, transaction processing software is designed to support large numbers of users executing short, repetitive tasks whereas Windows is designed to support a single user performing multiple long-running tasks.) Web-based server software is also evolving in a similar way to transaction processing systems, to execute many short tasks efficiently.

Transaction processing software can give the end user the feeling of being in a "conversation" with an application, so that once some information has been entered, the application remembers it. Thus, the user should not have to retype information, for example, name and address, with respect to an application. Transaction processing systems include facilities to simulate conversations and maintain server-side state efficiently across user interactions. Similar techniques are also evolving in Web software to provide conversation support.

Examples of specialized transaction processing systems software include Encina, IMS, CICS, TPF (Transaction Processing Facility), Unikix, and Tuxedo, which provide an infrastructure to run and manage applications that access and update a variety of data types. It is possible to write transaction processing–style applications without using specialized software. However, if the data types are diverse and/or distributed, and the number of users is potentially very large and unpredictable, then development and administration effort is reduced when using specialized transaction-based software.

WHAT IS A TRANSACTION?

In the field of computing, the term *transaction* is used in a number of ways. Here are just a few of them:

- The execution of a collection of updates to files and/or databases with integrity, such that all updates in a transaction occur or do not occur. This is important in many business applications; for example, money must be removed from one account and placed in another account as a unit. It would be unacceptable if money were deducted from an account, and then, because of a system failure, it never arrived at the destination account. The most commonly used protocol for coordinating updates, known as *two-phase commit*, appeared in the mid 1970s a few years after the first commercial transaction processing software shipped (see Figure 10.1). The protocol involves having a third party, known as a transaction manager, mediate between the various resources being updated and the application program (rather like a lawyer; see Figure 10.2). In IBM's software products, the term *unit of recovery* or *logical unit of work* is often used to denote a transaction.
- The execution of an application that performs a business function, which typically accesses shared data (e.g., running a credit transaction).
- The application program or collection of application programs that performs a business function (e.g., an airline reservation transaction).

The fact that there are different interpretations of the word *transaction* can cause confusion. In this book, we use the term *unit of recovery* (UOR) to denote the formal all-or-nothing transaction as described in the first definition listed above. Database management systems usually support UORs

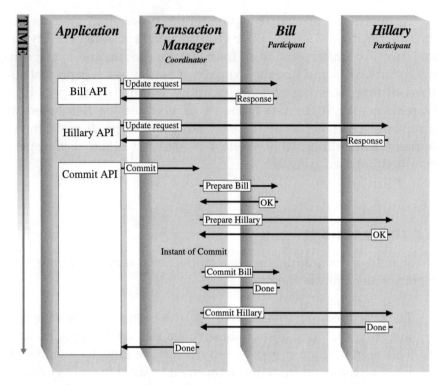

Figure 10.1 Two-phase commit—UOR successfully completed.

within and across databases of the same type (e.g., DB2 supports UORs across multiple DB2 databases). Transaction processing systems usually support units of recovery across multiple heterogeneous data sources (e.g., DB2 and Oracle).

MORE ON TRANSACTIONS AND UNITS OF RECOVERY

In Figure 10.1, the application program is transferring money from the Bill database to the Hillary database. While the updates are performed, *locks* are held on the modified data, preventing other users and programs from making changes to the same data concurrently. When the application program completes all necessary updates, it issues a commit request to the transaction manager to complete the UOR. The transaction manager proceeds with the first phase of two-phase commit and checks that the Bill and

Transaction Processing Systems and the Internet

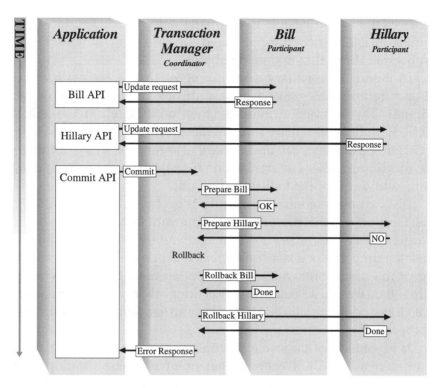

Figure 10.2 Two-phase commit—UOR failed and all updates removed.

Hillary database managers (the participants in this transaction) are agreeable, and they both reply *OK*. The transaction manager then commits the UOR by recording the fact externally on a disk log, just as a lawyer would record the completion of a transaction in a public document. The transaction manager then proceeds with the second phase of the two-phase commit, notifying the participants of the success of the UOR. At this point the participants remove any locks held on their data, enabling other applications and users to access to the modified data. After hearing from the participants a second time, the transaction manager then returns to the application, notifying it of the successful completion of the UOR.

When designing commercial applications, it is usually quite important to have short UORs, to avoid locking out data for considerable periods and preventing access. This is especially true if applications are maintaining total records that are updated in most UORs. These total records could become a significant bottleneck when long-running UORs execute, as no other UORs would be able to complete until the long-running UORs terminate. It is also necessary to avoid long-running UORs when building Web applications that update databases.

In Figure 10.2, Hillary does not agree to proceed with the UOR, so Hillary returns a negative response during the first phase of two-phase commit. The transaction manager then notifies Bill of the failure of the UOR. Both Bill and Hillary remove the effects of any updates in the failing UOR. If appropriate, Bill and Hillary also remove all locks they acquired for the failing UOR. The transaction manager then returns to the application, notifying it of the failure of the UOR.

The two-phase commit protocol has become quite elaborate. For example, there are various performance optimizations to reduce communication flows between the transaction manager and the participants and to reduce disk logging. The *in-doubt resynchronization* procedure governs the behavior of the participants and the transaction manager after system failures while the two-phase commit is executing. (For more information, please see Gray and Reuter, listed in the For Further Reference section at the end of this book.)

It is sometimes desirable to implement parts of systems by using an extension to the UOR concept that involves linking multiple UORs together. The linkage is usually achieved by updating well-defined sections of data consecutively or concurrently, with the goal of ensuring that all updates ultimately complete. Linked UORs are often required when updates cross company boundaries, for example, when transferring money from one account to another across two different banks, and where a single UOR is impractical (see Figure 10.3). Message queuing software such as IBM MQSeries is helpful in such cases.

In Figure 10.3, three participants are involved in UOR 1: CICS, SQL, and MQSeries, in the first bank. In addition, CICS also acts as the transaction manager. The first bank's application performs updates and writes the information to be transmitted to the second bank into an MQSeries queue (queue 1) which resides in the first bank's system. MQSeries itself then ships the information from queue 1 to queue 2, which resides in the second bank's system, in UOR 2. MQSeries ensures that the information appears in either queue 1 or 2, and is not lost while being transmitted across the network between the banks. In UOR 2, MQSeries is both the participant and the transaction manager, and it uses its own performance-optimized protocol as an alternative to two-phase commit. When the information appears in queue 2, an application at the second bank processes

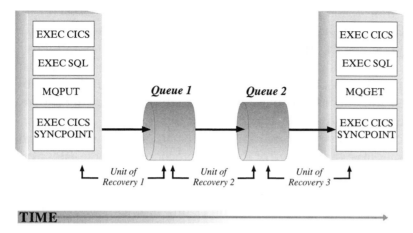

Figure 10.3 MQSeries—Three UORs to update two systems reliably.

it and updates its own databases in UOR 3. There could be some undesirable side effects if the whole operation were conducted as a single UOR instead of three UORs with MQSeries, for example, if locks were held on data in the first bank's system that the second bank wanted to access. MQSeries provides a reliable way of linking UORs, and supports heterogeneous systems, so the two banks' computer systems could be completely different.

WHAT IS CONVERSATIONAL PROGRAMMING?

It is often convenient for an interactive application to respond to a user's requests while remembering what the user said in earlier interactions. For example, when the user types in a password for authentication purposes, it would be very tedious if all systems were to repeatedly ask users to authenticate themselves on every interaction.

Systems avoid asking users for the same information by saving user input in the following places (often in combination):

- Long-term storage, such as a database, if the data (e.g., customer address) is required over a long period.
- Memory, if the information is required for a few user interactions. This type of information is usually known as *state*.

In transaction processing systems, the term *conversation* (or in the case of CICS, *pseudoconversation*) is used to denote the duration over which certain types of state information are stored on behalf of an individual user.

A conversation can also be used to maintain system state, usually for performance reasons (e.g., maintaining cursor positions in a database). The conversation avoids the overhead of opening up the connection to a database on consecutive user interactions.

Conversational (or pseudoconversational) programming is when the programmer takes advantage of the state mechanisms (or creates application-specific state functions) to maintain information about the end user.

Figure 10.4 illustrates some of the state mechanisms CICS provides for application programmers. For example, CICS creates the Common

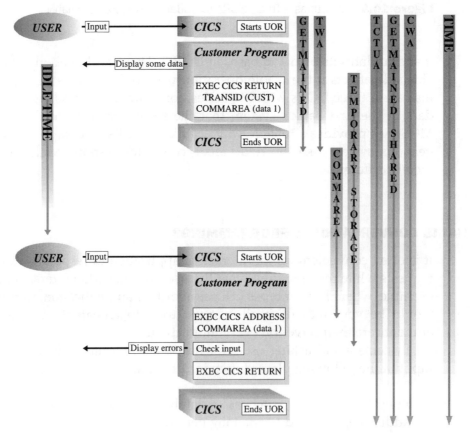

Figure 10.4 State management techniques for a CICS pseudoconversational application.

Work Area (CWA) as a global area that survives for the duration of the execution of the whole CICS system and can be used by application programs. Application programs can also acquire global memory themselves, using the *GETMAIN SHARED* command and the memory lasts until it is explicitly freed, or until the CICS system shuts down. The Terminal Control Table User Area (TCTUA) represents an entity in CICS called a terminal, which is created by CICS and is allocated to an individual user. The TCTUA survives across pseudoconversations. The Task Work Area (TWA) is created by CICS and can be used by application programs within an element of a pseudoconversation for an individual user. The same is true for *GETMAIN*ed memory, which the application program can acquire. The most popular CICS mechanisms for managing state across pseudoconversations are the Communications Area (COMMAREA) and Temporary Storage. Their use is described in more detail in conjunction with the CICS Web Interface and the CICS Gateway for Java in Chapter 11.

TRANSACTION PROCESSING FACILITIES

Transaction processing systems usually provide:

- Tools to help programmers design and write applications and user interfaces
- APIs for use in programs (e.g., for state, conversation, and UOR management); security checking
- A runtime environment for the programs
- Utilities to administer and audit the system

A number of the functions in a transaction processing system relate to performance. For example, system-level security checking, which can incur a high number of instructions, is often performed at the application level (e.g., a check to ensure that the individual user is allowed access to the overall application). The application itself then determines the appropriate subset of data a particular user can access.

The desirable functions of a transaction processing system include the ability to provide consistent response times, efficiency of execution, reliablity, data integrity, and support for large numbers of concurrent users.

EVOLUTION OF TRANSACTION PROCESSING SYSTEMS

When transaction processing systems were first developed, the user interface was typically a terminal device or terminal emulator, and the application ran (almost) completely at the server. More recently, transaction processing systems have evolved so that the *business logic* portion of the application that accesses and updates business data runs on the server system, whereas the *user interface logic* portion executes on the client user system. When designing such client/server applications, here are some issues to consider.

- Whether to write stateful or stateless server applications; in other words whether to store application state (e.g., user name and order number) totally on the client, totally on the server, or on both. Figure 10.5 shows an example of a client/server application where the state information is stored on the client.

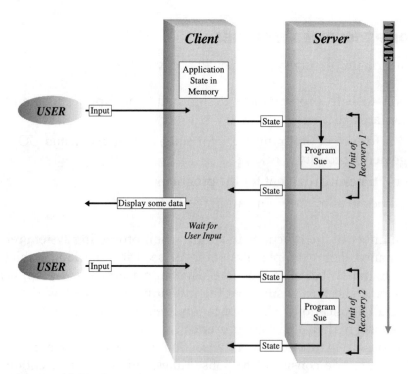

Figure 10.5 A stateless server application.

- Whether to accumulate user input gradually on the client for a particular application and then perform all corresponding database updates in a single invocation of the server or whether to perform the updates gradually, step by step, on the server on each user interaction.

The criteria for determining the best approach depend on the application type, the volume of input data, the number of interactions with the end user, and the importance of cross-checking the input with the up-to-date content of the database.

Thus, transaction processing systems have evolved from being the complete environment where the application executes to provide the infrastructure for the server portion of the application.

Many transaction processing systems have also incorporated object-oriented constructs to make it simpler to access the server programs from object-oriented clients and write object-oriented server applications.

Another trend in transaction processing systems is to support very large numbers of users by running the same application on multiple processors. This is achieved by incorporating workload balancing techniques to utilize the processors efficiently and allocate work to the least busy processors. To administer such an environment, systems management facilities have been introduced that enable a collection of systems to be managed as a single entity.

EVOLUTION OF WEB SERVER ENVIRONMENTS

Web servers provide many facilities, including serving a variety of static objects such as Java classes, images, and HTML files. They also offer the ability to execute application programs at the server (e.g., CGI or NSAPI programs), which take their input parameters from Web forms and produce HTML pages that they build dynamically. These programs typically access shared data such as indexes, files, and databases.

The functions that a Web server provides to run applications are similar to some of the functions that transaction processing systems provide. Both systems usually offer logging and auditing facilities to determine, for example, who has been accessing an application and the frequency of access.

In addition, some aspects of Web server evolution are similar to those of the evolution of transaction processing systems, except they have occurred over a much shorter period. Here are some examples:

- The introduction of long-running processes in Web servers and appropriate APIs for programmers, as an alternative to CGI, thus improving performance by eliminating the overhead of initiating and terminating a process on every request.
- The use of workload balancing techniques to deal with large numbers of concurrent users, as in the case of the Web server for the Atlanta Olympics. (See the Web Object Manager section in Chapter 13.)
- The introduction of client/server programming with Java applets in the client as an alternative to running the whole application on the server.
- The introduction of object-oriented Web server constructs, such as in the Java Jigsaw Web server from Conseil Européen pour la Recherche Nucleaire (CERN), where it is possible to write server applications in Java.

WEB SERVER AND TRANSACTION PROCESSING DIFFERENCES

In this section, we describe some of the areas where Web servers and transaction processing systems differ.

Many Web servers offer options to encrypt flows between browsers and servers because of the use of Web technology on public networks. This type of function traditionally has not been available in transaction processing systems because they have been used mainly within corporations. Where encryption has been available, it has been based on private rather than public key encryption.

Web servers are expected to provide reasonable support for dealing with large objects (multimedia), whereas this has not usually been a strength of transaction processing systems.

Some Web server configurations (proxies) offer caching support on the network. Typically, users in an organization access the Web through a proxy cache, which is physically located near the users (see Figure 10.6). Thus, many of the pages and multimedia objects that users access will be resolved locally by the proxy cache, assuming the users have common interests, without having to access remote Websites frequently. Proxy caching can improve performance considerably. The HTTP protocol makes it possible to ensure that versions of objects that have been cached are refreshed periodically. Proxy caching can be viewed as a form of on-demand replication.

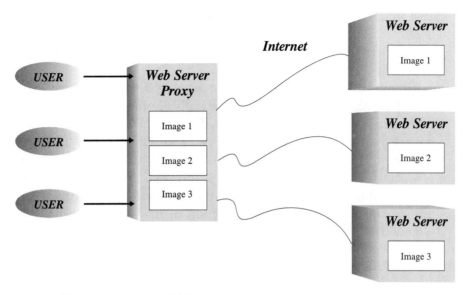

Figure 10.6 Proxy cache Web server.

In transaction processing and database systems, caching is usually performed near the data rather than near the users (see Figure 10.7) to improve the concurrency of accesses to the disk, which can become a bottleneck in high-volume systems.

Caching data on the client is an integral part of the Web. Thus, browsers typically offer a variety of configuration options to enable the end user to select the level of client caching (e.g., the number of images to be stored and the duration of the cache). This function has not been automatically avail-

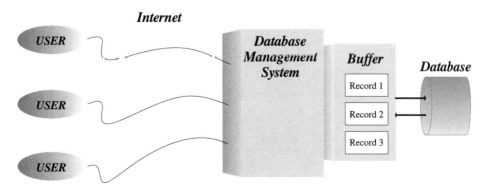

Figure 10.7 Caching in a database or transaction processing system.

able to transaction processing applications, although they can take advantage of the facility in Web clients when they use the browser as a client. Client-based caching can cause added complexity in conversation-based applications.

Replication is supported by database and transaction processing systems where updated data is automatically copied to another site to provide more efficient access at that site (see Figure 10.8). Web servers typically do not support automatic replication yet, although a number of major Websites are replicated around the world through specialized techniques.

Database replication techniques can take into account UOR commit scope, that is, that items are only replicated and only become visible at the remote site when the whole collection of updates in the UOR has completed at the local site. As Web servers do not support the UOR concept, this function is not available.

Web servers do not typically offer functions to help application programmers deal with application state across Web requests. Transaction processing systems do provide such facilities, in a variety of guises, such as the scratch-pad in IMS and the COMMAREA in CICS.

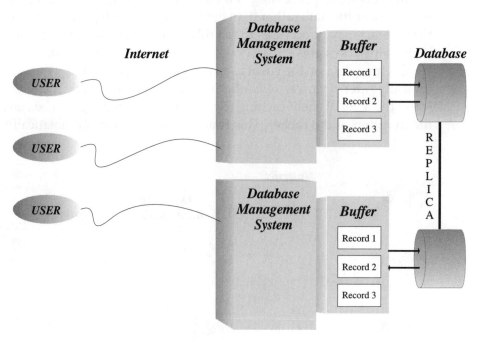

Figure 10.8 Database replication.

Web servers do not usually offer specific server-to-server support, other than through the server proxy mechanisms. Thus, HTTP is primarily a client-to-server protocol. Transaction processing systems have traditionally supported a variety of server-to-server communication mechanisms.

Web servers do not typically offer functions specifically intended to manage server applications, such as disallowing access at certain times. In addition, it is not always straightforward to manage multiple test and production environments, nor is it easy to manage applications distributed across multiple sites. Transaction processing systems have traditionally included such functions.

Web servers do not currently incorporate software to coordinate updates of distributed resources with integrity. Transaction processing systems have traditionally featured such functions, with two-phase commit coordination and its many variations, and performance optimization schemes.

Thus, Web servers have functions that support diverse data format access across a network through a simple and pleasant end-user interface, whereas transaction processing systems have functions that emphasize program execution efficiency and data integrity and consistency.

TRANSACTION PROCESSING AND THE WEB

Thus far we have shown that although Web servers and transaction processing software have completely different origins, they provide some overlapping functions. Transaction processing software can be used in combination with Web server software in various ways to support commercial Internet applications. Here are some examples:

- *Using a Web server adapted for transaction processing support.* The application server described in Chapter 14 illustrates such an approach in conjunction with a database management system and Net.Data.
- *Using a Web server together with a traditional transaction processing system.* This can be achieved using either a customized CGI or NSAPI program to perform the integration or specialized software such as the CICS Internet Gateway. Some of the earliest commercial systems on the Internet, such as the package tracking systems, used a customized approach to make an existing transaction processing application available on the Web.

- *Using a transaction processing system adapted to support Web protocols.* An example is the CICS Web Interface, where CICS itself responds to HTTP requests (see Figure 10.9). This facility makes it possible to write Web applications that support large numbers of concurrent users and interact directly with browsers. It provides a configuration that has fewer components to manage than a system that involves separate gateways. To overcome the problem that transaction processing systems are not well suited to managing large multimedia files, it is relatively straightforward to use a regular Web server to manage and deliver large static objects such as images, in conjunction with the CICS transaction processing system that has been adapted to support HTTP. For example, the HTML generated from a CICS application can refer to multimedia objects accessible from another server. In Chapter 11, we describe how to write CICS applications that respond directly to HTTP requests from browsers.

There are a number of issues to consider when using Web software and transaction processing software together, particularly in view of the overlapping functions in both types of systems. Here are just a few of the issues:

- *Which security functions to use:* As both Web servers and transaction processing systems include access control facilities, it is possible to select security elements from both systems (e.g., Web security for static multimedia objects, and transaction processing resource access security for

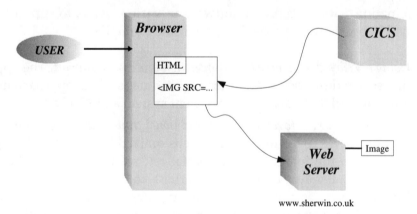

Figure 10.9 Static Web information held on a different server.

applications). Where an existing application is being made available on the Web, it may turn out to be simpler to use the existing transaction processing security control mechanisms. However, if the numbers and types of users of the application are going to change, it may be necessary to consider modifying the security checking.

- *Where to store application conversation state:* As both Web servers and transaction processing systems have techniques for managing state, it is possible to store application state in at least three places; the transaction processing system, the Web gateway, and the HTML page (in addition to using mechanisms such as Netscape cookies). It is generally simpler to use the minimum number of methods because synchronizing the state mechanisms can itself become a problem. For example, deleting the relevant conversation state in the various components can be difficult to do consistently, especially when failures occur. Each component may define the duration of a conversation differently, thereby causing inconsistencies.

In general, it is advisable to keep things as simple as possible, and concentrate on using the functions in one or two components. It can be difficult to predict the behavior of a system when related functions are used in different elements.

CONCLUSION

Transaction processing software emphasizes consistent response time, efficient execution, reliability, data integrity, and large numbers of concurrent users. Web-based software concentrates on ease of use and access, pleasant end-user interfaces, diverse data formats, and low initial startup costs. However, each type of software is trying to adopt some of the characteristics of the other.

Until a single integrated piece of software becomes available to support the desirable attributes of large-scale commercial Web applications, some combination of customized code and/or gateways will continue to be used in the immediate future, particularly for making legacy data and applications available on the Web.

CHAPTER 11

Accessing CICS Applications from the Internet

Today, more and more companies are looking to make their mainframe Customer Information Control System (CICS) applications and the data they manage available to Internet and Intranet users. Sometimes, however, it is inappropriate to migrate CICS applications to another environment because they form part of a well-established, integrated system that should not be disturbed. It is easier to access the applications through an Internet gateway or even to adapt them to communicate directly with Web browsers. In this chapter, we describe some of the ways you can access and use CICS from the Web.

We assume that as an application or system programmer you are familiar with CICS and have some understanding of the Web (having read the introductory chapters in this book). After reading this chapter, you will be able to identify the methods of accessing CICS applications across the Internet and select the most appropriate method for your applications.

CICS OVERVIEW

CICS is one of the earliest transaction processing systems. IBM introduced CICS in the late 1960s initially to support applications for public utility companies, literally for their customer information control systems. CICS has a large application programming interface (API) of about 100 verbs and replaces many of the regular operating system APIs for performance usability and failure handling reasons.

A CICS application is typically made up of many programs, screens, data layouts for work areas, queues, files, and databases. Associated with this collection may be one or more *transaction identifiers* or *transaction codes*. A transaction code consists of four characters that, when typed in, determine the name of the first application program to be executed.

Over the years, the CICS transaction code has accumulated many attributes, in addition to the name of the first program. Examples include security and execution priority. Thus it is often convenient to think of the transaction code as a grouping mechanism for a set of characteristics that can be associated with a CICS execution unit (or task) at runtime. Selecting and changing transaction codes at the appropriate times can be vital to achieving desirable behavior and performance characteristics in a CICS system.

Usually each user interaction causes a number of application programs to be executed within one CICS execution unit. A general recommendation is that CICS applications should be *pseudoconversational;* that is, the application should terminate instead of waiting for the human user to respond.

Pseudoconversational applications conserve computer resources such as memory and tasks. The application can name the transaction code to be used the next time the same user (or device) initiates work in that CICS system. The application can also save some context in a scratch pad or temporary work area, known as a communications area (COMMAREA) (see Figure 10.4). CICS presents the saved COMMAREA to the program associated with the next transaction code when it is initiated. In CICS terminology, a program that waits for a human to respond is called *conversational* (see Figure 11.1).

You will notice in Figure 11.1 that various resources, such as the Task Work Area (TWA) and the program itself, are preserved while the system and user are idle, whereas in pseudoconversational applications (see Figure 10.4) most resources are freed. In addition, you will notice that the conversational application program has to explicitly issue an EXEC CICS SYNCPOINT (a commit request) to terminate the UOR and free any data locks held. In pseudoconversational applications, CICS takes care of terminating UORs at the appropriate points.

Accessing CICS Applications from the Internet

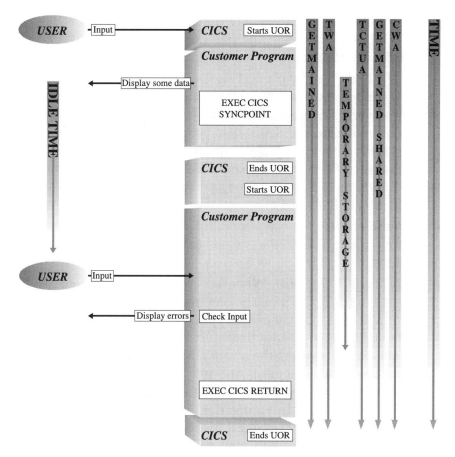

Figure 11.1 A conversational CICS application.

These are some of the main CICS APIs mentioned in this chapter:

- *Distributed program link (DPL).* The ability of a CICS program to invoke another CICS program across a network, without either program knowing that the other program is remote. Data conversion, for example, ASCII to EBCDIC, of the parameters is performed by CICS outside the application program. The local version of DPL is known as a *link*. Multiple DPL requests can be part of the same UOR as the calling program's UOR, or they can be in separate individual UORs when the SYNCONRETURN option is used. The calling program places its input parameters and receives its output parameters in a data area called a COMMAREA, not to be confused with the pseudoconversational

COMMAREA. The lifetime of the DPL COMMAREA is the lifetime of the DPL request itself. (The pseudoconversational COMMAREA lasts across requests, as illustrated in Figure 10.4.)

- *External call interface (ECI).* This is a call request to enable a non-CICS program to invoke a CICS program synchronously or asynchronously. The server CICS program does not know that the invocation is any different from a local or distributed program link nor whether the request is synchronous or asynchronous. Multiple invocations can be part of the same UOR or run in separate UORs. The calling program places its input parameters and receives its output parameters in a COMMAREA in a way similar to DPL.

- *External presentation interface (EPI).* This request enables non-CICS programs to simulate 3270 terminals to invoke existing unchanged applications.

- *SYNCPOINT (commit).* When an application terminates and returns control to CICS, CICS issues a commit request (a SYNCPOINT in CICS terminology) on behalf of the application. If the application itself issues a SYNCPOINT, CICS automatically begins another UOR for the application after processing the commit. Most CICS applications do not contain SYNCPOINT requests and rely on CICS to take care of recovery considerations. The main exception is CICS conversational applications, as illustrated in Figure 11.1. A CICS conversational application issues a SYNCPOINT request just before displaying data to users, to free data locks and allow concurrent access to retrieved and updated data while the user is idle.

In the rest of this chapter we describe several approaches to accessing CICS applications from the Web:

- *Using server-side programming:* a Web gateway with a Web server
  - A Web server with the CICS Internet Gateway for 3270 applications
  - The MVS/ESA Web server with a CGI sample for CICS
  - The Lotus Domino server with the CICS Gateway for Lotus
- *Using client-side programming:* the CICS Gateway for Java
- *Integrating the HTTP protocol:* the CICS Web Interface

The following are some general issues to consider for all of these approaches:

Accessing CICS Applications from the Internet

- The design guidelines for a CICS application that relate to performance still apply, whether the application is executed over the Internet or across an internal network. The CICS applications should continue to be pseudoconversational.

- The design guidelines for Web applications, as described in Chapter 4, still hold; for example, test hypertext links for their validity and avoid large images.

- If the number of potential users of your existing applications increases significantly, because you have made the applications available on the Internet or Intranet, you must consider all of the implications of such an increase on security mechanisms and administration as well as performance.

CICS INTERNET GATEWAY

The CICS Internet Gateway is one of the first software components to provide Web access to CICS applications in conjunction with a Web server and a CICS Client. It provides access to CICS 3270 applications. The software is available on OS/2, AIX, and Windows NT. Application programming is not required as the Gateway code provides automatic translation of 3270 datastreams to HTML. Program function keys, such as F5 and F6, which are common in 3270 applications, are simulated in HTML by using buttons or images (see Figure 11.2). The Gateway does not affect UORs and how they are handled in CICS. Thus, each user interaction causes one or more UORs to occur, just as in a regular CICS transaction. The CICS Internet Gateway supports both conversational and pseudoconversational applications.

How It Works

The CICS Internet Gateway is stateful CGI server software, as described in Chapter 5, that processes inbound forms requests from browsers. The requests reach the CICS Internet Gateway through a Web server and are then sent to access CICS applications (see Figure 11.3).

The Gateway translates the input into the appropriate CICS EPI request, which in turn is passed to the appropriate 3270 CICS application. The CICS application cannot detect that a Web browser is being used to access it. The application performs its usual processing; that is, it accesses

Figure 11.2 CICS Internet Gateway—3270 screen on an HTML page.

and updates data, creates output for the user, and commits the updates (completes the UOR). The Gateway takes the 3270 output from the application and turns it into HTML.

On the first request from a user, the Gateway asks CICS to create an entity called a *terminal*. The terminal is associated with the user's request and the sequence of requests that are to follow. On subsequent invocations,

Accessing CICS Applications from the Internet

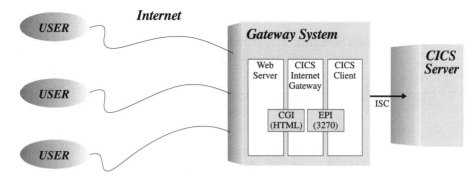

Figure 11.3 CICS Internet Gateway overview—accessing 3270 applications.

the Gateway detects that the request is part of a sequence that constitutes a session with the browser. A *browser session* can be made up of one or more conversations or pseudoconversations with CICS. The Gateway maintains operating system threads and memory to represent the request sequence and refers back to the original terminal in CICS on each subsequent user invocation. Eventually, the session with the browser is terminated (see Figure 11.4).

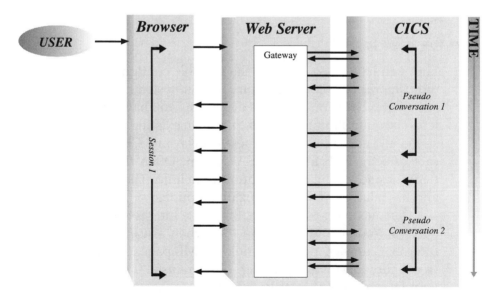

Figure 11.4 CICS Internet Gateway browser sessions and CICS pseudoconversations.

Configurations

As illustrated in Figure 11.3, the CICS Internet Gateway software runs on an intermediate server between the Web browser and the target CICS system (a three-tier configuration). The following are the options for the software running on the intermediate (second-tier) system:

- An OS/2 (or Windows NT) system (Web server, CICS Internet Gateway, and CICS Client) that communicates with a CICS for OS/2 (or CICS for Windows NT), which in turn routes the transactions to CICS/ESA or CICS/VSE system
- An OS/2 (or Windows NT) system (Web server, CICS Internet Gateway, and CICS Client) that communicates directly with a CICS/ESA or CICS/VSE system
- An AIX system (Web server, CICS Internet Gateway, and CICS Client) that communicates with a CICS/6000 system, which in turn routes the transactions to a CICS/ESA or CICS/VSE system

It is possible to use a two-tier configuration, for example, if the target CICS system is CICS for Windows NT or OS/2. In this case, the CICS Client and the CICS server would reside on the same computer.

What You Have to Do

First you have to select from the possible configurations listed above the most appropriate configuration for your system. In most cases, the initial selection is based on the types of systems you have installed. For example, it can be quite straightforward to take an existing OS/2 system with a Web server and add the CICS Internet Gateway and CICS Client that communicate directly with a CICS/ESA system. Often the most difficult part is defining and testing the communication links. The Gateway itself is simple and has relatively few customization options.

Your next step is to select the CICS Internet Gateway customization options. You should be aware that when a user first accesses the CICS Internet Gateway, a default initial HTML page, cigstart.htm, is displayed (see Figure 11.5 for an example). When reinstalling the CICS Internet Gateway, take care not to overwrite your customized cigstart.htm file.

It is possible for you to query the number of active users and various Gateway settings and turn the CICS Internet Gateway trace on and off from the Web. These are appropriate options for systems administrators.

Accessing CICS Applications from the Internet

Figure 11.5 An initial page for the CICS Internet Gateway.

You can also query the CICS systems that are available as well as initiate CICS transactions such as sign-on. These are suitable options for users. The list of CICS systems available is derived from the CICS Client initialization file, cicscli.ini, which includes all CICS systems that the client can access.

The CICS Internet Gateway customization options consist of two kinds of settings, default and override, as we describe next.

Default Settings

The default settings remain constant for the lifetime of a particular instance of the Gateway. Any changes in their values take effect only when the Gateway is restarted.

> *Cursor*—Cursor key equivalent
> *Error*—Error file name for the server
> *Info*—Information file name for the server (for AIX only)
> *MaxUsers*—Maximum number of concurrent Gateway users
> *TimeOutCICS*—Maximum time to wait for CICS to respond
> *TimeOutGateway*—Maximum time to wait for the Gateway daemon to respond
> *TimeOutInternet*—Maximum time to wait for the user to respond
> *Trace*—File name for the trace file for the server

Use the *Error, Info,* and *Trace* settings for logging and tracing.

Use the *Cursor* setting to define the character that will act as a 3270 datastream cursor. When information is being displayed from a CICS 3270 program, you can specify where the cursor should be positioned to make it more obvious to the user where to type in data. On completion of user input, the final location of the cursor, for example, row 5 column 7, is transmitted back in the 3270 datastream to the program. Because some CICS 3270 programs rely on knowing the cursor position, it is important for these applications that the cursor be simulated in the HTML pages and forms produced by the CICS Internet Gateway. The simulation is achieved by specifying a character to represent the cursor in the default settings. The user types the cursor character into the HTML form in the appropriate position (see Figure 11.6).

Use the *TimeOutInternet* setting to avoid consuming resources when users do not complete a sequence of requests in a CICS conversation or pseudoconversation. For example, if you set the option to five minutes, and the Gateway does not hear from a user who is in the middle of a sequence of requests (a browser session) for five minutes, it will notify CICS to delete the appropriate terminal. The Gateway itself will free any resources such as threads and memory that were dedicated to the sequence. Figure 11.7 shows the *TimeOutInternet* value as t1.

Use the *TimeOutCICS* setting when the Gateway does not hear from CICS in the specified period. In this case, the Gateway also frees up the resources associated with the request. Figure 11.7 shows the *TimeOutCICS*

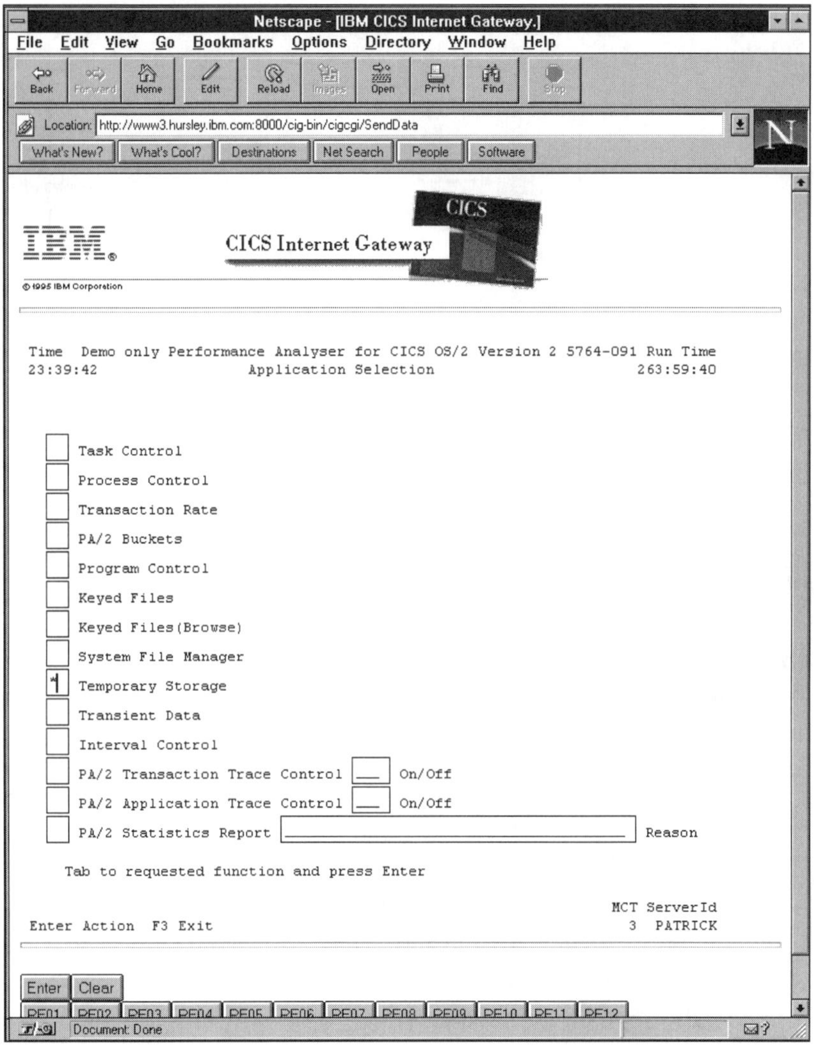

Accessing CICS Applications from the Internet

Figure 11.6 CICS Internet Gateway—3270 page with cursor simulation.

value as t2. The same behavior occurs when two of the Gateway components, the CGI program and the long-running process (the daemon), do not hear from one another other in the specified period, *TimeOutGateway*, during the execution of an individual user request.

MaxUsers specifies the maximum number of concurrent users of the Gateway. Users who access the Gateway when the maximum has been reached receive an error message from the Gateway.

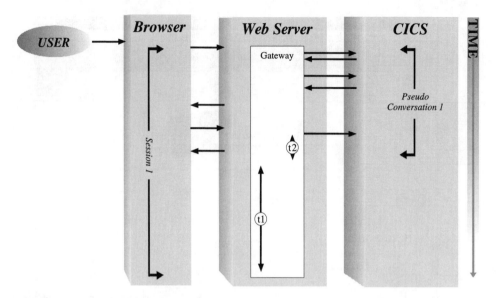

Figure 11.7 CICS Internet Gateway: t1=TimeoutInternet, t2=TimeoutCICS.

Override Settings

The override settings can change each time the transaction code associated with the CICS application changes.

```
AutoExit—Single transaction
ExitAid—Exit key equivalent
ExitPage—URL for the HTML exit page
GraphicKeys—Display the keys as GIFs
Header—File name for the HTML header
ImbedHTML—Allow embedded HTML
PAKeys—Display the PA keys
PFKey24—Display an extra row of PF keys
Trailer—File name for the HTML trailer
```

Most of these settings concern the visual aspects of representing a 3270 screen on an HTML page, such as the number of program function keys shown, or whether the generated pages should be customized with headers and footers. Examples of headers and footers include company logos and hypertext links to other pages and applications. Although the gener-

Accessing CICS Applications from the Internet

ated HTML looks different, no change is required to the CICS application that produces the 3270 datastream.

The *ImbedHTML* setting enables CICS applications to include HTML in the 3270 datastream, for example, in the CICS basic mapping support (BMS) map, and to cause the HTML to be interpreted and acted on by the Web browser (see Figure 11.8). When you set *ImbedHTML* to on, the CICS

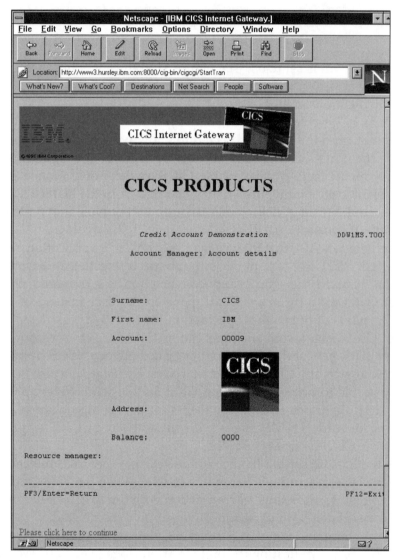

Figure 11.8 CICS Internet Gateway—using *ImbedHTML* set to on.

Internet Gateway does not modify the < and > characters (the HTML tag delimiters), and they reach the Web browser unchanged. The browser then interprets them as HTML tag delimiters. For example, setting *ImbedHTML* to *on* enables the inclusion of images in a CICS 3270 application on the Web. Thus, you can include HTML in a 3270 datastream, e.g.:

```
<img src=http://malaika.hursley.ibm.com/gifs/flowers.gif>
```

If *ImbedHTML* is set to *off,* (see Figure 11.9) the CICS Internet Gateway will modify any < or > characters in the 3270 datastream so they are displayed by the browser as < or >.

A blank 3270 screen is usually displayed at the end of a CICS pseudoconversation, and the user is expected to know what to do next, for example, type the next CICS transaction code. Of course, some systems include an initial menu listing all available CICS applications. Notice that the default blank page (see Figure 11.10) generated from the blank 3270 screen includes a quit button. Clicking on this button is equivalent to typing in the CICS sign-off transaction, CESF.

When you set *AutoExit* to on, each time the CICS application issues an EXEC CICS RETURN statement without specifying the next transaction code, that is, each time the pseudoconversation is terminated, the CICS Internet Gateway returns an HTML page to the user instead of a blank page. The name of the page is specified in the *ExitPage* parameter. Thus, a series of CICS pseudoconversations can be linked together through intermediate *ExitPages,* and users can navigate between CICS applications without knowing any CICS transaction codes. *ExitPage*s can also be used to make it simple to navigate between CICS and general Web applications. Figure 11.11 illustrates an *ExitPage* that is used to combine a presentation consisting of static HTML pages with invocations of CICS applications through the CICS Internet Gateway.

Use the *ExitAid* setting to specify the key that the CICS Internet Gateway should use to terminate a transaction (e.g., when the TimeOutInternet value expires). Terminating the transaction with the *ExitAid* key causes the terminal associated with a pseudoconversation to be deleted.

After customizing your CICS Internet Gateway, you can start using it to access CICS 3270 applications. Monitor various logs (e.g., your Web server logs) to anticipate any problems that may arise.

Accessing CICS Applications from the Internet

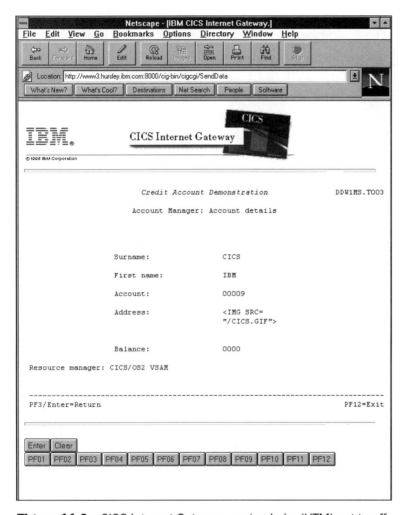

Figure 11.9 CICS Internet Gateway—using *ImbedHTML* set to off.

Initiation and Termination of Browser Sessions

A browser session is made up of one or more CICS conversational or pseudoconversational applications (see Figure 11.4). During a browser session with the CICS Internet Gateway, the Gateway maintains state information in the form of variables held in memory and operating systems threads for the user as follows:

Figure 11.10 CICS Internet Gateway—default blank page in a 3270 CICS system.

- *Browser session creation.* A browser session with the CICS Internet Gateway is initiated when a user starts his or her first CICS application (conversational or pseudoconversational) using the CICS Internet Gateway, usually from the initial page (see Figure 11.6). The first application is often the CICS sign-on transaction. At this point the CICS terminal is created.

- *Transmitting browser session state.* Browser session state remains in the Gateway component. When the Gateway creates a browser session, it also creates a session identifier and places it in a hidden field on every HTML page transmitted between the Gateway and the browser, until the session is terminated (see Web Forms Programming in Chapter 5). The Gateway also records the terminal identifier created by CICS when the Gateway first makes contact with CICS (using EPI) in a particular browser session. The Gateway includes that terminal identifier on all subsequent EPI requests until that browser session is terminated.

- *Terminating the browser session.* A browser session with the CICS Internet Gateway is terminated, and the corresponding CICS terminal is removed, when any of the following events occur:

Accessing CICS Applications from the Internet

Figure 11.11 A CICS Internet Gateway *ExitPage*.

- The *ExitAll* setting takes effect at the end of a pseudoconversation and the *ExitPage* is displayed (see Figure 11.11).
- The user presses the quit button (see Figure 11.10).
- The user uses the CICS sign-off transaction.
- Any of the time-out values expire (see Figure 11.7).

When the browser session with the Gateway is terminated, all state information in the Gateway for the user is deleted.

UORs

The CICS Internet Gateway does not affect UORs. If the application is pseudoconversational, the UOR will commit before the display of any application data in the browser. If the application is conversational, it is up to the application itself whether the UOR is committed before the display.

Security

With the CICS Internet Gateway, you can continue to rely on your existing CICS security mechanisms for authentication and access control. However, you may have to consider encryption for passwords and sensitive data. You can use the SSL functions of the Web server to encrypt the user input to the Gateway when it travels across the Internet.

You may also consider placing your Web server and CICS Internet Gateway system outside your firewall, if you want your CICS applications to be accessed by users over the Internet, illustrated in Figure 5.6. Your CICS system can remain behind the firewall.

Considerations

The Gateway is very suitable for proof of concept projects. It can be used to show Web access to existing CICS applications without much effort, particularly if the IBM Internet Connection server is installed on AIX or OS/2. In one Gateway project, users were able to run CICS applications written in the 1970s on the Web in a matter of days from the initial Gateway installation. (The source code for those CICS applications had been lost many years before.)

The CICS Internet Gateway does not require TCP/IP on the mainframe, as it communicates with CICS/ESA through an intermediate CICS system (either a client or a server or both), which in turns uses Systems Network Architecture (SNA) to communicate with CICS/ESA.

The CICS Internet Gateway cannot be used with non-CICS 3270 applications because it relies on some aspects of the behavior of the CICS Client. It cannot be used with applications that issue EXEC CICS START statements to the user's terminal. (EXEC CICS START is used as a way of changing the CICS transaction code while the CICS application executes and without dis-

Accessing CICS Applications from the Internet

turbing the user.) The CICS Internet Gateway cannot be used with applications that issue the EXEC CICS RETURN IMMEDIATE statement either.

THE MVS/ESA WEB SERVER CGI SAMPLE PROGRAM FOR CICS

The MVS/ESA Internet Connection Server (Web server) can be used in conjunction with a CGI program to access a mainframe CICS system. There are many ways for the CGI program to then invoke a CICS application, for example, it can use TCP/IP sockets, SNA conversations, or the External CICS Interface (EXCI); see Figure 11.12. The EXCI is similar to ECI in that it enables a non-CICS program to invoke a CICS program passing parameters in a COMMAREA. However, the EXCI can be used in a mainframe program only. It is always synchronous, and each invocation is a separate UOR. A sample CGI EXCI program is available at http://www.hursley.ibm.com/cics/txppacs/ca80.html. The sample program illustrates the CGI programming techniques needed to invoke a CICS application.

How It Works

The CGI program is invoked from a browser through the Web server. The CGI program can then call the appropriate CICS programs in accordance with the input data after creating a suitable COMMAREA. Multiple invocations of CICS applications are possible in one user interaction. (Each invocation is a separate UOR if EXCI is used.) The CGI program can shield the CICS application from understanding FORMS input and HTML, or it can pass on most of the parameters unchanged to the CICS program. In the former case we refer to the CICS application as *HTML-unaware,* and in the latter case, as *HTML-aware.*

Configurations

All components run on the mainframe system, including TCP/IP. You have to have MVS Open Edition 5.2 (or later) if you want to use IBM's MVS Web server.

What You Have to Do

Install an MVS Web server and have TCP/IP running on the mainframe. You can install the CICS EXCI CGI sample. Note that to use EXCI requires

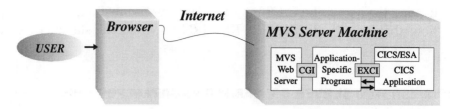

Figure 11.12 Using the CICS EXCI in a CGI program.

CICS/ESA 4.1 or higher. You will have to tailor the CGI sample program to suit your application.

Initiation and Termination of Browser Sessions

A browser session is made up of one or more CICS EXCI invocations. During a browser session, state information can be maintained in CICS, for example, in CICS temporary storage. If you require a stateful application, your CICS programs can manage the browser session identifiers and their transmission in hidden fields. You can use the techniques described in the CICS Web Interface section of this chapter (below) to store the state information in CICS temporary storage or getmained storage.

UORs

Each invocation of a CICS program through the EXCI is a separate UOR. The CICS program you invoke can itself call other CICS programs, possibly in remote CICS systems. The CICS programs will complete all their updates in a single UOR before returning to the CGI program, unless, for example, the CICS programs themselves use SYNCONRETURN, which commits portions of what would normally be a single UOR. You can invoke multiple CICS programs from a single invocation of the CGI program using multiple EXCI requests, but in this case each CICS program invocation will be a separate UOR.

Security

You can encrypt the flows between browsers and the IBM MVS Web server, as Version 2.1 of the server supports SSL. The EXCI request accepts a User ID (username) and password, so it is possible to ask the user to type in user information that would then be passed to CICS through the CGI program. CICS security checking would then be enforced. For example, a user-authorization check could be made, as well as further checks to ensure that the user is permitted to access files and programs, and so on.

Considerations

A CGI program that uses the EXCI is appropriate if you are running a Web server on the mainframe and require occasional access to mainframe CICS from the Web. The MVS Web server uses more mainframe resources than the CICS Web Interface (below), because the MVS Web server initiates a process (an address space in MVS terms) for each CGI request.

You cannot use the sample to invoke existing or new 3270 applications without processing the 3270 datastreams yourself, for example, by using the CICS Front End Programming Interface (FEPI) or by providing a new HTML-aware program that drives the business logic portion of the 3270 application.

USING THE LOTUS DOMINO SERVER TO ACCESS CICS

The Lotus Domino Web server, described in Chapter 9, can be used in conjunction with the CICS Gateway for Lotus Notes to access CICS applications from Web browsers. See Figure 11.13.

How It Works

The CICS Gateway for Lotus Notes is an interface that enables a Lotus Notes application to communicate with a CICS application and thus gain access to CICS data. The CICS application does not have to be altered in any way. It receives requests from Lotus Notes through the ECI just as it would receive requests from any other CICS Client. It processes the requests and returns the results to the client. The CICS Gateway for Lotus Notes supports both mobile and remote Lotus Notes users.

Considerations

This approach involves many components. The results of running the CICS application are returned asynchronously to the user, because Lotus Notes

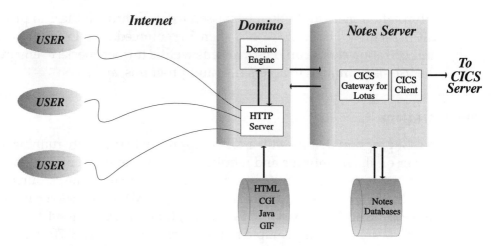

Figure 11.13 Using Lotus Domino to access CICS.

mail mechanisms are used in the CICS Gateway for Lotus Notes. Currently, this solution is suitable only for occasional access to CICS systems from Lotus Domino applications. With the Domino CGI support described in Chapter 9, improved integration between Domino and CICS is likely, giving access to both Lotus Notes and CICS applications and data from the Web.

THE CICS GATEWAY FOR JAVA

The CICS Gateway for Java enables Java applications and applets to invoke remote CICS applications across the Internet or Intranet through ECI requests. There are two main components:

- *The Client:* Runs on users' systems and supports ECI requests from local Java applets or applications which it sends to the Gateway component over TCP/IP. The client component for Java returns the ECI response from the Gateway back to the Java applet or application.
- *The Gateway:* Supports multiple concurrent ECI requests from Java Gateway clients and directs them to either a local CICS Client or server. The Gateway sends the responses from CICS back to the client.

Figure 11.14 illustrates the use of the CICS Gateway for Java in a three-tier environment.

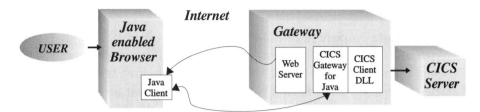

Figure 11.14 CICS Gateway for Java overview.

Just as with the CICS Internet Gateway, users of applications that access CICS programs over the Internet or Intranet through the CICS Gateway for Java do not have to install any CICS-specific software on their client systems. However, the user interface for applications that use the CICS Gateway for Java can be significantly better than that for CICS Internet Gateway applications (compare Figure 11.2 with Figures 6.4 and 11.15). The quality of the Java user interface depends on how the client application is written. The CICS Gateway for Java uses the client-side programming approach described in Chapter 6.

How It Works

The client component of the CICS Gateway for Java transmits requests across TCP/IP to the CICS Gateway for Java. The CICS Gateway for Java is multithreaded and supports concurrent users. There is no affinity between a thread and a user, as in the CICS Internet Gateway. The CICS Gateway for Java selects one of the threads to issue the ECI request to a local CICS Client or server system and returns the response to the CICS Client component for Java, using the same thread (if the request is synchronous).

All communication between the client and server components of the CICS Gateway for Java is through a protocol that is specific to the Gateway.

The initial prototype CICS Gateway for Java used communication flows that could be processed directly by a CICS server, eliminating the requirement for a Java Gateway alongside the CICS server. All that was required was a form of the traditional CICS Client written in Java that was downloaded when required. Having a Java Gateway on the server is a more flexible approach, enabling changes in the data that flows across the Internet or Intranet without modifying the CICS system itself to process new flows. For example, the Java classes for SSL can be used between the Java client component and the CICS Gateway for Java.

Configurations

The client component of the CICS Gateway for Java is in Java, and so will run in a Java-capable browser or any operating system with a JVM. The server component of the Gateway is written in Java with a small amount of platform specific code that issues the ECI request to the local CICS Client or CICS server. It can run on OS/2, AIX, and Windows NT.

As illustrated in Figure 11.14, the server component of the Gateway runs on an intermediate server between the Java client component and the target CICS system (a three-tier configuration). The following are the options for the software running on the intermediate (second-tier) system:

- An OS/2 (or Windows NT) system (Web server, CICS Gateway for Java, and CICS Client) that communicates with a CICS OS/2 (or CICS for Windows NT), which in turn sends DPL requests to a CICS/ESA or CICS/VSE system
- An OS/2 (or Windows NT) system (Web server, CICS Gateway for Java, and CICS Client) that communicates directly with a CICS/ESA or CICS/VSE system through DPL
- An AIX system (Web server, CICS Gateway for Java, and CICS Client) that communicates with a CICS/6000 system, which in turn sends DPL requests to a CICS/ESA or CICS/VSE system

It is possible to use a two-tier configuration, for example, if the target CICS system is CICS for Windows NT or OS/2. In this case, the CICS Client and the CICS server would reside on the same computer.

What You Have to Do

First, you have to select the most suitable configuration from those listed above. You install the CICS Gateway for Java on the same computer as your Web server that will be used to download the Client for the CICS Gateway for Java. The CICS Gateway for Java runs on port 2006 by default, but you can use any port number. You can run multiple Gateways on the same computer by using different port numbers. In addition, you install the CICS Client on the same computer, which should be configured to access the appropriate CICS servers.

Your next step is to write a Java client application that uses the client for the CICS Gateway for Java. Here is an example of how you might code the constructor (the Java creator) for the client object for the CICS Gateway for Java:

Accessing CICS Applications from the Internet

> **The constructor for an asynchronous call with callback requires:**
>
> ```
> ECIRequest eciRequest = new ECIRequest("hurcics", /* CICS server
> system      */
> "malaika",                  /* Userid          */
> "secret",                   /* Password        */
> "VERDI",                    /* CICS Program Name */
> "AIDA",                     /* CICS Transaction Code   */
> ECIRequest.ECI_ASYNC,       /* Call Type       */
> Commarea.length,            /* Communications Area Length */
> Commarea,                   /* Communications Area     */
> ECIRequest.ECI_NO_EXTEND,   /* Extend mode for UORs    */
> Msg_Qual,                   /* Message Qualifier */
> ECIRequest.ECI_LUW_NEW,     /* UOR Token       */
> calBack                     /* Callback        */);
> ```

Here is some more information about the parameters:

- *CICS server system.* The name of the CICS system to be accessed by the CICS Gateway for Java and which usually contains the CICS program to be executed.
- *Userid.* The User ID to be used by CICS to run the CICS program.
- *Password.* The password corresponding to the User ID. The Client transmits both the User ID and password without encryption to the CICS Gateway for Java.
- *CICS Program Name.* The name of the CICS program to be executed.
- *CICS Transaction Code.* The name of the transaction code to be associated with the CICS task running the program.
- *Call Type.* Specifies whether the request will be transmitted to the CICS Gateway for Java (and the CICS program will be executed) synchronously or asynchronously with respect to the client.
- *Communications Area Length.* The maximum of the lengths of the input and output communication areas.
- *Communications Area.* The area to contain the input and output parameters for the CICS program.
- *Extend mode for UORs.* If set, then this request is one of a series within a UOR. CICS supplies the UOR token in response to the first request within a series. On subsequent requests the client application sup-

plies the appropriate UOR token. On the final request in a series the client application does not set the extend mode parameter, causing the UOR to commit in CICS. Alternatively the client can set extend mode to rollback, causing all updates so far in the UOR to be rolled back (undone).

- *Message Qualifier.* Required if the client application uses polling to retrieve parameters from an asynchronous request.
- *UOR Token.* Also known as the Logical Unit of Work (LUW) token. Created and returned by CICS on the first CICS Gateway for Java invocation for a particular UOR. The client application must supply the UOR token on all subsequent requests to CICS for the same UOR.
- *Callback.* Determines the mechanism for returning the response from the CICS program in the case of an asynchronous invocation (polling or callback).

Here is an example of how your client application might invoke the CICS Gateway for Java in asynchronous mode:

```
try
    {
/* Open a connection to the Gateway. This constructor requires
the gateway and the port. */
        JavaGateway jgaTest = new JavaGateway("gateserv",
        2006);
/* Send the ECI Request. */
        jgaTest.flow(eciRequest);
/* Close the Gateway connection. */
        jgaTest.close();
    }
    catch (IOException e)
    {
        GatewayTrace.traceln("Caught Exception: " + e);
    }
    return;
    }
}
/* Callback class. */
class TestCallback implements Callbackable
```

(continued)

Accessing CICS Applications from the Internet

```
{
   ECIRequest eciResults = null;
   public TestCallback
   public void setResults(GatewayRequest gatReply)
   {
   eciResults = (ECIRequest) gatReply;
      }
   public void run()
   {
   /*Use eciResults*/
      }
}
```

As illustrated in the example above, your first step is to open a connection to the Gateway. You can omit the Gateway port number, which defaults to 2006. You then send any number of ECI requests. Finally you terminate the connection to the gateway. The example also illustrates how you code a callback routine to process the output from asynchronous requests.

The classes that give your Java application access to a CICS server are downloaded from a Web server to your user's Java-enabled browser. The Java application itself can also be downloaded as an applet. Here is an example of the HTML you would use to download your application applet class, which in turn would download the other classes it requires:

For testing purposes, it may be more convenient to use the Java applet viewer instead of a Java-enabled browser.

```
<applet codebase="../classes"
code="ibm.cics.jgate.demo.CatalogueView" width=608 height=341>
<param name=server value=documentbase>
<!-- set to "documentbase", "codebase" or to the host to
connect to --!>
<blockquote><hr><em>
Sorry, you're viewing this page with a browser that doesn't
understand the APPLET tag.
</em><hr></blockquote></applet>
```

Initiation and Termination of Browser Sessions

A browser session is made up of one or more CICS ECI invocations that constitute a single UOR. During a browser session with the CICS Gateway for Java, the Gateway maintains state information in the form of variables held in memory as follows:

- *Browser session creation.* A browser session with the CICS Gateway for Java is initiated when the first (or only) ECI request within a UOR is requested from the CICS client for Java. The Gateway invokes the appropriate CICS program and CICS returns the newly created UOR (LUW) token that represents the browser session.
- *Transmitting browser session state.* The browser session state remains in the gateway. The CICS UOR (LUW) token is transmitted between the client component and the gateway as part of the explicit ECI parameters.
- *Terminating the browser session.* A browser session with the CICS Gateway for Java is terminated, and the corresponding CICS UOR is committed, when the Gateway:
    - Responds to a client's ECI no extend mode request
    - Responds to a client's ECI commit or rollback request
    - Detects a time out and sends an ECI rollback request to the CICS program

When the browser session with the Gateway is terminated, all state information in the Gateway for the user is deleted.

UORs

Each ECI request can be a separate UOR, or a sequence of ECI requests can constitute a UOR. The CICS program invoked by the ECI can itself invoke other local or remote CICS programs whose updates will all be committed when the response to the final (or only) ECI request in the browser session is returned.

Security

With the most prevalent browsers today, a default restriction known as *host applet security level* applies. The Java applets (the client code in this case) can communicate only with software that resides on the same machine as the Web server that manages the applet. This restriction will diminish as trusted sites that supply Java applets become more common. The security restriction implies that the CICS Gateway for Java must reside on the same system as the Web server from which the client component of the CICS Gateway for Java was downloaded.

You can continue to use CICS facilities for user authorization and access control noting that the User ID and password are transmitted between the Client for Java and the CICS Gateway for Java without encryption.

Considerations

The performance of the CICS Gateway for Java is better than the CICS Internet Gateway because the Java Gateway is multithreaded and does not initiate a process on every request, in contrast with Web server CGI programs. There are limits on the number of threads in a process. For example, on AIX the limit is 512, which in turn imposes a limit on the maximum number of concurrent users of the CICS Gateway for Java.

The CICS Gateway for Java also supports unchanged 3270 applications. However, the CICS Gateway for Java does make it possible to provide significantly better user interfaces for CICS applications, without expecting users to install software that is specific to CICS (see Figure 11.15).

THE CICS WEB INTERFACE

The CICS Web Interface enables mainframe CICS application programs to communicate directly with Web browsers without an intermediate gateway or a separate Web server (see Figure 11.16). CICS itself supports HTTP. When a user selects the CICS Web Interface URL from a browser, the request is sent to CICS through HTTP. CICS determines the appropriate application to run from the URL. The CICS applications are invoked by using the CICS LINK interface, and any forms variables are placed in the input COMMAREA with the HTTP header information. After processing the input, the CICS application builds an HTML page as output and puts it in the output COMMAREA, which CICS then returns to the user's browser through HTTP.

The CICS Web Interface supports ASCII to EBCDIC data conversion as well as an HTML template mechanism. Encryption, such as SSL, is not currently supported in the CICS Web Interface but can be used in conjunction with a Web server proxy.

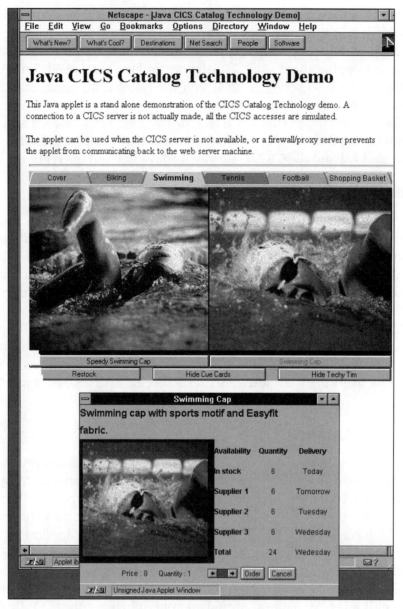

Figure 11.15 CICS Java Gateway sample application.

Accessing CICS Applications from the Internet

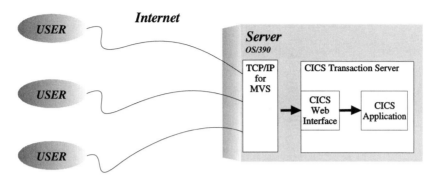

Figure 11.16 CICS Web Interface overview.

How It Works

The CICS Web Interface is initiated when an administrator uses the CICS-supplied transaction known as the *Connection Manager* (CWBC). The Connection Manager starts a long-running CICS transaction called the *Server Controller* (CWBM), which monitors inbound TCP/IP requests, such as HTTP requests, and routes them to the appropriate CICS applications to be processed. Only one instance of the Server Controller can be running in any given CICS system at a time. It is possible to initiate the Server Controller automatically at CICS system startup by placing the name of the Server Controller program in the CICS Program List Table.

For each inbound TCP/IP request, the Server Controller starts an *Alias Transaction* (CWBA) using an EXEC CICS START command (see Figure 11.17). The Alias Transaction initiates the *Alias Program*, which in turn issues an EXEC LINK CICS request to invoke the CICS application that will process the user's input.

Running all HTTP server applications in CICS using the CWBA transaction code may be unsatisfactory because specific performance tuning and access control checks by application may be required. It is possible to define application-specific transaction codes to run the Alias Transaction, by tailoring the *Analyzer* (see below) user-replaceable module.

Before the Alias Transaction invokes the CICS application, two CICS user-replaceable modules are called through EXEC CICS LINK (see Figure 11.17):

- *The Analyzer (compulsory)*. This program receives the HTTP input request and determines the CICS application program, converter, trans-

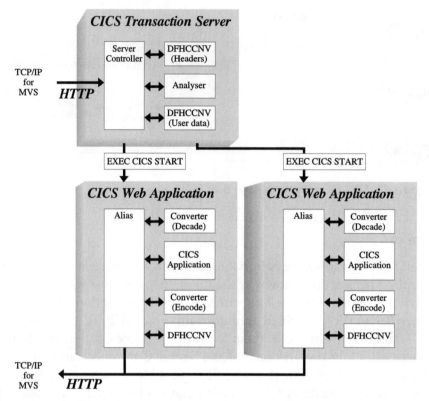

Figure 11.17 CICS Web Interface application structure.

action code and User ID for the Alias Transaction, and the code page data conversion to be used. There is one Analyzer module for the whole CICS system, and it is always invoked by the Server Controller.

- *The Converter (optional).* The *Decode* function in this program receives the output from the Analyzer and prepares the input COMMAREA for the CICS application program using the HTTP header and Web forms input formats. The Decode function also supplies lengths of input data. The *Encode* function takes the output COMMAREA for the CICS application program and converts it to a suitable HTTP response format. There can be many application-specific Converters in a CICS system, and they are invoked by the Alias Transaction. See "CICS Web Interface Sample Converter in C" at the end of this chapter for an example (see Figure 11.19 for the corresponding application).

When the input information is in ASCII, that is, when the user's browser is not running on a mainframe, the server controller invokes a standard CICS program called DFHCCNV to convert the HTTP header data from ASCII to EBCDIC. The Alias Transaction invokes DFHCCNV again after running the Analyzer to convert the user data (e.g., the forms input) in the HTTP request.

Eventually the CICS application program is invoked. It parses the content of the COMMAREA prepared by the Converter, processes it, and builds an output HTML page. A number of utilities are supplied to help the application program perform its processing. They are described in the What You Have to Do subsection below.

As the CICS system supports HTTP, a simple URL such as:

```
http://www.mycompany.com/
```

can lead directly to the CICS system. The default supplied Analyzer interprets the URL path to determine the Converter name, Alias Transaction code, the application program name, and the browser session identifier as follows:

```
/converter-program-name/alias-transaction-code/application-
program-name?session-identifier
```

By modifying the Analyzer, it is possible to adopt different naming structures in the URL.

Configurations

The CICS Web Interface is part of the CICS Transaction Server for OS/390 Release1. It is also available as a feature for CICS/ESA 4.1. TCP/IP is required on your MVS system to use the CICS Web Interface. Thus, you need a mainframe computer, without any intermediate gateway systems, as browsers communicate directly with your mainframe CICS system. You can choose to have a proxy server or firewall between the browsers and your CICS system (see Figures 11.20 and 11.21).

What You Have to Do

You can either install the CICS/ESA 4.1 Web Interface feature or the CICS Transaction Server. You should then configure the CICS Web Interface by updating the CICS Web Interface data set using the Connection Manager transaction. Options you can specify include:

> *Trace*—CICS Web Interface tracing activity
>
> *Trace Level*—The level of detail for the trace
>
> *CWBM Userid*—The CICS User ID for the server controller
>
> *Analyzer Program*—Program name for the server controller to use to analyze inbound requests
>
> *Automatic Enable*—If set, the interface is enabled using the values in the CICS Web Interface data set by typing CWBC (the Connection Manager transaction code)
>
> *TCP/IP port number*—The number for inbound HTTP requests (default 80)
>
> *Backlog*—The maximum number of unprocessed requests queued by TCP/IP for MVS. Further requests are rejected. The default is 5.

You should also define the resources used by the CICS Web Interface to your CICS system, for example, the transactions and user-replaceable modules.

Writing Your CICS Application Programs

Your first step is to decide whether your CICS application programs should be aware of HTTP, HTML, browser session management, and CICS conversation management, or whether to isolate these functions in the Converter module. In this section, we assume that you will isolate the functions in the Converter (or Analyzer) module, but most of the descriptions apply even if you do not separate the functions. (The 370 assembler sample at the end of this chapter illustrates how HTML and HTTP can all be managed within the application program bypassing the Converter.)

A CICS environment program has been introduced called DFHW-BENV, which the Converter (or CICS application program) can invoke to determine the contents of the HTTP header. The Converter can use the CICS Web Interface HTML Template Manager, DFHWBTL. The templates are held in an MVS partitioned data set and each template is made up of HTML and a set of symbols which are denoted by the character &. Here is an example of an HTML template that incorporates the values of the environment variable (see Figure 11.18 for the browser display that corresponds to the template):

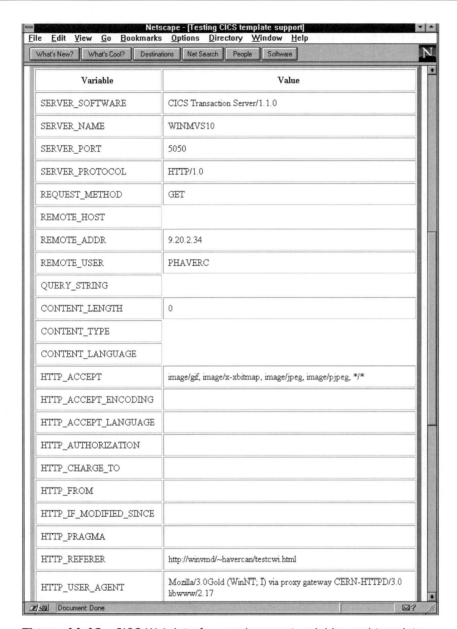

Figure 11.18 CICS Web Interface environment variables and templates.

```
h4>Environment variables</h4>
<p>With the environment variables program, you can define
environment variables as symbols:
<table border="8" cellpadding="8">
<tr><th>Variable</th>                   <th>Value</th></tr>
<tr><td>SERVER_SOFTWARE</td>            <td>&SERVER_SOFTWARE;
</td></tr>
<tr><td>SERVER_NAME</td>                <td>&SERVER_NAME;
</td></tr>
<tr><td>SERVER_PORT</td>                <td>&SERVER_PORT;
</td></tr>
<tr><td>SERVER_PROTOCOL</td>            <td>&SERVER_PROTOCOL;
</td></tr>
<tr><td>REQUEST_METHOD</td>             <td>&REQUEST_METHOD;
</td></tr>
<tr><td>REMOTE_HOST</td>                <td>&REMOTE_HOST;
</td></tr>
<tr><td>REMOTE_ADDR</td>                <td>&REMOTE_ADDR;
</td></tr>
<tr><td>REMOTE_USER</td>                <td>&REMOTE_USER;
</td></tr>
<tr><td>QUERY_STRING</td>               <td>&QUERY_STRING;
</td></tr>
<tr><td>CONTENT_LENGTH</td>             <td>&CONTENT_LENGTH;
</td></tr>
<tr><td>CONTENT_TYPE</td>               <td>&CONTENT_TYPE;
</td></tr>
<tr><td>CONTENT_LANGUAGE</td>           <td>&CONTENT_LANGUAGE;
</td></tr>
<tr><td>HTTP_ACCEPT</td></td>           <td>&HTTP_ACCEPT;
</td></tr>
<tr><td>HTTP_ACCEPT_ENCODING</td><td>&HTTP_ACCEPT_ENCODING;
<br></td></tr>
<tr><td>HTTP_ACCEPT_LANGUAGE</td><td>&HTTP_ACCEPT_LANGUAGE;
<br></td></tr>
<tr><td>HTTP_AUTHORIZATION</td>         <td>&HTTP_AUTHORIZATION;
<br></td></tr>
<tr><td>HTTP_CHARGE_TO</td>             <td>&HTTP_CHARGE_TO;
<br></td></tr>
<tr><td>HTTP_FROM</td>                  <td>&HTTP_FROM;
<br></td></tr>
```

(continued)

```
<tr><td>HTTP_IF_MODIFIED_SINCE</td><td>&HTTP_IF_MODIFIED_SINCE;
<br></td></tr>
<tr><td>HTTP_PRAGMA</td>           <td>&HTTP_PRAGMA;
<<br></td></tr>
<tr><td>HTTP_REFERER</td>          <td>&HTTP_REFERER;
<br></td></tr>
<tr><td>HTTP_USER_AGENT</td>       <td>&HTTP_USER_AGENT;
</table>
```

The HTML Template Manager, which is linked to the Converter, substitutes each of the symbols in the predefined HTML at runtime. The Converter can construct a single output HTML page by concatenating a number of HTML templates together. To concatenate the templates, the Converter invokes DFHWBTL multiple times. The actual values of the set of symbols in a collection of HTML templates used by a particular Converter to construct a single output HTML page is called a *symbol table*.

DFHWBTL can be invoked in a number of ways by specifying the appropriate function in the COMMAREA. The following table describes the functions.

> *BUILD_HTML_PAGE.* Combines the functions of START_HTML_PAGE, ADD_HTML_TEMPLATE and END_HTML_PAGE.
>
> *START_HTML_PAGE.* Establishes an environment for the next three functions, and allows the program to place values in the symbol table.
>
> *ADD_HTML_SYMBOLS.* Adds symbols to the symbol table. It also modifies the values of symbols already defined in the symbol table.
>
> *ADD_HTML_TEMPLATE.* Adds a template to the HTML page, replacing symbols in the template with the values defined in the symbol table.
>
> *END_HTML_PAGE.* Destroys the environment established in START_HTML_PAGE.

At the end of this chapter, there is a 370 assembler program that accesses the environment variables and places them in the HTML template listed above. Notice that it uses a templates held in the program itself, rather than in separate files. It also refers to RGB values as described in Chapter 4. See Figure 11.19 for a another sample CICS Web Interface application.

Figure 11.19 CICS Web Interface sample application.

Initiation and Termination of Browser Sessions

An Analyzer, a Converter, or a CICS application program can use one of two sample programs to manage a browser session (as described in Chapter 5) by passing the browser session identifier:

- in hidden fields in HTML forms
- in the URL query field in HTML forms or hyperlinks

The sample programs to maintain browser session state in the CICS system are:

- DFH$WBST, which uses CICS GETMAIN and FREEMAIN requests to manage the session state in memory

- DFH$WBSR, which uses CICS temporary storage records to maintain the session state

These session management programs include the following functions:

> - *Create new token*
> - *Store state associated with a previously created token*
> - *Retrieve state previously associated with a token*
> - *Invalidate a token and destroy all associated state*

You can use the:

- Analyzer to maintain browser session state, which lasts for the duration of a user sign-on and sign-off session. The session identifier can be transmitted in the URL.
- Converter to maintain the browser session state or the application conversation state (they can be identical in this case). The session identifier can be transmitted in forms hidden fields.

Here is a description of how the Converter can be used (the description for the Analyzer is very similar):

- *Browser session creation.* A browser session with the CICS Web Interface is started when a user invokes his or her first CICS program, usually from the initial page for the CICS Web Interface. The first program is a CICS sign-on program. During the first user interaction your Converter Encode routine invokes the *create new token* function (to create a new browser session token), followed by the *store state* function (to preserve any session state on the server). In addition, it places the browser session identifier in a hidden field in the output HTML page.
- *Transmitting browser session state.* The browser session state remains in the CICS transaction server, in memory or temporary storage depending on whether DFH$WBST (memory) or DFH$WBSR (temporary storage) is used. The browser session identifier is transmitted between the browser and the CICS transaction server in hidden fields.

In intermediate user invocations (neither the first nor the last), your Converter Decode routine invokes the *retrieve state* function using the browser session identifier. Your Converter Encode routine uses the *store state* function (to preserve any session state on the server). In addition, it places the browser session identifier in a hidden field in the output HTML page, as in the first invocation.

- *Terminating the browser session.* A browser session with the CICS Web Interface is terminated when the Converter issues the *invalidate token* request, which also destroys all associated state. The sample programs provide a timeout mechanism to destroy state information that has not been used for a given period.

UORs

Each user invocation of the CICS Web Interface runs in a separate UOR, which can encompass a number of CICS applications across multiple systems (because the invoked program can call other programs). All updates are committed before returning the response to the browser. It is not possible for a UOR to consist of a number of user requests.

Security

The CICS Web Interface does not support SSL, however it is possible to use SSL with CICS Web Interface applications by installing a proxy server that supports SSL alongside the CICS system (on any platform, including MVS). The proxy server could then forward the HTTP requests to the CICS system, having decrypted the information (see Figure 11.20). It is also possible to use the CICS Web Interface in conjunction with a firewall. (see Figure 11.21). You can continue to use the CICS functions for authorization and access control.

Considerations

This support requires CICS/ESA 4.1 or greater, and it requires TCP/IP on MVS. When initiating multiple CICS systems concurrently on a single MVS image, all running the CICS Web Interface applications directly, then it is necessary to use different TCP/IP port numbers. This is the usual approach when running multiple Web servers on a single system.

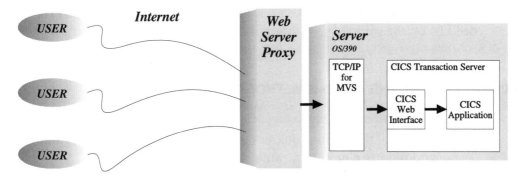

Figure 11.20 The CICS Web Interface with a Web server proxy.

The CICS Web Interface can be used to process non-HTTP TCP/IP requests by making appropriate modifications in the Analyzer module.

Currently, the CICS Web Interface does not support unchanged 3270 Web applications. It is necessary to write a FEPI program to invoke 3270 applications from the CICS Web Interface.

The maximum size of a CICS COMMAREA is under 32KB, thus it is necessary to have a separate Web server to serve images (and other multi-

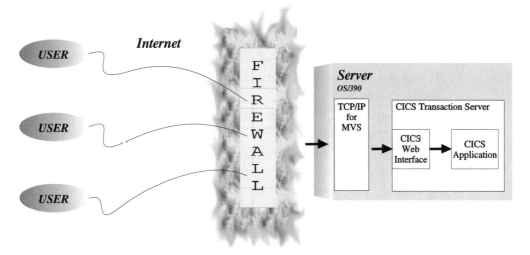

Figure 11.21 CICS Web Interface with a firewall.

media objects) for the CICS Web applications to use. Of course, that server could be on the same MVS system or on a different system.

CHOOSING AMONG THE ACCESS METHODS

1. *Use a customized gateway (as described in Chapter 5)*
   - If none of the options below satisfy your requirements; for example you require a nonmainframe, non-Java-based Gateway
2. *Use the CICS Internet Gateway*
   - If you want to proceed with simple proof of concept projects
   - If you and your users are content with a 3270 interface on the Web
   - If you do not require a high-performance solution
   - If you do not run TCP/IP on your mainframe
3. *Use the MVS Web server CGI sample for CICS*
   - If you are running an MVS Web server
   - If you require occasional access to CICS applications from Web browsers
   - If you do not require a high-volume solution
4. *Use the CICS Gateway for Java*
   - If you require a sophisticated user interface
   - If you are writing new CICS applications
   - If you do not run TCP/IP on your mainframe
5. *Use the CICS Web Interface*
   - If you use or plan to use TCP/IP on your mainframe systems
   - If you plan to maintain your data and applications on your mainframe systems
   - If you require high performance both in throughput and numbers of concurrent users
   - If you have application programmers with CICS skills

It is possible to develop common applications that run in CICS/ESA and respond to requests from both the CICS Web Interface and the CICS Gateway for Java, by isolating all HTML and HTTP knowledge in the CICS Web Interface Analyzer and Converter modules. In that way, it is possible to get the best from both interfaces.

CICS WEB INTERFACE APPLICATION IN 370 ASSEMBLER

```
*ASM XOPTS(SP NOPROLOG NOEPILOG)
    TITLE 'TESTWBTL -- Test DFHWBTL'
*
* This program is used to test DFHWBTL
*
COMMOUT DSECT
*
* Following fields are used to communicate with DFHHTTPD
*
OUTLEN DS F            Length of buffer to be output
OUTRESP DS CL9         HTTP Version
OUTRC DS CL6           response code
OUTRCC DS X            Linefeed to say end of header
OUTRCL DS X            Carriage Return
OUTHDR1 DS CL23        Header data
OUTHDR1C DS X          Carriage return at end of header
OUTHDR1L DS X          Linefeed at end of header
OUTMSGC DS X           Carriage return at end of header
OUTMSGL DS X           Linefeed at end of header
OUTMSG DS XL(32767-*+COMMOUT) Space for webpage text
CARRIAGE EQU X'0D'     Carriage return value
LINEFEED EQU X'25'     Linefeed value
CRLF EQU CARRIAGE*256+LINEFEED Carriage return + linefeed
DELIM EQU C'&&'
    COPY DFHWBTLD
    DFHREGS ,
TESTWBTL CSECT
TESTWBTL AMODE ANY
TESTWBTL RMODE 24
    DFHEIENT DATAREG=R13,CODEREG=R12,EIBREG=R11
    L R10,DFHEICAP
    USING COMMOUT,R10
    EXEC CICS LINK PROGRAM('DFHWBENV') *
      COMMAREA(ENVVARS) LENGTH(ENVVARSL)
*
* Now set up the commarea with HTTP protocol information
*
    LA R0,OUTMSG-COMMOUT Initialize length
```

(continued)

```
         ST R0,OUTLEN     Save in first word of commarea
         MVC OUTRESP,=CL9'HTTP/1.0' Initialize protocol
         MVC OUTRC,=CL6'200 OK' Initialize return code
         MVC OUTHDR1,=CL23'Content-Type: text/html'
         MVC OUTRCC(2),=AL2(CRLF) Set carriage-return/linefeed
         MVC OUTHDR1C(2),=AL2(CRLF) Set carriage-return/linefeed
         MVC OUTMSGC(2),=AL2(CRLF) Set carriage-return/linefeed
         LA R9,WBTL_PARMS
         USING DFHWBTL_ARG,R9
         XC WBTL_PARMS,WBTL_PARMS Clear the parameters
*-----------------------------------------------------------------
* Start the page, set up symbols
*-----------------------------------------------------------------
         LA R0,WBTL START_HTML_PAGE
         LA R2,SYMBOLS
         L R3,=A(SYMBOLS_L)
         LA R4,OUTMSG
         LH R15,EIBCALEN  Get total length of commarea
         LA R5,0(R15,R10)  Address of end of commarea
         SR R5,R4         Subtract addr of point reached so far
         STH R0,WBTL_FUNCTION
         ST R2,WBTL_SYMBOL_LIST_PTR
         ST R3,WBTL_SYMBOL_LIST_LEN
         ST R4,WBTL_HTML_BUFFER_PTR
         ST R5,WBTL_HTML_BUFFER_LEN
         MVI WBTL_VERSION_NO+1,1
         EXEC CICS LINK PROGRAM('DFHWBTL')    *
            COMMAREA(WBTL_PARMS) LENGTH(COMMAREA_LEN)
         CLI WBTL_RESPONSE+1,WBTL_EXCEPTION
         BNE CHECK01
         CLI WBTL_REASON+1,WBTL_TEMPLATE_TRUNCATED
         BNE CHECK01
         EXEC CICS ABEND ABCODE('WBTT')
CHECK01  CLI WBTL_RESPONSE+1,WBTL_OK
         BE GOODSTART
         EXEC CICS ABEND ABCODE('WBSP')
GOODSTART DS 0H
*-----------------------------------------------------------------
* Add the environment variables as symbols
*-----------------------------------------------------------------
ADD_SYMS DS 0H
```

(continued)

```
         LA   R0,WBTL_ADD_HTML_SYMBOLS
         LA   R2,ENVVARS+4
         L    R3,ENVVARS
         STH  R0,WBTL_FUNCTION
         ST   R2,WBTL_SYMBOL_LIST_PTR
         ST   R3,WBTL_SYMBOL_LIST_LEN
         EXEC CICS LINK PROGRAM('DFHWBTL')   *
             COMMAREA(WBTL_PARMS) LENGTH(COMMAREA_LEN)
         CLI  WBTL_RESPONSE+1,WBTL_OK
         BE   GOODSYM
         EXEC CICS ABEND ABCODE('WBAS')
GOODSYM  DS   0H
*--------------------------------------------------------------------
* Loop through a list of templates
*--------------------------------------------------------------------
         LA   R5,TTFIRST
         LA   R6,L'WBTL_TEMPLATE_NAME
         LA   R7,TTLAST
TEMPLOOP DS   0H
         LA   R0,WBTL_ADD_HTML_TEMPLATE
         STH  R0,WBTL_FUNCTION
******** XC   WBTL_HTML_BUFFER_LEN,WBTL_HTML_BUFFER_LEN
         MVC  WBTL_TEMPLATE_NAME,0(R5)
         EXEC CICS LINK PROGRAM('DFHWBTL')   *
             COMMAREA(WBTL_PARMS) LENGTH(COMMAREA_LEN)
         CLI  WBTL_RESPONSE+1,WBTL_EXCEPTION
         BNE  CHECK02
         CLI  WBTL_REASON+1,WBTL_PAGE_TRUNCATED
         BNE  CHECK02
         EXEC CICS ABEND ABCODE('WBPT')
CHECK02  CLI  WBTL_RESPONSE+1,WBTL_OK
         BE   TEMPLOK
         CLI  WBTL_REASON+1,WBTL_TEMPLATE_NOT_FOUND
         BE   NOTFOUND
         EXEC CICS ABEND ABCODE('WBAT')
NOTFOUND DS   0H
         L    R14,WBTL_HTML_BUFFER_PTR
         L    R15,WBTL_HTML_BUFFER_LEN
         MVC  0(NFMSG_L,R14),NFMSG
         MVC  NFTEMP1-NFMSG(8,R14),WBTL_TEMPLATE_NAME
         MVC  NFTEMP2-NFMSG(8,R14),WBTL_TEMPLATE_NAME
```

(continued)

```
         LA R0,NFMSG_L
         ALR R14,R0       Increase buffer address
         SLR R15,R0       Decrease length remaining
         ST R14,WBTL_HTML_BUFFER_PTR
         ST R15,WBTL_HTML_BUFFER_LEN
TEMPLOK DS 0H
         BXLE R5,R6,TEMPLOOP
*----------------------------------------------------------------
* Close the document by appending closing markup
*----------------------------------------------------------------
         LA R0,WBTL_ADD_HTML_TEMPLATE
         LA R2,TEMPLAT4
         L R3,=A(TEMPLAT4_L)
         STH R0,WBTL_FUNCTION
         ST R2,WBTL_TEMPLATE_BUFFER_PTR
         ST R3,WBTL_TEMPLATE_BUFFER_LEN
         EXEC CICSLINKPROGRAM('DFHWBTL')        *
            COMMAREA(WBTL_PARMS) LENGTH(COMMAREA_LEN)
         CLI WBTL_RESPONSE+1,WBTL_OK
         BE CLOSEOK
         EXEC CICS ABEND ABCODE('WBAZ')
CLOSEOK DS 0H
*----------------------------------------------------------------
* Tell template manager to clean up
*----------------------------------------------------------------
END_PAGE DS 0H
         LA R0,WBTL_END_HTML_PAGE
         STH R0,WBTL_FUNCTION
         EXEC CICS LINK PROGRAM('DFHWBTL')      *
            COMMAREA(WBTL_PARMS) LENGTH(COMMAREA_LEN)
         CLI WBTL_RESPONSE+1,WBTL_OK
         BE GOODEND
         EXEC CICS ABEND ABCODE('WBEP')
GOODEND DS 0H
*----------------------------------------------------------------
* Set up the commarea length
*----------------------------------------------------------------
         LH R0,EIBCALEN
         S R0,WBTL_HTML_BUFFER_LEN
         ST R0,OUTLEN
         DFHEIRET        Return
```

(continued)

```
*
* Table of templates
*
TTFIRST DC CL8'TEMPLAR0'
       DC CL8'TEMPLAR1'
       DC CL8'TEMPLAR2'
TTLAST DC CL8'TEMPLAR3'
TEMPLAT1 DC C'<html>'
       DC C'<head><title>'
       DC C'Testing CICS template support'
       DC C'</title></head>',AL2(CRLF)
       DC C'<body>',AL2(CRLF),C'<h1>'
       DC C'Testing CICS template support'
       DC C'</h1>',AL2(CRLF)
       DC C'This is a handy test file that contains symbols:'
       DC AL2(CRLF),C'<ul>',AL2(CRLF)
       DC C'<li>Name=&&Name;',AL2(CRLF)
       DC C'<li>Birthday=&&Birthday;',AL2(CRLF)
       DC C'<li>Salary=&&Salary;',AL2(CRLF)
       DC C'<li>Car=&&Car;',AL2(CRLF)
       DC C'<li>Undefined=&&Undefined;',AL2(CRLF)
       DC C'</ul>',AL2(CRLF)
TEMPLAT1_L EQU *-TEMPLAT1
TEMPLAT2 DC C'<p>'
       DC C'This sentence contains &&text;'
       DC C'that is not delimited by punctuation.'
       DC AL2(CRLF)
       DC C'This sentence contains (&&text;)'
       DC C'enclosed in parentheses.'
       DC AL2(CRLF)
       DC C'This sentence includes a '
       DC C'<!--#config timefmt="HH:MM:SS"-->'
       DC C'server-side include.',AL2(CRLF)
       DC C'This sentence would include '
       DC C'<! #include file="another"-->'
       DC C'another, if we supported SSI.',AL2(CRLF)
TEMPLAT2_L EQU *-TEMPLAT2
TEMPLAT3 DC C'<p>Here is some more SSI, courtesy of Dennis Plum.'
       DC C'<!--#set var=one value=111 -->'
       DC C'<!--#set var=two value=222 -->'
       DC C'<!--#set var=six value=666 -->'
```

(continued)

```
       DC    C'<p>This is one '
       DC    C'<!--#echo var=one -->'
       DC    C'<p>This is two '
       DC    C'<!--#echo var=two -->'
       DC    C'<p>This is six '
       DC    C'<!--#echo var=six -->'
TEMPLAT4 DC  C'</body></html>',AL2(CRLF)
TEMPLAT3_L EQU *-TEMPLAT3
TEMPLAT4_L EQU *-TEMPLAT4
SYMBOLS DC   AL1(DELIM),C'text=a piece of substituted text'
       DC    AL1(DELIM),C'Name=Peter Havercan'
       DC    AL1(DELIM),C'Car=Mitsubishi Space Wagon'
       DC    AL1(DELIM),C'unused=not used'
       DC    AL1(DELIM),C'Salary=%26#163;128,000 (you wish!)'
       DC    AL1(DELIM),C'Birthday=17 July 1946'
       DC    AL1(DELIM),C'title=Testing+CICS+template+support'
       DC    AL1(DELIM),C'bgcolor=#ffffff'
       DC    AL1(DELIM),C'txtcolor=#000000'
       DC    AL1(DELIM),C'linkcolor=#00ff00'
       DC    AL1(DELIM),C'vlinkcolor=#ff0000'
       DC    AL1(DELIM),C'product=Hello'
       DC    AL1(DELIM),C'HTTP_ACCEPT_ENCODING='
       DC    AL1(DELIM),C'HTTP_ACCEPT_LANGUAGE='
       DC    AL1(DELIM),C'HTTP_AUTHORIZATION='
       DC    AL1(DELIM),C'HTTP_CHARGE_TO='
       DC    AL1(DELIM),C'HTTP_FROM='
       DC    AL1(DELIM),C'HTTP_IF_MODIFIED_SINCE='
       DC    AL1(DELIM),C'HTTP_PRAGMA='
       DC    AL1(DELIM),C'HTTP_REFERER='
       DC    AL1(DELIM),C'HTTP_USER_AGENT='
SYMBOLS_L EQU *-SYMBOLS
COMMAREA_LEN DC Y(DFHWBTL_ARG_LEN)
ENVVARSL DC  Y(L'ENVVARS)
NFMSG  DC    C'<html>',AL2(CRLF)
       DC    C'<head><title>'
       DC    C'Template '
NFTEMP1 DC   CL8'********'
       DC    C' not found.'
       DC    C'</title></head>',AL2(CRLF)
       DC    C'<body>',AL2(CRLF),C'<h1>'
       DC    C'Template '
```

(continued)

```
NFTEMP2 DC CL8'********'
   DC C' not found.'
   DC C'</h1>',AL2(CRLF)
NFMSG_L EQU *-NFMSG
   LTORG ,
   DFHEISTG
WBTL_PARMS DS XL(DFHWBTL_ARG_LEN)
DAYNO DS F
MONTHNO DS F
LTIME DS CL8
LDAY DS CL4
LDATE DS CL8
LMONTH DS CL4
   DS 0D
ENVVARS DS XL1024
   DFHEIEND
   END
```

CICS WEB INTERFACE SAMPLE CONVERTER IN C

```
/*************************************************************/
/* This program provides html decoding and encoding to receive */
/* form data input, send it to a legacy user program and convert */
/* the output back to html for return to the browser           */
/*************************************************************/
/* Includes                                                  */
/*************************************************************/
#include <ctype.h>
#include <string.h>
#include <stddef.h>
#include <stdlib.h>
#include <stdio.h>
#include <stdarg.h>
/******************************************/
/* Data constants                         */
/******************************************/
#define NL     "
"
```

(continued)

```c
#define MAXSIZE         10000
#define TRUE        1
#define FALSE       0
#define URP_OK      0
#define URP_DECODE      1
#define URP_ENCODE      2
#define URP_INVALID     8
#define COMMSIZE        30000
#define DECODE_EYECATCHER_INIT ">decode "
#define ENCODE_EYECATCHER_INIT ">encode "
#define wbtl_build_html_page 1
#define wbtl_start_html_page 2
#define wbtl_add_html_symbols  3
#define wbtl_read_html_template  4
#define wbtl_add_html_template  5
#define wbtl_end_html_page  6
#define wbtl_ok        0
#define wbtl_exception     4
#define wbtl_invalid      8
#define wbtl_disaster     12
#define wbtl_invalid_function  1
#define wbtl_feature_inactive  2
#define wbtl_template_not_found  3
#define wbtl_template_truncated  4
#define wbtl_getmain_error  5
#define wbtl_freemain_error  6
/****************************************************************/
/* Template Manager parameter list                              */
/****************************************************************/
typedef struct
{
 signed short int wbtl_version_no;
 signed short int wbtl_function;
 signed short int wbtl_response;
 signed short int wbtl_reason;
 char wbtl_connect_token[8];
 char wbtl_template_name[8];
 char wbtl_template_abstime[8];
 char * wbtl_template_buffer_ptr;
 signed long int wbtl_template_buffer_len;
 char * wbtl_symbol_list_ptr;
 signed long int wbtl_symbol_list_len;
```

(continued)

```
  char * wbtl_html_buffer_ptr;
  signed long int wbtl_html_buffer_len;
} template_parms;
/*****************************************************************/
/* Coverter parameter list                                       */
/*****************************************************************/
typedef struct
{
  char converter_eyecatcher[8];
  unsigned long int converter_function;
  unsigned long int converter_response;
  unsigned long int converter_reason;
  char *converter_parmlist;
} converter_parms;
/*****************************************************************/
/* Decode parameter list                                         */
/*****************************************************************/
typedef struct
{
  char decode_eyecatcher[8];
  unsigned long int decode_function;
  unsigned long int decode_response;
  unsigned long int decode_reason;
  unsigned long int decode_client_address;
  char decode_client_address_string[15];
  char ignore;
  char *decode_data_ptr;
  unsigned long int *decode_method_ptr;
  unsigned long int *decode_http_version_ptr;
  unsigned long int *decode_resource_ptr;
  unsigned long int *decode_request_header_ptr;
  char *decode_user_data_ptr;
  signed short int decode_method_length;
  signed short int decode_http_version_length;
  signed short int decode_resource_length;
  signed short int decode_request_header_length;
  signed long int decode_input_data_len;
  signed short int decode_user_data_len;
  signed long int decode_output_data_len;
  char decode_server_program[8];
  char decode_user_token[8];
} decode_parms;
```

(continued)

```c
/*******************************************************************/
/* Encode parameter list                                           */
/*******************************************************************/
typedef struct
{
 unsigned long int outsize;
 char data[3000];
} data_parms;
typedef struct
{
 char encode_eyecatcher[8];
 unsigned long int encode_function;
 unsigned long int encode_response;
 unsigned long int encode_reason;
 data_parms * encode_data_ptr;
 signed long int encode_input_data_len;
 char encode_user_token[8];
} encode_parms;
/*******************************************************************/
/* Parcel data returned from legacy application                    */
/*******************************************************************/
typedef struct
{
 unsigned long int length;
 char Date_Received[9];
 char Dest_Address[80];
 char Transport_Method[10];
 char Location[80];
 int weight;
 int insured;
 char refno[14];
} parcel_data;
/*******************************************************************/
/* Prototypes                                                      */
/*******************************************************************/
void Decode(void);
void Encode(void);
char * GetField(char *, char *);
/*******************************************************************/
/* Global variables                                                */
/*******************************************************************/
converter_parms *converter_parms_ptr;
```

(continued)

```
/********************************************************************/
/* Main Function                                                    */
/********************************************************************/
main()
{
 EXEC CICS ADDRESS EIB(dfheiptr);
 EXEC CICS ADDRESS COMMAREA(converter_parms_ptr);
 /***************************************************/
 /* Identify which converter function is required */
 /***************************************************/
 {
  case URP_DECODE:
  {
   Decode();
   break;
  }
  case URP_ENCODE:
  {
   Encode();
   break;
  }
  default:
  {
   converter_parms_ptr->converter_response = URP_INVALID;
  }
 }
  EXEC CICS RETURN;
}
/********************************************************************/
/* Decode Routine                                                   */
/********************************************************************/
void Decode(void)
{
 decode_parms * decode_parms_ptr;
 /***************************************/
 /* Map Decode Structure onto Commarea */
 /* and establish commarea is valid    */
 /***************************************/
 decode_parms_ptr = (decode_parms *)converter_parms_ptr;
 if (strncmp(decode_parms_ptr->decode_eyecatcher,
    DECODE_EYECATCHER_INIT,8) == 0)
  decode_parms_ptr->decode_response = URP_OK;
```

(continued)

```
    else
     {
     decode_parms_ptr->decode_response = URP_INVALID;
     EXEC CICS RETURN;
     }
    /*********************************/
    /* Get parcel code from HTML form */
    /*********************************/
    sprintf(decode_parms_ptr->decode_data_ptr,
     "%s",       GetField(decode_parms_ptr->decode_user_data_ptr,"PARCEL
     CODE"));
    /***************************************************************/
    /* Set a reasonable comm area size, big enough to fit a big    */
    /* HTML template                                                */
    /***************************************************************/
    decode_parms_ptr->decode_input_data_len = COMMSIZE;
    decode_parms_ptr->decode_output_data_len =
         strlen(decode_parms_ptr->decode_data_ptr);
    }
    /***************************************************************/
    /* Encode Routine                                               */
    /***************************************************************/
    void Encode(void)
    {
     template_parms * template_parms_ptr;
     encode_parms * encode_parms_ptr;
     data_parms * data_parms_ptr;
     parcel_data * parcel_data_ptr;
     char queue[] = "LOG ";
     char prog[] = "DFHWBTL ";
     char data[100];
     char symbol[1000];
     char * buffer;
     int resp, resp2;
     short int size = 10000;
     short int size2 = 3000;
     short int size3 = 3010;
    encode_parms_ptr = (encode_parms *)converter_parms_ptr;
    /**************************************/
    /* Map Encode structure onto Commarea */
    /* and establish commarea is valid    */
    /**************************************/
```

(continued)

```
if (strncmp(encode_parms_ptr->encode_eyecatcher,
  ENCODE_EYECATCHER_INIT,8)== 0)
  encode_parms_ptr->encode_response = URP_OK;
 else
 {
  encode_parms_ptr->encode_response = URP_INVALID;
  EXEC CICS RETURN;
 }
/****************************************/
/* Map legacy application Commarea data */
/* structure over returned data         */
/****************************************/
 parcel_data_ptr = (parcel_data *)encode_parms_ptr->encode_data_ptr;
/*******************************************/
/* Build variables list for template Manager */
/*******************************************/
 sprintf(symbol,
"VAR1=%s&VAR2=%s&VAR3=%s&VAR4=%s&VAR5=%d&VAR6=%d&VAR7=%s&",
  parcel_data_ptr->Date_Received,
  parcel_data_ptr->Dest_Address,
  parcel_data_ptr->Transport_Method,
  parcel_data_ptr->Location,
  parcel_data_ptr->weight,
  parcel_data_ptr->insured,
 parcel_data_ptr->refno);
/****************************************************************/
/* Getmain storage for template structure and template buffer */
/****************************************************************/
EXEC CICS GETMAIN SET(data_parms_ptr) FLENGTH(size3);
 EXEC CICS GETMAIN SET(template_parms_ptr) FLENGTH(size);
 EXEC CICS GETMAIN SET(buffer) FLENGTH(size2);
/*********************/
/* Clear New storage */
/*********************/
memset((void *)template_parms_ptr,0x00,sizeof(template_parms));
/************************************/
/* Establish environment for Web page */
/************************************/
template_parms_ptr->wbtl_version_no = 0;
 template_parms_ptr->wbtl_function = wbtl_start_html_page;
EXEC CICS LINK PROGRAM(prog) COMMAREA(template_parms_ptr)
     LENGTH(sizeof(template_parms))
```

(continued)

```
          RESP(resp) RESP2(resp2);
if(resp != DFHRESP(NORMAL))
 {
 sprintf(data,"Failed to LINK resp(%d) resp2(%d)",resp,resp2);
EXEC CICS WRITEQ TS QUEUE(queue) FROM(data)
     LENGTH(strlen(data));
 }
/********************/
/* Add HTML Symbols */
/********************/
template_parms_ptr->wbtl_function = wbtl_add_html_symbols;
 template_parms_ptr->wbtl_symbol_list_ptr = symbol;
 template_parms_ptr->wbtl_symbol_list_len =
 (unsigned long) strlen(symbol);
EXEC CICS LINK PROGRAM(prog) COMMAREA(template_parms_ptr)
     LENGTH(sizeof(template_parms))
     RESP(resp) RESP2(resp2);
if(resp != DFHRESP(NORMAL))
 {
 sprintf(data,"Failed to LINK resp(%d) resp2(%d)",resp,resp2);
EXEC CICS WRITEQ TS QUEUE(queue) FROM(data)
     LENGTH(strlen(data));
 }
/*********************/
/* Add HTML Template */
/*********************/
template_parms_ptr->wbtl_function = wbtl_add_html_template;
 memcpy(template_parms_ptr->wbtl_template_name,"TEMPL1  ",8);
 template_parms_ptr->wbtl_html_buffer_ptr = buffer;
 template_parms_ptr->wbtl_html_buffer_len = 3000;
EXEC CICS LINK PROGRAM(prog) COMMAREA(template_parms_ptr)
     LENGTH(sizeof(template_parms))
     RESP(resp) RESP2(resp2);
if(resp != DFHRESP(NORMAL))
 {
  sprintf(data,"Failed to LINK resp(%d) resp2(%d)",resp,resp2);
EXEC CICS WRITEQ TS QUEUE(queue) FROM(data)
     LENGTH(strlen(data));
 }
/*****************/
/* End HTML Page */
/*****************/
```

(continued)

```c
  template_parms_ptr->wbtl_function = wbtl_end_html_page;
  EXEC CICS LINK PROGRAM(prog) COMMAREA(template_parms_ptr)
       LENGTH(sizeof(template_parms))
       RESP(resp) RESP2(resp2);
  if(resp != DFHRESP(NORMAL))
   {
    sprintf(data,"Failed to LINK resp(%d) resp2(%d)",resp,resp2);
  EXEC CICS WRITEQ TS QUEUE(queue) FROM(data)
       LENGTH(strlen(data));
   }
  /*************************************************************/
  /* Null terminate the buffer to allow use of string functions */
  /*************************************************************/
  template_parms_ptr->wbtl_html_buffer_ptr[0] = '\0';
  /******************************************////
  /* Now Freemain allocated storage for user */
  /* program response and point to template  */
  /* output                                  */
  /******************************************/
  EXEC CICS FREEMAIN
       DATAPOINTER(encode_parms_ptr->encode_data_ptr);
  strcpy(data_parms_ptr->data,buffer);
   encode_parms_ptr->encode_data_ptr = data_parms_ptr;
   data_parms_ptr->outsize = strlen(data_parms_ptr->data) + 4;
  }
  /*************************************************************/
  /* GetField routine                                          */
  /*************************************************************/
  char * GetField(char * data, char * field)
  {
   char outdata[80];
   char * out;
   char * token;
  out = (char *) &token;
  /*********************************************************/
  /* Tokenise HTML form data looking for specified field */
  /*********************************************************/
  for (token = strtok(data,"&");token != NULL;token = strtok
  (NULL,"&"))
   {
   if (strncmp(token,field,strlen(field)) == 0)
    {
```

(continued)

```
        out = strstr(token,"=");
        out++;
return(out);
        }
  }
return(NULL);
}
```

CHAPTER **12**

Accessing Encina, IMS TM, and MQSeries Applications from the Internet

In Chapter 11, we discussed a variety of approaches for accessing CICS applications from the Web. There are many other types of transaction systems software, such as Transarc's Encina and IBM's IMS. In this chapter we describe how Transarc's Encina and IBM's IMS applications can be accessed from the Internet. Encina and IMS include UOR support, both as coordinators and participants. UORs enable programmers to build applications with the knowledge that either all data modifications within a UOR will be completed or rolled back. UORs are particularly useful for applications, such as funds transfer or stock purchase, that cannot afford to have partial or repeated entries even when system failures occur.

We also describe how the MQSeries Messaging and Queuing software can be used to access and run various business applications from the Web. MQSeries supports UORs as a participant. MQSeries also includes specific support for invoking IMS applications.

After reading this chapter, you will be able to identify the methods of accessing Encina, IMS TM, and MQSeries applications across the Internet and select the most appropriate method for your applications.

ENCINA OVERVIEW

Transarc produced the Encina series of products in the early 1990s to support three-tier applications on a variety of UNIX systems where users manipulate databases and files. The tiers are:

- *Client systems* that support the user interface and issue requests to application servers.
- *Shared application servers* that implement business logic to satisfy client requests, interacting with resource managers, such as database and file managers, on behalf of clients.
- *Shared resource managers* that enable access to data. These can be relational databases, queuing systems, or mainframe-based services.

The origins of the Encina software are described in a book entitled *Camelot and Avalon*, listed in the For Further Reference section at the end of this book. Encina uses the Distributed Computing Environment (DCE) software from the Open Software Foundation (OSF).

DCE

Transarc provides an implementation of Distributed Computing Environment (DCE). The goal of DCE is to provide the functions for developing and running distributed applications across various operating systems and networks.

The components of DCE are as follows:

- *Remote Procedure Call* (*RPC*) mechanism enables programs to invoke remote programs. You use the Interface Definition Language (IDL) to define the structure of the parameters passed between the programs so that DCE can transmit the parameters across a network. The client program can link consecutive RPC requests together in a conversation, using an RPC context handle that is returned on the initial RPC request.
- *Security Service* enables processes on different machines to be certain of each other's identities (authentication), allows a server to determine whether a given user is authorized to access a particular resource, and supports several protection levels for information as it travels across the network. DCE authentication is based on Kerberos from the Massachusetts Institute of Technology (MIT), where each process involved in

an RPC operation consults a third-party (Kerberos) to check the identities of the client and the server. Access Control Lists (ACLs) are used for authorization checks.

- *Distributed Time Service* (*DTS*) enables the synchronization of clocks across different computers.
- *Threads Service* supports applications that perform multiple tasks concurrently. Threads use resources more efficiently than operating system processes.
- *Cell Directory Service* (*CDS*) is the mechanism for naming objects within a DCE cell (a collection of client and server machines). Applications identify resources by name, without knowing where the resources are. DCE cells can also participate in a worldwide directory service such as the Internet Domain Name Service (DNS). Every cell must run the CDS, DTS, and Security Service.
- *Distributed File System* (*DFS*) is a high-performance, secure way of sharing remote files. DFS provides access to files anywhere in the network for any user at any location, with the same local filename (uniform file access). In addition, DFS includes caching and security support.

Some DCE services, such as DFS, can be replicated for improved availability and performance.

Encina Components

The major components of the Encina systems software are made up of Encina Base Services and Extended Services. Here are the Encina Base Services:

- *Transactional-C* supports an API for programs to define the start and end of UORs (transactions). There is no specific support to link multiple UORs in user conversations as in CICS and IMS beyond the RPC context handle.
- *Transactional Remote Procedure Call* (*T-RPC*) supports an extension of DCE RPC for distributed UORs across a number of systems.
- *Distributed Transaction Service* supports the two-phase commit protocol described Chapter 10 to ensure the integrity of UORs. Nested UORs (*nested transactions*) are supported as well as regular UORs. So you can

write an application that contains a number of subordinate UORs that you can roll back without rolling back the overall UOR. All subordinate UORs must terminate before the overall UOR can commit. Nested UORs are helpful when encapsulating sections of an application thereby preventing errors detected in one portion of an application from causing the updates performed by the whole application to roll back.

Here are the Encina Extended Services:

- *Encina Monitor* provides an environment for developing, running, and administering distributed transaction processing applications. The Encina monitor enables servers to be replicated for increased availability and performance. It supports automatic load balancing and restart of failed application servers. In common with other transaction processing systems, such as IMS and CICS, Encina can perform automatic authorization checking for security but it does not provide explicit support for user conversations and conversation state beyond the use of RPC context handles.
- *Encina Structured File Server* (*SFS*) is a record-oriented file system that supports two-phase commit as a participant, enabling multiple SFS servers and other resource managers such as relational databases to be used in a single UOR. SFS supports B-tree clustered, relative, and entry-sequence access methods, and provides interfaces similar to both Indexed Sequential Access Method (ISAM) and Virtual Storage Access Method (VSAM). SFS supports online backup and restore.
- *Encina Recoverable Queuing Service* enables enqueuing and dequeuing of data, allowing tasks to be queued for later processing while ensuring that system failures do not result in lost information. RQS provides multiple levels of priority. RQS queues can participate in the two-phase commit protocol.
- *Encina PPC Executive* supports peer-to-peer communications using the Common Programming Interface—Communications (CPI-C) and Common Programming Interface—Resource Recovery (CPI-RR) application programming interfaces to provide SNA LU6.2 connectivity over TCP/IP. It enables cooperating Encina systems to participate in transactions using SNA LU6.2 sync-levels 0 (no coordination), 1 (single-phase commit), and 2 (two-phase commit).

- *Encina PPC Gateway/SNA* provides interoperability over an Systems Network Architecture protocol implementation of LU6.2 in conjunction with the Encina PPC Executive. The Encina PPC Gateway allows Encina applications to ship or accept applications from mainframe transaction processing systems that use LU6.2, such as IMS and CICS, without requiring Encina software on the mainframe. The Encina PPC Gateway/SNA module delivers sync-level 2 (two-phase commit) services from an open, distributed environment to the mainframe.

DE-Light

You can use the DE-Light (lightweight DCE Encina) API in client applications to access Encina applications through the DE-Light Gateway. DE-Light consists of two components:

- The *DE-Light Client*, which runs on client systems and provides an API to access Encina application server applications. The API includes options for selecting a Gateway server, supplying User ID and password information, issuing RPC and T-RPC requests, and UOR management. UORs can span multiple DE-Light T-RPC requests and multiple-application servers.
- The *DE-Light Gateway*, which runs on server systems and processes the DE-Light Client requests. The Gateway includes an RPC interpreter and can invoke various application servers.

DE-Light Client applications are not linked with IDL stub files, which is the case for ordinary DCE and Encina clients. Instead, a DE-Light Client builds a string describing the RPC it wants the Gateway to execute on its behalf. The DE-Light Client collects any additional parameters required by the target RPC, opens a TCP/IP connection to the appropriate DE-Light Gateway, and sends the string and parameters to the Gateway for execution. The DE-Light Gateway is a DCE client that accepts requests from DE-Light Web Clients and translates them into RPC or T-RPC requests.

The RPC interpreter in the Gateway dynamically builds a DCE RPC or Encina T-RPC and calls the server. Servers can be any existing DCE or Encina application. When the call returns, the interpreter collects the result and any return parameters and sends them back to the DE-Light Client. The DE-Light protocol is compact and suitable for low-bandwidth environments, such as dialup, common with Web configurations.

ACCESSING ENCINA APPLICATIONS FROM THE WEB

In this section we describe two methods for accessing Encina applications from the Web.

Using Server-Side Programming—Using a CGI Program

You can use a CGI program to access Encina application servers from the Web. The CGI program translates the HTML forms input into the required T-RPC request as command line arguments, parses the arguments into local variables, and issues a T-RPC request. The CGI program is also responsible for formatting any results into a suitable HTML stream for return to the browser through the Web server (see Figure 12.1).

An advantage of using the CGI approach is that Encina application servers can be integrated into Web environments very quickly with existing Web technology. The usual CGI characteristics described in Chapter 5 apply, such as starting up a separate operating system process for each user interaction. You can use one of the techniques described in Chapter 5 to maintain application state information across user requests within a browser session.

The CGI interface is a fast way of prototyping Web-based client access to Encina applications. You have to build your own application-specific gateway software if you want to use CGI programming with Encina.

Using Client-Side Programming—The DE-Light Web Client

You can use the *DE-Light Web Client*, which is written in Java to access Encina application servers through the DE-Light Gateway (see Figure 12.2).

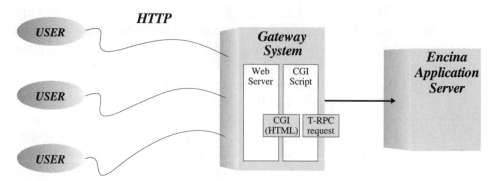

Figure 12.1 Accessing Encina applications using a CGI program.

Accessing Encina, IMS/TM, and MQSeries Applications from the Internet

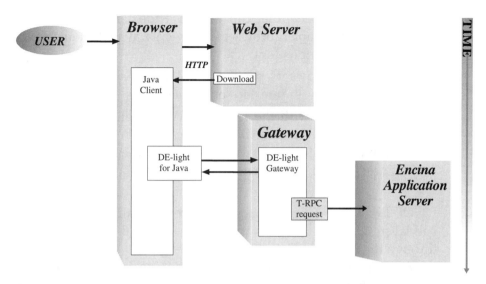

Figure 12.2 Accessing Encina applications using the DE-Light Web client.

The DE-Light Web Client supports a subset of the regular DE-Light Client API. A DE-Light Web Client is downloaded and executed on demand by a Java applet running in a Web browser.

Using the DE-Light Web Client provides a number of benefits that are generally common to using Java-based clients:

- The DCE and Encina runtime client libraries do not have to be present on the client platform for applications to run. Given the size of the libraries, downloading them on demand can be time consuming. In contrast, the Java runtime library is built into most popular browsers, Java automatically locates and downloads any applets that are not already cached locally, and no setup is required on the client. The applets themselves are generally quite small, minimizing transfer times.
- When applets change, you can ensure that users are running the latest version. Clients that have an old version of the applet, or no version at all, automatically receive the new version the next time it is referenced from a Web page from a new instance of the browser.
- Individual client systems do not require specific versions of the DCE and Encina client runtime libraries, or the application itself, in order to

operate. A single applet can cross a wide range of client platforms because Java-enabled browsers are widely available, and Java applets are machine independent.

- Java-enabled browsers present a look and feel that is well integrated with the native user interface on all platforms.
- Java, combined with the DE-Light Web Client, makes it practical to extend DCE and Encina client applications from the Intranet into the Internet. Client functions can be distributed across the Internet while business logic and data remain behind corporate firewalls.

DE-Light Web Client consists of several small Java classes that use a special programming API to issue DCE RPC and Encina T-RPC requests through the DE-Light Gateway.

At execution time, the Java applet is downloaded to the client browser from a standard Web page via HTTP. The applet contains presentation logic, and a small amount of application logic that includes DE-Light calls. To execute an RPC, the applet builds a string describing the RPC, then passes the string to the DE-Light Gateway using a TCP/IP connection. The Gateway builds a DCE RPC or (Encina T-RPC) and makes the appropriate call. When completed, the outbound arguments are returned to the runtime client and the applet's presentation logic is invoked to format the data and display it to the user.

Here is a typical application request sequence from the Java DE-Light Client:

- Connect to the Gateway
- Login supplying a user identifier and password
- (List available RPC requests—optional)
- Transaction begin (start UOR)
- RPC .. RPC
- Transaction commit (commit UOR)
- Transaction begin (start UOR)
- RPC .. RPC
- Transaction commit (commit UOR)
- Terminate connection to the Gateway (automatically causes a logout)

Accessing Encina, IMS/TM, and MQSeries Applications from the Internet

If you require multiple concurrent UORs from a single DE-Light Web Client, then you must issue multiple Gateway connection requests, one for each UOR.

You cannot use RPC context handles to maintain conversation state using the DE-Light Web Client. You can pass application tokens and state information as RPC variables between your client and server applications in order to maintain a user conversation across requests.

The DE-Light Gateway uses a protocol based on HTTP headers when communicating with the DE-Light Web Client, although the HTTP content is specific to DE-Light. The use of HTTP headers means that DE-Light Web Clients can usually communicate with DE-Light Gateways outside corporate firewalls without any additional configuration.

As illustrated in the request sequence above, the DE-Light Web Client can send user identifiers and passwords to the DE-Light Gateway for authentication in DCE. Login requests cannot be issued when a UOR for the Gateway Connection is outstanding, and not yet committed. The DE-Light Gateway, along with the DE-Light Web Client, supports SSL to encrypt the data that flows between the Client and the Gateway.

The DE-Light Gateway supports all DE-Light Clients, the ordinary DE-Light Clients and the Java-based DE-Light Web Clients, whereas the CICS Gateway for Java supports the Java-based CICS clients only and not the regular CICS clients. The DE-Light Gateway is written in C, whereas the CICS Gateway for Java is written in Java (apart from a small portion of operating system–specific code).

Using DFS on the Web

Although DFS is a shared file system and does not play a significant role in providing Web access to Encina applications, it is worth mentioning using DFS in conjunction with a Web server for managing static or fragments of Web content such as HTML files and images (see Figure 13.3).

IMS OVERVIEW

IBM introduced IMS DB/DC (Data Base and Data Communications) in the late 1960s, at the same time as CICS. The two products appeared in one IBM announcement document in 1969. In general, IMS and CICS are used for similar types of applications on mainframes.

Unlike CICS, IMS uses a common API to interface, called DL/I, with shared hierarchical data structures and with terminals. The number of verbs in the IMS API is much smaller than CICS.

A single IMS system initiates and manages a number of address spaces (similar to processes) and routes users' requests, which typically have a short duration, through the IMS address spaces. At any point in time, each IMS address space runs one user request at most. In contrast, a CICS address space usually runs many user requests concurrently and CICS itself manages the priorities and dispatching of requests. CICS's unconventional use of operating system address spaces on the mainframe means that it provides its own APIs to replace operating system APIs, as operating systems expect requests on behalf of one user only to execute in an address space at one time. The difference in address space usage is another reason for the extensive CICS API compared to IMS.

Unlike CICS and Encina, IMS provides explicit support for long-running batch applications that contain intermediate commit requests enabling restart in the event of failures from the most recent UOR, instead of from the start of the batch job.

IMS applications process device (and human user) input and output using Message Format Services (MFS). IMS places device input onto IMS input message queues for applications to process using MFS. Similarly, IMS places the application output to the device in output message queues. The structure of an IMS application is as follows:

```
Read input queue
Application logic
Insert reply into output queue
Commit (sync)
```

The removal of an input message from a queue and the placement of the corresponding output message onto a queue each form separate UORs and are different from the application's UOR.

IMS has a structure to link consecutive invocations from the same device (or user), called a *conversation*. Conversations in IMS are analogous to pseudoconversations in CICS. An IMS application program can place state information associated with a conversation in a *scratch pad area* (SPA), which IMS restores on the next invocation from the same device or user.

IMS includes support for high-performance applications, for example, through the Fast Path option that is made up of:

- *Expedited Message Handler,* where the removal of an input message from a queue and the placement of the corresponding output message onto a queue form part of the application's UOR instead of separate UORs.
- *Data Entry Databases,* where special data elements, called *sequential dependent segments,* can be used for very frequent data inserts without reducing concurrent user access.
- *Main Storage Databases,* where data is held in memory, eliminating disk access.

All Fast Path data updates take place during or after commit processing.

In the early 1990s, IMS DB/DC was repackaged as IMS TM (Transaction Monitor) and IMS/DB (Data Base).

Open Transaction Manager Access (OTMA)

OTMA enables MVS programs, known as OTMA clients, to invoke IMS programs in such a way that the IMS program thinks it has been invoked from a human user through a terminal. It is also possible to write an OTMA client program that interfaces with devices not supported by IMS, thus extending IMS device support. OTMA uses MVS Cross System Coupling Facility (XCF), which is an efficient way for MVS programs to invoke one another within or across instances of the MVS operating system in a Sysplex (a mainframe multiprocessor).

In the MQSeries section in this chapter, you will see that IMS applications can be accessed from the Web using the MQSeries Internet Gateway or the MQSeries Client for Java in conjunction with the MQSeries Bridge for IMS that uses OTMA.

ACCESSING IMS APPLICATIONS FROM THE WEB

You can download a sample CGI program to use in conjunction with the MVS Web server from: http://www.software.ibm.com/data/ims/.

Using Server-Side Programming—The MVS Web Server CGI Program

Using the CGI gateway approach enables your users to access IMS applications directly from their Web browsers (see Figure 12.3).

Figure 12.3 Accessing IMS/TM applications using an MVS Web server.

There are a number of communication mechanisms that you can use in the CGI program to access IMS applications:

- MQSeries
- DCE RPC using the Application Support/IMS facilities on the mainframe
- IMS TCP/IP Sockets support
- Application Program to Program Communications (APPC) support
- 3270 emulation
- Secondary Logical Unit Program (SLUP) support, traditionally associated with Banking controllers

Using Server-Side Programming—Generic 3270 Gateways

There are a number of generic CGI gateway products available that translate CGI forms requests to 3270 datastreams, thus providing Web access to existing IMS 3270 applications. These products include Salvo from Simware, which requires TCP/IP support on the mainframe, and Corridor from Teubner. Often these types of products require an intermediate Web server gateway system as they do not run on the mainframe.

Using Server-Side Programming with the IMS Web

You can use the IMS Web to access your IMS applications from regular Web browsers. The IMS Web provides a complete end-to-end solution by generating both the HTML input and the corresponding CGI program for an IMS application. It provides the solution according to the MFS source for the application. The IMS Web requires IMS Web server DLLs to be installed on the Web server and the OTMA TCP/IP adapter to be installed on the mainframe. The IMS Web supports multiple Web server platforms (including Windows NT).

At development time you use the IMS Web Studio tool to produce an HTML input form and a corresponding CGI program from an existing or new IMS MFS file. You then place the generated CGI program and the HTML file in the appropriate Web server directories.

At runtime, users can access the IMS application by clicking on the URL that invokes the generated HTML input form. After filling out the input fields on the form, users click on the submit button and the generated CGI program and server DLLs format, which sends the request to the mainframe across TCP/IP and then to OTMA. The server DLLs take the output messages from the IMS application and convert and format them for the CGI program, which generates the output HTML page. The page will then be delivered to the user's browser through the Web server.

Using Client-Side Programming—Generic 3270 Clients

There are products such as OC://WebConnect Gold from Open Connect which provide client-side 3270 emulation, thereby supporting access to IMS applications from Java-enabled browsers.

MQSERIES OVERVIEW

IBM introduced the MQSeries (Messaging and Queuing) software in the early 1990s to help programmers write reliable distributed applications that communicate across many operating systems, such as various forms of UNIX, MVS, OS/2, OS/400, and Windows NT, and across different types of networks, such as TCP/IP, SNA, and Netbios.

MQSeries makes it possible for a program to send data to another program even when the second program is not available, or the network between the two programs is not operating correctly. MQSeries achieves the resilience against failures by writing the data to be sent (the message) on queues held on disk. First the message is written to a local queue near the sending program. If the network is available, MQSeries places the message on a queue near the target program and removes it from the original local queue. If the network is unavailable, MQSeries continues to check for its availability and sends the message on as specified. Finally, MQSeries makes it possible for the target program to remove the message from the queue when the target program becomes available. If a message never reaches its destination, for example, because it was wrongly addressed, MQSeries places the message on a special queue called a *dead letter queue* for subsequent processing, and for possible scrutiny by the system administrator.

The MQSeries software that provides the queuing service for applications is called the *queue manager.* Queue managers have names. Applications can *put* and *get* messages from MQSeries queues. Each queue is owned and maintained by a single queue manager and has a name that a programmer can use, possibly in conjunction with the queue manager name.

There are four types of messages defined by MQSeries:

- *Datagram,* which you use when you do not require a reply from the program that receives your message.
- *Request,* which you use when you require a reply from the program that receives your message.
- *Reply,* which you use when you reply to another message.
- *Report,* which you can use when you find a severe error, such as not being able to understand the content of a message you have been sent. MQSeries also generates report messages. When you place a message on a queue you can choose to receive message reports of these types: *exception, expiration* (message discarded), *arrival confirmation* (message placed on target queue), *delivery confirmation* (message read by receiving application).

MQSeries has a simple set of verbs with many options:

- *Connect* and *Disconnect* programs to the queue manager.
- *Open* and *Close* a queue.
- *Put* a message.
- *Get* a message. A message can be removed from a queue or just browsed and left on the queue. There is an option that allows you to wait for a precise time limit if the message is not yet available.
- *Inquire* about or *Set* the attributes of queues and messages.
- *Commit* and *roll back* changes made within an MQSeries UOR. If other resources are included in the UOR, then the commit or rollback API of

the UOR coordinator, such as a transaction processing system, should be used (see Figure 10.3).

An application programmer typically connects to a queue manager and opens a queue. It then issues a few queue requests (get or put) and eventually closes the queue and disconnects from the queue manager. If the program runs within a transaction processing system, then it may not be necessary for the programmer to connect and disconnect from the queue manager, as the transaction processing system issues these requests on behalf of the programmer.

MQSeries requests can be issued locally to the queue manager or remotely via *MQSeries Client* API connection. The MQSeries Client itself does not include a full queue manager nor any local queues on disk. MQSeries API options include the queue manager connection handle and the queue handle to identify the appropriate queue manager and queue.

An MQSeries message consists of control information and application. The control information includes the required report options (such as confirmation or delivery), expiration time, reply-to queue name, and reply-to queue manager name.

You must design your MQSeries programs to cope with the asynchronous nature of MQSeries. Your program will typically regain control from MQSeries to a message put request before the message has reached its final destination, and before the target program has responded. So, your program should check for replies from the target program by issuing appropriate get requests.

The MQSeries system administrator can cause MQSeries messages to be forwarded on to various queue managers and queues by modifying queue definition information, without requiring any changes to the corresponding MQSeries programs. Many other changes can be made without affecting MQSeries applications, such as altering the underlying network protocol.

Grouping MQSeries Messages

There are a number of ways of grouping messages together that correspond in some way, such as message replies with message requests, for example:

- *The message identifier (24 bytes)*: If a program that issues a put request does not specify a message identifier of its own, MQSeries creates a unique message identifier and places it in the message control information. The message identifier is returned to the application after a put request. The structure of the MQSeries-generated message identifier is a 4-byte product code, followed by a 12-character queue manager name, followed by a value derived from the system clock.

- *The correlation identifier (24 bytes)*: In contrast with the message identifier, the correlation identifier is always set by the application program and not by MQSeries.

When processing get requests, MQSeries retrieves messages that match the message identifier and correlation identifier specified on the request itself. You can set parameters on the get request to retrieve the first message irrespective of the values of the identifier.

You can group related messages together using a combination of message identifier and correlation identifier fields. The sending application can place the MQSeries-generated message identifier, for the first message in a group, in the correlation identifier field for all subsequent related messages in order to group those messages together. Receiving programs can also propagate the initial generated message identifier in the correlation identifier field in messages they produce that are part of the same message group.

Here is an example of a group of three messages using the Correlation Identifier as described above:

1. Message Identifier: MI1, Correlation Identifier: all 'FF'X (high values)
2. Message Identifier: MI2, Correlation Identifier: MI1
3. Message Identifier: MI3, Correlation Identifier: MI1

Note that it is recommended that the message identifier always be unique, ideally generated by MQSeries itself. You can set the correlation identifier for the first message in a group to some specific value that the receiving application can use to find the first item in a group, such as all 'FF'X (high values), as shown in the message group above.

When processing a group of messages, the receiving application can search for any message that contains all 'FF'X in the correlation identifier, for example, to discover the start of a new a group and its initial message identifier value. To process subsequent messages in the group, the receiving application issues get requests specifying any message identifier and using the initial message identifier value in the correlation identifier field.

Triggers

MQSeries provides a facility called *triggering* to initiate applications when certain events occur. If triggering is enabled for a queue and a *trigger event* occurs, such as a certain number of messages arriving in a specified queue, the queue manager sends a trigger message to an *initiation queue*. A long-running program, called a *trigger monitor application,* reads the initiation queue and takes an appropriate action, such as starting another program to process the contents of the original queue.

The MQSeries-IMS Bridge

MQSeries on MVS supports OTMA access to IMS through the MQSeries-IMS Bridge, which places and retrieves MQSeries messages on the IMS queues. So you can write an application that issues an MQSeries put request that causes an IMS application to execute, and your application can then issue a get request to process the output from the IMS application.

The MQSeries bridge is part of the MQSeries software on MVS. One queue manager can connect to one or more IMS systems, and one IMS system can connect to one or more queue managers.

When you use the MQSeries-IMS Bridge, you should include information in your MQSeries messages to invoke IMS applications as described in the *MQSeries Application Programming Reference,* such as the IMS transaction code and the reply-to queue for the replies from IMS.

If you simulate a 3270 terminal to an IMS application with OTMA, you must consider information contained in the inbound message to IMS, such as the key pressed (Enter, PF1, etc.) and the cursor location. On the outbound message (the reply) from IMS you must consider the attribute settings (high, normal, or dark). You can also simulate IMS conversations using the MQSeries-IMS Bridge application.

ACCESSING MQSERIES APPLICATIONS FROM THE WEB

There are a number of ways of accessing MQSeries applications from the Internet.

Using Server-Side Programming—The MQSeries Internet Gateway

Currently, the MQSeries Internet Gateway is a CGI program and associated software that communicates with an MQSeries application running on the same or different system as the Gateway. The Gateway maps the synchronous HTTP requests to asynchronous MQSeries messages. You can use the MQSeries Internet Gateway in conjunction with the MQSeries-IMS Bridge to access existing and new IMS applications from any Web browser.

When the Gateway receives an HTTP POST request, it sends an MQSeries message to the target application that includes the form input data. The Gateway waits for the corresponding reply message from the target application before sending the HTTP reply back to the browser through the Web server.

As described in Chapter 10 (see Figure 10.3), there are at least three UORs involved when processing MQSeries messages; however, only one of them is the application UOR. The first and last UORs are to ensure the arrival of the messages, or their placement in a dead letter queue eventually for further processing.

You can use the MQSeries Internet Gateway to invoke applications in parallel as illustrated in Figure 12.4. You can invoke non-HTML-aware applications from the Gateway by including all the HTML-sensitive code in a Gateway module.

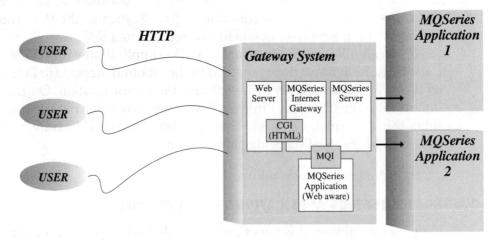

Figure 12.4 Accessing MQSeries applications using the MQSeries Internet Gateway.

You'll find more information on the MQSeries Internet Gateway at: http://www.hursley.ibm.com/mqseries/.

Using Client-Side Programming—The MQSeries Client for Java

The MQSeries Client for Java provides access to MQSeries queue managers from a Web browser through a Java applet without any MQSeries code being installed on the client system. In general, the MQSeries queue manager system must reside on the same system as the Web server from which the MQSeries Client for Java was downloaded.

You can use the MQSeries Client for Java in conjunction with the MQSeries IMS Bridge to access existing and new IMS applications from a Java-enabled Web browser.

In contrast with the Encina DE-Light Web Client and the CICS Gateway for Java Client, the MQSeries Client for Java communicates directly with a remote queue manager instead of an intermediate gateway system. In the main, the MQSeries Client for Java is the same as the regular MQSeries client except that it is written in Java; for example, it does not include any local queues. However, the MQSeries Client for Java supports the TCP/IP protocol only.

The MQSeries Client for Java has no access to environment variables, and so does not make use of the MQ_USER_ID, MQ_PASSWORD, and MQ_SERVER environment variables as the C client would. Instead, the Java client has a class called MQEnvironment, with static data members for hostname, channel, port number, User ID, and password.

Three exits are defined by the client:

- *The Send Exit* is invoked whenever a transmission is sent to a queue manager. The send exit is passed all the data that is to be transmitted and can encrypt, sign, or otherwise process the data before it is sent.
- *The Receive Exit* is invoked whenever a transmission is received from a queue manager. The receive exit is passed all the data that has been transmitted and can encrypt, sign, or otherwise process the received data before control is returned to the client applet.
- *The Security Exit* is invoked when security exchanges are performed during the establishment of a connection to a queue manager. The exit can be used to send security messages to the queue manager such as User ID and password.

A typical sequence of requests to the MQSeries Client for Java consists of the following:

- Connect to the queue manager.
- Log on (optional) using the security exit.
- Open a queue.
- Issue sequence of get and put requests.
- Commit UOR.
- Issue sequence of get and put requests.
- Commit UOR.
- Close the queue.
- Disconnect from the queue manager.

If you require multiple concurrent MQSeries UORs then you must have multiple concurrent connections to the relevant queue managers, one connection for each concurrent UOR.

Here is a code fragment illustrating the interfaces to the MQSeries Client for Java:

```
// MQSeries Client for Java sample applet
//
// This sample runs as an applet using the appletviewer and HTML file,
// using the command :-
//           appletviewer MQSample.html
// Output is to the command line, NOT the applet viewer window.
//
// Note. If you receive MQ error 2 reason 2059 and you are sure your MQ and TCPIP
// setup is correct (see advice in "What do I do if something goes wrong?"),
// you should click on the "Applet" selection in the Applet viewer window
// select properties, and change "Network access" to unrestricted.

import MQ.*;            // Include the MQ package

public class MQSample extends java.applet.Applet
```

(continued)

Accessing Encina, IMS/TM, and MQSeries Applications from the Internet

```java
{
  // define the name of your host to connect to
  private String hostname = "your_hostname";
  // define name of channel for client to use
  private String channel = "server_channel";
                          // This assumes MQ Server is listening on
                          // the default TCP/IP port of 1414

  // define name of queue manager object to connect to.
  private String qManager = "your_Q_manager";

  // define a queue manager object
  private MQQueueManager qMgr;

  // When the class is called, this initialisation is done first.

  public void init()
  {
    // Set up MQ environment
    // Could have put the hostname & channel string directly here!
    MQEnvironment.hostname = hostname;
    MQEnvironment.channel = channel;   //

  } // end of init

  public void start()
  {

    try {
      // Create a connection to the queue manager
      qMgr = new MQQueueManager(qManager);

      // Set up the options on the queue we wish to open...
      // Note. All MQ Options are prefixed with MQC in Java.

      int openOptions = MQC.MQOO_INPUT_AS_Q_DEF |
                        MQC.MQOO_OUTPUT ;

      // MQOO_INQUIRE & MQOO_SET are always included by default.

      // Now specify the queue to open, and the open options...
```

(continued)

```java
            MQQueue system_default_local_queue =
                qMgr.accessQueue("SYSTEM.DEFAULT.LOCAL.QUEUE",
                                 openOptions,
                                 null,       // default q manager
                                 null,       // no dynamic q name
                                 null);      // no alternate user id

// Define a simple MQ message, and initialise it in UTF format..
MQMessage hello_world = new MQMessage();
hello_world.writeUTF("Hello World!");

// specify the message options...

// accept the defaults, same as MQPMO_DEFAULT constant
MQPutMessageOptions pmo = new MQPutMessageOptions();

// put the message on the queue
system_default_local_queue.put(hello_world,pmo);

// get the message back again...
// define a MQ message buffer to receive the message into
MQMessage retrievedMessage = new MQMessage();
retrievedMessage.messageId = hello_world.messageId;

// Set the get message options..
// accept the defaults same as MQGMO_DEFAULT
MQGetMessageOptions gmo = new MQGetMessageOptions();
// get the message off the queue...

   system_default_local_queue.get(retrievedMessage,
                                  gmo,
                                  100);      // max message size

// Prove we have the message; display the UTF message text

   String msgText = retrievedMessage.readUTF();
   System.out.println("The message is: " + msgText);

   // Close the queue

   system_default_local_queue.close();
```

(continued)

```
      // Disconnect from the queue manager

      qMgr.disconnect();

  }

  // If an error has occured in the above, identify what went wrong.
  // Was it an MQ error?

  catch (MQException ex)
  {
    System.out.println("An MQ error occurred : Completion code " +
                       ex.completionCode +
                       " Reason code " + ex.reasonCode);
  }
  // Was it a Java buffer space error?
  catch (java.io.IOException ex)
  {
    System.out.println
  ("An error occurred whilst writing to the message buffer: " + ex);
  }

  } // end of start

} // end of sample
```

In common with the other Java clients that use their own protocol to communicate with their servers, difficulties may arise when using the MQSeries Client for Java through a firewall to access an MQSeries server outside the firewall. Firewalls are not usually configured to permit outbound requests other than standard TCP/IP requests such as HTTP and e-mail.

CONCLUSION

In this chapter we discuss Internet access to Encina, IMS, and MQSeries applications. The server gateway approach is available for all the systems, without making any changes on the target system itself. Both Encina and MQSeries have introduced Java clients.

You can use the MQSeries Internet Gateway or the MQSeries Client for Java to access various server applications, including IMS and CICS. You can use the Java client for DB2, MQSeries, Encina, and CICS together in one Java applet. However, you cannot rely on Java clients to coordinate UORs in different server systems. If you require updates to be coordinated then you must select an appropriate server system that supports two-phase commit as a coordinator to synchronize the updates.

CHAPTER 13

Electronic Commerce on the Internet

When setting up an Intranet or Internet system that incorporates electronic commerce, you must examine certain areas that may not be relevant in other systems. In this chapter, we highlight those areas and review the relationship between electronic commerce and traditional transaction processing systems. We also provide some examples of electronic commerce.

After reading this chapter, you will be able to identify the areas that require attention when creating a system that supports buying and selling on the Internet and communicates with your existing computer applications.

INTRODUCTION

Electronic commerce on the Internet usually refers to the exchange of goods and services in return for money. On the Internet, the payments are often between individuals and organizations, such as ticket sales for the 1996 Olympics in Atlanta, Georgia. The Internet portion of the ticket sale occurred between the buyer and the merchant selling the tickets. All other portions of the transaction (e.g., contact with the relevant credit card company) occurred on a private network. Increasingly, however, commercial exchanges occur between organizations and other organizations across the Internet. The SET protocol, which is outlined later in this chapter, is an example of a procedure that enables secure exchanges between individuals, banks, and merchants.

Just as there are many ways of making payments in the real world—cash, checks, traveler's checks, credit cards, and debit cards—there are many ways of making payments in the digital world on the Internet. The payments fall into two main categories:

- *Account-based money such as credit cards:* Account-based money is money stored in a trusted third-party ledger such as a bank. This approach is used when the amounts exchanged are more than about five dollars. It is not used for smaller amounts because the cost of processing a credit card transaction, for example, would be relatively high in comparison with the amount exchanged.

- *Token-based money, such as digital cash:* Token-based money is made of packets of bits traded like coins. If you possess the bits you possess the money. This approach is used when small amounts of money are involved, but it presents many difficulties. For example, some of the early digital cash schemes did not incorporate adequate precautions to prevent double spending and the owner of the cash was able to spend it more than once. There are also political problems associated with digital cash when governments want to track its flow, particularly across countries.

Currently, the efforts for securing credit card transactions are developing much faster than those for digital cash payments, and a number of major companies are involved.

Intelligent agents can be used in conjunction with electronic commerce applications to help buyers find the best value product to suit their needs. Software is already available that compares the prices of identical goods for sale on the Internet and reports back to the potential buyer. Intelligent agents could be used to create more sophisticated purchasing applications, however, that take personal preferences into account, such as shopping for birthdays and for special holidays such as Christmas. In the future we are likely to see, intelligent agents that pay their way with digital cash or assess the competition.

Purchasing habits and styles may change as a result of widespread use of the Internet, even before electronic commerce on the Internet becomes generally accepted. The press has reported instances of potential buyers making contact with one another. The benefits of such communication are well illustrated in the case where consumers living in the same town contacted one another electronically and were able to get a group discount of 25 percent on the price of a new car that they all wanted. Such communication also helps decision making. It makes it easy, for example, to find out whether recent buyers are satisfied or dissatisfied with their purchase.

Easy access on the Internet to price and product information, the views of other consumers and competitors may transform commerce generally. As an example, certain items are cheaper in the United States than in Europe, even when the price of postage is included. Some small companies in the United States are doing well by placing their product catalogs on the Internet and selling to Europeans. Another example occurred during the Olympics when sites appeared on the Internet that specialized in helping people resell their tickets if they could not use them.

THE INTERNET IS WORLDWIDE: IMPLICATIONS

A major difference between electronic commerce that does not involve the Internet and electronic commerce on the Internet is that the Internet is worldwide. You may have to consider the laws and regulations of the country where your application is running as well the laws of the country of the purchaser. Some electronic commerce applications restrict their use to certain countries, by stating, for example, that the sale can be made only in the United States. It is often possible to check the domain name associated with the IP address of the inbound request of the buyer and thus determine the country from which the purchase is being made. This is not a completely reliable technique, however, as many organizations around the world have been acquiring U.S.-style domain names with a com suffix.

Although English is widely used on the Internet, in many countries, such as Japan, users expect to have an interface in their own language. Thus, you may want to provide a choice of languages to enable purchasers to use the application comfortably. You may also consider providing prices in a variety of currencies, but do so with care. Multiple prices in a single window quickly become cluttered and confusing.

Traditional payment schemes vary by country. For example, in the United States it is relatively uncommon for public utilities to provide mechanisms for the automated payment of household gas and electricity bills, whereas the automated payment of such bills is routine in the United Kingdom. Another example is credit card payment, which is only just coming into general use in some countries such as India. Thus, you should take into account customs and habits in the various countries in which you are trying to make Internet sales when devising or adopting global payment schemes.

You also have to consider the side effects of application maintenance when you make your electronic commerce application unavailable in the early hours of the morning in the United States (eastern standard time). It becomes unavailable at peak times to people in countries in the Far East. The weekend and public holidays vary considerably around the world, so you have to take that variability into account.

Patterns of access also differ. For example, in the United States there is considerably more Internet use from the workplace than from home, although this may change. In many systems, audit logs enable you to monitor the frequency and origins of the accesses. You may even find that some of the accesses are from your competitors!

When a credit card number is used on the Internet, it is critical to ensure that the credit card number cannot be accessed by unauthorized individuals or organizations. Encryption is the main technique used to protect this type of data. Many governments limit the export of cryptographic technology to ensure the interests of national security and crime prevention. It is now recognized, however, that the implementation of electronic commerce will require the widespread use of strong cryptography. Key recovery techniques enable authorized agencies to locate private keys. These techniques will allow the widespread use of strong cryptography while preserving the legitimate needs of national security and law enforcement agencies and protecting legitimate users from the risks associated with losing encryption keys.

Several organizations from around the world have formed the Key Recovery Alliance with the objective of defining a worldwide standard and infrastructure to support key recovery. Companies involved in the alliance include Apple, IBM, and HP.

You should also be aware that some countries have restrictions on the import of encryption software, such as France and Russia. The restriction could mean that it is illegal for someone in that country to download or use your software if it includes support for encryption.

Ensure that you use your own material, diagrams, images, and the like. If you use the material of other owners, you must obtain their permission first. It is usual on the Internet to use images, such as GIFs and JPEGs, and Java applets from a variety of sources, but a commercial organization should aim to create and use its own material.

In the majority of cases, commercial sites have relatively few hypertext links to other sites, according to the survey run by Open Text and published in the proceedings of the Fifth World Wide Web Conference held in May 1996. If you do include such links (e.g., to advertise the use of your product by another company), it is both advisable and courteous to obtain the permission of the other company first. Obtaining use permission is also recommended when you are preparing material for presentations and documentation that include Web pages from other companies.

Take care to ensure that you do not use any language or material that could be considered offensive by various groups of people, such as small communities or people in other countries. Indeed some countries are beginning to introduce Internet censorship. In 1996, there was a well-known case in a European country where an Internet service provider had to remove access to certain material on the Internet as it was in conflict with the laws of that country.

Ensure that the information you make available is current. The price information must be clear, and the countries in which the prices apply must be clearly identified. There have been cases where companies have had to withdraw portions of their Websites because the bargain prices quoted were no longer valid. Potential buyers complained to the legal authorities when the company did not honor the prices quoted on the Internet. As a result restrictions were placed on that company in the country of the buyers.

If you plan to introduce your own digital payment scheme, check any existing patents in this area. There are numerous such patents, such as methods for electronic transactions with digital signatures, verification and fraud protection systems for credit cards, and smart card validation.

THE SECURE ELECTRONIC TRANSACTION (SET) PROTOCOL

Secure Electronic Transaction (SET) is a protocol for ensuring that credit card transactions can be processed securely over an open network. SET was developed by Visa and MasterCard, along with a number of other companies, including GTE, IBM, Microsoft, Netscape, Terisa, and Verisign. A standard way for processing credit card payments safely is essential for the success of electronic commerce on the Internet. Thus, other credit card companies, such as American Express, have agreed to support SET.

SET uses public key encryption and assumes three major participants in any transaction: the credit card holder (the buyer), the merchant, and the bank (see Figure 13.1). All three participants have digital certificates issued by a trusted common third party known as the certification authority. The certification authority could be the credit card company or any other trusted company.

The SET protocol defines how the sensitive data in a transaction is encrypted to ensure that the merchant cannot see the buyer's credit card number, and the bank does not get information about the goods purchased (see Figure 13.2).

The SET specification is available from: http://www.visa.com/cgi-bin/vee/sf/set/intro.html.

PROTECTING COPYRIGHT INFORMATION ON THE INTERNET

One aspect of running a worldwide electronic commerce application is protection of digital information copyrights. This can be difficult, particularly as copyright laws vary significantly around the world. Techniques such as digital signatures, watermarks, and cryptolopes are evolving to protect digital information.

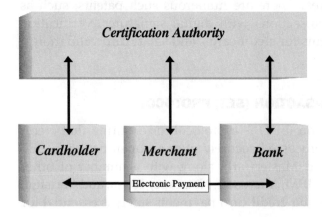

Figure 13.1 The SET participants.

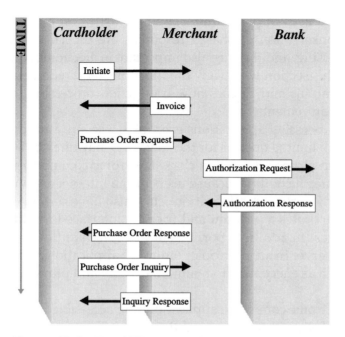

Figure 13.2 The SET message flow.

Cryptolope containers are a packaging technology developed by IBM to help prevent the unauthorized distribution of electronic media across the Internet. The authors, publishers, and redistributors of information can track the actions that are performed and then ensure that the appropriate royalties are paid. A cryptolope container package consists of the document, in encrypted form, that a user wants to purchase and some additional information. When users view the cryptolope container with a browser, they see some information in clear text, such as a document abstract, and the cost of the document, but they do not see the document itself. A browser helper application is needed to view cryptolopes. In the future, however, a Java applet will be used to enable cryptolopes to be processed.

TRANSACTION PROCESSING AND ITS ROLE IN ELECTRONIC COMMERCE

Transaction processing is the software and techniques needed to ensure the successful execution of many short, concurrent requests that update resources, possibly in multiple locations, with security and integrity. Performance and conservation of shared resources are crucial elements of transaction processing, and they are also important in electronic commerce applications. In this section we review the functions required in electronic commerce applications and discuss how transaction processing software supports those requirements.

Transaction processing applications execute in a secure and controlled environment, with limited options for the user, who may often be a trained person, such as an airline reservation clerk. Electronic commerce applications require greater flexibility because users of the Internet are untrained with respect to any particular application. They also have certain expectations of what constitutes a pleasant and friendly interface for purchasing goods and services. In addition, portions of the data that flows between the user and the server in an electronic commerce application require special attention, such as encryption to maintain privacy and provide authentication.

Typically, electronic commerce applications are accessible from a much greater number of diverse users around the world. Therefore, supporting customized heterogeneous interfaces, as well as system availability, is becoming more and more important.

Many of the extensions to transaction processing software that are required to support Internet electronic commerce are in the portions of the software that involve customers: security and the user interface. Security, agreed data formats, and audit trails are also vital for electronic commerce and Electronic Data Interchange (EDI) between companies over the Internet. The term *Extranets* has been used to describe a secure network linking the Intranets of multiple companies.

Software is evolving that combines some elements of transaction processing and of Internet electronic commerce. Below we describe two examples: The Web Object Manager (WOM), which is general-purpose software for high-volume systems on the Internet, and Net.Commerce, which is software specific for a particular application such as a store or a shopping mall on the Internet.

The Web Object Manager

WOM was originally developed in IBM in the United Kingdom and Germany to support major Websites with requirements for high volumes of users and accesses. Its first major application was to provide the results of the Wimbledon Tennis Championships on the Web. Its most recent, major application was the Atlanta Olympics, where WOM handled 3600 user accesses per minute and received 425 million hits during the period of the Olympics. The difference between the Olympics Website and some of the other busy sites on the Internet was that the results data presented to the user was changing constantly. The higher the rate of change in the underlying data delivered, the more difficult it is to provide a consistent response time. Processor cycles and disk resources are busy making the alterations as well as responding to users, thereby causing significant contention. By buffering information in memory, one can usually alleviate disk contention, but when data is being updated, the buffers have to be refreshed constantly.

WOM emphasizes scalability and the customized presentation of information that is constantly changing. As well as providing a framework for defining and creating information to be returned to users, it responds efficiently to end user requests from browsers (that is, HTTP requests).

To avoid bottlenecks and help with scalability, WOM supports multiple replicated server systems. When the first request arrives from a user, a component known as WomBat in the main server selects the most appropriate site to respond to an individual user. Wombat makes the choice by comparing the times to PING the user from the various sites. (PING stands for Packet Internet Groper and is a simple way of sending communication packets). All subsequent requests from that user are then automatically rerouted to the most responsive site without the user noticing any change.

The WOM component known as the WomSprayer also helps with scalability, as it routes requests to the least busy processor at a particular site, once the site has been selected. WOM uses virtual IP addressing, that is, IP addresses are used to refer to applications, not systems (processors), making it simpler to add or remove systems when necessary.

WOM uses the Distributed File System (DFS) from Transarc as the basis for the elements that make up the Web pages (see Figure 13.3). DFS files can be replicated on many systems, but a particular file is always retrieved by using the same name, irrespective of whether it is a replica or the original copy. Thus the DFS file name does not include the server name, which makes it easier for WOM servers to access files in many places. WOM caches the file records when they are retrieved. Information stored and used by WOM in DFS is tagged and is self-defining, so the same piece of information can be used and presented in many ways, for example, according to user preferences. With a Java-enabled browser, results can be incorporated into a Java applet. With a simpler browser, the results could be presented in a dynamically built image. If the users communications link is slow, the results could be transmitted as text.

WOM has a WomCanvas which consists of a number of objects. The application designer selects the various tagged WOM objects to make up a WomCanvas, which is used when responding to an end user request. Thus the pages returned to users are assembled at runtime according to the Wom-Canvas. WomCanvas objects can also include portions of legacy systems.

WOM is not yet available as a separate product. However, it is being used in major applications and its concepts are important when creating large-scale systems.

Net.Commerce

Net.Commerce is software that helps you build a store or shopping mall on the Web (see Figure 13.4). It enables you to define and make available a catalog of products which can be purchased securely by using a Web browser. Net.Commerce also provides a framework for calculating various charges, such as taxes and shipping costs. The IBM Internet Connection Server and Net.Data are packaged with Net.Commerce.

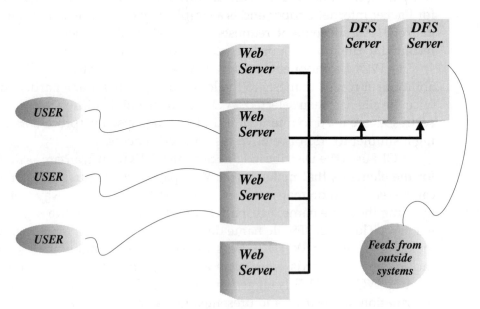

Figure 13.3 Distributed File System and its use with WOM.

Electronic Commerce on the Internet

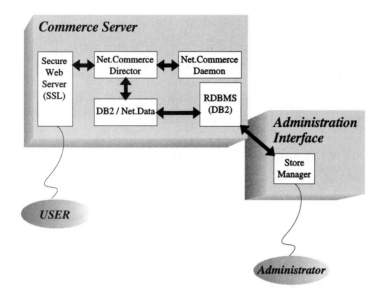

Figure 13.4 Net.Commerce architecture.

Net.Commerce has a store manager, which enables the merchant to manipulate pricing, product, customer, and merchant information. Product information can be classified into categories. Shoppers may also be grouped (e.g., by frequency of access) to provide special discounts.

The commerce server itself (see Figure 13.4) is the main runtime element. It is the interface between the Web server and Net.Data and runs the store application code. Its functions include maintaining application state. It also maintains a set of hot connections to the database (e.g., DB2 through Net.Data) to avoid initiating a new connection on each user request. Among the application functions it runs are order processing, taxation and shipping calculations, shopping cart (server-side state), and interfaces to legacy systems.

Net.Commerce supports secure transactions, in conjunction with a secure Web server. Sensitive information can be encrypted, and users can be certified. SET protocol support is planned for Net.Commerce release 1.1 as is a template editor for creating the store pages. SSL can be used to encrypt all Net.Commerce transactions.

The case study in Chapter 14 sets out the issues to consider when building an application server such as Net.Commerce.

CONCLUSION

The term *electronic commerce* is used in many different ways. It is clear that some basic functions are necessary to conduct business (to buy, sell, and deal with sensitive information and goods) safely and successfully on the Internet. If you have a commercial application that will be accessed through an open network, you must consider:

- The privacy of the information transmitted
- The laws of the various countries in which the transaction is being conducted
- An appropriate payment scheme, such as the SET protocol

Transaction processing software supports important functions such as predictable performance and response times and data integrity. However, when conducting electronic commerce on the Internet, you have to pay special attention to security, the end user interface, and international law and customs. New types of software infrastructure are being created that combine the functions of traditional transaction processing software with the needs of electronic commerce.

SECTION 5

A Case Study

CHAPTER **14**

An Application Server

Web application servers facilitate the solution of business- or academic-related problems over the World Wide Web, permitting a consumer located anywhere in the world to use a Web browser to transact with a Web application server to accomplish a given task. The task could be as simple as posting a comment to an Internet news group, or as complicated as booking an entire itinerary for an international trip, including travel, accommodations, and automobile rental, charging it to multiple different credit cards, or withdrawing money directly from a bank account to cover the costs of the trip.

The use of a Web browser to access information began as an attempt to bring together many different protocols and data access paradigms into a single, easy-to-use environment. Previously, multiple client programs were required to access files using FTP, log in to hosts using telnet, and view collections of data using gopher or other TCP/IP clients. A technological revolution occurred when the Web browser was created to combine all of these clients into a single, graphical user interface.

Initially, a Web browser could easily access "static pages," or files containing HTML and stored in a file system accessible by the Web server, through the use of the HTTP GET command. A user familiar with Web browser usage would either select a URL highlighted on the browser screen or type in a URL, such as: http://www.ibm.com/index.html.

This command instructs the Web browser to build a set of HTTP command lines that sends a message to the Web server located at the host named www.ibm.com. The HTTP command lines could contain many functions describing to the Web server who the caller is, the information the caller is seeking, the Web browser (or user agent) used to request the information, and the types of information that could be sent back and displayed by the Web browser. All of these command lines are examined in depth elsewhere in this book; a key essential line specifies arguments to the HTTP GET method. The above URL, http://www.ibm.com/index.html, translates to the HTTP command line, GET/index.html, which is the method GET, sent with argument/index.html to the Web server listening on TCP/IP port 80 on the machine with the domain name server (DNS) address of www.ibm.com.

The web server accepts this GET method as a request for the index.html file in the document root directory located on the same system as the Web server. The file would then be sent through an HTTP connection down to the Web browser and stored in a temporary file in the Web browser's system. The Web browser would examine the file, decode the information contained therein, and use a user interface (most often graphical in nature) to display the data.

WEB SERVER APPLICATION PROGRAMMING INTERFACES

HTTP has become increasingly more complicated. The above URL syntax creates a request for a static page. One of the limitations of an early version of the HTTP protocol was the lack of a standard method for creating dynamic pages, that is, executing a program on the Web server that would dynamically create the content and then pass the content through the Web to a browser. To satisfy this problem, the Common Gateway Interface was defined to manage communications between the Web server and application programs that can be run on the same system as the Web server.

In a CGI application, HTML forms communicate with a process executed by the Web server when a given URL is selected. An HTML form is one that contains the clause <FORM> ... </FORM>, and within it, <INPUT> tags signifying input. The clause accepts input from the user of the Web browser and translates that input into a URL of the form: http://<hostname>/cgi-bin/<program>?name1=value1[&name2=value2 . . .].

If the URL above seems confusing, it can be easily separated into pieces. An HTML form describes Name=Value pairs through the use of the <INPUT> tag for example:

An Application Server

```
<FORM ACTION="http://myhostname/cgi-bin/getpwd" METHOD="GET">
<INPUT type="field" name="myfield">
<INPUT type="submit" value="Make it So!">
</FORM>
```

Once the above HTML page is displayed, if the method of the form is GET, the following URL is generated after the user types in myvalue in the input field: http://myhostname/cgi-bin/getpwd?myfield=myvalue.

The primary deficiency of CGI is that a new process is generated every time a user enters data on a page and clicks on the button to submit the data. To alleviate this problem, other interfaces have been defined to enable a program to accept input from an HTML form. These interfaces include NSAPI and ISAPI, which allow a long-running process or dynamic link library (DLL) to register entry points with the Web server that can override the default processing of the Web server. This approach results in a far more flexible specification than CGI affords for building high-performance Web application servers.

Nevertheless, despite the fact that CGI is less efficient than NSAPI or ISAPI, it is a considerably easier interface for beginning application server programming, so this chapter focuses on the use of CGI.

Whichever server load you anticipate, however, it is important to far overestimate the number of hits that your application server will have to accept and to choose the interface appropriately. The Atlanta Olympic Games Ticket Server, for example, was initially designed to take around 100,000 hits per day and sell perhaps 10,000 tickets during its six-month lifetime. Instead, the Atlanta Olympic Games Ticket Server accepted 40,000 ticket orders in the first six weeks, accepting an average load of 650,000 hits per day. Over time, ticket sales amounted to 20 percent of the total tickets sold at the Atlanta Olympic Games. Rapid redesign and performance tuning of the Atlanta Olympic Games Ticket Server led to much of the development and deployment of concepts and technologies discussed later in this chapter.

WEB APPLICATION PLATFORMS

This book discusses technologies to gain access to data stored in databases or alternatively processed through transactional systems. Examples include DB2 World Wide Web Connection, CICS Internet Gateway, and Lotus Domino Server interfaces into Lotus Notes. These data access gateways convert data managed in a data system so it can be accessed with a

Web browser. Typically, these gateways rely on the intelligence of the data system and a set of procedural directives or templates to process and display the data in an HTML context. However, these gateways are becoming increasingly more complex, providing a degree of programmability previously unseen. They are evolving into Web server middleware.

Figure 14.1 illustrates how a Web application server acts to manage data either through direct access to a data system or by using a data access gateway as an intermediary. A Web application server is designed to make use of all of the componentry and middleware available and to add the necessary interfaces (or "glue") to develop a solution to a problem. Web browsers, Web servers, web server APIs, data access gateways, and data storage and management systems together provide a Web application platform, now also referred to as an Internet operating system, on which web application servers can be designed and developed.

DESIGNING A WEB APPLICATION SERVER

The key to designing and developing Web application servers is understanding how they process HTML forms. Here is a simple example of an

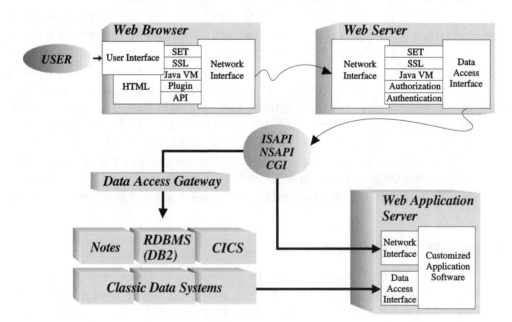

Figure 14.1   A Web application server architecture.

An Application Server

HTML form that prompts the user for a User ID and password and then passes this information to a CGI program that validates the User ID and password against a registry:

```
<FORM ACTION="/cgi-bin/getpwd" METHOD="get">
<p>Enter Userid: <INPUT TYPE="field" NAME="userid" VALUE="">
<p>Enter Password: <INPUT TYPE="field" NAME="password" VALUE="">
<INPUT TYPE="submit" VALUE="Register">
</FORM>
```

Figure 14.2 shows how the user will view this.

A CGI program written in the C language to process a CGI GET method from this input looks like this:

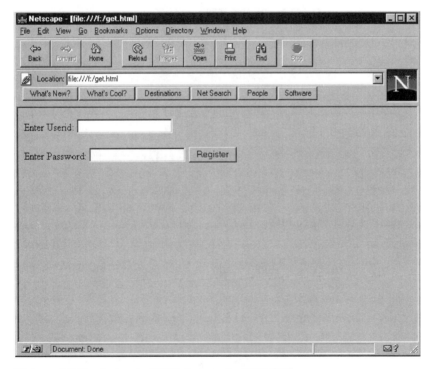

Figure 14.2 A simple HTML form using CGI GET.

```c
#include <stdlib.h>
#include <stdio.h>

int main(int argc, char *argv[])
{
    char *query_string;
    char *uid;
    char *pwd;
    char *qptr;

/* Read the parameters set by the web server from the environment
   variable
   QUERY_STRING */

    qptr = getenv("QUERY_STRING");

    if((qptr == NULL) || (strlen(qptr) == 0))
    {
          printf("<li>ERROR: This program must be executed using
          the GET method.\n");
          return 0;

    }

/* Make a copy of the environment variable, some systems don't
   like manipulation of this space */

    query_string = (char *) malloc(strlen(qptr)+1);
    strncpy(query_string,qptr);

/* Retrieve the userid part of the query string */
    qptr = strstr(query_string,"userid");
    if (!qptr)
    {
          printf("<li>ERROR: No userid specified!\n");
          return 0;
    }
    uid = strchr(qptr,'=')+1;

/* Retrieve the password part of the query_string */
    qptr = strstr(query_string,"password");
    if (!qptr)
    {
```

(continued)

```
            printf("<li>ERROR: No password specified!\n");
            return 0;
     }
     pwd = strchr(qptr,'=')+1;

  /* Null terminate the fields within the string */
     for (qptr = query_string; qptr !=0; qptr++)
        if (*qptr == '&') *qptr=0;

  /* Print out the result */
     printf("<li>userid: !%s!\n",uid);
     printf("<li>password: !%s!\n",pwd);

     return 0;
  }
```

The above program reads the QUERY_STRING environment variable for the contents of the input fields. Using an HTTP GET method, the parameters encoded after the anchor (those characters after the ? symbol) are stored by the Web server in the QUERY_STRING environment variable before the CGI program that will process the request is called. If the HTML form had been encoded by using the HTTP POST method, the parameters would be passed to the program through the stdin (standard input) stream. Here is a CGI program that reads and processes the HTTP POST method. Note that the HTML form is the same as the previous HTML form, with the sole exception that the method has been changed to POST from GET.

```
<FORM ACTION="/cgi-bin/getpwd" METHOD="post">
<p>Enter Userid: <INPUT TYPE="field" NAME="userid" VALUE="">
<p>Enter Password: <INPUT TYPE="field" NAME="password" VALUE="">
<INPUT TYPE="submit" VALUE="Register">
</FORM>
```

Figure 14.3 shows how the user will view this.

The CGI program written to process a POST method looks like this:

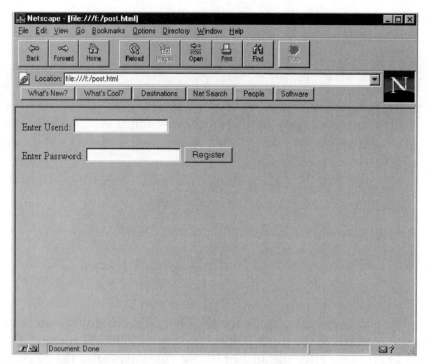

Figure 14.3 A simple HTML form using CGI POST.

```
#include <stdlib.h>
#include <stdio.h>

int main(int argc, char *argv[])
{
   char *query_string;
   char *uid;
   char *pwd;
   char *content_lenth;

/* Instead of putting the content in the QUERY_STRING environment
   variable, the results will be read from stdin (standard input).
   Read the parameters set by the web server from the environment
   variable QUERY_STRING
*/

   content_length = getenv("CONTENT_LENGTH");            (continued)
```

```
        if ((content_length == NULL) || (strlen(content_length) == 0) ||
            (atoi(content_length) == 0))
        {
                printf("<li>ERROR: This program must be executed using
                        the POST method.\n");
                return 0;
        }

/* Read stdin into a variable */

    query_string = (char *) malloc(atoi(content_length)+1);
    memset(query_string,content_length,0);
    fread(query_string,content_length,1,stdin);

/* Retrieve the userid part of the query string */
    qptr = strstr(query_string,"userid");
    if (!qptr)
    {
            printf("<li>ERROR: No userid specified!\n");
            return 0;
    }
    uid = strchr(qptr,'=')+1;

/* Retrieve the password part of the query_string */
    qptr = strstr(query_string,"password");
    if (!qptr)
    {
            printf("<li>ERROR: No password specified!\n");
            return 0;
    }
    pwd = strchr(qptr,'=')+1;

/* Null terminate the fields within the string */
    for (qptr = query_string; qptr !=0; qptr++)
       if (*qptr == '&') *qptr=0;

/* Print out the result */
    printf("<li>userid: !%s!\n",uid);
    printf("<li>password: !%s!\n",pwd);

    return 0;
}
```

EXTENDING THE APPLICATION SERVER

Our examples provide a simplistic way of accepting input from and providing output to a user. Several technical hurdles still must be overcome, however, to create a robust and secure environment on which to build Web application servers. First, HTTP currently provides no inherent mechanism to preserve *state*. State involves the ability to track users as they request pages from the Web server. Without the ability to track the progress of an individual through a Website, there is no way of mapping a single transaction from beginning to end. In addition, the above examples do not discuss methods for the interaction between a Web browser and a Web server involving authentication, authorization, and encryption, to ensure that the users of Web browsers are who they say they are, are permitted to access the information they are requesting, and are prevented from eavesdropping on or altering information while it is in transit between the Web browser and Web server.

MAINTAINING STATE IN A WEB APPLICATION SERVER

There are five ways of relating users and their actions as they conduct Web transactions:

- Stateless, or a transaction generated by the use of a single Web page or form
- Out-of-band, or through information provided by a proprietary protocol or mechanism, such as the use of Java applets or Netscape cookies
- Embedded, maintaining a link by embedding a field that is passed through the use of the GET or POST mechanisms
- HTTP basic authentication, using the basic authentication mechanism in HTTP to identify a user and the REMOTE_USER environment variable to track the user
- URL-embedded, also called server-side state, created by dynamically filtering all pages and remapping URLs to embed a state variable

Some Web browsers and servers set two environment variables: the PATH_INFO environment variable and the REFERRER_URL environment variable. Setting these variables enables a rough identification of the path being traveled through the Web site. If a person were to access a page, /foo.html, that has a link to /bar.html, the REFERRER_URL environment variable received by the Web server would be set to /foo.html, and the PATH_INFO environment variable would be set to /bar.html. However, this mechanism does not preserve state on behalf of an individual user. Two individuals could be accessing page /foo.html at the same time, and then could, at different times, access page /bar.html.

Stateless transactions in a shopping environment could provide a user with a page that prompts users to enter information about themselves (credit card number, name and address) and identify the item they are purchasing. There is no concept of a shopping basket—each item is purchased one at a time. The HTTP GET and POST examples above are stateless transactions.

Out-of-band transaction states depend on the Web browser and Web server sharing a common convention or mechanism for passing information between them without the knowledge or intervention of the user. Cookies, for example, use a protocol that enables a Web server to set variables in the Web browser's environment and store data on a section of the user's hard disk, which then may be queried at a later date by that Web server, or potentially another Web server. There are three main problems with using cookies. One is that not all Web browsers support them. Netscape's Merchant Server, for example, uses cookies, so it requires the use of a Netscape Navigator to permit purchases over the Web, because most other Web browsers do not support cookies. A second problem with cookies involves the possibility of large amounts of data being passed over the network, thereby reducing network performance. Storing a shopping basket on the client's system makes the client heavier—it is more economical to store as much data as possible at the Web server, where processing is performed. A third problem with using cookies is that there is no way of permitting a user to move to a different browser to complete a transaction. Picture yourself at work adding an airline ticket to a destination to a virtual shopping basket, and then driving home to consult your wife before making the final decision. When you reach home and turn on your home PC, the contents of the shopping basket stored in your Web browser at work are inaccessible.

HTTP basic authentication uses an out-of-band variable, defined by the HTTP protocol, to track and maintain state. An HTTP server administrator can set the pages that require authentication before they are delivered to a Web browser. Each time a user requests one of these pages, the Web browser must supply a User ID and password to the Web server. If the User ID and password have not been set in the Web browser for the page requested, the user is prompted to enter his or her User ID and password. Once the User ID and password are entered once, the Web browser keeps track of the information and supplies it at each subsequent request. The Web server passes the identity of the user who is requesting data to the Web application server by setting the REMOTE_USER environment variable to match the User ID, after performing a check against a user registry to ensure that the User ID and password match. The drawback of requiring *HTTP basic authentication* when designing a Web application that maintains state is that it forces users to identify themselves before accessing pages on your Website, which is a detraction for those who want to surf the Web anonymously.

Embedded state variables are implemented in a Web application server by making every single Web page presented into an HTML form. Each subsequent page is reached by selecting a Submit button, and the data is passed on in this manner. For example:

```
FOO1.HTML:
<FORM ACTION="/foo2.html" METHOD="post">
<p>Enter Userid: <INPUT TYPE="field" NAME="userid" VALUE="">
<p>Enter Password: <INPUT TYPE="field" NAME="password" VALUE="">
<INPUT TYPE="submit" VALUE="Register">
</FORM>
```

```
FOO2.HTML:
<FORM ACTION="/foo3.html" METHOD="post">
Your userid is: $(userid)
<INPUT TYPE="hidden" value="$(userid)">
<INPUT TYPE="submit" value="CONTINUE">
</FORM>
```

```
FOO3.HTML:
<FORM ACTION="/foo4.html?userid=$(userid)" METHOD="post">
Your userid is STILL $(userid)
Enter a number:<INPUT TYPE="text" name="newvar" value="">
<INPUT TYPE="submit" value="CONTINUE">
</FORM>
```

Two very obvious problems are encountered here. If the programmer puts another input name-value pair into the HTML with the name of

USERID, the environment variable may be overridden or concatenated, depending on the Web server. This can have unexpected results. One version of Netscape's Commerce Server, for example, had the bad habit of creating the URL /foo4.html?userid=whatever?newvar=1234, which would then cause everything between the two question marks to be deleted by Netscape's Navigator. In addition, the Web browser user interface imposes this limitation: The user has to continuously select a button on the Web page rather than a hypertext link, which eliminates the usability of hypertext links.

URL-embedded, or server-side state, is slightly more complicated. It involves turning a CGI program into a Web proxy server that filters all data requested from a Web server. Each page fetched using a server-side state Web application server is turned into a dynamic page, as each URL embedded in the Web page is remapped into a call back to the CGI program with arguments for the program to pull in the next Web page dynamically. IBM's Net.Commerce system uses this process to maintain state, until a user decides to log in to the Web server, at which point it uses SSL-protected HTTP basic authentication to maintain state. This process eliminates the need for a Web browser that supports cookies, allows embedding of any page from any Website, and enables the creation of *directed content,* that is, content that is customized to an individual user. It also enables reuse of any other CGI program, as content can be passed from multiple URLs that may reference other CGI programs.

Maintaining Server-Side State

To maintain server-side state, the state variable must be embedded into each URL before any of the data that would normally be generated by a GET request and subsequent to that understood by the Web server to access a CGI program. The dynamically generated URL http://www.ibm.com/cgi-bin/nph-msrvr/;session_id=1234/command/args?a=1 embeds the state variable right into the information received by the PATH_INFO environment variable. The Web server calls nph-msrvr, which is the IBM Net.Commerce system director program. The nph-msrvr program reads the PATH_INFO environment variable and parses out session ID 1234 from the URL, checks the command and arguments, and processes them appropriately. The GET method argument "a=1" is passed for HTML form processing as usual. The nph-msrvr program is a non-parse-header CGI (NPH-CGI) program. The nph- prefix essentially instructs the Web server to pass through unmodified all information generated by the CGI program. Typically, the Web server would add an HTTP header to the information generated by the CGI program. NPH-CGI scripts allow a CGI program to send back the appropriate header, enabling direct manipulation of the HTTP protocol to affect the Web browser. One effective use of NPH-CGI direct manipulation is to return an HTTP/1.0 Moved header to the Web browser, which causes the Web browser to transmit an HTTP GET command at another URL rather than the URL originally specified.

Here is source code that combines the above two program fragments that process HTML forms by handling the HTTP GET and POST methods. It first receives data submitted by either a GET or POST method and then parses the session ID out of the URL:

```
/*      ParseSessionID
 *
 *      Function to parse the session id out of an embedded-URL
 */
#define CMDSEP          ';'     /* This will separate out state */
                                /* and command from the URL     */
char *ParseSessionID(char *session_data)
{
      char *sptr = NULL;

      char *SESSION_ID = NULL;

      if(session_data == NULL)
        return NULL;

      sptr = strstr(session_data,"session_id");
      if (!sptr)
        sptr = strstr(session_data,"SESSION_ID");

      if (sptr) {
        char *slashptr = NULL;
        char *cmdsep = NULL;

        sptr = strchr(sptr,'=');
        slashptr = strchr(sptr,'/');
        cmdsep = strstr(sptr,CMDSEP);
        if((cmdsep && slashptr) && (cmdsep < slashptr))
          slashptr = cmdsep;
```
(continued)

An Application Server

```c
        if(!slashptr)
          slashptr = cmdsep;

        if(!slashptr)
          slashptr = strchr(sptr,0);

        SESSION_ID = (char *)malloc(1024);
        memset(SESSION_ID,0,1023);
        strncpy(SESSION_ID,sptr+1,(slashptr-sptr-1));
    }/* endif */

      return SESSION_ID;
}
int main(int argc, char *argv[])
{
  char *SESSION_ID = NULL;
  char *newsid = NULL;
  int content_length;
  char *content_data = NULL;
/* Check for METHOD=GET */
  char* pstr = getenv("PATH_INFO");
  char* qstr = getenv("QUERY_STRING");
  cgistr[0]=0;
  if (qstr==NULL || *qstr=='\0') /* Check for Method=POST */
{
  char *cl = getenv("CONTENT_LENGTH");
  if (cl)
  {
                content_length=atoi(cl);
                if (content_length > 0)
                {
                        qstr = (char *)malloc(content_length+1);
                        fread(qstr,content_length,1,stdin);
                }
      }/* endif */
   }/* endif */

  if(pstr==NULL || *pstr=='\0') qstr=NULL;
  if(qstr==NULL || *qstr=='\0') qstr=NULL;
```

(continued)

```
    /* pstr is the contents of the path_info string */
    /* qstr is the contents of the submitted data from the form */

    if (pstr)
        SESSION_ID = ParseSessionID(pstr);

    /* At this point, SESSION_ID is NULL or contains the contents
    of the session id imbedded in the URL */

    }/* end of main */
```

EMBEDDING CONTENT FROM ANOTHER WEBSITE

Once all pages are built dynamically out of content stored on a single site, with an extension of the program fragments above, it is relatively simple to build a function to pull data from another Web site or Web server:

```
#include <stdlib.h>
#include <stdio.h>
#include <string.h>
#include <math.h>
#include <sys/types.h>

#include <sys/socket.h>
#include <netinet/in.h>
#include <netdb.h>

   #include <errno.h>
   #include "sendrcv.h"
   #include "defines.h"

   /* Globals. */
   struct sockaddr_in ServerAddress;
   struct hostent *HostEntry;
/*     MS_SendMessage

*      Send a message down a socket.

*/
```

(continued)

```
int MS_SendMessage(int Socket, char *Message)
{
  int rc, len;
  char *tmpMessage = (char *)(malloc(strlen(Message)+3));

  strcpy(tmpMessage,Message);

  strcat(tmpMessage, "\015\012");
  len = strlen(tmpMessage);
  while (len > 0) {
    rc = send(Socket, tmpMessage, len, 0);
    if (rc <= 0) {
      return(1);
    }
    len -= rc;
    tmpMessage += rc;
  }
  free (tmpMessage);
  return(0);
}

/* send_text

   Dump a buffer of text to a file, stripping off linefeeds.
*/

int send_text(FILE *fp, char *buffer, int bufsize)
{
  char *i;
  for (i=buffer;i<buffer+bufsize;i++)
  {
    if (*i == 0)

    break;
    if (*i !=26)
      fputc(*i, fp);
  }/* endfor */

  return 0;
}

/* GetResponseHunk
```

(continued)

```
      Receives a response from the server, storing it in Buffer
   */

int GetResponseHunk(int Socket, char *Buffer, int BufferSize)
{
   int rc;

   rc = recv(Socket, Buffer, BufferSize - 1, 0);
   if (rc > 0) {
     Buffer[rc] = '\0';
   }
   return(rc);

}

   /* http_command
    *
    * Runs the command stored in the command lines against
    * the web server located at host HostName:Port, eg www.ibm.com:80
    *
    * Sets the result in the open stream passed in, OutputFile.
    */

int http_command(char *HostName, char **commands, int cmdlines,
   FILE *OutputFile)
{
   long PortNumber = 80;
   char *port;
   int rc;
   int i;
   int status;

   /* Parse hostname for a port number. */
   port = (char *)strchr(HostName, ':');
   if (port != NULL) {
     *port = '\0';
     ++port;
     PortNumber = atoi(port);
   }

   /* Set up our address. */
   memset((char *) &ServerAddress, (char)0,
   sizeof(ServerAddress));
```

(continued)

```
   ServerAddress.sin_family = AF_INET;
   ServerAddress.sin_port = htons(PortNumber);

/* First, check to see if it's a dotted decimal address hostname! */
   ServerAddress.sin_addr.s_addr = inet_addr(HostName);

   if (ServerAddress.sin_addr.s_addr == -1)
   {
/* If that failed, try to resolve from a nameserver */
   HostEntry = gethostbyname(HostName);
   if (HostEntry == NULL)
   {
/* The name server didn't recognize this host name or address. */
     printf("A host machine at \"%s\",
port %d cannot be contacted. Check the address or the nameserver.\n",
HostName,PortNumber);
     exit(4);
   }
   memcpy((char *) &ServerAddress.sin_addr,
      (char *) HostEntry->h_addr_list[0],
      HostEntry->h_length);
   }


   /* Create the socket. */
   Sock = socket(AF_INET, SOCK_STREAM, 0);
   if (Sock < 0) {
     printf("Sock could not be created. TCP/IP stack is down.\n");
     exit(4);
   }

   /* Connect to the remote server. */
   if ((rc = connect(Sock,(struct sockaddr *) &ServerAddress,
            sizeof(ServerAddress))) < 0)
   {
     char errtxt[1024];
       sprintf(errtxt,
"<p>Director could not connect to a Web server at hostname \"%s\",
port %d. Please try again later.",
          HostName,PortNumber);
     printf(errtxt);

     exit(4);
```

(continued)

```
    }

  /* Send the request. */

  for (i=0;i<cmdlines;i++) {
    char *crfind = (char *)strchr(commands[i],'\n');
    if (crfind) *crfind=0;
    if (!((*(commands[i]) == '%') && (*(commands[i]+1) == '%')))
    {
      MS_SendMessage(Sock, commands[i]);
    }
  }
  MS_SendMessage(Sock,""); /* Final Line */

  /* Read the response, discarding the header for now. */
  past_header = 0;
  while (GetResponseHunk(Sock, Buffer, BUFFER_SIZE - 1) > 0) {
   char *outbuffer;
   int outbuflen;

   if (strstr(Buffer,"Error 404"))
           return 404;

   if (!past_header && strstr(Buffer,"\r\n\r\n"))
   {
     past_header = 1;
     outbuffer = strstr(Buffer,"\r\n\r\n")+4;
     outbuflen = strlen(outbuffer);
   }
   else
   {
     outbuffer = Buffer;
     outbuflen = BUFFER_SIZE - 1;
   }

     send_text(OutputFile, outbuffer, outbuflen);
  }

  /* close the socket */

#ifdef OS2
 soclose(Sock);
#endif
```

(continued)

```
#ifdef AIX
  close(Sock);
#endif
#ifdef WIN32
  if(closesocket(Sock) == SOCKET_ERROR )
   status = WSAGetLastError();
#endif

  return 0;
}
```

The http_command() function in the above code calls a Web server with a set of HTTP methods contained in a set of command lines. Here's another example of the function that uses the GET method to request the document root page from a Web server:

```
char *hostname;
char *cmd;
char **cmd_p;
char fname[256];
FILE *fp_tmp;

hostname = strdup("www.ibm.com:80");

sprintf(cmd,"GET / HTTP/1.1",cmd_action);

tmpnam(fname);

/* Create a temp file to store the results from the server in */
fp_tmp = fopen(fname,"w");

/* Run the HTTP command */
cmd_p[0]=cmd;
cmd_p[1]=(char *) malloc(256);

User_Agent = getenv("HTTP_USER_AGENT");
if (User_Agent == NULL)
    User_Agent = strdup("Unknown");

sprintf(cmd_p[1],"User-Agent: %s via %s",User_Agent,"My Director Program/1.0");

http_rc = http_command(hostname,cmd_p,2,fp_tmp);
```

The Web server located at host www.ibm.com, listening on port 80, would receive the request for the document root page, requested by the User_Agent "Unknown via My Director Program/1.0," and would serve it up and store it in the file pointed to by fp_tmp.

USER_AGENT is another environment variable that is received by a CGI program. It holds the unique identifier (by convention) of a Web browser. One version of IBM's WebExplorer, for example, would have caused the Web server to set the HTTP_USER_AGENT environment variable to "WebExplorer/1.0." It is important to specify this variable, by including this line in any HTTP request that you may make of a Web server.

Web servers often screen out requests from clients that do not provide a USER_AGENT string. The screening prevents destructive agents from causing damage to a Website by repeatedly requesting a page—destructive, or unwanted agents can be ignored by screening the USER_AGENT string and rejecting requests from certain clients.

In fact, Microsoft used the USER_AGENT environment variable to its advantage when writing the Internet Explorer. One of the emulation modes provided made Microsoft's Internet Explorer look to a Web server as a Netscape Navigator user agent. This request caused the Web server to send a more complicated version of the HTML code to the browser, which the Internet Explorer was then able to exploit.

In the example above, the USER_AGENT string is set to the previous USER_AGENT (if previously set in an environment variable) plus a "via My Director/1.0." This tells the Web server that the request is being filtered through a proxy of some sort. Once the data is retrieved from a Web server, it is easy to filter the file and replace all requests for URLs to be tracked back through a proxy. For example, if a page was retrieved that had the anchor:

```
<A HREF="http://www.ibm.com/foobar.html">
```

a simple piece of code could be written to take the URL in the file and convert it to:

```
<A  HREF="http://www.ibm.com/cgi-bin/nph-msrvr;session_id=1234/
    display/http/www.ibm.com/foobar.html">
```

An Application Server

Then, the director program, nph-msrvr, would return the modified HTML file to the Web browser that requested it, and any subsequent URL selected from the page would maintain state through the use of the session_id embedded state variable, and every subsequent URL selected would pass back through the director script to request the next page.

The code examples provided add up to something very simple, but very powerful: They permit server-side state, support any Web browser, support forms posted by either POST or GET, and provide the entire framework necessary to support transactions on the Web from any Web browser.

In addition, any of the other Web middleware CGI programs, such as Net.Data, DB2 World Wide Web Connection, or CICS Internet Gateway, can be used by these functions simply by passing all access to these HTML-generating programs through the director filter.

CONNECTING TO DATABASES (RELATIONAL AND NONRELATIONAL)

Once a single variable is maintained throughout the entire session, a transaction can be traced through to completion. In addition, the variable can be used to index any relational or nonrelational database and to track usage or any user profile information. This could include information stored in a shopping basket, which would simply be a set of records indexed by the session ID. Adding to the shopping basket is as simple as embedding a command in the URL that will add an item identified by a name-value pair created through an HTML form to the records stored in the database. DB2 World Wide Web Connection, also known as Net.Data, can be used to key off the session ID to expose the contents of any data indexed by the session ID. It can provide a template-driven interface to data stored in any relational database, as well, so the shopping basket could be customized for the individual customer or business, within the same application server infrastructure.

BUILDING DIRECTED HTML

Directed HTML takes dynamic HTML one step further. Once the identity or session of an individual is known, an environment can be customized for that user. By identifying a user with a previously used session ID, information about previous sessions that has been built up and stored on the server can be accessed and used to remember user profile information.

Statistical analysis tools such as IBM's Knowledge Utility (see http://www.aqui.ibm.com/) can compile the list of pages that a user most probably wants to view and compose an experience that is unique to the individual. As the volume of content continues to increase on Websites around the world, the amount of information presented to a user will have to be filtered by statistical analysis tools or more complex intelligent agents before being presented to the user, in order to make some sense of the enormous volumes of data. This may seem manipulative, but it could come to be something users demand.

DESIGNING A DIRECTOR/DAEMON APPLICATION SERVER

In designing an application server of any sort, consider the following:

- *Reliability:* Will the server stay available under load? If the server crashes, is cleanup performed, and is the server automatically restarted?
- *Scalability:* What is the maximum number of hits that the server will support? How long does a single GET request take to be executed, in the worst case? How many concurrent "transactions" can the server handle?
- *Performance:* Does the performance of the server degrade gracefully under load? How long does a single GET request take to be executed? Is there any way to speed up the processing of a GET request?

Reliability, scalability, and performance are three of the most important criteria for designing a Web application server, excluding, of course, security. Several basic steps can be followed to ensure that an application server is *reliable:*

- Check to see whether there are any memory leaks in the system, using a tool such as *purify.* Memory leaks occur when memory is allocated by the program and the system is not notified that the memory space is no longer required.
- Ensure that you have an exception handler that can catch fatal exceptions and clean up after the error. Expect a system error under load in the most unusual place in your source code, as the operating system gets confused by the enormous amount of activity.

- When dealing with TCP/IP sockets, ensure that you close or free up the socket after use. One bug found in the Atlanta Olympic Games Ticket Server caused it to crash after the amount of socket resources reached the system limit! So, after 2,000 successful connections, the application server started blocking the Web server from accepting connections remotely and eventually crashed the operating system.

- When using NSAPI or ISAPI to interface between Web servers and Web application servers, be extremely careful that your application server, if it crashes, can restart the entire environment, including the Web server. As your application server runs as a DLL in the same space as the Web server, if it crashes it is more than likely that the Web server will also crash. For reliability, consider using a central Web server and several satellite Web servers, the central Web server listening on port 80, and the satellites listening on other ports which are redirected to by the central Web server when the relevant section of the central Web server is accessed.

In designing an application server, it is also very important to consider your application scale. Issues to consider when ensuring the *scalability* of your application server include:

- If the application server accesses static Web pages or files in a file system, it is a good idea to ensure that the file system used does not reside on networked file system: a file system provided by the network file system (NFS), the Andrew file system (AFS), or the distributed file system (DFS). These mounts imply a TCP/IP network connection to another system. When the network load on the system that is running the application server increases, the amount of bandwidth will be restricted to the performance of the entire network around the Web server and will also reduce the amount of traffic the Web server can accept. If it is necessary to share files with other systems, share them by replication—that is, copy the files from system to system instead of creating links between the systems.

- If the application server needs to build dynamic Web pages out of a database of any sort, consider splitting the logic into two parts, a *director* and a *daemon*. The *daemon* is a long-running process that listens for requests on TCP/IP sockets and either maintains "hot" connections to a relational database, or caches, in memory, contents of the frequently accessed pages. Daemons are designed to stay running all the time and are most often multithreaded to accept and handle multiple director requests. A *director* is a small, lightweight CGI program or DLL (depending on the interface used) that simply filters the Web server commands and sends the daemon requests that the director cannot handle by itself. It directs the results of the daemon response back out through the Web server to the Web browser. A director can also be used as a proxy server to filter the results produced by the daemon and remap or tag portions of the HTML before serving them back to the Web browser. This mechanism can be used for maintaining state within a Web server. Finally, a director can be written as an NPH-CGI script which enables it to override the Web server's response to the Web browser with custom code, for instance, enabling it to redirect requests to alternative Web servers, prompt for and receive basic authentication requests, and return standard HTTP messages such as "Document not Found" when an error occurs, providing familiar feedback to the end user.

Finally, remember to make your application server as fast as possible. Very tight, lightweight, uncomplicated code should provide the quickest possible code path to the results that the application server should provide. The *performance* of a Web application server is key to the success of the overall application: Given today's network bandwidth and topologies, the speed of the application should never be slower than the latency of the network. Current computer system processing speeds are orders of magnitude greater than the speed of the network connection into your system, even using a full, nonpartitioned T3 line. The performance of your application server should degrade only when the number of simultaneous threads of control multiplied by the complexity of the task being performed exceeds the total capacity of the system. At this point, Web performance tricks to make multiple systems look like a single system can come into play:

- *Use DNS round-robin tactics.* When a single server is accessed through identification by a DNS address (for example, www.lotus.com), trick DNS into routing the request to multiple, different IP addresses. You can do this with a simple modification to most standard routers.
- *Use an IP sprayer.* Similar to the DNS round-robin solution described above, an IP sprayer routes requests to multiple systems. However, the IP sprayer actually plays with the interface between the open systems interconnection (OSI) data link and physical parts of the network stack

to modify the media access control (MAC) address in each packet, as it is transmitted to a destination server. The MAC address of the destination system in the cluster replaces the default MAC address. This technique was first used successfully in IBM-sponsored sporting events and in the Atlanta Olympic Games Ticket Center, where it was used to simulate seven different ticket wickets and a central system to route the request to each ticket wicket.

CONCLUSION

When building a Web application server, it is critical to ensure that you create an architecture before writing the necessary programming instructions. Understanding how forms work, how to make best use of the appropriate method to parse input from the Web browser user, and how to build dynamic HTML is all that is necessary to design a primitive Web application server. Designing a Web application server to support financial transactions over the Web requires an understanding of how to maintain state for individual users while they access sections of the Website maintained through the Web application server. Finally, understanding reliability, scalability, and performance considerations when building a Web application server enables the implementation to proceed smoothly and enhances the overall effectiveness of the Website. By combining these concepts into a rational whole, we can expect to see variations on the current Web application server themes well into the next millenium.

List of URLs

The URLs to interesting sites that we provide here are for reference only. We are not endorsing any company or their products. Because we have no control over these external sites, the content pages that the URLs reference may no longer exist or may have become irrelevant. If you come across an invalid URL, you can try to reduce the URL to its host name and search for the document from the host machine. If you still do not succeed, you may want to use one of the Internet search products to find the information you need. Find more URLs at http://www.ibm.com/technology/books/webgate/.

AlphaWorks
http://www.alphaworks.ibm.com, Java technologies from IBM.

Art sales
http://www.canyonart.com, the Canyon Country Original Web page, enables you to purchase art work online.

Atlanta Olympics Games
http://www.atlanta.olympic.org, the 1996 Atlanta Olympics Games home page.

Bookstore
http://bookzone.com/bookzone, the Bookzone home page, which contains its online catalog. http://www.wiley.com, the Wiley publisher home

page, which contains product information, information for authors, and online products and services.

CERN
http://www.cern.ch, home page of the European Laboratory for Particle Physics.

CERN Jigsaw server
http://www.w3.org/pub/WWW/Jigsaw, a Web server written in Java and developed by CERN.

CICS
http://www.hursley.ibm.com/cics, the CICS home page.

http://www.hursley.ibm.com/cics/internet, the CICS Internet software page

Cryptolope
http://www.cryptolope.ibm.com, the IBM Cryptolope page.

DB2
http://www.software.ibm.com/data/db2, the DB2 home page.

http://www.software.ibm.com/data/db2/support/servinfo/index.html, contains the DB2 Product and Service Technical Library.

DB2 World Wide Web Connection
http://www.software.ibm.com/data/db2/db2wgafs.html, the DB2 WWW home page which contains product information, customer examples, and free downloads.

DFS
http://www.transarc.com/afs/transarc.com/public/www/Public/ProdServ/Product/DFS/dfs_broc.htm, the distributed file system (DFS) home page.

DNS registration
http://ds2.internic.net/ds-home.html, the InterNIC registration page, which contains information about registration procedures, including how to register your domain name if you are outside the United States.

Domino
http://domino.lotus.com, the Domino Website where you can download product trials and sample applications.

Electronic mall

http://maingate.net/mall, the Main Mall

http://net.commerce.ibm.com, the Net.Commerce home page enabling secure electronic shopping around the world.

Encina

http://www.transarc.com/afs/transarc.com/public/www/Public/ProdServ/Product/Encina/index.html, the Encina home page.

For kids only

http://www.4Kids.org Web page, designed for kids only, highlights fun, educational, and safe spots for kids to visit on the Web.

http://www.theinfoguide.com/kid.htm, the information guide for kids-only Websites.

FTP shareware and freeware

http://www.net.link.net/faq/ftpfaq.html, FTP shareware and freeware.

Gopher manual

http://www.unidata.ucar.edu/projects/ieis/manual/manual/gopher.html, the "World of Gopher" manual.

Home banking

http://ihbprod1.bankamerica.com:444/ihb-bin/ihbcgi, Bank of America's home banking, where you can transfer money from one account to another and pay your bills online.

Hotel reservations

http://www.corretti.com, provides online hotel reservations as well as airline tickets and rental cars.

HTML converters

http://www.yahoo.com/Computers_and_Internet/Internet/World_Wide_Web/HTML_Converters/Commercial_Products, lists HTML converters.

HTML guide

http://www.ncsa.uiuc.edu/General/Internet/WWW/HTMLPrimer.html, a guide to HTML.

http://www.w3.org/pub/WWW/MarkUp/Wilbur, the HTML 3.2 specification.

http://www.w3.org/pub/WWW/MarkUp/html.spec, the HTML 2.0 specification.

http://lcweb.loc.gov/global/internet/html.html, the HTML resources at the Library of Congress.

HTTP
http://www.ics.uci.edu/pub/ietf/http, HTTP working group at the Internet Engineering Task Force (IETF).

Hypertext guide
http://www.w3.org/hypertext/WWW/Provider/Style, Berners-Lee, T., "Style Guide for On-Line Hypertext."

IBM
http://www.ibm.com, the IBM home page, which has a different theme each month and generates various news items selected from a collection for a particular period.

http://www.hursley.ibm.com, the IBM Hursley home page, which contains information about the development group, advanced software services, IBM Hursley forums, and tourist information.

IBM software
http://www.software.ibm.com, the IBM software home page, which contains press releases, news, products, downloads, partners, support, and feedback pages.

Image map editor
http://www.boutell.com/mapedit, the Web image map editing software from Boutell.com, Inc.

IMS
http://www.software.ibm.com/data/ims/imsfamly.html, the IMS home page.

InfoMarket
http://www.infomarket.ibm.com, the IBM Internet search product that enables pay per view.

Insurance company
http://www.statefarm.com/agents/near.htm, a State Farm Insurance Web page that enables State Farm clients to locate an agent in their own neighborhood.

InterNIC
http://ds2.internic.net, the InterNIC home page, which contains information about directory and database services, registration services, support services, and Net Scout services.

Java

http://www.javasoft.com, the Java home page at Sun.

http://ncc.hursley.ibm.com/javainfo, the Java home page at IBM.

http://www.gamelan.com/index.shtml, Gamelan-Java sources on the Internet.

JavaScript online tutorial

http://gmccomb.com/javascript/index.html, the *JavaScript Sourcebook* tutorial page.

Java remote method invocation

http://chatsubo.javasoft.com/current, contains information about Java RMI.

JDBC

http://splash.javasoft.com/jdbc, JDBC at Sun.

http://www.software.ibm.com/data/db2/jdbc, JDBC at IBM.

Jobs

http://www.careerpath.com/info.html, advertisement on job openings.

Knowledge utility

http://www.aqui.ibm.com, a middleware to help each user find and share the most relevant information based on their individual preferences.

Lotus Notes:Newsstand

http://www.newsstand.lotus.com, the Lotus Notes:Newsstand Website for delivering information product subscriptions and managing those subscriptions in a way that suits the needs of the corporate environment.

Medical center

http://www.chmcc.org, the Children's Hospital Medical Center in Cincinnati provides a physicians' referral guide, patient education programs, and library resources for parents.

MQSeries

http://www.hursley.ibm.com/mqseries, the MQSeries home page, which contains product information, headlines, services, and downloads.

Net.Commerce

http://net.commerce.ibm.com, the Net.Commerce home page enabling secure electronic shopping around the world.

Net.Data
http://www.software.ibm.com/data/net.data, the Net.Data home page containing information about the product, documentations, live demonstrations, downloads, and services information.

NetRexx
http://www2.hursley.ibm.com, the NetRexx home page.

Netscape
http://www.netscape.com, the Netscape home page.

Pizza
http://round-table.com, the Round Table Pizza home page, which enables online pizza ordering.

PointCast
PointCast Network (http://www.pointcast.com) provides a free subscription to monitor news weather in cities of your choice and the prices of your selected stocks.

Search products
http://altavista.digital.com, the AltaVista home page.

http://www.excite.com, the Excite home page.

http://www.infomarket.ibm.com, the InfoMarket home page.

http://www.infoseek.com, the Infoseek home page.

http://www.lycos.com, the Lycos home page.

http://www.mckinley.com, the Magellan home page.

http://www.yahoo.com, the Yahoo! home page.

Server-side includes
http://hoohoo.ncsa.uiuc.edu/docs/tutorials/includes.html, contains information about server-side includes (SSI).

SHTTP
http://www.commerce.net/software/Shttpd, secure HTTPD Reference Manual, Enterprise Integration Technologies, 1995.

Supermarket coupons
http://www.SuperMarkets.com contains coupons for various supermarkets.

Transaction processing facility (TPF)
http://www.s390.ibm.com/products/tpf/tpfhp.html, the transaction processing facility (TPF) home page.

Virtual cities
http://www.planet9.com, contains attractions in U.S. cities.

VisualAge family
http://www.software.ibm.com/ad/visage, the IBM VisualAge family home page, which contains information about the IBM VisualAge for Smalltalk, C++, COBOL, BASIC, RPG, PACBASE, and Java programming environments.

W3C
http://www.w3c.org, the World Wide Web Consortium home page.

Weather report
http://www.intellicast.com/weather, the weather report for the United States and world.

White pages
http://www.angelfire.com/pages0/ultimates, the Ultimate White Pages, which contain U.S. telephone white pages.

Wine sales
http://www.newtech.it, enables online wine purchase—directly from Italy.

WITI
http://www.witi.com, the International Network of Women in Technology Campus, which offers live chats and interaction with a wide variety of professional experts.

Web Object Manager
http://www.womplex.ibm.com, the Web Object Manager home page, which was used to provide the results of the Wimbledon Tennis Championships and 1996 Atlanta Olympic Games on the Web.

WWW user surveys
http://www.cc.gatech.edu/gvu/user_surveys, the Graphic, Visualization and Usability Center (GVU) of Georgia Technical University's World Wide Web User Survey page.

http://www.cc.gatech.edu/gvu/user_surveys/survey-04-1996/graphs/use/shopping.htm, lists frequency of online shopping by location.

WWW5 Conference
http://www5conf.inria.fr/fich_html/papers/P8/Overview.html, the conference proceedings.

Glossary of Terms and Acronyms

ACRONYMS

2PC
two-phase commit

ACL
access control list

AFS
Andrew file system

APPC
application program to program communication protocol

ARPANET
Advanced Research Projects Administration Network

AWT
abstract Windowing toolkit

BBS
bulletin board system

BMP
bitmap

BMS
basic mapping support (CICS)

CA
certification authority

CBC
cipher block chaining

CDS
cell directory service (DCE)

CERN
Conseil Européen pour la Recherche Nucleaire

CFB
cipher feedback

CGI
common gateway interface

CICS
Customer Information Control System

COMMAREA
communication area (CICS)

CWA
common work area (CICS)

DB2
DATABASE 2

DBMS
database management system

DCA
Defense Communications Agency

DCE
distributed computing environment

DES
data encryption standard

DFS
distributed file system

DL/I
data language/1

DLL
dynamic link library

DMV
Department of Motor Vehicles

DN
distinguished name

DNS
domain name server

DPL
distributed program link

DTS
distributed time service

DSVD
Digital Simultaneous Voice Data

ECB
electronic codebook

ECI
external call interface

EIT
Enterprise Integration Technologies

EPI
external presentation interface

FAQ
frequently asked questions

FTP
file transfer protocol

GIF
graphic interchange format

GVU
Graphic, Visualization, and Usability Center of Georgia Technical University

HTML
hypertext markup language

HTTP
hypertext transport protocol

HTTPD
hypertext transport protocol daemon

HTTP-NP
hypertext transfer protocol-new generation

IETF
Internet Engineering Task Force

ICAPI
IBM Internet server application program interface

IDL
interface definition language

IIOP
Internet inter-object request broker protocol

IKP
Internet keyed payment protocol

IMS
Information Management System

IMS TM
Information Management System Transaction Manager

IP
Internet protocol

IRC
Internet relay chat

IS
information systems

ISAM
indexed sequence access method

IT
information technology

ISAPI
Microsoft Internet server application program interface

ISDN
integrated services digital network

JDBC
Java database connectivity

JDK
Java developers' kit

JIT
just-in-time compiler

JPEG
Joint Photographic Experts Group

JPG
a file name suffix for JPEG files

JVM
Java virtual machine

LAN
local area network

MAC
media access control

MFS
message format services

MIME
multipurpose Internet mail extensions

MIT
Massachusetts Institute of Technology

MPEG
Motion Picture Experts Group

MQI
message queue interface (MQSeries)

NCSA
National Center for Supercomputing Applications

NFS
network file system

NPH
non-parse header

NSAPI
Netscape server application program interface

NTTP
Network News Transfer Protocol

ODBC
open database connectivity

OFB
output feedback (CICS)

OSF
Open Software Foundation

OSI
open systems interconnection

OTMA
open transaction manager access

PC
personal computer

PCN
PointCast Network

PEM
Internet privacy-enhanced mail

PGP
pretty good privacy

PKCS7
public key cryptography standard 7

PING
packet Internet groper

PPC
peer-to-peer communication

PPP
Point-to-Point Protocol

RFTP
socksified FTP client

RGB
red, green, blue

RMI
remote method invocation

RPC
remote procedure call

RQS
recoverable queuing service (Encina)

RSA
Rivest, Shamir, and Adleman

RTF
rich text format

SET
Secure Electronic Transaction Protocol

SFS
Encina structured file server

SGML
standard generalized markup language

SHTTP
secure hypertext transport protocol

SLIP
serial line interface protocol

SLUP
secondary logical unit program

SNA LU 6.2
Systems Network Architecture logical unit 6.2

SPA
scratch pad area

SQL
structural query language

SSI
server-side includes

SSL
secure sockets layer

TCP/IP
Transmission Control Protocol/Internet Protocol

TCTUA
terminal control table user area

TIFF
tagged image file format

tn3270
3270-type terminal emulator

TPF
transaction processing facility

T-RPC
transactional remote procedure call

TWA
task work area (CICS)

UOR
unit of recovery

URL
uniform resource locator

VBScript
Visual Basic script

VGA
video graphics adapter

VRML
Virtual Reality Modeling Language

VSAM
virtual storage access method

W3C
World Wide Web Consortium

WAIS
wide area information server

WOM
Web object manager

WWW
World Wide Web

WYSIWYG
what you see is what you get

XCF
MVS cross system coupling facility

TERMS

access control
Regulates who (subject) has which kind of access right to which objects or services. Access control is usually classified as discretionary or mandatory. Discretionary access control is a means of restricting access to objects according to the identity of a user. Mandatory access control is a means of restricting access to objects according to the sensitivity of the information in the objects and the formal authorization (clearance) of subjects to access information of such sensitivity.

access control list (ACL)
A list of (subject, access right) pairs associated with each object.

account-based money
Money stored in a trusted third-party ledger such as a bank. Credit cards are examples of account-based money.

Advanced Research Projects Administration Network (ARPANET)
Funded by the United States Department of Defense to develop a network to connect computers among universities, government agencies, and companies that have government contracts for information sharing. In 1975, ARPANET was converted from an experimental network to an operational network, and the administration of the network was transferred to the Defense Communications Agency (DCA).

AltaVista
Digital Equipment Corporation's Web search product. See http://altavista.digital.com.

anchor
Synonym for hot spot.

Andrew file system (AFS)
A distributed file system that enables cooperating hosts (client and servers) to efficiently share file system resources across both local area and wide area networks. AFS is marketed, maintained, and extended by Transarc Corporation. It is based on a research project called "Andrew" at Carnegie Mellon University. See http://www.transarc.com/afs/transarc.com/public/www/Public/ProdServ/Product/AFS/index.html.

applet
A small application written in Java that is automatically downloadable by the browser to be executed in the client. The browser imposes security restrictions on Java applets.

authentication
The process of establishing that the party you are talking to is really the party he or she claims to be.

bitmap (BMP)
One of the file formats for images often used with Windows.

bookmark
A personal URL address book, supported by browsers, that enables users to get where they want to go quickly.

browser
A program that runs in the client environment to retrieve information from the Internet.

browser session
A series of related requests from a particular browser to a particular server application. To manage a browser session, one must create or use a token called a *browser session identifier,* which represents the session and is passed between the browser and the server application.

cell directory service (CDS)
A mechanism for naming objects within a distributed computing environment (DCE) cell.

certification authority (CA)
A trusted authority that issues digital certificates. The role of a certification authority is similar to the authority that issues driver licenses. A well-known CA is Verisign.

common gateway interface (CGI)
Provides a simple mechanism for executing within an HTTP server a program requested by the returned HTML document. The HTTP server passes control to the program to be executed with parameters in the form of "Name=Value" pairs as specified by the client. The program can interface with other resources outside an HTTP server to read from or write to a file, make a database request, or perform other operations.

communication area (COMMAREA)
An area used to pass data between different programs within a task in CICS. A COMMAREA can also be used to pass data between tasks that communicate with the same terminal.

Conseil Européen pour la Recherche Nucleaire (CERN)
The European Laboratory for Particle Physics in Geneva, where Tim Berners-Lee worked when he introduced the World Wide Web technologies. See http://www.cern.ch.

conversation
A collection of consecutive related requests from a user to an application.

cryptography
A way of scrambling a message such that it is unintelligible to those who do not have the associated key. The original message is often called *plaintext*, and the resulting scrambled message is called *ciphertext*.

Cryptolope
IBM's Cryptolope (derived from the words *encrypted envelope*) is a mechanism for charging for electronic data on a per-item-delivered basis. Instead of sending the data directly to the consumer, a link to the data is provided, which must be viewed with a viewer equipped to decrypt the contents of

the Cryptolope. The viewer decrypts the media only after it receives information from a central server that a payment has been processed for the media. See http://www.cryptolope.ibm.com.

Customer Information Control System (CICS)
An IBM licensed program that enables transactions entered at remote terminals to be processed concurrently by user-written application programs. It includes facilities for building, using, and maintaining databases. See http://www.hursley.ibm.com/cics.

DATABASE 2 (DB2)
The IBM DB2 family of relational database products is designed to offer open, industrial-strength database management for decision support, transaction processing, and a line of business applications running not only on IBM platforms such as personal computers, AS/400 systems, RS/6000 hardwares, and IBM mainframes, but also on non-IBM machines from Hewlett-Packard and Sun Microsystems. See http://www.software.ibm.com/data/db2.

Data Encryption Standard (DES)
The best-known symmetric key encryption algorithm, originally developed by IBM. DES has four modes of operation: electronic codebook (ECB), cipher block chaining (CBC), cipher feedback (CFB), and output feedback (OFB).

data language 1 (DL/I)
The IMS/ESA data manipulation language—a programming interface between a user application and IMS/ESA. DL/I is invoked from PL/I, COBOL, or Assembler language programs by means of ordinary subroutine calls. DL/I also refers to the database subsystem. DL/I enables a user to define data structures, relate structures to the application, load structures, and reorganize structures.

DCE cell
A collection of client and server machines.

DE-Light
A lightweight DCE Encina

digital certificate
Contains information about a person that is sealed with the signature of a certification authority.

digital money
Token-based money, that is packets of bits traded like coins. Possessing the bit means possessing the money. Digital money is used when small amounts of money are involved. Also called digital cash, electronic money, or cybercash.

digital signature
Essentially a digital fingerprint. It is a message encrypted by using the sender's private key. The receiver can use the public key of the sender to decrypt the message and be sure that it really comes from the sender.

distributed computing environment (DCE)
Provides the functions for developing and running distributed client/server applications across various operating systems and networks.

distributed file system (DFS)
A system software application built on top of the industry-standard Open Software Foundation Distributed Computing Environment (OSF DCE), functioning as an integral part of the DCE. DFS enables collections of computers to share files as a single unit, within and across enterprises located in one site, or in multiple sites around the world. DFS is marketed, maintained, and extended by Transarc Corporation. See http://www.transarc.com/afs/transarc.com/public/www/Public/ProdServ/Product/DFS/index.html.

distributed program link (DPL)
Provides a remote procedure call (RPC)-like mechanism in CICS.

distributed time service (DTS)
A DCE service enabling the synchronization of clocks across different computers.

domain name server (DNS)
A system that maps Internet protocol (IP) addresses to the names assigned to network devices. See http://ds2.internic.net/ds-home.html, the InterNIC registration page that contains information about registration procedures, including how to register a domain name from outside the United States.

Domino
The Lotus Domino Server delivers the contents of a Notes application database to both Notes clients and Web browsers and provides the platform for Lotus Internet Applications, business solutions enabling the deployment

of Internet and Intranet technology in the organization. See http://domino.lotus.com.

Domino.Action
Provides the platform and tools for designing, creating, and maintaining an electronic presence on either the Internet or Intranet. Domino.Action provides templates for creating an Internet or Intranet presence quickly and effectively.

Domino.Broadcast for PointCast
An information delivery system based on the Lotus Domino Server technology, the Lotus Notes application engine, and the Internet broadcast technologies developed by PointCast Incorporated. It is an authoring, communication, and information delivery platform for corporate Intranets that combines external news with internal communications.

Domino.Merchant
Supports marketing and sales on the Internet, from activities as simple as registering prospects and distributing product literature to more complex activities such as accepting a credit card, processing a payment, and delivering a digital product.

dynamic HTML
The creation of Web pages dynamically by a program as a result of user interaction.

electronic commerce
The exchange of goods and services on the Internet in return for money.

Encina
Enterprise computing in a new age. A set of DCE-based products from Transarc Corporation. The Encina family of online transaction processing products includes:

- Encina Toolkit Executive
- Encina Server
- Encina Structured File Server (SFS)
- Encina Peer-to-Peer Communication Executive (PPC)
- Encina PPC Gateway/SNA

See http://www.transarc.com/afs/transarc.com/public/www/Public/ProdServ/Product/Encina/index.html.

Excite
An Internet search product by Excite Incorporation. See http://www.excite.com.

external call interface (ECI)
An application programming interface (API) that enables a non-CICS client application to call a CICS program as a subroutine. The client application communicates with the CICS server program through COMMAREA.

external presentation interface (EPI)
An application programming interface (API) that allows a non-CICS application program to appear to the CICS system as one or more standard 3270 terminals. The non-CICS application can start CICS transactions and send and receive standard 3270 data streams to those transactions.

extranet
A secure network linking the Intranets of multiple companies.

file transfer protocol (FTP)
Used mainly for sending and retrieving files over the Internet. To perform an FTP operation between their computers and a remote computer, users must have a logon ID to the remote computer, unless an anonymous ID with null password has been set up. Once users have logged on to a remote server with the FTP service, they can see the directory of files that they can transfer. For more information about FTP shareware and freeware, see http://www.yahoo.com/.

finger
An Internet service that provides a convenient way of finding detailed information about networked users, such as their full name, login status, and telephone number. It can also be used to find out information about all users who are currently logged on in a networked computer.

firewall
A barrier that sits between an internal, "safe" network, such as a corporate network, and a public, "unsafe" network, such as the Internet. A firewall serves two purposes: It regulates internal users' information exchange with outside networks and prevents outside users from attacking private networks.

frames
An important HTML feature that helps display complex data and information in a friendly way. With frames, an HTML author can display multiple HTML pages concurrently within a single browser window. Each HTML page is known as a *frame*, and the whole set of frames within the browser is known as a *frameset*.

gopher
An Internet protocol and software to enable users to research and browse distributed documents held on servers. Many browsers support the gopher protocol in delivering documents from gopher servers. See http://www.unidata.ucar.edu/projects/ieis/manual/manual/gopher.html, "The World of Gopher" manual.

graphics interchange format (GIF)
One of the file formats for images developed for use on CompuServe.

HotJava
The HotJava browser incorporates the Java virtual machine and runs compiled Java programs (in byte code form) known as applets.

hotlist
See bookmark.

hyperlink
A capability in HTML to reference or link to other documents.

hypermedia
A capability in HTML to include multimedia documents such as image, audio, video, and animation.

hypertext markup language (HTML)
A document scripting language. HTML is derived from the Standard Generalized Markup Language (SGML). It consists of tags starting with a left angle bracket (<), a tag name, and a right angle bracket (>), for example, <H1> for Heading 1. See http://www.ncsa.uiuc.edu/General/Internet/WWW/HTMLPrimer.html, a guide to HTML.

hypertext transport protocol (HTTP)
An application-level protocol for retrieving documents with a fast response time over the Internet. It is a generic, stateless, object-oriented protocol. See http://www.ics.uci.edu/pub/ietf/http, the HTTP working group at the Internet Engineering Task Force (IETF).

image map
Enables a user to click on a portion of a displayed image and cause an action, such as selecting another URL to be displayed, to take place at a server. For an image map editor, see http://www.boutell.com/mapedit.

InfoMarket
An IBM Internet search product that enables pay per view. See http://www.infomarket.ibm.com.

Information Management System (IMS)
An IBM database and transaction manager system that can manage complex databases and networks. See http://www.software.ibm.com/data/ims/imsfamly.html, the IMS home page.

Infoseek
An Internet search product from Infoseek Corporation. See http://www.infoseek.com.

Internet
Public network where computers are connected through Transmission Control Protocol/Internet Protocol (TCP/IP). The Internet is also called the *Net, information superhighway,* or *cyberspace.*

Internet address
The numbering system used in Transmission Control Protocol/Internet Protocol (TCP/IP) Internetwork communications to specify a particular network or a particular host on that network with which to communicate. Internet addressees are commonly denoted in dotted decimal form.

Internet connection server application interface (ICAPI)
An IBM Internet connection server API to address performance and security enhancements over the CGI.

Internet Engineering Task Force (IETF)
An open, international group of volunteers responsible for the standards and implementation of Internet technologies. See http://www.ietf.org.

Internet Explorer
Microsoft's browser for its operating systems.

Internet inter-object request broker protocol (IIOP)
A communication protocol used between an object and an object request broker (ORB).

Internet phone
Software that enables users to communicate verbally with other users over the Internet. Users can conduct long distance or international conversations through Internet phone for the cost of a local Internet connection. Using Internet phone is simple—users click on a hypertext link to a Web forum that supports Internet phone, and the browser automatically connects them with the forum.

Internet protocol (IP)
A protocol used to route data from its source to its destination in an Internet environment.

Internet server application program interface (ISAPI)
Microsoft Web server API to address performance and security enhancements over the CGI.

InterNIC
A collaborative project between AT&T and Network Solutions Inc., funded by the National Science Foundation, to provide services on directory and database, registration, and Internet support. See http://ds2.internic.net.

Intranet
The Internet inside a company; the implementation of Web technologies within a corporation over the enterprise network inside the firewall.

Java
A small footprint (compact code) and a safe (crash-proof) language invented by Sun Microsystems. See http://www.javasoft.com, the Java home page at Sun and http://www.ibm.com/javainfo, the Java home page at IBM.

Java byte codes
A concise intermediate language into which Java is compiled. Java programs are then distributed in Java byte code form and processed by the Java virtual machine (JVM; sometimes known as the *Java interpreter*) at runtime on the target system.

Java Database Connectivity (JDBC)
Enables programmers to issue SQL requests to a local or remote relational database from Java applets and applications and receive and manipulate the results from the requests. See http://www.software.ibm.com/data/db2/jdbc, JDBC at IBM.

JavaScript
An object-based, interpretive scripting language invented by Netscape Communications Corporation. Although Netscape named the language JavaScript, it is not the same as the Java language. JavaScript statements are embedded in HTML documents. They describe links between events such as clicking on a push button.

JavaTel
A Java telephony application interface (JTAPI) developed by Sun along with Lucent Technologies, IBM Intel, Northern Telecom, and Novel, to provide a uniform interface for computer telephony applications in the Java environment.

Java virtual machine (JVM)
Interprets and executes the Java byte codes and acts as the interface between the Java program and the target operating environment. A compiled Java program can run on any system provided that the JVM exists on that system.

Jigsaw server
A Web server written in Java and developed by CERN. Jigsaw server enables the dynamic addition of Java-based functions for use by server programs. See http://www.w3.org/pub/WWW/Jigsaw.

Joint Photographic Experts Group (JPEG)
One of the file formats for images designed for maximal image compression.

JPG
A file name suffix for JPEG files.

Kerberos
An authentication system for distributed computing networks developed in the Athena Project at the Massachusetts Institute of Technology.

Knowledge utility
A middleware to help with information overloaded. It helps each user find and share the most relevant information based on their individual preferences.

Lotus Notes:Newsstand
A system on the Web for delivering information product subscriptions and managing those subscriptions in a way that suits the needs of the corporate

environment. Users can visit the Lotus Notes:Newsstand on the Web site and sign up for a sample publication at http://www.newsstand.lotus.com.

Lycos
An Internet search software from Carnegie Mellon University. See http://www.lycos.com.

Magellan
An Internet search product from McKinley Group Incorporated. See http://www.mckinley.com.

Mosaic
The first browser, built by the National Center for Supercomputing Applications (NCSA), to create a graphical user interface (GUI) to the World Wide Web for UNIX systems. Mosaic became available in the first half of 1993. Although it provides an easy, point-and-click interface, it did not capture attention until November 1994, when it was ported to Macintoshes and PCs. It has since become universal client software that users can find in almost all operating systems on many hardware platforms.

Movie Photographic Experts Group (MPEG)
One of the file formats for compressed movies.

MQSeries
MQSeries messaging software enables business applications to exchange information across different operating system platforms in a way that is easy for programmers to implement. See http://www.hursley.ibm.com/mqseries.

multipurpose Internet mail extensions (MIME)
A specification for information exchange among computer systems using the Internet mail standards. The browser can use the MIME type in the response header to determine whether it should use a helper application, or it can offer the user the option of selecting such an application to view the downloaded file if the browser does not know how to display or process it.

Net.Commerce
Software that helps users build a store or shopping mall on the Web. Net.Commerce enables users to define and make available a catalog of products that can be purchased securely by using a Web browser. Net.Commerce also provides a framework for calculating various charges, such as taxes and shipping costs. See http://net.commerce.ibm.com.

Net.Data
Delivers a powerful framework for Web applications accessing heterogeneous data sources such as files, DB2, Lotus Notes databases, IMS, Oracle, and other sources through ODBC drivers and supporting various programming languages such as Java, Perl, REXX, C, and C++. See http://www.software.ibm.com/data/net.data.

NetRexx
An IBM programming language that is an extension of REXX and incorporates some features of Java. NetRexx programming is simpler than Java programming in a number of ways: Punctuation is not required, the language is not case sensitive, and variables do not have to be declared. The NetRexx compiler takes NetRexx source and produces a Java class file that can execute wherever there is a Java virtual machine (JVM). Thus, NetRexx is suitable for writing applets as well as applications. Just-in-time Java compilers can be used with NetRexx generated classes to reduce execution time. Java classes can be called from NetRexx programs.

Netscape cookie
Name=Value pairs (cf. under CGI) that a Web application typically returns when a browser visits the Website where the application resides. The browser keeps track of the cookies it receives from different Websites, and it may discard cookies that have expired or are taking up too much space. When a browser revisits a site, it returns to the server any cookies that are applicable to the URL being accessed. The server makes any received cookies available to Web applications by means of the HTTP_COOKIE environment variable. For more information about the Netscape cookie specification, see http://www.netscape.com/newsref/std/cookie_spec.html.

Netscape plug-in
User-supplied components that enable a Netscape browser to view special data types such as video and IBM Cryptolope documents.

Netscape server application program interface (NSAPI)
Netscape Web server API to address performance and security enhancements over the CGI.

network computer
A relatively inexpensive computer (under $1,000) that supports Internet access through a browser with a Java virtual machine for running Java-based applications. Network computers are also known as *thin clients,*

Internet appliances, Java stations, Java machines, Net boxes, bare metal, and *hollow PCs*.

Network News Transfer Protocol (NTTP)
NTTP is an Internet protocol enabling users to participate in user groups, bulletin board systems (BBSs), and forums, which are essentially public e-mail.

non-parse header (NPH)
The nph- prefix to a program essentially instructs the Web server to pass through unmodified all information generated by the CGI program. Typically, the Web server would add an HTTP header to the information generated by the CGI program. NPH-CGI scripts allow a CGI program to send back the appropriate header, enabling direct manipulation of HTTP to affect the Web browser. One effective use of NPH-CGI direct manipulation is to return an HTTP/1.0-moved header to the Web browser, which causes the Web browser to transmit an HTTP GET command at a URL other than the URL originally specified.

open transaction manager access (OTMA)
Enables MVS programs, known as OTMA clients, to invoke IMS programs in such a way that IMS program thinks it has been invoked from a human user through a terminal.

out-of-band
Information provided by a proprietary protocol or mechanism, such as the use of Java applets or Netscape cookies. Out-of-band transaction states depend on the Web browser and Web server sharing a common convention or mechanism for passing information between them without the knowledge or intervention of the user.

packet filter
Controls the flow of IP packets between the internal and external networks. Basically, all incoming and outgoing IP packets must go through a gateway that is responsible for passing over all IP packets. By installing a packet filter in the gateway, users can control the kind of IP packets that are allowed to come in or go out.

PointCast Network (PCN)
Combines the SmartScreen screensaver and the ability to receive broadcast channels from a central source. When the system running the PCN client is idle, a dynamically updating screensaver opens to display the latest news

organized by channel or topic area. The PCN currently provides six channels of information to registered users. To register and download the SmartScreen software, visit PointCast's Website at http://www.pointcast.com/.

packet Internet groper (PING)
A simple way of sending communication packets; often used to check whether a local machine is connected to a remote host. It also displays statistics about packet loss and delivery time.

proxy server
Provides a way of protecting a private network at the application level. Conceptually, a proxy server running in a gateway acts as a liaison between an application and the external network. To access services outside the firewall, a user first uses a client such as FTP or telnet to access the gateway. Usually, to use the proxy server, a user must first be authorized by supplying a User ID and password to the gateway. After successful authorization, the proxy server connects the user to the outside network, just as if the user were talking directly with the outside server. Most common use is to cache.

pseudoconversation
A type of CICS application design that appears to the user as a continuous conversation but consists internally of multiple tasks.

pixel
Dots of color in an image.

red, green, blue (RGB)
A method of storing and displaying color information about computer videos.

remote method invocation (RMI)
Permits Java objects to communicate with one another across Java virtual machines (JVMs), that is, across network connections. RMI is intended for a homogeneous Java environment, not for use by non-Java programs, so, for example, Java remote objects are garbage collected as though they are running locally. See http://chatsubo.javasoft.com/current.

Rivest, Shamir, and Adleman (RSA)
The most popular asymmetric key encryption system, named after its three inventors, Rivest, Shamir, and Adleman. The security of RSA is based on

the computational difficulty in factoring large numbers. To be safe, one has to pick very large keys, which are awkward to store and transmit.

scratchpad area (SPA)
In IMS/VS conversational processing, a work area in main storage or on direct access storage used to retain information from the application program for execution of the application program from the same terminal.

Secure Electronic Transaction (SET)
A protocol for ensuring that credit card transactions can be processed securely over an open network. Visa and MasterCard, along with a number of other companies, including GTE, IBM, Microsoft, Netscape, Terisa, and Verisign, developed SET. Other credit card companies, such as American Express, have agreed to support SET.

secure HTTP (SHTTP)
EIT's secure HTTP protocol to authenticate HTTP transactions only. Clients and/or servers can sign and/or encrypt with public or private keys.

secure socket level (SSL)
Netscape Communications Corporation's SSL provides mutual authentication, data encryption, and data integrity to protect any high-level protocol built on sockets such as FTP and HTTP.

Server Side Includes (SSI)
Makes it possible for a Web server to insert variable items into static and dynamic Web pages at runtime. SSI is useful for boilerplate information such as copyright notices and data of last modification. It is not necessary to use a CGI program with SSI as the Web server itself acts on directives included in HTML just before transmitting a page to the server.

socks server
Checks the origin of the request. If the request comes from an authorized source, it is granted, and the socks server creates a pipe that connects the requesting machine to the outside server. All subsequent interactions between the client and the outside server flow through the pipe without further interference from the socks server.

sync point
An intermediate or end point during processing of a transaction at which an update or modification to one or more of the transaction's protected resources is logically complete and error free. Synonymous with *synchronization point* and commit.

tagged image file format (TIFF)
One of the file formats for images commonly used in the publishing world.

telnet
Method of connecting to a remote computer with a user logon ID and password. Once users are connected, they can perform operations as if they were on a local machine.

tn3270
A 3270-type terminal emulator.

Transmission Control Protocol/Internet Protocol (TCP/IP)
A set of communication protocols that support peer-to-peer connectivity functions for both local and wide area networks.

two-phase commit
A two-step process by which recoverable resources are committed. First, the resources managers are polled to ensure that they are ready to commit. Then, if all resources managers respond positively, they are told to execute commit processing.

uniform resource locator (URL)
A scheme for addressing distributed requests over the Internet. A URL indicates which Internet service is used, where to send the request, and what the request is. The browser retrieves a document specified by a URL. A URL is used in an HTML document to reference or link to another document.

unit of recover (UOR)
A sequence of operations within a unit of work between commit points.

unit of work (UOW)
Same as UOR.

Virtual Reality Modeling Language (VRML)
A scene description language for describing three-dimensional (3D) graphics and their environments on the Web. VRML is a file syntax for defining nodes, or 3D objects, and their behaviors. VRML was first developed by Mark Pesce and Tony Parisi in late 1993. It was presented to the First International Conference on the World Wide Web in Geneva, where the name VRML was introduced.

VisualAge
The IBM VisualAge family of products provides visual application development environments for Smalltalk, C++, COBOL, BASIC, RPG, PACBASE,

and Java programming languages. See http://www.software.ibm.com/ad/visage.

Visual Basic Script (VBScript)
A subset of Visual Basic that works with ActiveX controls to support interactive elements on the Web. VBScript is supported by Microsoft Internet Explorer version 3.0 and higher.

Web crawler
A program to gather information for a client.

Webmaster
The person who manages Websites.

Web Object Manager (Wom)
Originally developed at IBM in the United Kingdom and Germany to support major Websites with requirements for high volumes of users and accesses. Wom's first major application was to provide the results of the Wimbledon Tennis Championships on the Web. Its most recent, major application was at the Atlanta Olympics, where it handled 3600 user accesses per minute and received 425 million hits during the period of the Olympics. See http://www.womplex.ibm.com.

wide area information server (WAIS)
An attempt to standardize access requests to databases on the Internet. Thinking Machines Corporation invented WAIS in 1988. WAIS is now owned by WAIS Incorporated.

World Wide Web
A set of programs originally built at CERN for the research community, government, and industry to use to share information and collaborate through the Internet. The World Wide Web consists of a Web client or browser; different Internet servers, such as FTP, HTTP, NTTP; gopher servers; and a common interface, URL, for addressing distributed requests. The World Wide Web is also known as *WWW* or *W3* or the *Web*.

World Wide Web Consortium (W3C)
A consortium of companies such as IBM, Microsoft, and Netscape whose goal is to standardize Web technology. Many of the standards specifications developed by W3C can be found at http://www.w3c.org.

Yahoo!
An Internet search software. See http://www.yahoo.com, the Yahoo! home page.

WORKS CITED

CICS Clients Unmasked. IBM International Technical Support Centers, GG24-2534-00, May 1995.

IBM Dictionary of Computing. Compiled and edited by George McDaniel. New York: McGraw-Hill, 1994.

For Further Reference

CHAPTER 3

Cheswick, William R. and Bellovin, Steven M. *Firewalls and Internet Security*. Reading, MA: Addison Wesley, 1994.

Comer, Douglas. *Internetworking with TCP/IP, Volume 1*. Englewood Cliffs, NJ: Prentice Hall, 1991.

Denning, D. E. *Cryptography and Data Security*. Reading, MA: Addison-Wesley, 1982.

Garfinkel, Simson and Spafford, Gene. *Practical Unix Security*. Sebastopol, CA: O'Reilly & Associates, 1991.

IBM Internet Connection Secure Server "UP and Running." User's manual. IBM Corporation, 1996.

International Technical Support Organization. Building a Firewall with the NetSP Secured Network Gateway. GG24-2577-00. IBM Corporation, 1995.

Russell, D. and Gangemi, G. T. Sr. *Computer Security Basics*. Sebastopol, CA: O'Reilly & Associates, 1991.

Won, William T. *Secure NASA httpd Reference Manual*. Enterprise Integration Technologies, 1995. Available from: http://www.commerce.net/software/Shttpd.

CHAPTER 4

Berners-Lee, T. *Style Guide for On-Line Hypertext:* http://www.w3.org/hypertext/WWW/Provider/Style.

Gilster, Paul. *The Web Navigator.* New York: Wiley, 1997.

Graham, Ian. *The HTML Sourcebook* (2nd edition). New York: Wiley, 1995.

HTML resources at the Library of Congress: http://lcweb.loc.gov/global/internet/html.html.

HTTP working group at the IETF: http://www.ics.uci.edu/pub/ietf/http/.

CHAPTER 5

Accessing CICS Business Applications from the WWW—IBM Publication GG24-4547

Echo script for testing forms:
   http://hoohoo.ncsa.uiuc.edu/htbin-post.post-query

Image maps:
   http://sunsite.unc.edu/boutell/mapedit/mapedit.html
   http://www.hursley.ibm.com/cics/
   http://www.hursley.ibm.com/mqseries/

Server-side includes:
   http://hoohoo.ncsa.uiuc.edu/docs/tutorials/includes.html

CHAPTER 6

alphaWorks—Internet technologies from IBM: http://www.alphaworks.ibm.com.

Anuff, E. *The Java Sourcebook.* New York: Wiley, 1996. ISBN: 0471148598.

CICS Gateway for Java and shopping demonstration: http://www.hursley.ibm.com/cics/.

Cowlishaw, M.F. *The NetREXX Language.* Englewood Cliffs, NJ: Prentice-Hall, 1997.

Cowlishaw, M.F. *The REXX Language* (2nd edition). Englewood Cliffs, NJ: Prentice-Hall, 1990. ISBN 0-13-780651-5.

Gamelan—Java sources on the Internet: http://www.gamelan.com/index.shtml.

Gosling, J.A., et al. *The Java Language Specification.* Reading, MA: Addison Wesley, 1996. ISBN 0-201-63451-1.

van Hoff, Arthur, et al. *Hooked on Java*. Reading, MA: Addison-Wesley, 1996. ISBN 0-201-48837-X.
Java home page at IBM: http://ncc.hursley.ibm.com/javainfo/.
Java home page at Sun: http://www.javasoft.com/.
Java Remote Method Invocation: http://chatsubo.javasoft.com/current/.
JavaScript Guide, Netscape Corporation, 1996.
JDBC at IBM: http://www.software.ibm.com/data/db2/jdbc/.
JDBC at Sun: http://splash.javasoft.com/jdbc/.
Jigsaw Web server from CERN.
NetREXX home page: http://www2.hursley.ibm.com/.
PointCast: http://www.pointcast.com.
W3 Consortium: http://www.w3.org/.
W3 Consortium: URL for HTML 3.2 and future intent of frames support.

CHAPTER 10

Bernstein, P. and Newcomb, E. *Principles of Transaction Processing*. San Mateo, CA: Morgan Kaufmann, 1996. ISBN 1-55860-415-7.
CERN Jigsaw server: http://www.w3.org/pub/WWW/Jigsaw/.
CICS: http://www.hursley.ibm.com/cics/.
Encina: http://www.transarc.com/afs/transarc.com/public/www/Public/ProdServ/Product/Encina/index.html.
Gray, Jim and Reuter, Andreas. *Transaction Processing: Concepts and Techniques*. San Mateo, CA: Morgan Kaufmann, 1993. ISBN 1-55860-190-2.
IMS: http://www.software.ibm.com/data/ims/imsfamly.html.
TPF: http://www.s390.ibm.com/products/tpf/tpfhp.html.

CHAPTER 11

Accessing CICS Business Applications from the WWW—IBM Publication SG24-4547.
Accessing a CICS/ESA system using the CICS EXCI from an MVS Web server CGI program: http://www.hursley.ibm.com/cics/txppacs/ca80.html.
CICS: http://www.hursley.ibm.com/cics/.
CICS Web Interface Guide—IBM Publication SC33-1825.
Lotus Domino Server: http://domino.lotus.com/.

CHAPTER 12

Blakeley, B., Harris, H., and Lewis, J.R.T. *Messaging and Queuing Using the MQI: Concepts and Analysis, Design and Development.* New York: McGraw-Hill, 1995.

Corridor server-side 3270 emulation from Teubner: http://www.teubner.com/corridor/corrhome.htm.

Eppinger, J. L., Mummert, L. B., Spector, A. Z. *Camelot and Avalon—A Distributed Transaction Facility.* San Mateo: Morgan Kaufmann, 1991.

IMS: http://www.software.ibm.com/data/ims/.

Kapp, D. and Leben, J. *IMS Programming Techniques.* New York: Van Nostrand Rheinhold, 1986. ISBN: 0-442-24655-1.

MQSeries: http://www.software.ibm.com/mqseries/.

MQSeries Application Programming Guide, SC33-0807.

MQSeries Application Programming Reference, SC33-1673.

OC://WebConnect Gold browser client-side 3270 emulation from Open Connect: http://www.oc.com/WebConnect/index.html.

Salvo server-side 3270 emulation from Simware: http://www.simware.com/salvo.

Transarc: http://www.transarc.com.

CHAPTER 13

Atlanta Olympics: http://www.atlanta.olympic.org/.

Bray, T. *Measuring the Web.* Proceedings of the Fifth World Wide Web Conference, May 1996, Paris: http://www5conf.inria.fr/fich_html/papers/P8/Overview.html.

DFS (Distributed File System): http://www.transarc.com/afs/transarc.com/public/www/Public/ProdServ/Product/DFS/dfs_broc.htm.

Net.Commerce: http://net.commerce.ibm.com/.

SET (Secure Electronic Transaction) specification: http://www.visa.com/cgi-bin/vee/sf/set/intro.html.

Wom (Web Object Manager): http://www.womplex.ibm.com/.

Index

A

Access control, 58
   Domino Server, 245–247
   Net.Data, 215–216
   See also Security
Access control lists, 246–247
ACL files, 64–66
Acronyms, 405–413
ActiveX control, 166–167
Advertising on the Internet, 29–30
Alias Transaction, 303–304
Applet host security, 128–129
ARPANET, 7
Authentication, 57–58, 379–380

B

Backgrounds, 94
Bookmarks, 95, 116
Browsers:
   caching, 115
   page refresh, 115
   testing, 99
   using multiple, 115
Browser session identifier, 113–114
Browser sessions:
   CICS Internet Gateway, 279
   creation, 138–139
   initiation and termination, 140
   CICS EXCI, 292
   CICS Gateway for Java, 300
   CICS Internet Gateway, 287–290
   CICS Web Interface, 310–312
   integrating with conversation, 117
   managing, 116–117
   managing state with Java, 132–133
   server-side programming, 113–118
   state management guidelines, 117–118
   storing state, 140
   transmitting state with Netscape cookies, 139
   Web environment, 114–116
Business applications, 25–47
   advertising and marketing, 29–30
   chat and collaboration, 37, 39
   downside, 27
   education and training, 32–33, 35
   electronic commerce. *See* Electronic commerce
   examples, 39–42
   Internet models, 28
   market research, 32–33
   planning, 42–47
   publishing, 30–32
   sales, 33–34, 36–37
   services and maintenance, 32, 34
   why go online, 25–27

C

Certificate imbed, 61
CGI, 10–11, 110–113
   alternatives, 113
   common uses, 111–112
   deficiency, 371
CGI Link Server, 165
Chat, 37, 39
CICS applications, 273–330
   accessing with Domino Server, 293–294
   choosing among access methods, 314
   Distributed Program Link, 275–276
   external call interface, 276
   external presentation interface, 276

CICS applications *(Continued)*:
   MVS/ESA Internet Connection Server, 291–293
   overview, 273–278
   pseudoconversational, 274–275
   pseudoconversational programming, 262–263
   security, 290
   SYNCPOINT, 276
   UOR, 292
   writing, 306–310
   See also CICS Gateway for Java; CICS Internet Gateway; CICS Web Interface
CICS Gateway for Java, 294–301
   configurations, 296
   how it works, 295
   initiation and termination of browser sessions, 300
   overview, 295
   parameters, 296–299
   security, 300–301
   UOR, 300
CICS Internet Gateway, 110, 277–291
   browser sessions, 279
   configurations, 278, 280
   customization options, 280–287
   default settings, 282–284
   how it works, 278–279
   initiation and termination of browser sessions, 287–290
   override settings, 284–287
   UOR, 290
CICS Web Interface, 301, 303–314
   Analyzer, 303–304
   application in 370 assembler, 315–321
   configurations, 305, 313
   Converter, 304–305
   how it works, 303–305
   initiation and termination of browser sessions, 310–312
   sample converter in C, 321–330
   security, 312
   UOR, 312
   writing CICS application programs, 306–310
Client/server application, 145
Client-side programming, 88–89, 123–143
   accessing Encina, 336–339
   generic 3270 clients, 343

   JavaScript, 134–141
   managing session state, 143
   mixing with server-side programming, 133
   MQSeries Client for Java, 349–353
   NetRexx, 141
   specialized non-Java clients, 142
   See also Java
Client-side state, 118
Code server protection setup, 64–66
Cold Fusion, 218
Collaboration, online, 37, 39
Color, use on HTML page, 93–94
Commercial sites, 359
Common Gateway Interface. *See* CGI
Composition Editor, 155–156
Computers, network, 21–22
Conditional logic, reports, 196–197
Conditional variables, 201–202
Connection Manager, 303
Connectivity, back-end, 147
Conversation, integrating with browser sessions, 117
Conversational programming, definition, 261–263
Cookie, generating, 215
Copyright information, protecting on the Internet, 360–361
Correlation identifier, 346
Crawlers, 95
Credit card transactions, secure, 356, 358
Cryptography, 53–56
Cryptolope, 230, 361
CRYPTOPTS, 63–65
Customer Information Control System. *See* CICS

D

Data:
   accessing
      Net.Data, 212–214
      non-HTML, 214–215
   postprocessing, 203–212
      built-in functions, 209–210
      calling user functions and applications from macros, 210–211
      with Java applet, 204–207
      Perl function, 208–209
      REXX function, 207–208

Database:
   access control, Net.Data, 215–216
   connecting to, 391
   replication, 268
   retrieval, 14, 16
   tailoring for use on the Web, 247–250
   updating, 119–120
Data Encryption Standard, 55
DCE, components, 332–333
Decryption, 53–56
DE-Light, 335
DE-Light Web Client, 336–339
DES, 55
DFS, 363
   using on Web, 339
Digital cash, 356
Digital certificate, 57
Digital signature, 56–57
Director/daemon application server, designing, 392–395
Distinguished name, 62
Distributed Computing Environment. *See* DCE
Distributed File System. *See* DFS
Distributed program link, 275–276
DLLs, developer's kit for building, 210
DNS round-robin tactics, 394
Domino.Action, 222, 226–228
   built-in interactivity, 228
   command and control for the Internet, 227
Domino.Merchant, 222–223
Domino Server, 223–224, 236–251
   access control lists, 246–247
   accessing:
      CICS, 293–294
      HTML files, 244–245
   customizing content, 249–250
   extending with Lotus Internet Applications, 225–226
   external links, 248–249
   home page, 248
   how it works, 238–239
   initializing, 243–244
   installation, 241
   introduction, 237–238
   links between pages, 248
   Lotus Notes extension, 237–238
   navigators and, 248
   registering Web users, 245–246

Index

sample registration application, 239–241
security and access control, 245–247
setting up Notes application, 241–243
SSL, 247
test searching, 250
user interface, 249
Drill-down report, 195–196
dtw_raddquote(), 209–210
Dynamic pages, 104
  hyperlinks, 97
  integrating with static pages, 97–98
  Net.Data, 176–181

E

Education, 32–33, 35
Electronic commerce, 35–38, 355–366
  Net.Commerce, 364–365
  payment methods, 356
  protecting copyright information, 360–361
  SET protocol, 359–361
  transaction processing, 361–365
  Web Object Manager, 362–364
  worldwide implications, 357–359
E-mail, tests, 98
Encina, 332–339
  Base Services, 333–334
  components, 333–335
  DCE, 332–333
  DE-Light, 335
  Extended Services, 334–335
  using client-side programming, 336–339
  using server-side programming, 336
Encryption, 45, 53–56, 358
End-user interfaces, 45
Error handling, customized, 198–200
External call interface, 276
External presentation interface, 276

F

Files:
  accessing, Net.Data, 212–214
  updating, 119–120
File Transfer Protocol. *See* FTP

Finger, 50–52
Firewall, 44, 58, 67–78, 120
  configuration example, 74–78
  packet filter, 68–69
  proxy server, 69–71
  security policy, 74–75
  socks server, 71–74
FORM ACTION and METHOD options, 105–110
Form Data, 159–160
Frames, JavaScript, 135–138
FTP, 12
  proxy server, 70–71
  socks server, 72–73
Functions:
  parameters, 211–212
  user, calling, 210–211

G

Gateway:
  application-specific, 88
  basic approach, 87
  to existing systems, 112
Generic 3270 clients, client-side programming, 343
Generic 3270 gateways, server-side programming, 342
GET method, 83, 107–108, 370, 389
GIF, 92
Gopher, 13
Graphics Interchange Format, 92

H

Home page, 247–248
HotJava browser software, 124
HTML, 9–10
  directed, 391–392
  frames, 135
HTML document:
  coding for SHTTP, 60–64
  security specification, 62–64
  server certificate, 61
HTML files, accessing through Domino Server, 244–245
HTML Form, 370
  CGI GET, 373–375
  settings, 156
HTML input form, 177–179
HTML page:
  design, 91–95
  dynamic, 104
  including APPLET tag, 124
  looking out of date, 94–95

setting, 154
size, 93
static, 104
testing using different browsers, 94
user interface, 169
HTML sections, 186–188, 190
HTML Table, 164
  customized report form, 194–195
HTML tags, 92, 146
HTML Template Manager, 309
HTTP, 10–11
  basic authentication, 379–380
  command lines, 370
  overview, 82–86
  protocol support, 89–90
  redirection option, 95–96
  requests through proxy server, 85
  statelessness, 85–86
  status codes, 84
Hyperlinks, 95, 195
  testing, 99
  URL, 106–107
  using in dynamic pages, 97
Hypertext links, 359
HyperText Markup Language. *See* HTML
HyperText Transport Protocol. *See* HTTP

I

IDL, 131
Image formats, 92
Image maps, 93
  clickable, 112
ImbedHTML, 285–287
IMS, 339–343
  accessing applications from the Web, 341–343
  MQSeries-IMS Bridge, 347
IMS Web, server-side programming, 342–343
In-doubt resynchronization, 260
Informix Webkits, 217–218
Internet:
  history, 6–7
  number of users, 3, 24
  present and future trends, 18–24
Internet phone, 23
Intranet, 16–18
  number of corporate users, 24
IP address, 43

J

Java, 18–19, 123–134, 143
  APPLET tag, 124–125
  differences from JavaScript, 134
  Interface Definition Language, 131
  managing state on browser, 132–133
  mixing server-side and client-side programming, 133
  Remote Method Invocation, 131
  security, 127–129
  using for server programming, 133–134
Java applets, 125, 166–169
  postprocessing with, 204–207
Java byte codes, 124
Java clients and gateways, 88–89
Java Database Connectivity, 129–131
Java Developer's Kit, 126–127
JavaScript, 20, 134–141
  differences from Java, 134
  frames, 135–138
  Netscape cookies, 138–141
Java Virtual Machine. *See* JVM
JDBC, 129–131
Joint Photographic Experts Group, 92
JPEG, 92
JVM, 124

K

Key recovery, 358

L

Legal issues, 46–47
Links:
  between pages, 248
  external, 248–249
List variables, 201
Lotus Internet Applications, 221–251
  Domino.Action, 222, 226–228
  Domino.Merchant, 222–223, 233–235
  Domino Server. *See* Domino Server
  strategic direction, 251
Lotus Internet Commerce, Domino.Merchant, 233–235
Lotus Internet Customer Service, 223, 235–236

Lotus Internet Publishing, 228–233
  benefits for publishers and media companies, 232–233
  broadcast, 230–231
  need for a framework, 229
  single-copy sales, 230
  subscription, 231–232
Lotus Internet Publishing Solutions, 222, 229–232
Lotus Notes, 221
  CICS Internet Gateway, 293–294
  customizing content, 249–250
  extension by Domino Server, 237–238
  setting up to use Domino Server, 241–243
  tailoring a database for use on the Web, 247–250
Lotus Notes:Newsstand, 231–232

M

Macros (Net.Data):
  calling user functions and applications from, 210–211
  sharing among applications, 202–203
Mailto, 13
Marketing, 29–30
Market research, 32–33
Message identifier, 345–346
MQSeries, 343–354
  accessing applications from the Web, 347–353
  grouping messages, 345–347
  message types, 344
  overview, 343–345
  queue manager, 344–345
  triggering, 347
MQSeries Client for Java, client-side programming, 349–353
MQSeries-IMS Bridge, 347
MQSeries Internet Gateway, server-side programming, 348–349
Multimedia, integrating objects, 121
Multiple Row Query, 161–163, 165
MVS/ESA Internet Connection Server, 291–293
  CGI program, server-side programming, 341–342
  security, 292–293

N

Navigators, Domino Server and, 248
Net.Commerce, 364–365
Net.Data, 74–78, 88, 175–219
  access control by database, 215–216
  accessing files, 212–214
  accessing non-HTML data, 214–215
  conditional logic, 196–197
  customized error handling, 198–200
  customizing reports, 191–203
  data postprocessing, 203–212
  db2www, 185
  drill-down report, 195–196
  dynamic Web pages, 176–181
  example2.d2w macro, 191–194
  function parameters, 211–212
  input form, 186–188
  list and conditional variables, 201–202
  report form, 188–191
  sharing macros among applications, 202–203
  simple database application, 181–191
  system overview, 176
  URL to access applications, 185–191
  variable definition sections, 189
NetRexx, 141
Netscape cookies, 138–141
Network computers, 21–22
News, 13, 15
Non-HTML data, accessing, Net.Data, 214–215
Non-Java clients, specialized, 142

O

Open Transaction Manager Access, 341
OTMA, 341

P

Packet filter, 68–69
Pages:
  links, Domino Server, 248
  See also HTML page; Web page

Index

Payments:
  handling, Domino.Merchant, 235
  methods, 356
Performance tests, 99
Perl function, postprocessing with, 208–209
Phone book application, 181–191
  accessing files, 213
  implementing, 185–191
  report form, 188–191
Pizza application, 148–166
  ConfirmAPizza, 158–168
  database access, 160–163
  dynamic content
    Form Data and, 159–160
    in table, 163–164
  HTML for pizza order form, 148, 150
  LPizza, 151–152, 167
  OrderAPizza, 152–158
  PayForPizza, 167–168
  sequence of events, 164–166
PointCast, 142
POST method, 107–109, 375–377
Proof-of-concept projects, 43
Proxy caching, 115
Proxy server, 69–71
Pseudoconversational programming, 262–263
  CICS, 274–275
Publishing:
  broadcast, 230–231
  Internet, 30–32
  need for a framework, 229
  single-copy sales, 230
  subscription, 231–232
  turning into business activity, 226–227
  Web delivery models, 228
  See also Lotus Internet Publishing

Q

Queue manager, 344–345

R

Report form, 188–191
Reports:
  conditional logic, 196–197
  customizing, 191–203
  drill-down, 195–196

REXX function, postprocessing with, 207–208
RMI, 131
RSA, 55–56

S

Sales, 33–34, 36–37
Search products, 16
Search tools, 100
  testing, 99
Secure Electronic Transaction Protocol, 359–361
Secure Hypertext Transport Protocol. *See* SHTTP
Secure Sockets Layer. *See* SSL
Security:
  access control, 58
  ACL files, 64–66
  authentication, 57–58
  basics, 52–53
  CICS applications, 290
  CICS Gateway for Java, 300–301
  CICS Web Interface, 312
  code server protection setup, 64–66
  cryptography, 53–56
  digital certificate, 57
  digital signature, 56–57
  Domino Server, 245–247
  HTML document, 62–64
  Java, 127–129
  MVS/ESA Web server, 292–293
  risk example, 50–52
  server's certificate, 61–62
  server-side programming, 120
  SHTTP, 60–66
  SSL, 59
  transaction processing, 270–271
  See also Firewall
Security policy, 74–75
Server programming, Java, 133–134
Server's certificate, 61–62
Server-side includes, 112
Server-side programming, 87–88, 103–121
  accessing Encina, 336
  FORM ACTION and METHOD options, 105–110
  generic 3270 gateways, 342
  IMS Web, 342–343
  managing browser session state, 113–118

  mixing with client-side programming, 133
  MQSeries Internet Gateway, 348–349
  multimedia objects, 121
  MVS Web server CGI program, 341–342
  security, 120
  updating databases and files, 119–120
  Web forms, 104–106
Server-side state, maintaining, 381–384
Services and maintenance, up-to-date information, 32, 34
SET protocol, 359–361
Settop boxes, 128
SHTTP, 60–66
  coding HTML document, 60–64
  differences from SSL, 66
  security transport mode, 62–64
Socks server, 71–74
SQL Statement, 160–162, 165, 190
  dynamic generation, 201–202
SSL, 59
  differences from SHTTP, 66
  Domino Server, 247
Standalone Web application, 97
Static pages, 104
  integrating with dynamic pages, 97–98
Surfing, 116
Sybase web.sql, 217
SYNCPOINT, 276
System availability, 46

T

Table, dynamic content, 163–164
TCP/IP, 7
  support, 45
Telnet, 13
Test searching, Domino Server, 250
TimeOutInternet, 282–284
Training, 32–33, 35
Transaction, definition, 257–258
Transaction processing, 255–271
  background, 255–257
  business logic portion, 264
  conversational programming, 261–263
  database replication, 268
  differences from Web server, 266–269

Transaction processing *(Continued)*:
  electronic commerce, 361–365
  evolution of systems, 264–265
  facilities, 263
  security, 270–271
  UOR, 258–261
  user interface logic portion, 264
  Web and, 269–271
Transmission Control Protocol/
  Internet Protocol, 7
Triggering, MQSeries, 347

U

Ultimate White Pages, 4–5
Uniform Resource Locator. *See*
  URL
Unit of recovery. *See* UOR
UOR, 119, 258–261
  CICS applications, 292
  CICS Gateway for Java, 300
  CICS Internet Gateway, 290
  CICS Web Interface, 312
  mode extension, 297–298
Updates:
  files and databases, 119–120
  partial, 119
URL, 11–14
  accessing Net.Data applications, 185–191
  hyperlink, 106–107
  initial, 95
  list, 397–404
  to Web applications, 157
Usenet, 13, 15
USER_AGENT, 390
User feedback, 94
User interface:
  Domino Server, 249
  guidelines, 90–101
  HTML and page design, 91–95
  integrating static and dynamic pages, 97–98
  maintaining quality of site, 98–100
  multiple, 169

  searching and being found, 100–101
  Website structure guidelines, 95–97

V

Variables, list and conditional, 201–202
VBScript, 20
Virtual mall, 35–38
Virtual Reality Modeling
  Language. *See* VRML
Visitor page counts, 111–112
VisualAge, 147–148
  Organizer, 151–152
Visual editor, 147
Visual programming:
  advantages, 146–147
  extending to cover Web application development, 146
  Java applets, 168–169
  maintaining state, 167–168
  multiple user interfaces, 169
  other Web applications, 166–167
  See also Pizza application
VisualWave, 147–148
VRML, 20–21

W

W3 Consortium (W3C), 10
WAIS, 13
Web, transaction processing, 269–271
Web application, 145
  configuration and operation, 146
  platforms, 371–372
  URL to, 157
Web application server, 369–395
  connecting to databases, 391
  designing, 372–377
  director/daemon, 392–395
  embedding content from another Website, 384–391
  extending, 378

  maintaining server-side state, 381–384
  maintaining state, 378–384
  scalability, 393–394
Web browser, 8–9, 369
Web Connection, parts, 170–172
Web environment, affect on browser sessions, 114–116
Web forms, programming, 104–106
Web Object Manager, 362–364
Web Oracle Web, 218
Web page:
  backgrounds, 94
  dynamic, 176–181
    standalone applications, 179–180
  structure evolution, 91
  visual and spatial properties, 155
Web server:
  application programming interfaces, 370–371
  differences from transaction processing, 266–269
  evolution, 265–266
  Lotus extensions, 223–224
  proxy cache, 266–267
Website:
  embedding content from another, 384–391
  keeping up-to-date, 45
  maintaining quality, 98–100
  major structural changes, 100
  navigational structures, 96
  registering, 100
  structure guidelines, 95–97
  testing, 46
  users finding, 46
  way of searching, 100
Web users, registering, 245–246
Wide Area Information Server, 13
WOM, 362–364
Wombat, 363
WomSprayer, 363
WOW, 218